LANGUAGE AND LITERACY SERIES

Dorothy S. Strickland and Celia Genishi

EDITORS

The Complete Theory-to-Practice
Handbook of Adult Literacy:
Curriculum Design and Teaching Approaches

*Rena Soifer, Martha E. Irwin, Barbara M. Crumrine, Emo Honzaki,
Blair K. Simmons, and Deborah L. Young*

Literacy for a Diverse Society:
Perspectives, Practices, and Policies

Elfrieda H. Hiebert (Editor)

LITERACY
for a
DIVERSE SOCIETY

Perspectives, Practices, and Policies

Edited by

ELFRIEDA H. HIEBERT

Foreword by Frederick Erickson

Teachers College, Columbia University
New York and London

Published by Teachers College Press, 1234 Amsterdam Avenue
New York, NY 10027

Library of Congress Cataloging-in-Publication Data

Literacy for a diverse society : perspectives, practices, and policies / edited by Elfrieda H.
  Hiebert.
      p.   cm. —(Language and literacy series ; no. 2)
  Includes bibliographical references and index.
  ISBN 0-8077-3098-X (c). —ISBN 0-8077-3097-1
    1. Language experience approach in education—United States. 2. Literacy—United
States. 3. Constructivism (Education) I. Hiebert, Elfrieda H. II. Series: Language
and literacy series (New York, N.Y.); v. 2.
LB1576.L554   1991
302.2'244—dc20   91-13045
                                                          CIP

Printed on acid-free paper

Manufactured in the United States of America

98 97 96 95 94 93 92 91   8 7 6 5 4 3 2 1

Contents

Foreword

When I read this book, I thought of Renee. She was an African-American second grader who was in trouble with her teacher for not finishing some of her worksheets. Both Renee and her teacher, who was white, seemed hurt and angry. Once, when the teacher was at the end of her patience for the day and we were walking together out to the playground for recess, she said to me, "Why do I bother trying to get her to finish? She'll be a hooker by the time she's 15."

That made me furious. But what was going on didn't seem to be blatant, overt racism. I knew the teacher was conscientious. As time went on I came to see some ways in which, from her point of view, her frustration with Renee made sense. I took account of what I was able to learn about her beliefs about teaching and about how children learn to read and write. Some aspects of those beliefs may have originated in—and were certainly sustained by—her school district's policies and conceptions of what was reasonable and desirable in literacy instruction. Yet, after straining to understand and not to condemn the teacher out of hand, I was still angry. I didn't agree with the sense that was being made. It seemed to me that Renee and her teacher had been caught by each other in a tragic bind. Each seemed partly responsible for producing the situation with the other. It seemed that from the bind they were in they were unlikely to escape all by themselves.

How did Renee and her teacher get into so tangled a knot? This collection of papers sheds light on that question by considering the social and cultural constitution of literacy and its acquisition. The book reviews a broad range of phenomena and issues. They include root conceptions and interests in literacy that are taken for granted as reasonable and just by persons and groups in society and that, in the press of doing daily business in schools, are rarely subjected to critical scrutiny. These are conceptions and interests that become institutionalized in school work, in intellectual discourse, and in the political and economic influences on how Americans try to understand, plan, conduct, and regulate educational processes and outcomes with the hope of improving them.

The book takes an approach that is distinctive in that while its papers focus on a single area of subject matter, they manage to consider a wide range of connected phenomena and issues. The contributors examine not only the arguments Americans have about how and what to teach as literacy in school but in how to do schooling itself. This book connects conceptual work on the nature of literacy and its acquisition, not only with empirical research on how literacy is taught in classrooms but also with the workings of school organization, governance, and policy within which local school practices are embedded. Those connections are rarely so comprehensively and so pointedly made. Yet it is just such a combination of scope and specificity that has been absent from current discourse on educational reform. The reform debates have failed, for the most part, to take account of the concrete struggles of classroom life and the particular unexamined beliefs and institutional arrangements that may be exacerbating those struggles. Without being at all doctrinaire, this book's analysis shows that the tugs of war over literacy in the classroom and in American society are fundamentally interest- and value-laden, which is to say, that they are political in nature.

A "constructivist" perspective on thinking, learning, and literacy is the conceptual thread that links the major sections of the book. In recent years, we have seen emerging a set of family resemblances in orientation by which current efforts in psychology and linguistics, sociology and anthropology, and literary theory and philosophy can be seen as joined in spirit. By collecting review articles that share in this family connection of perspectives, this volume shows literacy in American schooling as a set of constructing practices that are organized within and across the activities of individual learners, of classrooms as immediate scenes of pedagogical interaction and curricular engagement, of schools as formal organizations, and of society as a whole.

If you are familiar with the full range of issues presented, you may want to read this book from front to back. It begins with discussions of constructivist perspectives on literacy instruction, continues with papers that review classroom practices, and concludes with essays on policy and accountability processes that frame and influence the work of local teachers, students, and administrators. If you are more familiar with some topics than others, I suggest that you read the first few chapters in Part I, skip to the first and final chapters of the last section, and then work your way back through the rest of the book. This is because, for most of us, the connections between policy and the basic assumptions underlying literacy and its teaching are not at all well-known. On the issues we face in literacy instruction, there has been a very unfortunate separation between policy decisions and processes and the substantive choices practitioners must make about what and how to teach in the classroom. Reading all the sections of the book gives us a more comprehensive sense than we would otherwise have of what is necessary if real change is going to happen.

What we see is daunting—a multidimensional web of mutually reinforcing assumptions and practices in teaching, assessment, school organization, finance, and governmental decision, which result in the provision of the most marginal kinds of literacy for the poorest of our nation's children. Only by making the web visible can we begin to see how its structuring of countervailing tensions operates and where the crucial points in the system are located, toward which change efforts should be directed.

A final note on diversity. Some of the chapters in the middle section of this book point to a root assumption that research shows to be false but that normal policy and practice take for granted. This is the assumption that the children of marginally literate parents—and in America today that means persons from ethnic, racial, and linguistic minority groups who in another generation will be majority groups—come to school virtually lacking any knowledge of or desire for literacy. The school's job, in that view, is to motivate those children by placing them on the bottom rung of a ladder of skills and having them practice simple skills. Here is where literacy learning becomes a moral tale. Because in our society literacy is culturally defined as good—and inherently so—if a learner doesn't try hard and persist at practice on the rung where he or she has been placed, that can be seen as a sinful act. When Renee's teacher started to regard her as a potential teenage prostitute, I think it was because Renee's reluctance to finish her boring worksheets— her actions as framed by the school's definitions of them—had made her a sinner in that teacher's eyes.

Teaching literacy on a ladder of skills contradicts what we now know about children and their learning at home and at school. All children, from the most to the least socially advantaged family circumstances, come to school knowing and doing various kinds of literacy. Thus, schools start with every child a full child. The particular kinds of literacies children bring to school, however, differ in subtle ways that we are only beginning to see and comprehend. It follows that the kinds of literacy work and play that teachers and students begin to do in classrooms necessarily should look and sound different, given differing combinations of racial, ethnic, linguistic, and class backgrounds of actual sets of teachers and students. Such differences in kinds of practice, if they follow from the presumption that all children construct sense and use it actively, need not lead to the invidious processes and outcomes we now see in ordinary assessment and streaming. Simply to place differing students on differing rungs of a uniform ladder of school literacy skills—and then to teach them in bottom, middle, and top instructional groups or curricular tracks—is a phony response to diversity.

In our contemporary practice, the ladder of skills approach does not presume a range of variation in kinds of literacy knowledge and interests, nor does it presume differing modes and sequences of healthy and robust literacy acquisition. The same ladder of proper learning is built for all. The assumption behind the ladder of skills approach is that students are not qualitatively different in what they know, do, and want. Rather, they are just quantitatively different in how many successive skills they have acquired at a given moment in their history of development as learners. This book presents a far different image of literacy acquisition. It tells us that in human literacy learning and teaching there are many differing ladders, many ways to climb, many kinds of powers in climbing, and an amazing capacity in human learners of all ages to climb on more than one ladder at once. How to organize schools genuinely for diversity in literacy, treating its multidimensionality as a resource rather than as a liability and providing various ways to climb high, is a challenge we continue to face as educators and as citizens.

However you climb along and across the various ladders in this book, I hope you will come away with richer conceptions of literacy and its possibilities for acquisition in schools than the notions with which you started. As you read and argue with these chapters, do not forget Renee and her teacher. Do not fail to look for the webs in which they became entangled. Then go to them. Do not leave them where they are now, stuck and alone. They are still capable of changing if schooling changes with them.

Frederick Erickson
University of Pennsylvania

Preface

The origins of this book, in extended conversations among scholars with diverse backgrounds, befit its concern with literacy for a diverse society. In 1987, a number of new faculty members joined the School of Education, University of Colorado at Boulder and, with existing faculty, began collaborating on research and program development activities. Despite diverse backgrounds in disciplines like educational psychology, anthropology, sociolinguistics, and policy analysis, they soon saw that they shared a constructivist view of learning and a commitment to applying this perspective to the school learning of students with diverse backgrounds. Moreover, they asserted a strong commitment to studying thought, language, and participation structures in schools and the role of these structures in creating and maintaining a diverse, multicultural society.

To extend this conversation, an invitational conference on Literacy for a Diverse Society was held in Boulder in April of 1989. At this conference, presentations by scholars from other institutions made it clear that a constructivist view of literacy and its importance in a diverse society was shared by many. This volume is intended to identify the common themes that arose at the conference and share them in the broader community of educators. We are especially interested in engaging other practicing teachers in this conversation, for it is in daily practice that literacy for diversity becomes reality in schools.

The conference that gave birth to this book would not have been possible without funding from the Gannett Foundation and the University of Colorado-Boulder, as well as the enthusiastic support of the chancellor of the university, James Corbridge, and the dean of the School of Education, Philip DiStefano.

An edited volume such as this depends on the work of numerous individuals. The efforts of Michael Meloth, who contributed in numerous ways to the organization of the conference, and Carole Anderson, who made diverse computer systems compatible, are gratefully acknowledged. Special thanks are also extended to the authors whose commitments to the themes of this book were evident in their diligent work and adherence to demanding writing schedules.

1 | Introduction

ELFRIEDA H. HIEBERT
University of Colorado, Boulder

For some time now, a new perspective on literacy, and the learning processes through which literacy is acquired, has been emerging. This new perspective does not consist of old ideas with a new name, but rather it represents a profound shift from a text-driven definition of literacy to a view of literacy as active transformation of texts. In the old view, meaning was assumed to reside primarily within text, whereas, in the new view, meaning is created through an interaction of reader and text. This book examines the new perspective and its implications for fostering higher levels of literacy in an increasingly diverse society.

A wide variety of academic disciplines has contributed to the new view of literacy and literacy instruction. The chapters in this volume portray contributions made by cognitive psychologists, anthropologists, sociolinguists, and policy analysts. The labels that scholars use for this "new" perspective vary as a function of their disciplines. However, the diversity of labels should not obscure the similarity in the underlying views of literacy and learning held by these scholars. In this introduction, the general perspective is called *constructivism*. Other authors refer to the perspective, or its subthemes, as sociocognitive (Langer), ability-centered (Miramontes & Commins), and multiple literacies (McCollum). Various nuances in constructivist views of literacy, as well as their implications for literacy in a diverse society, are addressed in Part 1 of this book. Although chapters may differ in their emphases, the underlying principles share much common ground.

A VIEW OF LITERACY AS CONSTRUCTING MEANING

A view of literacy acquisition, or any other learning domain, as constructive is not new. Major components of this view can be found in the ideas of Dewey (1909), Piaget (1959), and others, although some philosophers place the origins much earlier (von Glasersfeld, 1983). What is new, however, is the consensus among American educators on the utility of this view.

Until now, American education has taken its underlying frameworks for conceptualizing learning, instruction, assessment, and intelligence, among other constructs, primarily from psychology. For decades, the view that psychology has offered has been heavily influenced by behaviorism. The outlines of behaviorism will be familiar to those who teach in schools and see its manifestations in norm-referenced testing programs, mastery learning, and compensatory remediation programs for students who differ from the "norm."

By contrast, constructivism views learners as active participants in the creation of their own knowledge. Because learners interact with and interpret the world, knowledge is a function of the learner's background and purposes. Learning often occurs in social contexts, and, therefore, the learner's relationships with other persons serve a vital function in the interpretation process. The social aspects of learning are especially relevant in homes and schools, where interaction between adults and children has a strong influence on what, how, and how much children learn.

Work by the Russian psychologist Vygotsky (1978) is a particularly important and frequently cited source for the constructivist view. By reconciling the functioning of individuals with that of the culture, Vygotsky provided a common framework for those primarily concerned with culture (anthropologists) and those primarily concerned with individuals (psychologists).

The implications of this view for literacy are momentous. Meaning no longer is viewed as residing in texts but is regarded as a function of readers interacting with texts in different contexts. This view of reading, which provided the framework for *Becoming a Nation of Readers* (Anderson, Hiebert, Scott, & Wilkinson, 1985), continues to be elaborated by cultural anthropologists and Vygotskians. An important thrust of this elaboration has resulted in greater attention to the contexts of literacy use and acquisition, especially to the forms and structures of social interaction in teacher-student and student-student classroom dialogues (see Chapter 9). These social interactions serve to structure and restructure meanings that readers make of text.

TWO MEANINGS OF DIVERSITY

There are two definitions of *diverse* that run throughout the book. One pertains to the "diverse" society of the late 20th century. In this diverse society, social and cultural boundaries are changing rapidly as technological advances create instantaneous communication among nations. Individuals and groups are increasingly required to process large amounts of information. Furthermore, as interaction among individuals from very different cultures increases, individuals are required to construct meanings from different perspectives and understand how one's meanings may differ from those of others. Successful performance in such situations demands what Brown (1989) calls the higher literacies. Without these higher literacies, individuals and groups may be disenfranchised from full participation in the economic, social, and political lives of their communities.

The second interpretation of diversity that underlies this book relates to the role of students' diversity in the process of literacy acquisition. In the old view, differences among students were seen as barriers to literacy acquisition, and, in some cases, programs were designed to reduce or remove these differences. In the new view, the higher literacies are acquired by recognizing and building on diversity among students. In this sense, differences among students constitute a valuable source of learning: springboards, so to speak, to higher literacies. With this shift in perspective, diversity among students becomes an asset to classroom instruction rather than a liability. For example, teachers and students might examine ways in which school and home cultures create and sustain different experiences for particular students. By broadening both teachers' and students' views of students' backgrounds and existing knowledge, the unique experiences that students bring to school make an important contribution to the process of literacy acquisition itself.

When a constructivist view is applied to school contexts, diversity is recognized and fostered as a strength rather than something to be reduced, erased, or displaced. New information is presented in relation to what students already know. Furthermore, when social interaction is regarded as an essential mechanism whereby information is structured and restructured, interaction patterns in classrooms shift to involve students as full participants rather than observers or spectators.

In this sense, the diversity present in many American classrooms can be seen as a means for acquiring literacy in the diverse society of the late 20th century. Artificial situations do not have to be created to demonstrate alternative interpretations to students. Within one classroom, children with different backgrounds interact with one another, listen to one another, and learn, firsthand, different ways in which the same text or information can be interpreted.

A constructivist view is commensurate with the higher literacies required in a diverse society containing many cultures and languages. Moreover, this view is useful for developing learning experiences that facilitate acquisition of these higher literacies.

THEORETICAL PERSPECTIVES, PRACTICES, AND POLICIES
FOR LITERACY ACQUISITION

It is an explicit intention of this book to address relationships between the constructivist perspective, policies intended to support implementation of this perspective, and enacted classroom practice. The tripartite structure of the book reflects this intention. Many would argue that literacy education in America has suffered from overspecialization and subsequent isolation of these domains. A common stereotype places sole interest in theory with university faculty, practice with classroom teachers, and policy with administrators and politicians. Clark and Peterson (1986), in partial support of this idea, note that university educators' emphasis on "theory" frequently conflicts with teachers' orientation toward "activities." Although it may be true that educational theorizing by academics has sometimes occurred with little heed to practice and policy, analogous statements about practitioners and policymakers also have some validity.

To the extent that specialization and isolation do exist, they constitute formidable impediments to substantial and lasting change in literacy programs. For example, a superficial grasp of the theoretical perspectives that underlie one's practice has typically left large numbers of educators vulnerable to what Feitelson (1988) calls the "fads" of literacy instruction. As the pendulum swings back and forth, the fundamental changes in policies and practices that are required to achieve the higher literacies in a diverse society simply do not occur. One popular method fades and is replaced by another.

Broader understanding of the theoretical perspectives underlying alternative approaches to literacy is particularly critical as a new wave of an old debate sweeps the field. This debate, argued in journals as different as *Phi Delta Kappan* (e.g., Carbo, 1988; Chall, 1989) and *Review of Educational Research* (e.g., McGee & Lomax, 1990; Stahl & Miller, 1989), is an extremely high-stakes event, especially for children of the poor and students for whom English is a second language. Responsible participation in this important debate demands a solid grasp of both the older behaviorist view and the newer constructivist view on the part of academics, practitioners, and policymakers. Some groups on both sides of the debate claim to have the one best methodology and at the same time eschew open inquiry that could provide insight into long-standing problems in literacy instruction. As Pearson (1989) suggests, such claims for exclusivity do not bode well for the overall transformation of the field.

Emergence of the constructivist perspective has challenged several of the dominant policies and practices in American literacy education and thereby heightened interest in this policy domain. In the 1950s and 1960s, literacy educators talked and wrote primarily about literacy materials and teaching methods. During the 1970s, the focus shifted to characteristics of readers and texts. Increasingly during the 1980s and now in the 1990s, concerns about the context of literacy are moving to center stage. In spite of this trend, literacy educators have rarely addressed the larger contexts of education wherein beliefs of the general public and elected officials shape and enact policies for literacy instruction. This scenario is starting to change, as indicated by the provocative policy analyses included in this volume (see Part III) and elsewhere (see, e.g., Fraatz, 1987).

Policies about literacy receive their ultimate interpretation from classroom teachers in the day-to-day enactment of instruction. In spite of this, teacher education programs rarely, if ever, address educational policy as a field of study or the impact of policies on practices. The mandates of various agencies regarding classroom practice often come as a surprise for beginning teachers. They have little background with which to interpret a state legislature's law that kindergarten children's promotion to grade 1 depends on attaining a particular level on a readiness test (Meisels, 1989) or a district administrator's mandate that 15 minutes of daily phonics instruction be provided all elementary-level children.

When literacy educators, whether academics, practitioners, or policymakers, bring both an understanding of the underlying theoretical perspectives and firsthand knowledge of students and classroom and community conditions, then substantive, well-grounded changes are more likely to be achieved. This volume provides educators with a solid understanding of the constructivist perspective and its application to literacy instruction. Numerous examples of classroom practices and policies are presented and their efficacy evaluated on the basis of constructivist principles. Teachers, school administrators, teacher educators, and policymakers should find information that assists them in designing and reorienting practices and policies to foster the higher literacies in schools.

SUMMARY

As the 21st century approaches, educators face many challenges, chief among them an ever increasingly diverse student population and a society that requires ever increasingly diverse literacy use. The chapters in this book illustrate the manner in which a constructive perspective provides the framework for school literacy experiences that accomplish the goals of higher literacies. In particular, literacy instruction from a constructivist view builds on the strengths of students with diverse backgrounds, so that all students acquire the literacy levels required for full participation in a complex and diverse society.

REFERENCES

Anderson, R. C., Hiebert, E. H., Scott, J. A., & Wilkinson, I. A. G. (1985). *Becoming a nation of readers*. Champaign, IL: Center for the Study of Reading.

Brown, R. (1989). Testing and thoughtfulness. *Educational Leadership, 46,* 31–33.

Carbo, M. (1988). Debunking the great phonics myth. *Phi Delta Kappan, 70,* 226–240.

Chall, J. S. (1989). Learning to read: The great debate 20 years later—A response to 'Debunking the great phonics myth.' *Phi Delta Kappan, 70,* 521–538.

Clark, C. M., & Peterson, P. L. (1986). Teachers' thought processes. In M. C. Wittrock (Ed.), *Handbook of research on teaching* (3rd ed., pp. 255–296). New York: Macmillan.

Dewey, J. (1909). *The school and society.* Chicago: University of Chicago Press.

Feitelson, D. (1988). *Facts and fads in beginning reading: A cross-language perspective.* Norwood, NJ: Ablex.

Fraatz, J. M. B. (1987). *The politics of reading: Power, opportunity, and prospects for change in America's public schools.* New York: Teachers College Press.

McGee, L. M., & Lomax, R. G. (1990). On combining apples and oranges: A response to Stahl and Miller. *Review of Educational Research, 60,* 133–140.

Meisels, S. J. (1989). High-stakes testing in kindergarten. *Educational Leadership, 46,* 16–22.

Pearson, P. D. (1989). Reading the whole-language movement. *Elementary School Journal, 90,* 231–241.

Piaget, J. (1959). *The language and thought of the child.* New York: Humanities Press.

Stahl, S. A., & Miller, P. D. (1989). Whole language and language experience approaches for beginning reading: A quantitative research synthesis. *Review of Educational Research, 59,* 87–116.

von Glasersfeld, E. (1983). Learning as a constructive activity. In J. C. Bergeron & N. Herscovics (Eds.), *Proceedings of the fifth annual meeting of the North American chapter of the International Group for the Psychology of Mathematics Education* (Vol. 1, pp. 42–69). Montreal: Universite de Montreal, Faculte de Sciences de l'Education.

Vygotsky, L. (1978). *Mind in society: The development of higher psychological processes.* Cambridge, MA: Harvard University Press.

Part I
PERSPECTIVES

The title of this section is plural denoting nuances in the constructivist view of literacy, rather than uniquely different perspectives. The different orientations of the first three chapters illustrate the manner in which several disciplines have contributed to development of constructivist themes. The broadly conceived chapter by Langer opens this section by identifying roots of constructivism in cognitive psychology, on the one hand, and anthropology and sociology, on the other. In the following chapters, Eisenhart and Cutts-Dougherty delineate contributions to constructivism from cultural anthropology, and Calfee and Nelson-Barber expand on contributions from cognitive psychology.

When paradigms shift, misinterpretations of the new paradigm often occur—frequently in the form of "new" labels for "old" concepts. It is as critical to understand what the perspective is *not,* as it is to understand what it is. The last two chapters in this section explore two themes of educational evaluation from the constructivist viewpoint. The chapter by House, Emmer, and Lawrence examines the current interest in cultural literacy and its implications for cultural diversity. The idea that diverse experiences impact readers' interpretations of text is recognized by E. D. Hirsch, a primary proponent of cultural literacy. House et al. show how Hirsch misconstrues the idea, creating an interpretation that eliminates diversity, rather than fosters it. The chapter by Miramontes and Commins considers a frequently taken perspective of the learning potential of students with diverse backgrounds—a deficit view. Miramontes and Commins spell out the consequences of such a view and its contradictions of what children know and how they learn.

Taken together, the chapters in this section provide a solid grasp of the constructivist perspective and what it means (and does not mean, in some cases) for practice. While many issues related to implementation of constructivist ideas are left to later sections of this book, it should be clear that constructivism has powerful and far-reaching implications for improving literacy in an increasingly diverse society.

2 | Literacy and Schooling: A Sociocognitive Perspective

JUDITH A. LANGER
State University of New York, Albany

Throughout the educational history of the United States, each generation has brought with it current concerns about the literacy development and instruction of its children as well as current notions of the literacy demands of the society and abilities of its adults to meet those demands. Attention to literacy has remained more or less constant, although the issues have changed. This can be seen in a survey of the titles of books and articles indexed by the Library of Congress, Education Index, and Educational References Information Clearinghouse (Langer, 1988), which indicates that across this century concerns about literacy have followed changing foci: the literacy abilities of immigrant populations, the testing and teaching of literacy to adults, literacy acquisition in K–12 schooling, literacy skills underlying reading and writing. However, it was not until 1965 that the Education Index used the word *literacy* in addition to *illiteracy* as a descriptor, reflecting concerns with how *well* students comprehended and wrote. This broader emphasis has been accompanied by an increased publication of books on literacy—particularly those dealing with relationships among literacy, culture, thinking, and learning.

Although notions of literacy and what it means to be a literate individual have taken on broader meanings and broader implications, underlying views of literacy instruction seem to have remained relatively stable (Langer & Allington, in press; Langer, 1984b). During the first half of the 20th century, the issues surrounding literacy and schooling generally focused on curriculum—what to teach and when (e.g., Gray, 1919; Pressey & Pressey, 1921)—as well as on underlying skills in an attempt to develop procedures to assess the presence or absence of these skills (e.g., Davis, 1944; Gates, 1921; Richards, 1929; Thorndike, 1917). Implicit in this view of literacy instruction was that skill acquisition preceded the ability to engage successfully in literate activities. From this view it followed that short-answer, fill-in, and multiple-choice exercises designed to teach and test literacy subskills could be useful instructional tools.

By mid-century, the work of cognitive and linguistic researchers (e.g., Brown, 1958; Bruner, 1978; Bruner, Olver, & Greenfield, 1966; Inhelder & Piaget, 1958) began to have a profound effect on literacy theory. Their work provided an alternative view of learning, suggesting that conceptual development is rule governed, characterized by gradually changing systems of representations of the whole (e.g., of literacy events) rather than by the additive acquisition of separate skills that do not necessarily occur in similar ways in actual use. This work shifted the research focus to the processes of coming to understand, which in turn strongly affected research into processes of reading and writing (Gregg & Steinberg, 1980; Spiro, 1980). Although there was an active line of research on general classroom practices (summarized by Doyle, 1983) in the 1970s and early 1980s, process-oriented literacy research tended to focus on cognitive behaviors alone, not also on what to teach and how to teach it, nor on the conditions that affect the learning enterprise; there was little direct concern about societal uses of literacy or about literacy instruction.

It was not until the 1980s, in response to the incorporation of sociolinguistic and anthropological conceptions of literacy events and literacy environments into studies of literacy (e.g., Cook-Gumperz, 1986; Erickson, 1977; Heath, 1983; Ogbu, 1983; Scribner & Cole, 1980), that research into literacy processes and instruction was united. Underlying this work is the belief that use shapes thinking and learning, and that the contribution of context and culture cannot be overstated in what is learned and how. Because it looks at learning in action, this work often provides a commentary on instruction (e.g., Bloome, 1987; Cazden, 1988; Dyson, 1984; Florio & Clark, 1982; Graves, 1983; Green & Wallat, 1981; Heath, 1983; Langer, 1991; Langer & Applebee, 1987; Sulzby & Teale, 1988; Wells, 1986). Although the studies of process effectively moved concerns of instruction well beyond issues of curriculum, it is in combination with the more recent culturally focused work that a coherent framework can be developed for considering issues of instruction.

Such a conceptual union is critical because at this point in the history of literacy education, we are at a crossroads (Applebee, Langer, & Mullis, 1989); we are faced with a tension between our own visions and our own reality. The institutional and societal demands of literacy have changed (e.g., see Kirsch & Jungeblut, 1986; Noyelle, 1985; Venezky, 1987), our scholarly knowledge about conceptions of literacy, how it is learned, and how it can be taught have changed, and related instructional advances are being undertaken in the name of whole language (Goodman, 1986), writing process (Graves, 1983), and writing across the curriculum (Martin, D'Arcy, Newton, & Parker, 1976). Yet, to date these movements remain nascent, having no widespread effect on achievement (Applebee, Langer, & Mullis, 1990a; Langer, Applebee, & Mullis, 1990). The materials of instruction as well as the underlying theories of teaching and learning that were developed during the first half of the century continue to shape people's underlying conceptions of literacy education. For changes in learning to occur, new notions of what literacy means and how it can be learned are in order.

WHAT IS LITERACY?

People generally associate literacy with the ability to read and write. This is the common dictionary definition, the mark of literacy in society at large, and the one generally thought of in regard to schooling. However, literacy can be viewed in a broader and educationally more productive way, as the ability to think and reason like a literate person, *within a particular society*. As Vygotsky (1979) suggested, because the practices of literacy and ways of understanding them depend upon the social conditions in which they are learned, the skills, concepts, and ways of thinking that an individual develops reflect the uses and approaches to literacy that permeate the particular society in which that person is a participant. In this view, literacy is culture-specific and needs to be considered in a multiple sense (see Chapter 8).

Thus, to prepare students to participate fully in the adult community, schools need to understand the ways of thinking that are involved in that society's uses of literacy and to use approaches to literacy instruction that will ensure that these ways of thinking become an intrinsic part of the school's context. Take the Vai society described by Scribner and Cole (1980) as an example. If people need and value memorization, as do the Vai who wish to learn to read the Koran, then an appropriate mode of instruction would be to teach the students to memorize. However, if the uses of literacy require reflection, objectification, and analysis (like the coursework demands of the English schools in the same Vai society), then in the English schools, instruction in these kinds of abilities would be appropriate. Writ large, there is no right or wrong literacy, just one that is more or less appropriate to the demands of a particular culture. Clearly, within a given society, several literacies can be valued, supported, and taught (both formally and informally), in response to the needs of the various subcultures to which the individual members belong or wish to belong.

It follows then, as Scribner and Cole (1980) and Traugott (1987) suggest, that thinking is *not* the result of literacy per se. Rather, thinking is human and reflects the particular oral and written ways of solving problems, organizing knowledge, and communicating that are learned early, have the potential to be—but not always are—reinforced by the schools, and have enormous consequences for the acquisition and uses of language and knowledge throughout life. And when the literacy of the classroom and the literacy of the society differ, we need to ask serious questions about the goals of schooling.

Although notions and uses of literacy vary among cultural groups, they also change within groups across time. In the United States, for example, early uses of literacy were relatively restricted (Kaestle, 1985; Resnick & Resnick, 1977), but the current era requires that students acquire the kinds of critical-thinking skills that are needed to use the communication devices and technologies we meet on a daily basis in our everyday living and in entry-level jobs (Langer, 1987b). These new demands have been discussed, for example, by Noyelle (1985), who describes the shift in both the American workplace and in daily life from tasks involving manual to those requiring cognitive processes. American schools, Noyelle thinks, need to reflect these societal shifts by training students in the more flexible thinking skills they will need for entry into today's job market. If we are to respond to these concerns, literacy instruction needs to go much beyond the acts of reading and writing, and to teach culturally appropriate ways of literate thinking as well.

Because literate thinking is a reflection of the uses of literacy within a *particular* culture, the kinds of intellectual functions with which we are familiar (analysis and synthesis, for example) are not necessarily the benchmarks of literate thinking in all cultures; ways of thinking follow function. This is in contrast to the assumption that people who are not literate are deficient in mental skills, suggesting instead that ways of thinking differ and it is these differing *approaches* to meaning that must be better understood. Scribner and Cole (1980), for instance, show that the same Vai people who do very poorly on general tests of cognitive abilities are seen to reason very well when called upon to use the particular cognitive skills they involve in completing tasks within their own culture. It is possible that because the literate-illiterate dichotomy has permeated our thinking, for the major portion of this century, educators have focused literacy instruction primarily on *acts* of reading and writing—with little attention to the complex ways of thinking that are used in nonreading and nonwriting situations as well. Attention to cultural ways of thinking associated with literacy allows literacy instruction to focus on how students *think,* as well as on the skills they use to read and write. It permits teachers and students to regard reading and writing as tools that enable, but do not ensure, literate thinking.

The kinds of literate-thinking skills valued in American culture are generalizable to many situations besides those where people read and write—situations where people talk about texts, compare their interpretations with others, and explain, rethink, and reformulate what they know. Literate thinking is not wholly reliant on the use of print, although the cognitive and linguistic activities involved are similar to those people use when they read and write.

For example, when a group of students reads a social studies textbook and then discusses the contents and the implications, most people would say that the students are engaging in literate thinking. But what if they had had that discussion after seeing a television news report about the same topic? It could be claimed that the students had engaged in literate thinking even though they had neither read nor written. Now, imagine a group of students who don't know how to read or write (in English or another language) engaged in the very same conversation about the television news report; it could be claimed that they too would have engaged in literate thinking. In contrast, imagine that the students had read the same social studies text and then completed end-of-chapter questions by locating information in the text and copying the information the questions asked them to itemize. In this case, it could be claimed that the kinds of literacy reflected in this activity do not reflect the kinds of literacy needed and valued by American society today—that the activity does not reflect literate behavior, even if the students get the answers right. These examples highlight the distinction between literacy as the act of reading and writing and literacy as *ways* of thinking.

Reading and writing as memorization or copying can be socially appropriate (as with Arabic for the Vai). However, this form of literacy is inappropriate to the present-day communication and technological demands of American society. It is the culturally appropriate way of thinking, not the act of reading or writing, that is most important in the development of literacy. Literate thinking manifests itself in different ways in oral and written language in different societies, and educators need to understand these ways of thinking if they are to build bridges and facilitate transitions among ways of thinking.

THE STATE OF LITERACY IN AMERICAN SCHOOLS

How well are our schools currently doing in teaching the more thoughtful literacy skills used in today's society? The best available evidence comes from the National Assessment of Educational Progress (NAEP). Reports, based on the 1984 and 1986 assessments, provide an overview of achievement in reading since 1971 (Applebee, Langer, & Mullis, 1990b) and achievement in writing since 1974 (Applebee, Langer, & Mullis, 1986)—over a decade of achievement in both subjects, in the elementary, middle-school, and secondary grades.

NAEP findings indicate that in both reading and writing, achievement among language-minority school-age students has increased across the past 10 to 15 years. In reading, the *rate* of increase for minority students was higher than that of the white students of the same age. White students were still performing better, but the gap was substantially narrowed. However, NAEP findings also indicate that in reading and writing none of the groups of students—neither the minority nor the majority students—are performing well. Improvement in overall achievement levels has come about because more and more students are able to perform well at the lower levels of competence in reading and writing—and that is where the minority students' growth has taken place as well. When the texts become more complex or the questions become more difficult, when more thoughtful literate thinking is required, comprehension drops off.

In writing, students (minority and majority alike) seem to be developing at least minimal writing skills. They can write simple stories and reports but cannot write persuasive or analytic pieces that require them to mount a coherent argument or explain their position or point of view. These results were similar for all groups of students: relative success at the more "basic" tasks and relative failure with anything that required more thoughtful responses. Students do not seem to be learning the type of literate-thinking skills needed in present-day society.

Although these results are distressing, they reflect the success of American schools in teaching what they have set out to teach. Whether by accident or design, the school curricula and the tests that go with them have rewarded relatively simple performance, and they have undervalued the attainment of more thoughtful skills.

In a recent study, Langer and Applebee (1987) found that even teachers who are deeply committed to using writing for broader purposes, who have sought to learn new instructional approaches, and who are committed to using writing as a way to help their students think and learn, have great difficulty in carrying out their goals. Their attempts to focus on more thoughtful writing activities were undercut by their deeply rooted views of their role as "transmitter" of knowledge—and with it their overarching concern with diagnosing what students needed to learn, teaching the missing information, and testing to evaluate the success of that teaching. This pattern of test-teach-test left even the best intentioned teachers with little room to encourage students to think, muse, and grow as writers and readers.

Standardized tests reinforce these emphases. Studies of testing (Langer, 1985, 1987a) indicate that tests focus on small bits of information and make such unusual cognitive demands that it is difficult to know if a student got the right answer for the wrong reason or the wrong answer for the right reason. Thoughtful literate behaviors are not helpful to get through most tests used in school.

These results can be interpreted as a signal that more than a few schools are basing their instructional programs on an older and more restricted definition of literacy, focusing more on the acts of reading and writing than on the ways of thinking.

Example 1: María

María, a woman who arrived in California from El Salvador about 6 years ago (Langer, in progress), enrolled in a 2-year degree program in a local college. In addition to her regular courses, she was placed in a basic English-as-a-second-language (ESL) class as a result of her test scores. She got A's and B's in her economics, government, history, and accounting courses, and also passed her first ESL course. But she took her second ESL course three times and couldn't pass the required posttest.

Although she was never assigned anything more than a few paragraphs in length to read in her ESL class, she borrowed many novels from her American friends and acquaintances; she bought books as well. She read Ernest Hemingway, Toni Morrison, and Alice Walker and discussed them intelligently. She could also understand her academic course books and discussed the ideas outside of class.

But when it came to the exercises she had to do in class and the posttests she had to pass, she got caught in a particular type of question-answering skill: She couldn't figure out the difference between what her test labeled as direct statements, valid interpretations, and unjustified assumptions. She could explain very well whether a statement was true or not, and even how she knew it, but the terminology of the questions and its relation to what she had read continued to cónfuse her. She understood the passages but had difficulty completing the exercises. Whenever she thought she understood how to complete the worksheets, she would find an exception to her rule. She was a diligent student who arranged for tutorial help and bought extra workbooks to practice, but she simply couldn't "get" the answering skills needed to pass the tests. She finally left school without finishing her degree. She never had a chance to show how well she could read and reason and think critically in English.

Example 2: Jack

Jack is a high school English teacher whose class was observed for a full year (Langer & Applebee, 1987). Jack's class was studying *Romeo and*

Juliet, and at the end of the unit he wanted his students to understand the alternatives Juliet has at the end of the play and her choice to die instead of to live. Jack said he thought his students' personal experiences in making difficult choices might help them to understand Juliet's dilemma better. So, he planned a free-writing activity in which his students would describe a conflict. They were to pick a time when they had had to make a difficult decision, tell why they did what they did, and discuss the factors that influenced their decision.

Jack might have opened the class with a discussion of conflicts and decisions, assigned the writing, and used it as a basis for a discussion of *Romeo and Juliet* later on. But he did other things. The first 26 minutes of the class session were devoted to diagramming sentences from a grammar exercise book, followed by 7 minutes when he read aloud from *Romeo and Juliet* (to give them a "feel" for the play). Thirty-three minutes into the class, he said, "Now, we're going to do some personal free writing." It took another 3 minutes for him to give them instructions. When the bell rang, most of the students were still writing. Jack collected the papers, pleased that his students had had a chance to think about issues of personal conflict. He never mentioned the writing again.

At the end of the unit, when the class finished *Romeo and Juliet,* Jack asked the students to write about Juliet's decision and how she came to it. Not surprisingly, the students never made the connection between the free writing they had done earlier and Juliet's decision. Some didn't even remember having done the free writing. However, when we spoke with Jack later, we saw this really didn't matter, because Jack was looking for other things. He wanted his students to write about Juliet's decision based on the interpretation he had taught them and considered correct.

María's and Jack's classroom experiences are not unusual. Neither our old nor most of our present approaches to instruction encourage thoughtful literacy learning. The activities assigned in most classrooms are like those María and the students in Jack's class were required to complete—they are "exercises" that require students to use small bits of language and thought, abstracted from the literacy activities to which they once belonged. They do not probe students' understandings nor answer the questions students might have about what they read. The activities are separated from the literacy event itself—the text (or textbook) presents the exercise, it is done for the teacher, and its success will be judged by the teacher. This is in keeping with a traditional view of education that focuses on the teacher as transmitter of knowledge and the student as receiver. It produces what Barnes (1976) calls transmission instead of interpretation, where teachers transmit what they know for the students to receive. In such an instructional system the students' own backgrounds, experiences, and ideas are irrelevant. This is also the kind of education that is curriculum-goal driven: There is a set of skills or information to be learned, and the teacher tests to see what the students know and don't know, teaches what isn't known, then tests to see if it has been learned.

When instruction is driven by this model, the focus shifts toward discrete skills and small bits of information that are easy to test and away from deeper understandings that, although more complicated and time-consuming to consider, are more supportive of literate thinking. And clearly, the results from the NAEP suggest that such approaches have not been effective in teaching more thoughtful literacy skills.

THE SOCIOCOGNITIVE VIEW

Let us consider an alternative, a sociocognitive view (Langer, 1987). This view sees literate thinking as the ability to think and reason like a literate person within a particular society, literacy learning as socially based, and cognition (ways of thinking) as growing out of those socially based experiences. Within social settings, both at home and in school, students learn how literacy is used and how literate knowledge is communicated—what counts as a literacy event and what literacy behaviors "look like," what literacy-related values are respected, and what literate habits are to be cultivated. As children learn to engage in literate behaviors to serve the functions and reach the ends they see modeled around them, they become literate—in a culturally appropriate way; they use certain cognitive strategies to structure their thoughts and complete their tasks, and not others. Learners' literate thinking is selective, based upon the uses to which literacy is put and the learners' beliefs about "what counts" within that community. Thus, as children learn to interpret and use the linguistic signs and symbols of the culture for culturally appropriate purposes, they become part of the community (Langer, 1987); they become what that community considers "literate."

The sociocognitive view grows out of theory on language and literacy learning and out of more recent work in psychology, anthropology, and sociolinguistics. (See, e.g., Bruner, 1978; Chapter 3, this volume; Heath, 1983; John-Steiner, 1985; Luria, 1929/1978; Scribner & Cole, 1980; Vygotsky, 1979; Wertsch, 1985). It is rooted in the belief that learners do not learn rule-governed systems such as language by having the rules presented to them by others and then practicing the rules. On the contrary, they learn such rules in the process of interacting with others to complete tasks in meaningful and functional situations. Routines develop as learners internalize the principles of approaches that work—and they revise and refine their skills with repeated practice in functional settings (Applebee, 1984; Langer, 1984b; Langer, 1991; Langer & Applebee, 1986; Langer & Applebee, 1987).

This view leads to a substantive change in the ways in which literacy learning and issues of schooling are addressed. It forces us to look at ways in which literacy is used, what is valued as knowing, how it is demonstrated and communicated—and the kinds of thinking as well as content knowledge that result. Because schooling is an important community in which academically sanctioned literacy is used and learned, we need to rethink the sociocognitive context of that schooling—the ways in which more complex thinking can be encouraged, becoming the goals and values and underlying fabric of literate thought within that community.

From a sociocognitive perspective, what kinds of situations are likely to encourage students to think more deeply about what they are doing? The learning will take place in social contexts in which there are shared problems to solve or issues to discuss. In general, these will be situations where there is more than one right answer and where the answer that is given will need to be shared with and justified to other people who may disagree or misunderstand.

To be powerful educational contexts, these situations must also provide ways for students to learn the skills necessary to complete their tasks more successfully. There are many ways this learning can take place. Some of it can come about simply as a result of the interaction—students will see what works and what doesn't, and will shape their performance accordingly. Some of it will come from models that others provide either through discussion or in the materials they are working with. Some of it will come from the differing strengths that other students bring; they will learn from each other. And some, of course, will come directly from the teacher. This may take the form of direct instruction, help offered at appropriate points in the activity, questions that the teacher asks, and the structures included to guide the students through the overall activity. Thus, in this view a prewriting activity is not just a way to get a lesson going but also a strategy for thinking about new material—a strategy that a student should eventually be able to use alone. Such a view of instruction is at the heart of the sociocognitive approach.

A sociocognitive view means two things for instruction. First, more attention is paid to the social purposes to which the literacy skills are being put—students learn best when they are trying to accomplish something that is personally and socially meaningful. Second, more attention is paid to the structure as well as content of tasks that we ask students to undertake so that direct instruction in needed skills will be provided as part of the task, at points where it is needed. In this way students will have a better chance of understanding how the new skills and knowledge relate to the activities that are being completed. Rather than simply memorizing isolated rules and facts (as in María's case), they will be able to make sense of how the rules work in completing literacy tasks. To clarify what these notions look like in practice, the following section provides several examples of instruction from a sociocognitive perspective. (See Chapters 7 and 10 for related discussions of instruction.)

Learning Logs

Julian, a biology teacher (Langer & Applebee, 1987), began to use the last 5 minutes of each class period as learning-log time. The students were asked to jot down any thoughts they had about:

1. What they had learned
2. What they didn't understand
3. What they were unsure of
4. Something else they would like to know about what they had just studied

The teacher would read the logs and write notes back to the students, sometimes organize the comments to put on an overhead projector as the basis of class discussion, and use the logs in conferences with the students to discuss how their knowledge about biology was changing across the semester.

Why, from a sociocognitive perspective, is this activity likely to stimulate more thoughtful learning? First, it grows directly out of the social purpose of the learning activity and the writing of the logs. The students make the entries in order to communicate with the teacher about the lesson, and the teacher communicates back—in writing, class discussion, or individual conferences. The logs are not used as tests where the students need to display a right answer. Rather, the activity provides room for the kinds of uncertainty that accompany new learning. Because students can exhibit their uncertainties along the way, the teacher has a better chance of knowing the particular kind of help to offer.

Often this kind of learning-log activity leads the student to put ideas together in new ways, simply by thinking and writing about them. Because neither recitation nor right answers are expected by the teacher, the students' thoughts can turn inward—to explore and question the new learning, rather than outward—to guess what the teacher wants. This kind of reflection can be the basis of new strategies students acquire for both language and content learning—learned within a classroom culture that supports and values such thinking. But self-reflection and self-monitoring are not enough, and the activity can also open communication with the teacher, making future assistance potentially more successful because both teacher and student will have a good idea of where to begin.

Letter Writing

Shirley Brice Heath, a Stanford anthropologist, and Amanda Branscombe, a ninth-grade basic English teacher (Heath & Branscombe, 1985), had Branscombe's students gather data about language use in their community. Through this activity, students came to focus on issues of language use and language structure. They shared their new knowledge about language as well as their personal experiences with pen pals. Their varied audiences required them to engage in writing that became gradually more and more decontextualized. The students began by writing to older students in their school who knew something about them and their experiences. From direct feedback, they were able to learn when they had made themselves clear and when they had not been understood by their audience. They were also able to learn how to write better. Then they wrote to Shirley Brice Heath's daughter, close in age but geographically distant. They needed to explain more about themselves, the people, the places, and the activities they were writing about. Last they wrote to Shirley Brice Heath, who wrote back about her travels and encouraged them to learn from her experiences and to share their own.

From a sociocognitive perspective, this activity can be seen as being both personally and socially meaningful; the students focused on presenting their ideas in ways that worked for them and could also be understood by the different audiences. It helped the students to do more academic writing than they had ever done before, directing it toward a real audience and serving a real purpose. Instead of the usual writing exercise where the teacher marks their pretend letters for lack of clarity, this assignment allowed a real audience to provide feedback about what they did and didn't understand in the students' letters. The students had to become more explicit in their writing in order to be understood; they had to pay attention to such things as discourse structure, syntax, and mechanics. And because the letters were written to pen pals who were different from them, and about whom they knew less, they had to learn to provide increasingly more detail and elaboration and to become more logical and more academic in their use of language.

Uses of Language

Luis Moll and Stephen Diaz (1987) taught expository writing to junior high school students. They turned the students into ethnographers who were to learn about the language uses in their own communities. As a group, they developed an interview questionnaire and interviewed members of their community about such topics as their attitudes toward bilingualism and their uses of language. After completing the interviews, the students examined their data together and then wrote a report about their study and findings. During this experience the students used literacy skills on many levels, to plan, to gather information, to synthesize it, to analyze it for academic and social meaning, to elaborate upon their findings, and to present it in a coherent academic report. And they did it well.

From a sociocognitive perspective, the students had to communicate with each other about what to do and how to do it. They helped each other, and their teachers helped them. Those who understood the nature of this highly academic activity could help the others think the problem through. The students also needed to think analytically about the kind of information they wanted and how best to get it. Throughout the activity, including analyzing the data and writing the report, they worked cooperatively, each assisting others with the aspect of the task he or she understood and could do best. The teachers also helped them, and, in the end, students had learned a great deal about research, writing, and literate thinking.

Writing a Newspaper

Francoise Herrmann (1990) studied foreign-language learning in a sociocognitive context. She had college students who were learning French as a foreign language engage in a collaborative learning activity in which they wrote a newspaper using a computer network. The students determined what the paper would be like, what topics to write about, how and where to gather the data—everything from planning to production of the paper. They planned and talked among themselves, and they interviewed their informants. They became food critics, museum buffs, travel editors, and political columnists. And they saw their columns grow on the computer, where they communicated with each other, edited each other's work, and collaborated with their teacher via the computer network. (They also, of course, generated oral language around the computer—about use of the computer and about the newspaper itself.) Oral and written language, and talk about language as well as text, occurred in both the computer and noncomputer settings; the newspaper was the catalyst for language use.

From a sociocognitive perspective, this is a joint activity where the need for language and the uses of language grow out of the group's need to communicate with each other and to write messages. It also involves interactive teaching. The students helped each other with the content and language, and the teacher was available to help whenever needed. The language and literacy learning took place continuously, as the students made their commitments to work on the paper, develop their plans, write their articles, review each other's work, and publish the newspaper. The French language skills the students learned were embedded in a context where they had opportunity to think about and plan and practice their new learnings over time and to generalize their language learning to new situations. Because language was used in communication with others, vocabulary, syntax, verb forms, and text organization were discussed and learned in a way that is very different from the usual approach, even in activity-based foreign language texts.

A Prereading Plan

Not all activities need to be done in a group. When students read or write alone (as they so often do in high school and college classes), it is helpful to begin with a preliminary activity to help them think about what they already know about the topic. This lets them form ideas and language to express those ideas as well as develop connections (both topical and syntactic) as ways to link them.

Some years ago, Langer (1981, 1984a) developed the PReP activity, Prereading Plan, designed to do just this. In it the teacher asks the class to free associate about major concepts they will read for class. For example, recently, in preparing to read Bruner's (1986) *Actual Minds, Possible Worlds,* I asked the students in a graduate seminar to tell everything that came to mind when they heard the phrases "narrative thought" and "logical thought." They were asked to scribble their thoughts on paper in pairs, although they could as easily have called them aloud. In either case, their ideas would be discussed. Some students talked about logical thought as being scientific, formal, and ordered, whereas others said narrative thought was personal, subjective, and lifelike. During this portion of the PReP, students have a chance to discuss what made them think of what they did. In this situation, the students commented, "Olson talks about . . ." or "Rosenblatt says . . . ."

Next, in PReP, the teacher orchestrates a discussion to help the students think more deeply about what they already know about the concept, and what they have become aware of through discussion. In this case, the students were asked to think about some ways in which they thought the two modes were similar and different, and then to think about the comparative utility of each mode for both academic study and everyday life. My students described the utility of both the logical and narrative modes in everyday life but had a more difficult time doing so for academic study beyond the humanities classroom. A few students, however, argued for the value of historical narrative and personalizing scientific problems as a means to solving them.

Finally in PReP, the students are reminded to think about their course assignment—the reading they will do—and to predict how the ideas they've just discussed will relate to the reading. The seminar students tried to link the title of the book *Actual Minds, Possible Worlds* to the two modes of thought we had been discussing. And with these thoughts stirring, they were ready to read.

From a sociocognitive perspective, this activity is thought provoking because the class discussion provides a sharing of ideas, to remind students of what they know. The students interact in their sharing of knowledge, and the teacher helps structure the discussion and the thinking, leading the students toward the particular language and concepts they will read about (or need to have available for writing) and also the ways in which the ideas might be connected. Students actively think about what they know, changing and refining their own ideas and their own language as new information is discussed by themselves and others. The activity also provides them with a useful strategy to use on their own—a pulling together of relevant ideas to help make sense of new experience.

DISCUSSION

The literacy activities described above are rooted in an alternative view of literacy, one that focuses more broadly on literate thinking than on the acts of reading and writing. This view sees literacy as reflective of the uses of literacy within a culture and suggests that when the literacy demands of a society change, so too must the school uses of literacy. Such changes are necessary because there is ample evidence that the kind of literate thinking currently valued and used in the United States is generally not taught, learned, or tested in American schools; it is not the focus of schooling. A conceptualization of literacy instruction based upon a sociocognitive approach to literacy learning suggests that skills, structures, and routines are internalized en route to accomplishing purposeful and socially meaningful activities, and that the kinds of literate thinking that learners acquire is reflective of the social context in which literacy is learned. If schools are to teach higher levels of literate thinking, teachers must value and use these activities as part of the ongoing social-communicative fabric of the classroom. The examples discussed above illustrate what instruction from this point of view looks like.

In none of these activities is knowledge "transmitted." The role of the group members, the role of the teacher, and the goals of instruction are very different from the traditional view. There is cooperation and collaboration; there is a sense of a meaningful use to which language is put; there is talk and metatalk about language and about information. Further, the success of the learning is evaluated easily by both the learner and the teacher—in terms of how well the job gets done. Both the student and the teacher know what the student does not understand, and where more help is still needed.

All this is a far cry from the pretest, assign, and retest view of instruction that is prevalent in American schools. But it is difficult to adopt a socio-cognitive approach to instruction. The more traditional paradigm, with its pre- and posttests, marks a teacher's "success"—it tells what and how much the students have "learned." Also, it elicits the kinds of responses the students will need to give when they take standardized tests. However, the simplicity of these instructional activities prevents them from leading toward more reasoned thinking—because they don't involve the students as active and thoughtful learners in personally or socially meaningful tasks.

SUMMARY

Literacy instruction needs to help students think more deeply and more broadly about language and content and to use these as they engage in socially purposeful activities like the examples above. Teachers, tests, and instructional materials need to begin to look for successful learning not in isolated bits of knowledge but in students' growing ability to use language and literacy in more varied and more reasoned ways. And progress in learning needs to be judged by gauging students' ability to complete those activities more successfully. When this occurs, the nature of instructional activities will change dramatically—from pretend to real tasks, from parts to wholes, and from practice to doing. And literacy instruction will have begun to move from the focus on reading and writing exercises toward the teaching of literacy as a way of thinking appropriate to the demands of our present society.

REFERENCES

Applebee, A. N. (1984). Writing and reasoning. *Review of Educational Research, 54,* 577–586.

Applebee, A. N., Langer, J. A., & Mullis, I. V. S. (1986). *Writing trends across the decade, 1974–84.* Princeton, NJ: National Assessment of Educational Progress, ETS.

Applebee, A. N., Langer, J. A., & Mullis, I. V. S. (1989). *Crossroads in American education*. Princeton, NJ: National Assessment of Educational Progress, ETS.

Applebee, A. N., Langer, J. A., & Mullis, I. V. S. (1990a). *Learning to write in our nation's schools*. Princeton, NJ: National Assessment of Educational Progress, ETS.

Applebee, A. N., Langer, J. A., & Mullis, I. V. S. (1990b). *The reading report card, 1971–88*. Princeton, NJ: National Assessment of Educational Progress, ETS.

Barnes, D. (1976). *From communication to curriculum*. Harmondsworth, England: Penguin.

Bloome, D. (1987). *Literacy and schooling*. Norwood, NJ: Ablex.

Brown, R. (1958). *Words and things*. New York: Free Press.

Bruner, J. S. (1978). The role of dialogue in language acquisition. In A. Sinclair, R. J. Jarvelle, & W. J. M. Levelt (Eds.), *The child's conception of language*. New York: Springer-Verlag.

Bruner, J. S. (1986). *Actual minds, possible worlds*. Cambridge, MA: Harvard University Press.

Bruner, J. S., Olver, R. R., & Greenfield, P. M. (1966). *Studies in cognitive growth: A collaboration at the Center for Cognitive Studies*. New York: John Wiley & Sons.

Cazden, C. (1988). *Classroom discourse*. Portsmouth, NH: Heinemann.

Cook-Gumperz, J. (1986). *The social construction of literacy*. New York: Cambridge University Press.

Davis, F. B. (1944). Fundamental factors of comprehension in reading. *Psychometrics, 9*, 185–97.

Doyle, W. (1983). Academic work. *Review of Educational Research, 53*, 159–199.

Dyson, A. (1984). Learning to write/Learning to do school. *Research in the Teaching of English, 16*(3), 233–264.

Erickson, F. R. (1977). Some approaches to inquiry in school-community ethnography. *Anthropology and Education Quarterly, 8*, 515–544.

Florio, S., & Clark, C. (1982). Functions of writing in the classroom. *Research in the Teaching of English, 16*, 115–130.

Gates, A. I. (1921). An experimental and statistical study of reading tests. *Journal of Educational Psychology, 12*, 303–307.

Gray, W. S. (1919). *Principles of method of teaching reading as derived from scientific investigation*. (National Society for the Study of Education Yearbook, 18, Part II.) Chicago, IL: University of Chicago Press.

Graves, D. (1983). *Writing: Teachers and children at work*. Exeter, NH: Heinemann.

Goodman, K. (1986). *What's whole about whole language?* Exeter, NH: Heinemann.

Green, J., & Wallat, C. (1981). *Ethnography and language in educational settings*. Norwood, NJ: Ablex.

Gregg, L. W., & Steinberg, E. R. (1980). *Cognitive processes in writing*. Hillsdale, NJ: Erlbaum.

Heath, S. B. (1983). *Ways with words*. New York: Cambridge University Press.

Heath, S. B., & Branscombe, A. (1985). Intelligent writing in an audience community: Teacher, students, and researcher. In S. Freedman (Ed.), *The acquisition of written language* (pp. 3–32). Norwood, NJ: Ablex.

Herrmann, F. (1990). *Computers and communication: Learning to write in a foreign language*. Unpublished doctoral dissertation, Stanford University, Stanford, CA.

Inhelder, B., & Piaget, J. (1958). *The growth of logical thinking from childhood to adolescence*. London: Routledge & Kegan Paul.

John-Steiner, V. (1985). The road to competence in an alien land: A Vygotskian approach to bilingualism. In J. Wertsch (Ed.), *Culture, communication, and cognition* (pp. 348–371). New York: Cambridge University Press.

Kaestle, C. F. (1985). The history of literacy and the history of readers. *Review of research in education* (Vol. 12). Washington, DC: American Educational Research Association.

Kirsch, I. S., & Jungeblut, A. (1986). *Literacy: Profiles of America's young adults*. Princeton, NJ: Educational Testing Service.

Langer, J. A. (1981). From theory to practice: A prereading plan. *Journal of Reading, 152–156.*

Langer, J. A. (1984a). Examining background knowledge and text comprehension. *Reading Research Quarterly, 19,* 468–481.

Langer, J. A. (1984b). Literacy instruction in American schools. *American Journal of Education, 93*(1), 107–131.

Langer, J. A. (1985). Levels of questioning: An alternative view. *Reading Research Quarterly, 21*(5), 586–602.

Langer, J. A. (1987a). The construction of meaning and the assessment of comprehension. In R. Freedle & R. Duran (Eds.), *Cognitive and linguistic analyses of test performance* (pp. 225–244). Norwood, NJ: Ablex.

Langer, J. A. (1987b). A sociocognitive perspective on literacy. In J. Langer (Ed.), *Language, literacy, and culture: Issues of society and schooling* (pp. 1–20). Norwood, NJ: Ablex.

Langer, J. (1988). State of research on literacy. *Educational Researcher, 17,* 42–46.

Langer, J. A. (1991). *Literacy understanding and Literature instruction*. Report series 2.11, Center for the Learning and Teaching of Literature. Albany, NY: State University of New York at Albany.

Langer, J. A. (in progress). *María: A case study. Literacy and learning project*. Albany, NY: The University at Albany.

Langer, J. A., & Allington, R. L. (in press). Curriculum research in reading and writing. In P. Jackson (Ed.), *Handbook of research on curriculum*. New York: Macmillan.

Langer, J. A., & Applebee, A. N. (1986). Reading theory and instruction: Toward a theory of teaching and learning. In E. Rothkopf (Ed.), *Review of Research in Education* (Vol. 14). Washington, DC: American Educational Research Association.

Langer, J. A., & Applebee, A. N. (1987). *How writing shapes thinking: Studies of teaching and learning.* Urbana, IL: National Council of Teachers of English.

Langer, J. A., Applebee, A. N., & Mullis, I. V. S. (1990). *Learning to read in our nation's schools.* Princeton, NJ: National Assessment of Educational Progress, ETS.

Luria, A. R. (1978). The development of writing in the child. *Soviet Psychology, 16,* 65–114. (Original work published 1929)

Martin, N., D'Arcy, P., Newton, B., & Parker, R. (1976). *Writing and learning across the curriculum.* London: Ward Lock Educational.

Moll, L., and Diaz, S. (1987). Change as the goal of educational research. *Anthropology and Education Quarterly, 18,* 300–311.

Noyelle, T. J. (1985). *The new technology and the new economy: Some implications for equal employment opportunity.* Unpublished manuscript, The Conservation of Human Resources Project, Columbia University, New York.

Ogbu, J. (1983). Literacy and schooling in subordinate cultures: The case of black Americans. In D. P. Resnick (Ed.), *Literacy in historical perspective* (pp. 117–138). Washington, DC: Library of Congress.

Pressey, L., & Pressey, S. L. (1921). A critical study of the concept of silent reading. *Journal of Educational Psychology, 12,* 25–31.

Resnick, D. P., & Resnick, L. R. (1977). The nature of literacy: An historical exploration. *Harvard Educational Review, 47,* 370–385.

Richards, I. A. (1929). *Practical criticism.* London: Kegan Paul, Trench, Trubner & Co.

Scribner, S., & Cole, M. (1980). *The psychology of literacy.* Cambridge, MA: Harvard University Press.

Spiro, R. J., Bruce, B. C., & Brewer, W. F. (1980). *Theoretical issues in reading comprehension.* Hillsdale, NJ: Erlbaum.

Sulzby, E., & Teale, W. (1988). *Emergent literacy: Writing and reading.* Norwood, NJ: Ablex.

Thorndike, E. L. (1917). Reading as reasoning: A study of mistakes in paragraph meaning. *Journal of Educational Psychology, 8,* 323–332.

Traugott, E. C. (1987). Literacy and language change: The special case of speech act verbs. In J. Langer (Ed.), *Language, literacy, and culture: Issues of society and schooling* (pp. 111–127). Norwood, NJ: Ablex.

Venezky, R. L., Kaestle, C. F., & Sum, A. M. (1987). *The subtle danger.* Princeton, NJ: Educational Testing Service.

Vygotsky, L. S. (1979). The genesis of higher mental functions. In J. Wertsch (Ed.), *The concept of activity in Soviet psychology.* New York: Sharpe.

Wells, G. (1986). *The meaning makers.* Portsmouth, NH: Heinemann.

Wertsch, J. (Ed.). (1985). *Culture, communication, and cognition.* New York: Cambridge University Press.

3 | Social and Cultural Constraints on Students' Access to School Knowledge

MARGARET A. EISENHART
KATHARINE CUTTS-DOUGHERTY
University of Colorado, Boulder

The point we want to argue in this chapter is that access to knowledge, including literacy, is socially situated and culturally constructed. That is to say, access to knowledge is created in the way we collectively conduct our face-to-face social interactions and social relationships and in the way we give meaning to the pursuit and enactment of knowledge. What people are exposed to, what they are purposefully taught, and what they actually learn are constrained by social arrangements in which we convey who is supposed to know what and under what circumstances and by the meanings that cohere in these social arrangements. The argument, developed by Frederick Gearing (Gearing & Sangree, 1979) and extended by Clement and Eisenhart (1979; Clement, Eisenhart, & Harding, 1979) continues as follows: Most of the information that we acquire in schools, and elsewhere, is cognitively easy to learn. If we are exposed to the information, given supportive opportunities to practice it, and permitted to demonstrate our knowledge of it, most of us will learn it without much trouble. This does *not* happen because social barriers or cultural norms define and limit the type and the amount of information that is supposed to be exchanged within and between social groups.

These different patterns of knowledge use, learned first in community and family social interactions, instantiate and direct the meaning of knowledge displayed by social groups. In families and communities knowledge is made social property, with parcels of it belonging to certain groups, other parcels to other groups. Because conventional social practices and cultural norms limit the occasions for interaction among certain social groups as well as the knowledge that is considered appropriate or natural for people in certain groups to have, information, skills, understandings, beliefs, preferences, interests, and abilities become concentrated in certain social groups and are unlikely to appear in others (Clement & Eisenhart, 1979). If such patterns go undetected or are ignored, they create the foundation for unequal access to knowledge into the future.

Some would counter this argument by saying that this social distribution of knowledge is inevitable in nonschool settings, but schools are supposed to, and do, overcome such social factors. After all, schools take all kinds of children, mix them together in classrooms, try to teach all of them the same things, and try to evaluate all of them using the same measures. This argument continues: If some children get less of what the school offers, it is because they don't try, they don't have the "ability," or they don't get the support from home that they need. Schools are said to be, for example, "color-blind" and "gender neutral." On a theoretical level, we agree that schools could overcome the social and cultural channeling of access to knowledge, but in practice we are afraid that U.S. schools do not do so, at least not as well as they might. One reason why we who work in schools are not doing as much as we might is that we are often unaware of exactly how this channeling occurs.

In what follows, we will illustrate some of the ways that access to literacy is socially and culturally channeled. The examples begin with studies of children before entering school and in elementary school and move on to studies of young people in high school and college. The first example illustrates how the meaning of language use is first constructed in the social arrangements of children's families and communities; it is taken from Heath's work on language socialization. The second example demonstrates the role of the elementary school in organizing social groups and constructing meanings of literacy; it is based on Borko and Eisenhart's (1986) study of second-grade reading groups. The third example explores the contribution of high school and college peer groups, and it draws on the work of Fordham and Ogbu (1986) and of Holland and Eisenhart (1988a, 1988b). After presenting these examples, we will discuss some of our ideas about how problems associated with the social and cultural channeling of access to knowledge might be addressed in schools.

THE CHANNELING OF LITERACY BY COMMUNITY

Shirley Brice Heath (1982a, 1982b, 1983) examined children from different communities first in their homes and later in their schools. She was concerned with the way early experiences in the home generate patterns of communication that then may or may not correspond to those encountered at school. Drawing on Roland Barthes's description of "culture" as a "way of taking" from the world, she demonstrates how early communicative patterns taught in the home organize knowledge and mediate the way it is acquired in school. She compares African-American working-class children of Trackton, white working-class children in Roadville, and middle-class children, both African-American and white, living in Gateway (fictitious names).

In Trackton life is a continuous bustle of social interactions with no fixed schedules or formal routines. Children learn that in order to gain the attention of others they are expected to be entertaining and creative in their use of language. Parents are not interested in their children's rote learning of words and phrases; rather they emphasize the need for youngsters to extend ideas from one situation to another, to recognize similar situations, and to gain control of an audience through language use. Children are rewarded for being creative and innovative in their story telling, and from a very early age Trackton infants learn to assume the roles and guises of others as they recount stories. The type of questioning that predominates in the home is heavily dependent on analogical reasoning skills: Children are asked questions such as, "Now, what you gonna do?" or "What's that like?" with a demand for creative and oftentimes witty answers, and no exact standards for correctness. For Trackton parents, these linguistic skills are necessary for children so they can stand on their own in the world.

Children in Roadville grow up in an environment that is very different. Here children are held to strict eating and sleeping schedules, and they are carefully "taught" how to use words correctly from their first days. Parents spend much time giving directives to their children, and questions are predominantly of the kind "What is this?" or "Where is that?"—questions that test for the referential meaning of words and for knowledge of facts already known to the speaker. Special attention is given to telling the truth and not telling "stories" that depart from the facts.

From the above it is clear that the preschool worlds of Trackton and Roadville children are miles apart, despite their geographic proximity. Further, the middle-class children from the town of Gateway are different from both the Trackton and the Roadville children: They are directed along paths that will be consistent with the demands made of them in their school years, and later in their working life. From infancy, children are seen as conversational partners. Thus they learn to listen and respond to others. Gateway children are asked predominantly "what" questions (as are children from Roadville); however, they are also taught to link old information to new information and to search for creative solutions (in this way more similar to Trackton children, although Gateway children are given more structured experiences for acquiring information than Trackton children).

When they begin school, both the Roadville and Trackton children enter a world where its "ways with words" are somewhat orthogonal to what they have learned in their homes. Initially Roadville children are able to perform adequately as they find a place for their learned ability to follow rules, to give the referential meanings of words, and to tell the "truth." However, as the school begins to demand imaginative thinking, merging reality and fantasy, Roadville children are quickly confused as they find conflicting rules in the school and in their homes.

On the other hand, Trackton children are well practiced in the skills of learning by observing others when they begin school, but the rigid format of the classroom—the stringent spatial and time rules, the demand for exactitude, and the emphasis on correct answers—baffles these creative entertainers. Heath describes how the Trackton children would insist on trying to take the floor during story time (as they would do at home), and how teachers saw this initially as a lack of "normal manners" and later as evidence of "behavior problems." Over a period of time, the communicative differences between Trackton children and the "mainstream" children and teachers led most of the former to be labeled "potential reading failures," despite the incredible interpretive and linguistic skills evidenced by the same children at home.

After tracking the school progress of the children in her study, Heath found that success in school was closely associated with community membership. Middle-class students from Gateway did best, followed by those from Roadville and then by those from Trackton.

Many others have also drawn attention to the communicative breakdowns between teachers and students from different communities (see Chapters 6, 7, 8, and 11). They stress that what young children know about language and its use is learned as part of the interactional/communicative routines of the group in which they grow up. Early home social environments shape the way children go on to understand the world by providing them with a particular set of mediational tools by which they learn how to make and take meaning. The social routines and mediational tools may be quite different from community to community. Parents, community members, and later teachers distribute information through particular mediational channels, only insofar as they know how to "give" it, and students are able to acquire the knowledge presented only insofar as they know how to "take" it. If significant differences between ways of giving and ways of taking go undetected or unaddressed, exchanges of information are likely to be haphazard or unrewarding, and the best intentions of parents, teachers, or students may go unrealized. Only when early patterns of learning are consistent with, or can be attached to, those used in the schools are children likely to benefit from the instruction provided there.

THE CHANNELING OF LITERACY BY ABILITY GROUP

Our second example comes from a study conducted in four second-grade classrooms of a public elementary school in Appalachia, during the 1981–82 school year. The study was designed to investigate students' "conceptions," or ideas, about reading and their reading experiences in each classroom. We were particularly interested in whether students differed in their reading conceptions and whether any differences seemed to be reflections of different reading experiences in school (the following discussion is taken from Borko & Eisenhart, 1986; note the similarity of our findings to those of Allington in Chapter 17).

At the study school, there were no typical minority groups. With the exception of one African-American child in each classroom, all the students were white, and most were middle class; they shared the experience of growing up in a small town/rural county of Appalachia. The four teachers were white, middle class, residents of the area, and in their 20s, with at least 5 years' experience at the school.

Despite the absence of minority groups, we found evidence of distinct social groups and associated information distribution. Here, students were officially divided according to "reading ability" as measured by standardized tests administered at the end of first grade. They were apportioned into four reading groups, as required by the district in all second-grade classrooms.

In general, patterns in the data suggest that students' ways of thinking about reading were related to their reading-group experiences. Low-group students were consistently more likely than high-group students to comment on behavior and procedures, and teachers were more likely to focus on student behavior and instructional procedures in low groups. Reading skills, and, to a more limited extent, global reading ability were also recognized in low-group students' conceptions, although they were mentioned less frequently than behavior. This ordering reflects the higher frequency with which teachers stressed behavior and reading skills (as contrasted to global reading), particularly in public performances in the low groups. High-group students were consistently more likely than low-group students to comment on global reading ability, and teachers more often gave high-group students opportunities to engage in such reading. High-group students also mentioned global reading ability more often than behavior in expressing their conceptions, reflecting the higher frequency with which teachers were observed to focus on global reading in contrast to behavior.

In this school, each reading group, together with the teacher, seemed to be operating with a distinct and closed informational system. Each system was exemplified by its own set of mutually supportive and reinforcing reading activities, student and teacher behaviors, student understandings of reading, and criteria for successful performance. In low-ability second-grade reading groups, students defined learning to read as a process of attempting to behave appropriately while sounding out words, following procedures, and using materials correctly; and they identified as successful those students who performed accordingly. Correspondingly, the teachers (using the designated curriculum) stressed and rewarded correct decoding and appropriate behavior.

This system operated in marked contrast to the system in high reading groups. Here, students focused on "reading a lot" and "reading fast" and were beginning to orient toward reading for meaning. Teachers stressed and rewarded these activities while virtually ignoring student behavior and procedural aspects of the reading program. Together, teachers and high-group students constructed a system in which success was measured primarily in terms of global reading and comprehension.

Implicit in these reading systems were differing criteria for success. For students in high-ability groups, success in group is equivalent to success in class. Students' strong performances in high-group activities are likely to bring them good grades on report cards and high status in class as well as praise from teachers. For students in low groups, in contrast, success in group is not equivalent to success in class. Strong performances in group may bring praise from the teacher but are not likely to bring students good report card grades or high status in class. The reading program thus becomes a means not only of grouping students to facilitate instruction but also of manifesting different views of success and of the relationship between success in group and success in class.

The situation makes movement into a higher group very difficult for low-group students. In order to move up, not only must these students simply work harder and learn more; they must also learn qualitatively different information. To do this, they must learn to think differently about reading and must direct their efforts toward different aspects of learning to read. Yet the closed system of the reading group, with its set of mutually reinforcing knowledge, beliefs, and practices, does not provide the opportunities for these changes to occur, at least not quickly.

It is easy to see how such a reading program can produce a widening gap between high- and low-group readers as students progress through school. It is also easy to see how the self-perpetuating systems of knowledge, belief, and practice that operate within groups become the mechanisms by which some students—namely, those in low groups—learn that they do not have, and are unlikely ever to have, access to the "real" rewards of schooling. Thus, they may be encouraged to look elsewhere (e.g., to peers, to nonschool-sanctioned activities) for satisfaction and status. Regardless of background or home experiences, students in low groups are vulnerable to such pressures. Students from communities that offer alternatives to educational success (e.g., through family money or networks, illegal activities, or getting pregnant or married) will find it easier to turn away from the school, but the need to "turn away" can be created in the school setting when students acquire different information and, as a consequence, are not afforded equal access to school-based rewards.

The works of Fordham and Ogbu (1986), Holland and Eisenhart (1988a, 1988b), Ogbu (1974), and Willis (1977) powerfully illustrate how lack of success and status in the reward system of the school can lead older students not to want to (or not to care whether they) do well in school or subvert the purposes of schooling. We take up this body of work as our third example.

THE CHANNELING OF SCHOOL KNOWLEDGE
BY PEER GROUP

Fordham and Ogbu (1986) describe how making good grades and otherwise doing well in high school are defined by some African-American high school peer groups in Washington, D.C., as "acting white"—a socially enforced categorization that discourages bright young African-Americans from trying to do well in school. Willis's (1977) work reveals how the peer groups of working-class boys in Britain discourage their members from doing well in school, and Eisenhart's recent work with Holland (Holland & Eisenhart, 1988a, 1988b) suggests how the attraction of participating in the campus romance system diverts bright college women from their schoolwork and future careers.

The peer group at Capital High where Fordham and Ogbu did their study provided a definition of how its members should "take" from high school, and individuals had to learn how to conform in one way or another to its standards if they were to remain in the group. Fordham and Ogbu found that "studying hard" or "excelling" in school were viewed negatively by the African-American peer group. A deeper analysis of the group's structure and attitudes revealed that it emphasized an identity as "black" and constructed a culture (a way of taking) that directly opposed those activities that were viewed as being a valued part of white culture. Thus the African-American peer group opposed academic success and numerous other activities that were seen as "acting white," such as speaking standard English, reading poetry, or joining the "It's Academic" Club.

Fordham and Ogbu's research is a powerful demonstration of the tensions that arise between two opposing cultures and the hardships faced by students who attempt to defy their peer group and culture. In particular, academically competent African-American students either had to expend enormous efforts to displace attention from their academic success so as to remain acceptable to their peer group or had to disengage themselves from classroom work, hence becoming underachievers. Compliance or performance consistent with the school culture labeled "white" threatened them with being called "brainiacs" and with being ostracized by their peers.

Fordham and Ogbu's work speaks to the need for a greater understanding of the influence of the peer group in channeling learning in the school (see also Eisenhart & Holland, 1983). For whatever reason—whether it be the perceived job ceiling for African-Americans in society, the cultural identity of African-Americans in opposition to the "white" standards and values expounded in the schools, or some other factors—the peer group exerted an influence on its members that undermined academic success. In this way African-American students were encouraged not to take from the school, not to learn what the school had to offer.

Holland and Eisenhart's (1988a, 1988b) work is yet another illustration of the role of the peer group, this time defined in terms of gender, in mediating school learning and success. This research shows how schoolwork becomes marginalized in the lives of African-American and white college women, as another more salient identity becomes central to their lives: the identity of a female in a romantic relationship. Holland and Eisenhart describe three initial orientations to the world of college work held by the women in their study: "work in exchange for doing well," "work in exchange for getting [it] over," and "work in exchange for learning from experts" (1988b, p. 273). They show how it is mostly those women who initially held the latter orientation—work in exchange for learning from experts—who were able to go through college without losing enthusiasm for schoolwork, school achievement, and career aspirations. For most of the rest, early disappointments with schoolwork, combined with a pervasive peer culture that emphasized involvement in the campus "culture of romance" (1988a), soon overwhelmed career goals and minimized the perceived importance of school learning and achievements.

In a very real sense then, students' memberships in different social groups are an organizing factor in their experience of formal education, with serious implications for school success and academic achievement. Social groups not only act to structure ways of perceiving the world but also mediate what is perceived, what is learned, and what is transmitted in the school.

WHAT MIGHT BE DONE ABOUT ALL THIS?

The examples above as well as many others illustrated in this volume convince us of the need to think much more carefully about the social inter- actions and cultural norms that constrain what students learn. If we do not take into account the social and cultural aspects of learning literacy, or any other school subject, we as teachers are doomed to fail to achieve our own goals and aspirations for our work.

We think that anthropologists know some things about how we might address these social and cultural aspects of learning. We now turn to their work to guide our discussion of possible remedies.

Place Reading and Writing in Familiar Contexts

First, numerous studies by anthropologists of education demonstrate that the school performance of young nonmainstream children can be in- creased dramatically when steps are taken to create culturally familiar and comfortable classroom situations for them. For example, Heath (1983) de- scribes the efforts of several teachers to create effective learning environ- ments for the very different communities feeding into their school. One teacher, "Mrs. Gardner," began her year with a class of 19 African-American first graders—all labeled "potential failures" on the basis of reading- readiness tests. Angered that "these children were designated 'no chance of success' before [even] entering school" (p. 286), Mrs. Gardner set out to provide an exciting learning environment for them—an environment that would, at the same time, draw on experiences relevant to their own lives.

On learning who would be in her class, Mrs. Gardner visited the com- munities that fed into it, jotting down such features as store names and streets, churches, and the location of street lights and telephone poles in the areas. Noting that several parents worked in local garages, she called them up and asked them for old tires, which were then cut up and used to make letters of the alphabet. Her curious requests got several parents intrigued, and soon many came to the school to help her construct the letters which were then scattered just outside the classroom.

As the semester began, Mrs. Gardner attempted to introduce the alpha- bet to her students, not merely as symbols on paper but also as structured shapes apparent all over their neighborhoods. Children were asked to search for the big T's (telephone poles), to find the O's and the A's in such things as cups and saucers, tires, and street wires. They were also instructed to look for these shapes on license plates. As they became familiar with the shapes, Mrs. Gardner introduced the associated letter sounds—first by concentrating on the letters that began each child's name and then by having children recognize certain sounds in words heard throughout the day. Next, children used advertisements to separate lower-case from upper-case letters, then matched them. Mrs. Gardner also took pictures of her students that were then used to illustrate such concepts as "over," "under," "higher," and "lower."

By the end of their first year, benefiting from many more creative teaching activities, all but one child (who was later placed in a class for the emotionally handicapped) were reading on at least grade level—with eight at third-grade level, and six at second-grade level! The efforts to make classroom learning an integral part of the lives of the students—rather than isolated, nonmeaningful activities—allowed previously "doomed" individuals to reach outstanding levels of competence.

Heath (1983) also describes the efforts of "Mrs. Pat" to contextualize reading and writing for second graders in a rural school—again providing an excellent example of how cultural and linguistic differences in the classroom need not isolate certain individuals from the learning process but rather may serve to sensitize all children to the different "ways with words" that exist in society and that structure their own learning.

Most of Mrs. Pat's students came from poor farming families—35% of them African-American, the rest white. The first step in helping children along with their reading and writing was to show the relevance of these skills to the wider context of their lives. To this end, Mrs. Pat contacted parents, community members, the principal, lunchroom workers, and other students and had them come to her second-grade classroom to talk about their ways of communicating, to explain how and why they used reading and writing, and to show the children samples of their writing and reading materials.

Before every meeting, Mrs. Pat prepared her students to act as ethnographers—"detectives"—focusing on language in this case, by having them listen for answers to the following questions:

What sounds do you hear when _____ talks?
What did _____ say about how he talked?
What did _____ write?
What did _____ read?

At the same time, children were exposed to a variety of literature—dialect poetry, radio scripts, comics, biographies of famous baseball heroes, in conjunction with the traditional basal readers and workbook exercises. Students became familiar with a variety of language data, thereby learning more about the situational use of language and differing attitudes toward it. They learned the difference between dialect, casual, formal, conversational, and standard language use; the different oral and written traditions. "Throughout the year, the entire focus of the classroom was on language, its 'building blocks' in sound and in print, the ways its building blocks were put together, and how these varied in accordance with speaker and use in print or speech" (Heath, 1983, pp. 330–331).

Not surprisingly, by the end of the school year, Mrs. Pat's class had developed an amazing metalinguistic vocabulary and many ways of talking about language. They had also come to see school reading and writing as connected to activities in the wider world: "Learning to read and write in school was now linked to reading and writing labels and bills in the country store, the cafeteria worker's set of recipes, the church bulletin, or a notice of a local baseball game" (Heath, 1983, p. 333). Children had gained a sensitivity and understanding for the linguistic differences between people from all walks of life. Most importantly, however, these second graders now identified themselves as readers and writers.

Accommodate Different Cultural Traditions

As discussed by several authors in this volume, the researchers of the Kamehameha Elementary Education Program (KEEP) have shown how dramatic changes in school performance can take place when learning environments are modified to accommodate the different cultures within a classroom. These ethnographers have restructured classroom practices to cater more appropriately first to Hawaiian-American students' "ways of taking" and now to Navajo students (see, e.g., Vogt, Jordan, & Tharp, 1987).

Accommodate Peer Cultures

At the high school level, we also have evidence that when teachers make attempts to bridge the world of peers and that of the school, they can create the conditions for students, otherwise pulled away by peers and others, to perform successfully in school. The cases described by Dillon (1988), Kleinfield (1979), and Willis (1977), to name some, include examples of teachers who find ways to communicate their care for students' cultural traditions *and* to get across the subject matters of the school.

We think that recent work suggesting the success of cooperative learning groups, at least for black students (Slavin, 1983), is indicative of the kind of classroom reorganization that *could* draw on and perhaps accommodate, rather than alienate, student peer groups and their associated cultures. However, such reorganizations, to be successful, must be sensitive both to the power of peer group influences on students and the particular sociohistorical conditions that create and maintain peer group patterns and norms. We know, for example, that the peer culture of romance that diverts women's attention from schoolwork and careers is constructed quite differently from the racially oriented peer culture that diverts Fordham and Ogbu's students (Holland & Eisenhart, 1990). Cooperative learning groups that aim to tap the power of the peer group must take such differences into account.

Make Groups Flexible

About the problem of ability grouping that produces social and cultural differentiation in schoolwork activities, we encourage teachers and administrators to think more flexibly about ways to organize learning activities and to evaluate progress in language arts and other school subjects. Anthropologist Sylvia Hart (1982) suggests, for example, that children's reading style, situation, and taste, as well as their speed and accuracy ("ability"), could be used to group and regroup students for schoolwork.

Reorganize Teacher-Student Relationships

In addition and perhaps most importantly, teacher-student relationships might be reorganized to promote classroom learning. The relationship of teacher-as-authority and student-as-recipient is not the only available model. Anthropologists know, for example, from studies of primate socialization, of small-scale societies in which formal education plays a less important role, and of informal education in our own society that infants and youngsters can learn easily, with only a little *supervision*. Dobbert and Cooke (1987) sum up this anthropological knowledge as follows:

> Human adults . . . functioning as educators fail to note that human children are designed to learn. . . . [Instead] they deliberately set out to teach [in the sense of purposeful instruction] the young of the one species which least requires teaching. . . . Juvenile primates, including humans, when left to their own devices, with just a bit of supervision to prevent harm . . . will learn easily and well during all their pre-adult years to the point where they will be ready to step into and learn adult roles through practice when they reach that age. (p. 101)

Anthropologists have also found that young primates learn what they need to know to function as competent adults in warm, trusting, and caring environments where youngsters practice the skills, knowledge, beliefs, vocabularies, and social relations of those around them in safe and low-risk situations (Dobbert & Cooke, 1987). Warm, trusting, culturally sensitive environments are not created overnight; they require extended exposure to and involvement with the people of interest and then hard work to produce meaningful translations from what is already known to what might be learned. In this regard, McDermott (1977) suggests building teacher-student relationships *of trust*. Trust, according to McDermott, is a product of the work that people do to achieve a shared focus. Thus trust is context-sensitive; it can develop only when two or more people take the time to show they care for each other. It is an achievement that is managed through social interaction. According to McDermott, trusting relationships are a crucial first step for the success of any educational endeavor.

Build Scaffolds

Another thing anthropologists know is that in nonschool education children almost never learn directly from true experts. They learn from slightly older peers or (merely) competent adults, who, taken together and over time, can be viewed as providing the "scaffolding," or intermediate teaching and learning forms, that allow novices to develop into experts. Greenfield (1984) talks of such scaffolding as the activity of a teacher trying to close the gap between specific task requirements and the skill level of a learner. A good example of such scaffolding can be seen in the interactive processes occurring between a mother and her infant: The mother's actions are always contingent upon her child's responses—each time challenging her infant further and thereby producing effective learning situations.

Greenfield provides numerous other examples of this "scaffolding process," as do several authors in this volume (see Chapters 9 and 13). Central to Greenfield's notion of "scaffolding" is the idea that the scaffold supports what an individual can already do. In this way, a scaffold builds on what Vygotsky (1978) refers to as the "zone of proximal development" of a particular individual: The fuzzy temporary boundaries of knowledge and skill are continually being moved as individuals are helped through another stage of learning, only to uncover even more challenging boundaries ahead. The role of the teacher is to facilitate movement across boundaries—movement that is best achieved by providing effective bridges between what is already known and what remains to be learned.

Broaden School Knowledge

Anthropologists also know that most of what is really taught by and learned from adults in schools is social and procedural information and knowledge (the so-called "hidden curriculum" of schooling). If we judge by time spent and emphasis placed, students spend much more time learning how to use space, how to use time, how to follow directions and rules, how to use specialized language forms, and how to persist through tasks than they do learning how to use the subject matter information of school (see, e.g., Goodlad, 1984). From our point of view, there are no good reasons why *this* information and knowledge cannot be made sensitive to the social and cultural norms of the students being served. The work of Heath (1983) and Vogt et al. (1987) is testament to the fact that nonmainstream students can learn the subject matter of school quite well when social relationships and procedures are attuned to patterns that are already familiar to the students.

Finally, as things stand now, almost all school knowledge, including the subject matter material, comes from a narrow strand of U.S. cultural tradition, one that recognizes, rewards, and empowers only a very few members of our vast and heterogeneous society. We think this too should be changed, not just to be consistent with the rhetoric of equity but because anthropologists know that variation and alternatives in a social system are highly adaptive, especially in times of change. Students' experiences can be validated *and* enriched by incorporation into the curriculum of the abundant scholarly products of individuals and groups from around the world.

SUMMARY

Armed with all this knowledge, we should not allow the educational and the bureaucratic managers—and now the "cultural literacy" and the "English-only" types—to win most of the battles over how and what things should be taught in schools. This thrust of our current educational reform movement is *not* consistent with what anthropologists know about the social conditions conducive to equal access to knowledge. The school created by the present educational reform mania for programmed instruction at ever earlier grades, more homework, longer school days, tests of basic skills, minimum competencies, curriculum gates, and standardized achievement assessments could hardly be further from the educational world as depicted by Heath (1983), Vogt et al. (1987), Dobbert and Cooke (1987), McDermott (1977), Greenfield (1984), or many of the authors in this book.

When teachers are required to teach everyone the same curriculum or to prepare everyone for the same test at the same time; when schools allocate "professional development" or "in-service" time for speakers and programs related to new directions in classroom management but not for getting to know students in their homes, families, or peer groups, or for programs based on social or cultural perspectives; and when schools employ school psychologists but not school ethnographers, we are not giving teachers or students the time or resources they need to build trusting, warm, and culturally sensitive relationships or teachers the chance to become effective "brokers" between the children's worlds and that of the school.

The research discussed above and numerous other anthropological efforts demonstrate the impact of the classroom organization as a potential barrier or, at best, a facilitator, to student learning, depending on the extent to which it incorporates "ways of taking" that are familiar and accessible to students. It is imperative that teachers be made aware of the role they play in mediating the learning experiences of their students through the ways they organize their classroom. It is vital that teachers realize the need to understand the social groups and cultures of their students and to adjust the learning environment accordingly. However, the time and perseverance needed for "success stories" of the kind described above cannot be overstated. Heath (1983) spent 10 years as an ethnographer and teacher trainer in the communities and schools she describes, and Vogt et al. (1987) spent more than 10 years in theirs. But the results are clear: An understanding of the cultures present in the classroom led to marked changes in educational practice that, in turn, produced astounding improvements in student learning.

So let us end by charging you—and ourselves—to think about and investigate these matters much more critically. And let's see if we can't construct a better educational future for the wonderfully heterogeneous children who are trying to find their ways, to "take meaning," in the next generations of American society.

REFERENCES

Borko, H., & Eisenhart, M. (1986). Students' conceptions of reading and their reading experiences in school. *Elementary School Journal, 86,* 589–611.

Clement, D., & Eisenhart, M. (1979). Women's peer groups and choice of career [Project proposal]. Washington, DC: National Institute of Education.

Clement, D., Eisenhart, M., & Harding, J. (1979). The veneer of harmony: Social-race relations in a southern desegregated school. In Ray C. Rist (Ed.), *Desegregated schools: Appraisals of an American experiment* (pp. 15–64). New York: Academic Press.

Dillon, D. (1988, April). Showing them that I want them to learn. Paper presented to the American Educational Research Association, San Francisco.

Dobbert, M. L., & Cooke, B. (1987). Primate biology and behavior: A stimulus to educational thought and policy. In G. D. Spindler (Ed.), *Education and cultural process: Anthropological approaches* (pp. 230–244). Prospect Heights, IL: Waveland Press.

Eisenhart, M., & Holland, D. (1983). Learning gender from peers: The role of peer groups in the cultural transmission of gender. *Human Organization, 42,* 321–332.

Fordham, S., & Ogbu, J. (1986). Black students' school success: Coping with the "burden of 'acting white'." *The Urban Review, 8,* 176–206.

Gearing, F., & Sangree, L. (1979). *Toward a cultural theory of education and schooling.* The Hague: Mouton.

Goodlad, J. (1984). *A place called school: Prospects for the future.* New York: McGraw-Hill.

Greenfield, P. M. (1984). A theory of the teacher in the learning activities of everyday life. In B. Rogoff & J. Lave (Eds.), *Everyday cognition: Its development in social context* (pp. 117–138). Cambridge, MA: Harvard University Press.

Hart, S. (1982). Analyzing the social organization for reading in one elementary school. In G. Spindler (Ed.), *Doing the ethnography of schooling* (pp. 410–438). New York: Holt, Rinehart and Winston.

Heath, S. B. (1982a). Questioning at home and at school: A comparative study. In G. Spindler (Ed.), *Doing the ethnography of schooling* (pp. 102–131). New York: Holt, Rinehart and Winston.

Heath, S. B. (1982b). What no bedtime story means: Narrative skills at home and school. *Language in Society, 11,* 49–76.

Heath, S. B. (1983). *Ways with words.* New York: Cambridge University Press.

Holland, D., & Eisenhart, M. (1988a). Moments of discontent: University women and the gender status quo. *Anthropology and Education Quarterly, 19,* 115–138.

Holland, D., & Eisenhart, M. (1988b). Women's ways of going to school: Cultural reproduction of women's identities as workers. In Lois Weis (Ed.), *Class, race, and gender in American education* (pp. 266–301). Albany: State University of New York Press.

Holland, D., & Eisenhart, M. (1990). *Educated in romance: Women, achievement and college culture.* Chicago: University of Chicago Press.

Kleinfield, J. (1979). *Eskimo school on the Andreafsky: A study of effective bicultural education.* New York: Praeger.

McDermott, R. (1977). Social relations as contexts for learning in school. *Harvard Educational Review, 47,* 198–213.

Ogbu, J. (1974). *The next generation: An ethnography of education in an urban neighborhood.* New York: Academic Press.

Slavin, R. E. (1983). *Cooperative learning.* New York: Longman.

Vogt, L. A., Jordan, C., & Tharp, R. G. (1987). Explaining school failure, producing school success: Two cases. *Anthropology and Education Quarterly, 18,* 276–286.

Vygotsky, L. S. (1978). *Mind in society: The development of higher psychological processes.* (M. Cole, V. John-Steiner, S. Scribner, & E. Souberman, Eds. & Trans.). Cambridge, MA: Harvard University Press.

Willis, P. (1977). *Learning to labour: How working class kids get working class jobs.* Westmead, England: Saxon House.

4 | Diversity and Constancy in Human Thinking: Critical Literacy as Amplifier of Intellect and Experience

ROBERT CALFEE
SHARON NELSON-BARBER
Stanford University

We aim in this chapter to accomplish three tasks: (a) to review widely held but tacit assumptions about students' potential to become fully literate; (b) to present a model of *critical literacy,* the capacity to employ language as a tool for thinking and communicating; and (c) to describe instructional strategies that allow virtually every child to achieve high standards of critical literacy. We will argue that this goal can be accomplished with available resources, by effective application of current research and practice.

The chapter highlights a fundamental tension in American education. On the one hand, "everyone knows" that some children are more likely than others to become fully literate; on the other hand, our society is founded on the notion of equality of educational opportunity. In addition, our nation confronts an urgent economic and social need to develop fully the intellectual potential of every child.

We will use four themes to play out this tension, themes grounded in the interplay between diversity and constancy;

1. The first *constancy*—basic cognitive and linguistic resources are virtually identical for all individuals.
2. The first *diversity*—the worlds of experience vary tremendously among individuals in our society.
3. The second *constancy*—critical literacy comprises a curriculum for the formal use of language that can yield comparable outcomes for all students.
4. The second *diversity*—personal understandings and interpersonal connec-

tions can transform the elements of critical literacy into an infinite variety of creative shapes.

We intend the chapter for a broad audience: teachers, administrators, policymakers, and researchers. We address the practical as well as the conceptual, the here-and-now as well as the what-might-be. We do not attempt an extensive review of the scholarly literature but draw on our previous writings in cognitive psychology (Calfee, 1981), sociolinguistics (Nelson-Barber, in press), and individual differences (Calfee, 1983), along with our experience in school and policy settings.

BELIEF AND PRACTICE IN AMERICAN LITERACY

Prevailing Beliefs

What assumptions does our society hold about children and the role of schooling to promote competence in reading and writing? The answer is a welter of dreams, practices, and contradictions, mostly implicit. From this melange, we have chosen several tenets to challenge and critique. As you read each statement, ask yourself, "What if this claim were not true?"

1. *Learning capacity varies.* Conventional wisdom holds that some children possess greater potential than others to acquire academic knowledge and skill. The indicators of capacity are also well known—economic well-being, ethnicity, sex, family structure, and parent education ("Dealing," 1989, February, March; Reed & Sautter, 1990). Expectation bands in state testing programs concretize this assumption.
2. *Attention and motivation vary.* Whatever their basic potential, some children are better suited than others to the demands of schooling. Some children wiggle; other children fold their hands. Research shows that home experiences are correlated with school readiness, hence the pleas for parents to prepare children to pay attention to teachers. The implicit assumption is that schools can do little once the "twig is bent."
3. *Language varies.* Again, conventional wisdom says that some students are more fluent than others in the linguistic and conceptual domains. Schools anticipate problems for children who speak English as a second language or who speak a nonstandard dialect of English. Advocates of bilingual education may argue for the benefits of multilinguality, but the prevailing theme is that these students require remedial assistance.
4. *Schooling is fixed.* The belief is that all students should master the same

objectives in the same manner and the same sequence (Graham, 1987). Textbooks and curriculum frameworks embody this assumption. Variations in student progress are accommodated by changing the pace and adjusting the level. When these adjustments do not work, the child is removed from the mainstream for some or all of the school day.

Implicit in all of these assumptions is the notion that student diversity disrupts the effective operation of an educational enterprise organized around a fixed set of curricular objectives and methods. However, given our nation's current demographic trends, and the likelihood that our student population will continue to become more different rather than alike, we believe that each of these assumptions must be challenged. How real are observed differences in aptitude? Are low test scores a necessary concomitant of socioeconomic status? Need the curriculum be rigid and inflexible? Consider the possibilities inherent in a contrastive assumption, that *diversity provides opportunity.* From this perspective, the range of experiences and languages in today's classrooms offers an opportunity to engage students in the multiculture that is American society. To achieve this goal, however, schools need to change from "grading" to "growing."

Prevailing Practices

We have spoken of fixed curriculum and instruction. The reality is actually more complex. Research on classroom instruction shows that students from nonmainstream backgrounds often are believed to be less capable and, as a result, have classroom experiences that are different from those of their mainstream peers (see Chapter 17; Calfee, 1987; Chapter 10; Nelson-Barber & Meier, 1990, for summaries). The typical finding is that low-ability students are assigned to worksheets; the teacher interacts with them only when they ask for help, and the response is likely to be directive, telling them "Here is how to do it." By contrast, teachers engage mainstream students in more challenging discussions with the teacher, emphasizing "How could you do this?" Interactions for low-achieving students are specific and factual; for high-achieving students, exchanges are thematic and strategic. The result is the Matthew effect (Stanovich, 1986); the rich get richer, and the poor get poorer.

Exceptions to these trends appear on occasion, but teachers who are effective with minority students attain a mythical status. Observers attribute such unexpected success to shared language or culture; however, teachers who have been effective with minority students, like Marva Collins and Jaime Escalante, point to different assumptions and practices. They assume that all students can learn and then design an instructional program to fit this belief (e.g., Collins & Tamarkin, 1982; Meek, 1989).

Comparisons between communication patterns inside and outside the classroom show the strong effect of context on student performance (Cazden, 1988; Michaels, 1986). Typical classroom interactions resemble middle-class conversations. For instance, the adult is the "spectator" and the child is the "exhibitionist"; children are expected to show off for the grownups, which leads to appreciation and reward. A second feature of this communicative style is that adults ask children questions with known answers. Both parties understand that the purpose is for the child to demonstrate knowledge: It is not an authentic request to gain new information or discover the child's perspective on the issue. Third, text materials are often the focus of classroom discourse. The aim is seldom to address global and thematic issues but rather to state what is obvious and verifiable in the text.

Although these patterns fit middle-class dialogue, they are not typical of many cultures. In particular, children from poor homes are more accustomed to direct and genuine interactions. The stereotype may portray the poor home as deficient in both culture and language: "How can you teach students whose experience and language are limited?" But several investigations reveal home and peer discourse patterns that are quite rich and authentic.

For example, adults in the working-class African-American community studied by Heath (1983) seldom asked children questions where the answer was predetermined. Instead, questions called for open-ended answers based on the child's knowledge and experience: an analogy request like "What do you think you are?" to a child crawling under furniture; a "story starter" like "Did you see Maggie's dog yesterday?" or an "accusation-reply" like "What's that all over your face?" Wells (1986) reports similar findings from studies of lower-class English children: "Children at school play a much less positive role [compared with home] in conversation with adults and have less opportunity to explore their experience and develop their understanding through interactions with mature speakers who sustain their interests and encourage them to initiate topics, ask questions, and evaluate the answers they are given" (pp. 83–84). However, a growing literature, which includes a number of studies conducted by researchers of nonmainstream communities (e.g., Maldonado-Guzman, 1984; Smitherman, 1977; Swisher & Deyhle, 1987; Taylor & Matsuda, 1988), reveals home and peer discourse patterns that are quite rich and dynamic. Nevertheless, when the focus in classrooms is only on right answers, these home and peer discourse patterns may never manifest themselves there. Teachers may remain oblivious to students' capabilities or ability cues, as Miramontes and Commins (Chapter 6) call them.

On the other hand, as Resnick (1987) has pointed out, life after school places little premium on "right answers," at least not those that can be found in the back of the book. It makes sense, therefore, to reexamine the beliefs that support these practices.

CONSTANCIES AND DIVERSITIES IN LANGUAGE AND LITERACY: A MODEL OF CRITICAL LITERACY

The First Constancy: Cognitive and Linguistic Resources

Policies like standardized testing, tracking, and remedial programs all focus attention on variations in intellectual capacity. In this section, we want to reflect instead on the amazing commonalities in human potential to think and to use language. Several generalizations can be made about the cognitive and linguistic potential of virtually any kindergartner. Consider first the areas of memory, attention, and motivation:

- *Long-term memory* provides the child with unlimited capacity to store attended experience. No one runs out of space. Storing information is relatively easy; retrieving it is the challenge.
- *Attentional capabilities* are limited for everyone. Studies of short-term memory show that we must all juggle the complexities of experience by "chunking" complex realities into no more than five to seven distinctive entities. Effective use of long-term memory depends on the acquisition of organizational structures and strategies.
- *Motivational drives* are primarily social and derived. Human beings do not react in simple stimulus-response fashion to the environment. We are self-initiating and act through purpose and intention. Social goals quickly outweigh basic physiological drives; the kindergartner is driven by the need for success, affiliation, and power.

In human beings, cognition is joined by linguistic competence that qualitatively alters the nature of thought. Three domains capture the essence of the language system:

- *Phonology,* the capacity to perceive and produce a subtle and sophisticated code, is mastered within a couple of years after birth. A four-year-old may say "bus-ghetti," but we can understand her. And if we mock her pronunciation, she is likely to respond with annoyance, "That's what I said!"
- *Semantics,* the ability to detect and categorize related events, to form net-

works, and to label concepts and relations, is the ultimate foundation for language, for moving beyond immediate experience to symbol manipulation and reflection. The acquisition of conceptual networks and of labels for the nodes and linkages appears early in human development; the kindergartner possesses a rich array of words and ideas.

- *Discourse comprehension,* the capability to link concepts in novel but rule-governed ways, and to create sentences and texts, allows human beings to transcend experience, to imagine what might be, and to communicate those ideas to others. These systems are generative; the young child does not mimic the grammar of others but creates discourse based on abstract schemata. Societal patterns have an influence; television cartoons ensure that every kindergartner in this country has a particular narrative grammar (e.g., stories have happy endings).

These features of the cognitive-linguistic system are constancies. All children develop considerable potential in these areas within a few years of birth. Every student enters school with functioning cognitive and linguistic systems. All are capable of virtually limitless extension of their potential—and all want to succeed. These overarching commonalities distinguish us from other species. They provide the constant foundation for education.

The First Diversity: Worlds of Experience

In this section we look at individual differences from two perspectives: first, a broad view of the interaction of the individual in context, and then a more focused look at the context of a school as a social institution. In this discussion we make no effort to separate genetic and environmental sources; schools can do little to influence conditions outside the school walls.

The individual in context. From birth, children are surrounded by a widely variable range of events, which they absorb as experiential memories. The physical environment is one dimension; more important for present purposes are the variations in social settings. Two dimensions portray the range of variation in social experiences that surround the developing child (Calfee, 1983). One is the expanding network of influence from the preschool years through young adulthood. Here the main point is the emergence of the child from the protection of home and family to engagement with a broader world, with the school's becoming a central element in the preadolescent years, after which youngsters look more to peers.

The second dimension describes the range of community and family settings. As our nation has become more urbanized and as family structures have changed, the worlds of experience have also changed. For the child surrounded by an intact family, school success is promoted by adults who help the student understand and interpret the decontextualized events of the classroom. Many families spend the early years introducing their children to school-like experiences by helping them to understand and interpret decontextualized events, often with opportunities for reflection. For these children, the transition from home to school is considerably eased. Metacognition has become a significant part of their intellectual armamentarium. However, in culturally diverse classrooms, we might expect that students come to school with a variety of preschool experiences, some of which may have focused on other areas of development.

In all cases, by the time children enter kindergarten, they have acquired several worlds of experience. Some overlap and complement one another; others are disconnected. The combinations determine the store of knowledge, the language and dialect, the ways of knowing and expressing oneself. The end result is a complex web that defies easy analysis and interpretation.

The school as a special "world."   The classroom is a singularly significant world of experience, for both teachers and students. In the United States, youngsters spend 12 to 13 years in school, for two-thirds of their days and half their waking hours. It is the context that we share most as a culture.

Schools possess some features in common, but they also differ in significant ways, and the experience of schooling differs among students. A fundamental goal of American education, from Jefferson to the present, is the aspiration toward the fully educated person—competent, autonomous, and confident, effective in realizing individual potential and serving society. Against this common vision stands a harsh reality, the "factory" school in which youngsters are graded (literally), taught conformity, and trained in basic skills that enhance their economic value. The emphasis is not on personal growth but on "doing as you are told."

The tendency is for schools serving the well-to-do to reflect the visionary and those in poorer neighborhoods to resemble the second image. For most students, school blends the two extremes. Within the same classroom, ability grouping places some students (the cardinals) in one context, whereas others (the blue jays) find themselves at the other extreme. Tracking is a common approach for handling individual differences, but individual teachers vary in philosophy and style. Ms. Smith runs a language-experience kindergarten in which personal responsibility is emphasized and literature is the curriculum; Mr. Jones operates a skills-based first grade in which worksheets predominate. Within these variations, which can be found in a single school, individual students must figure out the "microclimates" and manage the transition from one context to another.

These variations reflect what McNeil (1988) has called "contradictions of control." On the one hand, teachers are encouraged to nurture each youngster as a unique individual. On the other, the teacher must manage a collective of two to three dozen disparate children. The standard American classroom, with its tension between the realities of crowd control and the ideal of individual autonomy, is indeed a contradiction.

The Second Constancy: The Literate Use of Language

The public school reflects the society, the coupling of individual differences and common tasks. The group needs to live together in reasonable harmony to support (or at least not hinder) fulfillment of collective goals while respecting the distinctive features of individuals. The situation parallels the everyday lives of grownups.

We view the attainment of *critical literacy* as the essential ingredient for supporting this undertaking. The key to the mutual empowerment of the individual and the group is the literate use of language—informal and intuitive methods of communication serve some purposes but not this one; basic literacy allows the individual to follow directions, but a higher level of discourse is needed to thrive in today's world (Tuman, 1987).

We characterize critical literacy as a constancy because a fixed set of strategies and structures provide the essential rhetorical core of a curriculum for the early years of schooling; by high school, distinctive interests and talents also need to be considered. We propose that the requisite skill and knowledge for acquiring critical literacy are within the reach of every student. Reading and writing need not displace the other subject matters in this method. Indeed, we envisage a school day where literacy is pervasive, but where reading and writing are embedded in literature, science, social studies, in art, music, and physical education, and even in the school's discipline policies. We know of situations in which reading and writing are not taught as separate subject matters.

The curriculum of critical literacy. What are the elements of the curriculum of critical literacy? One answer to this question is represented in Project READ, a program designed by Robert Calfee and implemented in several dozen schools throughout the country (Calfee, Henry, & Funderburg, 1988). Ten years ago, through a collaborative venture with an elementary school in Silicon Valley, California, a Stanford team developed a plan to integrate the prevailing reading/language arts curriculum—at that time, a basal series, process writing, a spelling series—with the rest of the day. The result was not a new reading technique but a staff-development, school-change program designed to change the way that elementary teachers thought about their work as individuals and as a collective (Calfee, in press).

The concept of an integrated language arts program is scarcely novel. Current emphases on whole language are philosophically oriented toward this goal. For our group, which included both researchers and practitioners, the starting point was neither "How to do it?" nor "Why to do it?" but "What is it?" We were dissatisfied with the skills-oriented approaches of the 1960s, and the literature-based programs emerging in the 1970s seemed to us lacking in substance. A critical breakthrough came as we reconceptualized the nature of literacy. The value of the exercise arose in the effort to shape the ideals of critical literacy to the realities of today's classrooms, to design and implement instructional strategies that brought the conception into reality.

What is the practical shape of critical literacy? In Project READ, the language arts curriculum takes shape as high-level *strategies* and *structures* that support the capacity to use language as a tool for thinking, for problem solving, and for communication. The techniques are grounded in the rhetoric and lead directly to an integration of curriculum across reading, writing, speaking, and listening. Reflective thinking (metacognition) is an essential feature of the curriculum.

Critical literacy begins with the decomposition of spoken language into the basic linguistic components of phonology, semantics, and discourse. For each of these components of natural language, a corresponding formal language component supports reading and writing. This model is not arbitrary but is the standard for linguistic analysis, hence its status as a constancy. Unlike the current debates about phonics versus comprehension, right- versus left-brain learning, and so on, the linguistic-rhetorical foundation of critical literacy has a well-established foundation.

In READ, we developed a set of distinctive structures, strategies, and technical language appropriate for each component, techniques that cut across all forms of perception and production. Within discourse, for instance, are two subdomains, narration and exposition. Each field includes rubrics that apply to reading, writing, speaking, and listening: plot and character, compare and contrast, cause and effect. The phonological component, which includes the parallel domains of phonics and spelling, employs a technical language quite different from discourse: consonants and vowels, syllabic and morphological elements.

The four components include a metalanguage for critical literacy, the basis for talking explicitly about language and literacy. The research on metacognition is compelling as to the advantages of explication, especially for students whose backgrounds have not supported the natural development of this competency. Some students seem to move naturally toward the analytic techniques that are the basis for reflective thought, but reliance on the growth of intuition is hazardous for students most at risk of school failure.

The READ curriculum builds on a top-down approach to language. The instructional strategies start with the question, "What is the purpose of this lesson or project?" Next comes the decision about the genre of the problem; handling a task that is narrational requires tools different from those for an expository task. The result is that higher level thinking becomes a habit of mind, a desirable feature of a curriculum that prepares students as citizens of tomorrow's world.

Critical literacy as an amplifier.   Natural language is the outgrowth of evolution; every child repeats the history of the species in some form or another. Literacy, in contrast, is an artifact or invention. The product of only a few millennia, this tool of thought and communication has changed markedly over the last few centuries and continues to develop with the appearance of new technologies. The printing press greatly amplified the power and scope of the invention. Equally significant, the personal computer makes possible the processing of words in ways that transcend the limitations of pen and paper. Whatever the future holds, good educational practice should lead students toward the acquisition of a small set of strategic tools for handling these technologies.

You are probably familiar with the consequences of the printing press and the personal computer, and so the amplifier metaphor seems comfortable. The events at Tianammen Square during the upheaval in China were transported by computers, electronic mail, and facsimile throughout the entire world in seconds. For the power of this technology to be fully realized, however, the "receiving station" must be able to interpret the information. To switch metaphors in midstream, we suggest that one consequence of critical literacy is captured by the image of *x-ray vision,* the capacity to see beneath the surface features of experience to the deeper realities.

The image may appear metaphysical, but it captures a significant facet of schooling for citizens of the future. The media messages that flood our world are valuable only as we can organize and analyze in systematic and communicable ways. For instance, millions of dollars are put into the selling of political candidates in this country. The surface messages are designed for broad appeal: "Lower taxes and better services!" There is nothing subliminal about the approach, and both rich and poor are subjected to a barrage of information. Today an increasing proportion of the electorate responds to such messages by deciding to sit out the election. Other messages are more demanding. Decisions to ignore tax forms can have hazardous consequences. Yet faced with complex and cumbersome instructions, the individual needs the analytic capacity to discover the point.

The Second Diversity: Personal and Interpersonal Creations

Like any invention, the tools of critical literacy can serve purposes either creative or mundane, illuminating or confusing, enjoyable or boring, engaging or alienating. Reflection and communication are difficult enterprises—the signals that we receive from ourselves and others are often weak. To the degree that the tools of the rhetoric foster communication, they expand appreciation of others, altering radically how we view human diversity. After all, art and literature rest not on uniformity but on variation.

The techniques of critical literacy, like any other technology, can be easily stultified. The important "aha" comes from the realization that literacy can put minds into contact with one another, that classroom walls can sustain imagination as well as boredom, that probing the recesses of individual minds can be both enlivening and illuminating. It is when the tools are employed to investigate content in novel and imaginative ways that the potential inherent in the amplification mentioned in the title is fully realized. It is at this stage that human diversity becomes a valued opportunity. Two examples from classroom observations illustrate the point.

Webbing.   Webbing, sometimes referred to as semantic mapping or brainstorming, is an instructional strategy designed to promote vocabulary and concept formation. The technique takes many forms, but the essence is to draw out students on a topic, and then guide them to cluster or organize their thoughts. The strategy can help students make contact with prior experience, analyze the content of a text, or prepare a composition. In Pam's second-grade class, the lesson was preparatory to a visit to the Monterey Aquarium, and the topic was *ocean*. Pam wrote the students' responses on chart paper, arranging them into clusters of flora, fauna, and environment. The paper was quickly filled with words; Pam then asked the youngsters to think about the clusters. "How are the words in each group related?"

Though familiar with the strategy, the students seemed hesitant. One boy ventured, "Those things don't make sense together." Another protested, "I wouldn't do it that way."

Pam countered, "How *would* you organize the ideas?"

"I'd put the things together that are fun and you can play with them. And there are things that you can eat. Then there's stuff that's junk and good for nothing."

The students' answers were more creative and insightful than the lesson as originally proposed—which led Pam to a discussion of how different structures served different purposes. By creating a situation in which students were encouraged to think freely, Pam validated their knowledge while bridging it to the scientific conception. Individual differences (between teacher and students, in this instance) became a virtue rather than a problem.

Imagery.   Imagery is a rare commodity in most classrooms. Increased interest in writing has led many teachers to encourage imagination, but student response is often disappointing. In Ed's third-grade lesson, he combined an innovative activity with READ structures to unleash the creativity of the group. He began his "Magic Carpet" trip simply enough: "Close your eyes. Imagine you are on a magic carpet. It lifts you from the floor, out the door of the classroom, up above the schoolyard, high over the neighborhood, and then away to another world—what do you see?"

He then connected the students' images with READ strategies: "Who do you see; who are the characters? What are they like? What's happening to them? Pick one of them that seems especially interesting, and spend some time visiting. What is happening in their lives that seems interesting?" His words guided the students through the creation of a story around the familiar rubrics of character, setting, plot, and theme. He then brought them back to the classroom, where they opened their eyes and reported their adventures. As the hour passed, the walls filled with images that became sharable resources for a rich variety of stories. The imagination of the entire class became available to every child. Rhetorical strategies allowed students to take advantage of their experiences and imaginations and to share this wealth.

SUMMARY

The capacity to connect with others is a significant educational goal. Our national principles emphasize equality and respect for all, regardless of background. During the past quarter-century, public schools have become the center of the tension between aspirations and realities. Most efforts to deal with these tensions have addressed political and managerial techniques; little has happened to modify curriculum and instruction to negotiate this tension. We propose that critical literacy, as conceptualized in this essay, provides a vehicle to address the challenge. Nor is the approach limited to the pragmatics of the school context. Beyond school, knowing how to deal effectively with others is an important skill for everyone.

We have focused here on literacy; the principles that distinguish critical literacy from functional reading and writing apply with equal force to other curriculum domains. We can imagine reshaping the study of social systems ("social studies") along similar lines. One of the more important "chunks" of this curriculum could be the examination of individual differences, including variations in culture, race, gender, and language. Such an examination would require an explicit and structured language for exchanging thoughts and ideas about our common heritage as a species as well as the features that distinguish us as individuals. It would require critical literacy.

REFERENCES

Calfee, R. C. (1981). Cognitive psychology and educational practice. In D. C. Berliner (Ed.), *Review of research in education*. Washington, DC: American Educational Research Association.

Calfee, R. C. (1983). Human diversity: Implications for schools. In E. W. Gordon (Ed.), *Human diversity and pedagogy*. Westport, CT: Mediax Associates.

Calfee, R. C. (1987). Curriculum and instruction: Reading. In B. I. Williams, P. A. Richmond, B. J. Mason (Eds.), *Designs for compensatory education*. Washington, DC: Research and Evaluation Associates.

Calfee, R. C. (in press). The *Inquiring School:* Literacy for the year 2000. In C. Collins (Ed.), *Expanding thinking abilities through reading instruction*. Hillsdale, NJ: Erlbaum.

Calfee, R. C., Henry, M. K., & Funderburg, J. A. (1988). A model for school change. In S. J. Samuels & P. D. Pearson (Eds.), *Changing school reading programs*. Newark, DE: IRA.

Cazden, C. (1988). *Classroom discourse*. Portsmouth, NH: Heinemann.

Collins, M., & Tamarkin, C. (1982). *Marva Collins' way*. Los Angeles: J. T. Tarcher.

Dealing with diversity: Ability, gender, and style differences. (1989, March). *Educational Leadership* [Whole issue].

Dealing with diversity: At-risk students. (1989, February). *Educational Leadership* [Whole issue].

Graham, P. A. (1987). *Achievement for at-risk students*. Unpublished manuscript, Faculty of Education, Harvard University, Cambridge, MA.

Heath, S. B. (1983). *Ways with words*. New York: Cambridge University Press.

Maldonado-Guzman, A. (1984). *A multidimensional ethnographic study of teachers' differential treatment of children in two Mexican American classrooms: The dynamics of teachers' consciousness and social stratification*. Unpublished doctoral dissertation, Harvard University, Cambridge, MA.

McNeil, L. (1988). Contradictions of control: Administrators and teachers. *Phi Delta Kappan, 70*(1), 334–350.

Meek, A. (1989). On creating "ganas": A conversation with Jaime Escalante. *Educational Leadership, 46*(5), 46–47.

Michaels, S. (1986). Narrative presentations: An oral preparation of literacy with first graders. In J. Cook-Gumperz (Ed.), *The social construction of literacy* (pp. 94–116). New York: Cambridge University Press.

Nelson-Barber, S. (in press). Considerations for the inclusion of multiple cultural competencies in teacher assessment. *Teacher Education Quarterly.*

Nelson-Barber, S., & Meier, T. (1990, Spring). Multicultural context a key factor in teaching. *Academic Connections.* New York: The College Board.

Reed, S., & Sautter, R. C. (1990). Children of poverty: The status of 12 million young Americans. *Phi Delta Kappan, 71*(10), K1–K12.

Resnick, L. B. (1987). *Education and learning to think.* Washington, DC: Academy Press.

Smitherman, G. (1977). *Talkin' and testifyin'.* Boston: Houghton-Mifflin.

Stanovich, K. E. (1986). Matthew effects in reading: Some consequences of individual differences in the acquisition of reading. *Reading Research Quarterly, 21,* 360–406.

Swisher, K., & Deyhle, D. (1987). Styles of learning and learning of styles: Educational conflicts of American Indian/Alaskan native youth. *Journal of Multilingual and Multicultural Development, 8,* 345–360.

Taylor, O., & Matsuda, M. (1988). Storytelling and classroom discrimination. In C. Smitherman-Donaldson & T. A. van Dijk (Eds.), *Discourse and discrimination* (pp. 206–220). Detroit: Wayne State University Press.

Tuman, M. C. (1987). *A preface to literacy.* University of Alabama: University of Alabama Press.

Wells, G. (1986). The language experience of five-year-old children at home and school. In J. Cook-Gumperz (Ed.), *The social construction of literacy* (pp. 69–93). New York: Cambridge University Press.

5 | Cultural Literacy Reconsidered

ERNEST R. HOUSE
CAROL EMMER
NANCY LAWRENCE
University of Colorado, Boulder

Recently a student in an American high school was asked on a test who Socrates was. He answered that Socrates was an Indian chief. Whether this incident is apocryphal is difficult to say. It does have the ring of authenticity: One can imagine the hapless student, in desperate search for an answer, associating Socrates with Seneca, the ancient Roman philosopher, then connecting Seneca to the Indian tribe of the same name. In any case the story is a favorite of former U.S. Assistant Secretary of Education Chester E. Finn, Jr., and has been used repeatedly to illustrate the cultural illiteracy of American students and to dramatize the urgency of restoring the nation's cultural knowledge. In fact, a formidable educational reform movement has developed, aimed at improving the teaching of American culture within the schools.

These ideas about public education, if carried forward, have strong implications for the school curriculum at both the elementary and secondary levels and for the content of standardized achievement tests at all levels. That is, both the content of what is now taught and tested for would be changed quite substantially if the schools were to focus on cultural literacy. In this chapter we will examine the core ideas of cultural literacy with a view to assessing their merit.

The phrase "cultural literacy" was popularized by E. D. Hirsch, Jr. (1987b), in his best-selling book *Cultural Literacy: What Every American Needs to Know.* The book has been lauded by top government officials as critical to the future of American education and lambasted by critics as "educational trivial pursuit." Hirsch published a sequel, *The Dictionary of Cultural Literacy* (1988c), and his organization, the Foundation for Cultural Literacy, also has been developing special tests. Another highly influential book about cultural literacy in higher education, Allan Bloom's (1987) *The Closing of the American Mind: How Higher Education Has Failed Democracy and Impoverished the Souls of Today's Students,* sold more than 650,000 hardback copies, a phenomenal number, and *What Do Our 17-Year-Olds Know?* by Diane Ravitch and Chester Finn, Jr. (1987), has also enjoyed popular success. All of these books have received considerable media attention, but we will concentrate here on Hirsch's ideas.

THE CONCEPT OF CULTURAL LITERACY

Hirsch (1983) contends that there is no doubt that our national cultural literacy has declined. The chief culprit is the pluralism of the school curriculum, which has diluted the content of the traditional English and history courses. Educators, afraid of attacks by minority groups accusing them of cultural imperialism, have promulgated a content-free curriculum focused exclusively upon formal cognitive skills. "Literacy is not just a formal skill; it is also a political decision. . . . Literacy implies specific contents as well as formal skills" (p. 162). This essential "canonical knowledge" Hirsch labels "cultural literacy."

In his view the United States is becoming so fragmented as to lose its coherence as a culture. He proposed a National Board of Education that would define broad lists of suggested literary works for the schools to teach. If such a national board could not be set up, other organizations should provide recommendations, including a lexicon of words and phrases that high school graduates should know and that could serve as a guide to instruction. Currently only the Scholastic Aptitude Test provides such guidance, Hirsch thought. "Is the Educational Testing Service our hidden National Board of Education? Does it sponsor our hidden national curriculum? If so, the ETS is rather to be praised than blamed" (Hirsch, 1983, p. 168). Hirsch later retreated from this position somewhat: "The common background knowledge required for literacy does not depend on specific texts" (Hirsch, 1986, p. 1). Perhaps the point Hirsch is trying to make is that "canonical knowledge" may be arrived at through a number of means, only one of which may be by reading a set of prescribed texts (Hirsch, 1984, 1987b, 1988b).

In 1987 Hirsch presented his full rationale: "The civic importance of cultural literacy lies in the fact that true enfranchisement depends upon knowledge, knowledge upon literacy, and literacy upon cultural literacy" (1987b, p. 12). In his view, reading requires background or "world knowledge"—cultural literacy. And this background knowledge is national in character rather than either local or international. The false doctrines of cultural pluralism and educational formalism were preventing our national culture from being taught, and the schools must teach specific national cultural content in the early grades.

There are four major strands to Hirsch's rationale. First, reading literacy depends upon background knowledge, and, similarly, getting along in society depends upon cultural literacy, that is, knowing the culture one lives in; second, modern industrial nations depend upon the development of homogeneous national cultures; third, traditional American pluralism does not preclude the necessity for conformity to the national culture; and fourth, education has fallen victim to romantic formalism and misguided pluralism, which has led to a diluted school curriculum and consequent cultural fragmentation. The solution is to reestablish the national culture as the core of the curriculum. Hirsch concludes his book by presenting a list of about 6,000 terms that comprise the national culture and that should be taught in the schools.

In the first argument Hirsch relies heavily upon research conducted by Anderson and his colleagues at the Center for the Study of Reading at the University of Illinois. In brief, this research demonstrates that specific background knowledge, called a *schema,* is critical to reading a given text. For example, in a study often cited by Hirsch, Americans reading about an American wedding understand the text much better than East Indians do, and East Indians understand the text about an Indian wedding much better. Hence, reading ability depends upon preexisting knowledge. The work by Anderson and his colleagues is highly regarded within the educational research community and is leading to significant changes in reading instruction in the schools.

There are problems with Hirsch's argument, however. Hirsch draws conclusions beyond the research studies: "What distinguishes good readers from poor ones is simply the possession of a lot of diverse, task-specific information" (p. 61). It is one thing to say that background information plays an important role in reading, consistent with the research, and quite another to say that such specific information is everything, which the research does not. One of Hirsch's own examples calls his extrapolation into question. He argues that master chess players recognize and employ chess schemata to organize and guide their play, which seems reasonable. However, it would seem highly unlikely that teaching a list of chess terms and concepts to chess novices would transform the novices into master chess players. Whatever chess schemata consist of, surely they are not simply lists of chess terms. Rather the novice must learn schemata by playing chess extensively and studying it intensively. The knowledge of the master entails much more than lists of specific knowledge. That is, schemata are different from a list of terms.

Hirsch's argument is by analogy: Reading ability is to reading schemata (as chess playing is to chess schemata) as succeeding in life is to achieving cultural literacy (cultural schemata). But the analogy does not hold very well when cultural literacy is defined as simple knowledge of a list of specific terms. What one might reasonably conclude is that reading ability is dependent in part on reading schemata, and that chess playing is dependent on chess schemata, and that knowledge of a list of specific cultural terms may help one do well in society but that cultural knowledge is neither necessary nor sufficient for doing well. Our opinion is that cultural knowledge is extremely desirable to have but that it is not necessary to or sufficient for "success in life," as that term is normally understood in American society. The fact that the upper social classes have more cultural knowledge in general and the lower classes do not is a relationship of correlation, not of cause and effect. So in our judgment Hirsch pushes his argument too far, although we would agree that cultural knowledge helps one interpret the social world.

It is also the case that Hirsch ignores the implications of his own argument as well as the research on the social context of learning. Eisenhart and Cutts-Dougherty in Chapter 3 survey the substantial research by anthropologists on how and what students learn in a particular context. Learning to read, or learning anything else, is highly dependent on the student's cultural background, as Hirsch asserts, but the anthropologists arrive at the conclusion that the student's own cultural background itself must be taken into account if the student is to learn. To use Hirsch's own example, teaching American students about an East Indian wedding will be much more successful if one recognizes the conceptions about weddings that the students already have. In other words, their own cultural backgrounds must be taken into consideration. Hirsch draws the opposite conclusion, that the students are culturally deficient and one must ignore their culture.

NATIONAL CULTURE

The second strand of Hirsch's rationale is an argument asserting the criticality of a national language and a national culture for the development of the modern industrial nation. He contends that a modern nation must have both a single national language and a homogeneous national culture. Hirsch first develops an argument for the necessity of a national language, essentially a case for standards: "Inside a national border, education helps to keep the national language stable by holding it to standards that are set forth in national dictionaries, spelling books, pronunciation guides, and grammars" (p. 71). Modern industrial societies do indeed require their citizenry to be literate, but that nations also deliberately "fix" their national languages is more contentious. The fact that the British, Australians, and Americans understand one another's dialects may have more to do with the pervasiveness of the mass media than with national governments' establishing language standards and holding their citizens to them.

Hirsch's account of how modern languages have become standardized is rather idiosyncratic. In his view, there is an international vocabulary, a national vocabulary, and a local vocabulary. The national language must be standardized by central authorities' imposing a particular dialect upon the general population in an arbitrary manner. "The fact of a common standard is much more important than the intrinsic character of the standard chosen" (p. 79). And regardless of the character of the accepted standards, such as the notorious inconsistency of English spelling, "It is much better to stick to them, whatever their intrinsic drawbacks" (p. 81). The idea that we must always accept what we are given runs throughout Hirsch's work.

Hirsch also seems to equate national language with written language, as opposed to oral dialects, though he discusses written and oral language interchangeably at times. Finally, and most importantly, "But in many other respects national languages are distinct from oral dialects. Among several distinctive features that make them unique linguistic phenomena, . . . one . . . is especially significant for the subject of this book: every national language is a conscious construct that transcends any particular dialect, region, or social class" (p. 82). In his view, national languages are the province of *all* the people of the country and do not disadvantage those from particular nonstandard dialects.

From this view of how national languages develop, Hirsch then takes a key intellectual leap: "What may be less obvious is that every national culture is similarly contrived. It also transcends dialect, region, and social class and is partly a conscious construct" (pp. 82–83). He posits a "national culture" development analogous to national language development. "For nation builders, fixing the vocabulary of a national culture is analogous to fixing a standard grammar, spelling, and pronunciation" (p. 84). In other words, the national culture must be fixed, homogeneous, and arbitrarily imposed for the good of the nation, just as the national language must be.

Hirsch cites an example of the formation of American national culture—Mason Weems's creation of the myth of George Washington and the cherry tree. Hirsch is admiring of this total fabrication, but we confess that we are bothered by authors' manufacturing untrue stories about famous personages and presenting them as the truth, even if in Hirsch's view, "Weems deduced that the public needed a domesticated Everyman whose life would serve as a model for American youth" (p. 89). McGuffey later introduced his own version of Weems's cherry tree myth in his *Reader,* which influenced many generations of young minds. No doubt Hirsch is correct in asserting that this is how some pieces of national cultures originate, but is it all right to make up facts if the cause is a good one?

Hirsch is steadfast in his belief that not only is the national culture difficult to change but it is wrong to attempt to do so. "Rapid, large-scale change is no more possible in the sphere of national culture than in the sphere of national language. It is no more *desirable* or practicable to drop biblical and legendary allusions from our culture than to drop the letter s from the third person singular" (p. 91, emphasis added). Not only can one not do it, but one should not do it. Hirsch is profoundly conservative on this matter. However, again his own examples give him difficulty. Did not the English introduce large-scale change in both language and national culture in Scotland—and rather successfully? Did not Weems deliberately introduce myths about George Washington and Abraham Lincoln into American culture in such a way as to instill certain values into generations of American school children, and, in Hirsch's own opinion, do so successfully and desirably? Hirsch's stated position on the immutability of culture is contradicted by his own examples. His actual position seems to be that it was possible and desirable to make such cultural changes in the past but that we cannot and should not do so in the present. We must passively accept the culture others have manufactured for us and extend it to everyone.

PLURALISM AND DIVERSITY

Where does this imposition of national culture leave our American tradition of pluralism? Hirsch is clear about this: "The brute fact of history in every modern nation has been the increasing dominance of the national culture over local and ethnic cultures" (p. 97). More prescriptively, "It is for the Amish to decide what Amish traditions are, but it is for all of us to decide collectively what our American traditions are, to decide what 'American' means on the other side of the hyphen in Italo-American or Asian-American" (p. 98). And how shall we decide what American culture consists of?

To resolve this problem, Hirsch divides the public culture into three parts: our "civil religion," which includes value commitments to freedom, patriotism, equality, and other core values, as well as supporting rituals and myths; the "culture proper," which includes the politics, customs, and legends that "define and determine our current attitudes and actions and our institutions" (p. 103); and the "vocabulary of national discourse," which includes the value-neutral language and cultural terms through which we engage in dialogue about the culture proper and which is synonymous with cultural literacy. The distinction here is similar to that between a language and the ideas expressed in that language, with certain ideas being sacred.

In Hirsch's view only items in the culture proper, the ideas themselves, should be argued about, but not the sacred ideas nor the medium of the national vocabulary. The national vocabulary is merely a convention that enables us to communicate with each other and is not subject to dispute. Why would one argue about vocabulary terms in English? Also, the national vocabulary has an "inherently classless character": "Nor does the national vocabulary reflect a coherent culture of a dominant class or other group in the same way that a local dialect does. It is primarily an instrument of communication among diverse cultures rather than a cultural or class instrument in its own right" (p. 104).

> Neither in origin nor in subsequent history have national languages been inherently class languages. It is true that after national dictionaries were formulated, the standard languages were more likely to be acquired by people who were rich enough to be educated than by poor people. But the distinction is one of schooling, which we have made universal, not of economic or social class. (p. 106)

Throughout his book Hirsch is at great pains to repeat again and again that cultural literacy has nothing to do with social class.

If it just so happened that some people acquired the national language, what about its content? Is it an adventitious, eclectic mix from all the various peoples who have inhabited America? Well, no. "By accident of history, American cultural literacy has a bias toward English literate traditions. Short of revolutionary political upheaval, there is absolutely nothing that can be done about this" (p. 106). If the ruling classes or social elites did not impose this national vocabulary, how did it emerge? "History has decided what those elements are" (p. 107).

And the emergence of this national vocabulary has nothing to do with merit:

> It is cultural chauvinism and provincialism to believe that the content of our vocabulary is something either to recommend or deplore by virtue of its inherent merit. . . . The specific contents of the different national vocabularies are far less important than the fact of their being shared. Any true democrat who understands this, whether liberal or conservative, will accept the necessary conservatism that exists at the core of the national vocabulary. (p. 107)

Apparently, then, we are not to decide what "American" means after all; it is already decided for us. In short, the national cultural vocabulary emerges from an agentless historic process, has nothing to do with intrinsic merit, is unattached to particular social classes or subcultures, is nonpolitical, and cannot be changed deliberately.

Frankly, these assertions are difficult to believe. First, the division of culture into three parts again is based upon an analogy with natural language and has no clear anthropological or sociological basis. Apparently, it is Hirsch's own invention. The national cultural vocabulary in fact differs from natural language vocabulary in important ways. Second, natural language itself is often political and historically closely allied with social class. The development of English itself through the Angles, Saxons, and Normans is proof of the great influence on language by the ruling classes.

In modern times the dialect employed by the BBC is the Cambridge-Oxford dialect of the British upper classes, and the same is true for written English. It is hardly accurate to portray this connection as accidental, because whether one obtains an Oxford or Cambridge education is not an accident but linked to social class. The current feminist attack upon pronoun gender usage is another contemporary example of the politics of language. In fact, examples of the political implications of language usage and their association with particular social classes, ethnic groups, and regions are simply too well known to belabor.

Third, cultural content itself is even more political and allied with social class than is natural language. Hirsch (1983) himself recognized this in his original paper: "Literacy is not just a formal skill; it is also a political decision. . . . Literacy implies specific contents as well as formal skills" (p. 162) . . . although I have argued that a literate society depends upon shared information, I have said little about what that information should be. That is chiefly a political question" (p. 167). By 1987, however, he had decided that cultural literacy is not political and that one should not argue about it because it cannot be changed—nor should it be, because it is inherently conservative (1987b). By declaring it nonpolitical, Hirsch hoped to remove it from debate, while at the same time obviously arguing the issue himself.

Again there is a curious contradiction in Hirsch's argument. In his view, the national cultural content cannot and should not be changed because it evolves in natural ways outside deliberate influence—yet if this is so, why is Hirsch writing a book about it and founding a movement? His own efforts are directed toward establishing a particular cultural content. If there is no intrinsic merit in any cultural content, why not allow the mass media or the schools as they currently operate to determine the cultural content of the nation? Why bother at all if the national vocabulary cannot be changed and the content doesn't matter? Hirsch's stance is inherently contradictory.

Both natural language and especially cultural content are in fact highly political, as evidenced by the explosive political nature of bilingual education, official English referenda, and controversies over standardized test performances, which determine access to educational institutions and better jobs. The daily headlines are full of reports of political encounters over such issues. And they are political precisely because they are allied with the fortunes of social classes, ethnic groups, and races. In reality, it is not that these issues are nonpolitical, as Hirsch suggests, but rather that Hirsch has a particular political position that he presents as nonpolitical.

SCHOOLING

Hirsch (1987b) focuses his reform agenda on the public schools almost exclusively. "But we should direct our attention undeviatingly toward what the schools teach rather than toward family structure, social class, or TV programming. No doubt, reforms outside the schools are important, but they are harder to accomplish" (p. 20). In his view the primary role of the schools is "acculturating our children into our national life" (p. 110), and cultural fragmentation is the fault of the schools:

> The decline of American literacy and the fragmentation of the American school curriculum have been chiefly caused by the ever growing dominance of romantic formalism in educational theory during the past half century. We have too readily blamed shortcomings in American education on social changes (the disorientation of the American family or the impact of television) or incompetent teachers or structural flaws in our school systems. But the chief blame should fall on faulty theories promulgated in our schools of education and accepted by educational policymakers. (p. 110)

According to Hirsch, educators mistakenly believe that reading is based upon formal skills when in reality it is based on cultural knowledge. The real reason low-income students are deficient in reading is because they lack cultural knowledge. Cultural deprivations and family inadequacies can be overcome through such knowledge.

According to Hirsch, these incorrect educational theories began to be implemented when the Cardinal Principles of Secondary Education of 1918 replaced the 1893 Committee of Ten recommendation of a traditional humanistic education. Social adjustment replaced subject matter. The origins of these destructive ideas were Rousseau's romanticism and Dewey's pragmatism, both focusing upon the romantic concept of "natural human growth." Unfortunately, in Hirsch's view, these ideas were accepted by educators and translated into curricula for individual differences and vocational education, thus implicitly accepting the permanent stratification of economic and social positions. Tracking and learning-by-doing, as opposed to book learning, came to dominate American education. According to Hirsch, these educational principles led to replacing history with social studies as a subject of study, and they culminated in the romantic formalism of the 1960s.

What can we make of these ideas? It seems rather farfetched to blame all the ills suffered by lower-class children upon educational theories taught in the schools of education, thus excluding such powerful social influences as poverty, unemployment, family dissolution, crime, and the mass media. Hirsch again reveals his conservative political orientation: These other social institutions cannot be changed; only the schools are at fault. We are also skeptical about the contention that Rousseau's ideas are the source of all the trouble in American education and American society. *Emile* was an influential book, but that is a long reach indeed. Hirsch's intent is to blame the Progressive Education movement for pernicious influences, that movement being a favorite target of conservatives over a number of years.

Actually, schools have been pressing for cultural homogeneity for decades, if not centuries, as Applebee notes in Chapter 16. Matthew Arnold in England saw the teaching of literature as an attempt to stem the evil tides of the industrial revolution, and the standard canon of literary works was established in both British and American schools long before the Progressives emerged. In one way Hirsch is reacting to attempts by various groups to expand the canon to include minorities and women. The switch is that whereas Arnold and others argued that the homogeneous literary canon would mitigate the influences of industrialism, Hirsch argues that cultural homogeneity is absolutely necessary for the development and expansion of the economy.

We leave the historical influences for others to consider and agree that Hirsch does have a valid point about the excesses of "educational formalism," the idea that literacy is a set of techniques that can be developed through coaching and practice. He is correct that literacy involves knowledge of some content that the learner must know, and that the content itself is important. Content matters, and not just skill. We think he is correct that educators and psychologists have sometimes lost their way in developing reading skills by having students practice abstract context-free skills. Having students memorize suffixes is not the way to learn to read. In our judgment Hirsch is also correct in castigating the educational tracking system in which lower-class students are shunted into vocational tracks where they have lessened opportunity to acquire academic knowledge necessary for admission to higher education and the best jobs. American education has had such a sorting mechanism in place for many decades, as Hirsch indicates. The idea of abolishing such a tracking system and allowing all students to acquire the same knowledge is an excellent one, it seems to us, and a surprisingly egalitarian one for Hirsch.

What content should all students learn? Hirsch advocates an "extensive" curriculum that covers the subject matter all Americans need to know, plus an "intensive" curriculum that investigates particular works in detail and that is adjusted to individual interests and abilities. The former (Hirsch's list) will provide what we share as a culture, he believes, and the latter will provide coherence and intellectual depth. However, it is the extensive curriculum that Hirsch's book is all about. Textbooks should convey the national cultural vocabulary, especially for young children. If students do not acquire this national vocabulary by 10th grade, they can rarely make up the loss, according to Hirsch. Schools should abandon romantic formalist ideas like "critical thinking" and "higher order skills" that denigrate facts. Facts and skills are inseparable.

THE LIST

What then are the essential cultural facts? Hirsch and two colleagues compiled a list of the contents literate Americans should know. The list was submitted to 100 consultants outside academia and published as the appendix of the 1987b book, with a revised list of 6,000 terms published in the 1988b paperback edition. The list itself is supposed to represent a high school level of cultural literacy, to be descriptive of what cultural literate Americans actually do know rather than prescriptive about what they should know, "to represent but not to alter current literate American culture" (1987b, p. 136). The exception is science because Hirsch and his colleagues thought that current scientific knowledge needed enhancement.

The list was deemed to be nonpolitical because schools "have a duty not to take political stands on matters that are subjects of continuing debate" (1987b, p. 137). Although a national core curriculum based upon such a list is neither desirable nor feasible, "an agreed-upon, explicit national vocabulary should in time come to be regarded as the basis of a literate education" (p. 139). Publishers and educators should reach an accord about both the contents of the national vocabulary and a sequence for presenting it, in Hirsch's view. Method of presentation would be left to teachers. A group of educators and public leaders might even develop a model grade-by-grade sequence of core information based on the list.

General knowledge tests should also be developed, perhaps at grades 5,

8, and 12. Such tests based on the list would be less arbitrary than the SAT because the SAT verbal test is essentially a vocabulary test whose makers have never defined the specific vocabulary on which it is based. Only a few hundred pages of information stand between the literate and nonliterate, between dependence and autonomy. In response to those who might object to such a list, Hirsch would say that they are objecting to literacy itself.

Hirsch's list then specifies the national cultural vocabulary, the knowledge that all Americans should know by 10th grade and preferably sooner. According to Hirsch, one does not have to know much about the terms on the list but only just a smattering of information about each item. For example, one does not have to know much about Socrates but should have a vague idea who he was. This is extensive knowledge. If one studies Platonic dialogues in detail, that is intensive knowledge, and not the type of knowledge required by the list.

What is on the original list? A great many proper names of Anglo-American origin, many English literary terms, a surprising number of foreign phrases, many cliches, and only a few historical dates. The original list is short on athletics, health, entertainment, social science, and military terms. It systematically omits terms associated with the 60s, such as the Age of Aquarius, the Beats, the Chicago Seven, counterculture, Bob Dylan, Allen Ginsberg, and Jack Kerouac. It omits writers such as Jack London, Henry Miller, Ezra Pound, Sam Shepard, and John Steinbeck. It omits ethnic terms such as Black Elk Speaks, the blues, Harlem Renaissance, soul (music, food) and musical references such as Billie Holiday, punk, reggae, rock and roll, but includes Fred Astaire, Ginger Rogers, and the Beatles. It omits references germane to social science, such as Margaret Mead, Thorstein Veblen, and weltanschauung. It omits health terms such as AIDS, carcinogenic, Lamaze, and stress.

Of course, any list will leave out some terms that should be included: It is the systematic exclusion and inclusion of certain ones that biases the list. One cannot help but think that unacknowledged criteria of propriety, acceptability, and politics were operating when the list was constructed. After all, this is supposed to be a list of what educated Americans do know, not what they should know (or should forget). But, of course, the list is transformed into a prescription of what should be taught. Hirsch's subtitle, after all, is "What Every American Needs to Know," not what they do know.

In 1988 the paperback edition of the book was published, and Hirsch deleted and added terms to the list, for what he claims was a net increase of 343. He says, "The deletions are few, totaling only about twenty-five, e.g. 'Edict of Nantes' and 'Occam's razor,' and other items that were questioned by several readers independently" (Hirsch, 1988b, p. xi). Hirsch seems a bit confused about the deletions. In fact, more than 300 items were deleted from the original list.[1] Apparently Hirsch has forgotten that a number of controversial political figures and terms were removed, as well as terms referring to human reproduction. Is there a politically conservative discrimination at work here?

Some of the omissions appear to be simple oversights, such as Cinderella, Indonesia, Italy, Japan, Mediterranean Sea, Poland, and Rome. A great number of terms were also added.[2] Hirsch expanded the list to include more terms referring to minorities, women, African-Americans, and Native Americans. On the other hand, both the Wounded Knee and Sand Creek massacres are missing, even though the Armenian massacres are included, which, horrible though they were, presumably would be much less relevant to Americans.

Terms from the 60s have also been added. The inclusion of some writers and artists and the exclusion of others must simply reflect the tastes of Hirsch and his colleagues. The deletion of terms with sexual references is compensated for by the inclusion of terms for sexually transmitted diseases. In spite of claims to the contrary, there do seem to be definite political biases creeping into the revision. Such a list of cultural terms can never be value neutral, as Hirsch claims. The best one can hope for is that the list reflect different sides, that it be impartial. Hirsch has not managed such balance.

CONCLUSIONS

After this analysis of Hirsch's arguments, several conclusions seem reasonable regarding the nature of cultural literacy, the politics of Hirsch's po-

---

[1] Including such terms as Spiro Agnew, art deco, civil liberties, Ralph Ellison, El Salvador, Jerry Falwell, Milton Friedman, ghetto, Barry Goldwater, Guatemala, Gulf of Tonkin, Lee Iacocca, Jeffersonian democracy, Edward Kennedy, Henry Kissinger, George McGovern, Ferdinand Marcos, Linus Pauling, Nelson Rockefeller, penis, phallus, Shylock, scrotum, sperm, Gloria Steinem, testes, vagina, Thornton Wilder, William Butler Yeats, and Wounded Knee massacre.

[2] Hank Aaron, AIDS, Aberdeen, Addis Ababa, Alas poor Yorick, Alzheimer's disease, Amazing Grace, Maya Angelou, Armenian massacres, bile, Gwendolyn Brooks, Ralph Bunche, Archie Bunker, Al Capone, Cato, CD (both), Chernobyl, concentration camps, Hernan Cortes, Crazy Horse, Bing Crosby, Demosthenes, Bob Dylan, Donald Duck, Dostoevsky, Paul Lawrence Dunbar, Amelia Earhart, Essay on Liberty, Federal Republic of Germany, Ella Fitzgerald, Freedman's Bureau, Anne Frank, William Lloyd Garrison, Marcus Garvey, herpes, Bob Hope, Langston Hughes, I am the very model of a modern Major-General, Kenya, La Fontaine, John Lennon, John L. Lewis, large intestine, La Scala, Nelson and Winnie Mandela, Metamorphosis (Ovid and Kafka titles), Carrie Nation, New Right, Nisei, Queen Elizabeths I and II, Queen Victoria, Chief Sequoyah, Junipero Serra, Frank Sinatra, B. F. Skinner, Jimmy Stewart, Shirley Temple, Trail of Tears, Uganda, Woodstock, Andy Warhol, John Wayne, Zambia.

sition, the appeal of cultural literacy to the general public, and what cultural literacy has to offer education in general. Cultural literacy, as advanced by its major proponents, is a particular view of the construction and generation of knowledge, the role of culture in that process, and the role of education in modern industrial society. In spite of references to research on reading, cultural literacy is not an intellectual ability akin to reading literacy. It is one thing to say that people need more cultural knowledge and something different to assert that there is a skill like the ability to read that enables one to succeed in society. Knowledge is necessary in both cases, and probably schemata as well, but these entail rather different abilities. Hirsch extends the analogy of cultural literacy and reading literacy too far. We suspect that there are quite a number of knowledge schemata in history, literature, and writing that enable one to do any number of things but not a coherent set of schema for cultural literacy per se. Cultural literacy is highly successful as a slogan, but its referent is obscure.

Formal education, culture, and literacy do play critical roles in modern industrial society but not necessarily in the way formulated by Hirsch. Hirsch is correct about the centrality of state-supported education to modern society, but we are skeptical about the role assigned education and culture by the particular theory of nationalism and economic development that Hirsch embraces. He interprets this theory in such a way as to make culture and education a driving force of the industrial state and to insist that everyone must assimilate to one dominant culture by means of the educational system.

In spite of protestations otherwise, Hirsch's position is politically conservative in several ways. In his view, nothing can be done about inequalities, social-class differences, social institutions other than the schools, or the dominant Anglo culture to which everyone must conform. The national culture itself is mandated by history and tradition, and we cannot challenge or change it. Social harmony and economic development depend on a homogeneous culture, he asserts. This conservatism does not make his arguments wrong, but his positions are often self-contradictory; for example, if none of us can change the national culture, why is he leading a movement to do so?

Furthermore, the list of what every American must know is politically conservative in what it includes and excludes. Such a list must withstand scrutiny as to its impartiality among the various races, ethnic, and interest groups in America, just as standardized achievement tests must. Minority groups strongly suspect that such a list would function to their further disadvantage, and in spite of Hirsch's assurances that their interests would be served, an examination of the list reveals that it is indeed biased in this regard.

The view of culture presented is one in which individuals passively receive culture rather than actively create it. No doubt one must learn cultural content before one is able to create products that contribute to that culture. However, Hirsch's denigration of creativity and critical thinking in favor of rote learning leans too far in the direction of educating passive consumers rather than producers of culture. Surely a liberal arts education should enable one to write well and think critically and not just recognize the names of classic authors. There is nothing in Hirsch's approach that emphasizes such an active, critical role for learners. Rote learning is not the education that Socrates would endorse.

Why is cultural literacy so attractive to so many people, in spite of the complex and often incorrect arguments? The deteriorating economic condition of the United States, the development of a seemingly permanent underclass, and the entry of vast numbers of non-English-speaking immigrants, legal and illegal, have created a situation in which many Americans feel threatened. Rising crime rates, welfare recipients, consumption of drugs, chronic poverty, and inadequate ghetto education highlight the problems of the so-called underclass. In addition, there is a pervasive sense of unease about the United States' slipping economically, as reflected in rising trade deficits and a stagnant standard of living. All this concern begs for an answer, and cultural literacy provides an explanation, a focus of blame, and a solution.

Why don't some ethnic groups do better in society? Because they are culturally deficient in the knowledge they possess, according to Hirsch, and they will no longer be disadvantaged when they acquire that cultural knowledge. Cultural knowledge alone allows one to succeed. This theme of cultural deprivation is repeated over and over in the United States in recent times and is a favorite of the neoconservatives in explaining why some ethnic groups succeed and some fail.

Cultural literacy promises a solution of traditionalism to an uneasy public by reasserting traditional American values and by promising that this reestablishment of tradition will recapture America's economic preeminence, eliminate the underclass, and transform millions of non-English-speaking immigrants into Americans. Anything that could do all these things has enormous appeal. Of course, the question is whether cultural literacy can do the things promised. We think not. On the other hand, although teaching humanities content will not solve the social ills that beset us, there are other reasons to introduce more cultural content.

Teaching more cultural content in the schools is an attractive idea. One can endorse teaching the poor more humanities content without believing that they are poor because they don't possess such content or that such knowledge will substitute for jobs and influence. The assertion that current texts and materials are deficient in humanities content seems reasonable. More myths, literature, history, and other changes proposed by the cultural literacy advocates make sense. However, we do not think that this material should be learned by rote or consist of exactly the content specified by Hirsch.

We would like to see a more active view of both culture and learning. Culture is constructed and produced by people and is transformed by both deliberate and nondeliberate modification and revision. American culture certainly has deep roots in Britain, but it is hardly a facsimile. The infusion of many different groups has produced a distinct culture that is reflected only partially by a Shakespearean play. We hold to the view that culture is actively produced and reproduced and is not an antique willed to us by ancestors. Portraying culture and education as passive is not a healthy perspective for a dynamic democracy.

The distinction between extensive and intensive knowledge, and Hirsch's endorsement of the extensive, suggests that tests of subject matter would cover many topics at a superficial level rather than a few terms in depth. This implies multiple-choice rather than essay tests, not a good choice in our opinion. Testing should be on intensive as well as extensive learning. As Langer points out in Chapter 2, the type of instruction best suited to learning is far removed from memorizing lists of terms.

Even though in our view cultural literacy cannot possibly accomplish the things claimed for it, whether, how, and to what extent we should test for more cultural content remains an important question. Though we doubt that such a thing as cultural literacy exists, we do agree that more and better humanities content should be taught and tested for in the public schools. However, this content should be more carefully defined and assessed than heretofore. Students should know when the Civil War took place, but we doubt that they need to know *annus mirabilis*. A list that serves as the basis for curriculum and testing with expectations of complete mastery should be more carefully worked out.

SUMMARY

Underlying the disputes between the cultural literacy advocates and their critics are differing visions of how culture is produced in society and what role the schools should play in transmitting that culture. Ultimately these are choices about what type of society we should have. The cultural literacy advocates have brought these important issues into focus by enunciating their own visions of society, culture, and the schools. Those who disagree must create their own persuasive alternative visions.

REFERENCES

Bloom, A. (1987). *The closing of the American mind: How higher education has failed democracy and impoverished the souls of today's students*. New York: Simon & Schuster.

Hirsch, E. D., Jr. (1983). Cultural literacy. *American Scholar, 52,* 159–160.

Hirsch, E. D., Jr. (1984a, January). Cultural literacy. Paper presented at the National Adult Literacy Conference, Washington, DC.

Hirsch, E. D., Jr. (1984b). English and the perils of formalism. *The American Scholar, 52,* 369–379.

Hirsch, E. D., Jr. (1985). Cultural literacy does not mean core curriculum. *English Journal, 74,* 47–50.

Hirsch, E. D., Jr. (1986). Cultural literacy does not mean a list of works. *ADE Bulletin, 84,* 1–3.

Hirsch, E. D., Jr. (1987a). Cultural literacy: Let's get specific. *NEA Today, 28,* 15–17.

Hirsch, E. D., Jr. (1987b). *Cultural literacy: What every American needs to know*. New York: Houghton-Mifflin.

Hirsch, E. D., Jr. (1988a). Brief response to Newman. *Social Education, 52,* 436–438.

Hirsch, E. D., Jr. (1988b). *Cultural literacy: What every American needs to know* (with an updated Appendix by E. D. Hirsch, Jr., J. Kett, & J. Trefil). New York: Vintage.

Hirsch, E. D., Jr. (1988c). *The dictionary of cultural literacy*. New York: Houghton-Mifflin.

Ravitch, D., & Finn, C. E., Jr. (1987). *What do our 17-years-olds know? A report on the first national assessment of history and literature*. New York: Harper & Row.

6 | Redefining Literacy and Literacy Contexts: Discovering a Community of Learners

OFELIA B. MIRAMONTES
University of Colorado, Boulder

NANCY L. COMMINS˙
University of Colorado, Denver

The theme of this book, the development of literacy for diverse populations, presents the opportunity to explore not only programmatic innovations but also the value positions from which our orientations toward diverse populations have evolved. An often repeated example portrays the essence of this chapter. One individual may see a glass of water as half-empty, whereas another sees the glass as half-full. The two interpretations represent profoundly different perspectives that can have serious consequences when the recipient of the interpretation is a child.

Why do so many educators perceive a half-empty glass when they look at culturally or linguistically diverse children? The answer lies in the fact that programs for these students are usually based on deficit perspectives of minority communities. In addition, students themselves may have gaps in linguistic development because of differential uses of language that help to reinforce negative stereotypes. In day-to-day interactions with students in the classroom, teachers may be unaware of the powerful historical and philosophical traditions that shape their perceptions of students, or how classroom interactions not only can limit students' academic performance but can also disrupt and undermine family and community ties.

This chapter examines how perspectives on students' literacy, language, and learning impact educational opportunities for language-minority students. It begins with a review of the deficit perspective, its manifestations in school programs, and its impact on home–school connections. An alternative, ability-centered perspective, developed within the social constructionist view of literacy, is presented to counter the deficit model, and its implications for school programs and reinforcement of home–school links are explored.

In describing an ability-centered view of students' academic performance we draw heavily on examples from our ongoing line of research. This work has focused on the unrecognized and untapped skills and abilities of language-minority students. We have been particularly interested in Spanish speakers who, after several years of schooling, do not show a clear dominance for Spanish or English or full proficiency in either language when assessed with traditional methods. The students we have studied have been underserved in a variety of educational programs for language-minority students in public schools including bilingual, English as a second language (ESL), and submersion into English.

THE PREVAILING PERSPECTIVE

Despite extensive work in language and cognition that suggests that children have linguistic and cognitive strengths whatever the first language (Labov, 1969; Vygotsky, 1978), educators have tended to take a deficit view of non-English-speaking children's existing linguistic and cognitive capabilities. Such views have a long tradition, as evidenced by George I. Sanchez's 1932 denunciation of the narrow and ethnocentric formulations of school policy that limited opportunities for culturally diverse students.

Even today, this perspective persists (Oakes, 1985), with lower-middle and minority homes seen as limited language-learning environments (Dunn, 1987), as providing faulty patterns of socialization (Moynihan, 1967), and as placing little value on education (Delgado-Gaitan, 1986). Although this view encompasses most culturally different populations, the deficit perspective is compounded when children have a language other than English. Often, bilingual children are perceived as lacking proficiency in two languages. The notions of bilingual children having "no language at all" and of "not possessing the means for logical thought" (Grosjean, 1982) are familiar characterizations of language-minority students. Because bilinguals' performance often varies as a function of languages and language contexts, students' differential abilities can impact perceptions of their abilities. Although they may display communicative competence (Hymes, 1974) based on their own sociocultural norms, their strengths can go unrecognized because of the nature of the demands of school tasks and the instruments used to assess them. As Garcia and Pearson in Chapter 18 argue, the definition of literacy underlying prevalent assessment tools has been limited, and misguided assessment processes have been used to reinforce deficit perceptions of students' abilities. When multiple measures are used, as has been the case in our research, a different view emerges of bilingual students' literacy and language abilities. Students do not have to be engaged in instruction that assumes deficits and compensates for these deficits with reductionist activities (see Chapters 7 and 10 for descriptions of these activities). When educators take a philosophical position that actively focuses on identifying student strengths or "ability cues" (Miramontes, 1990), by using alternative assessment tools and instructional tasks, they can begin to build on students' already established language repertoires.

School Programs From a Deficit Perspective

Educational interventions for limited-English-proficient students have typically been based on the compensatory or deficit perspective. Where special programs for language-minority students exist, they often represent a variety of loosely planned services, designed to make up for perceived deficits (Miramontes, 1991). Allington in Chapter 17 describes the manner in which special services often intermingle a variety of unrelated methodologies and lack mechanisms for sharing information about student progress. The situation is compounded for many language-minority students who, because of poorly conceived assessments, are placed in special education (Miramontes, 1987; Ruiz, 1989). Poor achievement test scores coupled with cultural differences, a two-language background, and limited familiarity with academic language skills in English become grounds for believing that students "lack" language and are therefore limited in their ability to perform cognitive tasks.

Program quality also varies radically, and programs tend to be understaffed, with students frequently receiving a majority of their instruction from paraprofessionals who speak their first language. Although well intentioned, paraprofessionals too often lack the training and skills necessary to design and implement instruction for language and literacy development. In addition, if students are afforded only limited access to the teacher, they are even less likely to encounter the notions of language development as expanding the capability to articulate arguments clearly, as a vehicle for learning to analyze ideas, and as an "expression of meaning."

Another difficulty that language-minority students encounter is a push to end ESL or bilingual services before students are ready. Special services may end when children are somewhat fluent in English but have not yet internalized the underlying structures of the second language. Furthermore, few provisions are generally made for a smooth transition into English across the content areas. One day students may be in a bilingual or ESL program and the next suddenly find themselves receiving instruction with no accommodation for their needs and competing for grades under the same criteria as native English speakers. Such students usually find themselves alone in their struggle to negotiate these new requirements.

Shannon (in press) profiles the fragile accommodations of a group of bilingual students beginning all-English instruction. In one example, Laura, a student whom her teacher praised extensively, achieved her academic excellence in English by translating what she could from Spanish using bilingual dictionaries at home and getting help from her sister. The teacher, completely unaware of Laura's struggle, was oblivious to the potential of Laura's sophisticated strategies. Unlike most second language learners, Laura was successful relying on her own resources.

Shannon's case studies demonstrate students' need for continued experiences in both languages and teacher awareness of their needs and strengths. Although research suggests that it takes 5 to 7 years for limited-English-proficient students to achieve academic proficiency in English (Cummins, 1986), students are rarely provided services for that length of time. More typically, they participate in programs for 2 to 3 years (Nadeau & Miramontes, 1988). In addition, data indicate that significant numbers of language-minority students (estimated 84%) receive no special ESL services at all (Olson, 1986). The level and quality of services play a major role in students' academic development.

Miramontes (1987) found that Spanish-dominant, Mexican-American students labeled as learning disabled evidenced many of the same reading miscue strategies as students considered proficient Spanish readers but that these skills had not been recognized in the special education assessment, resulting in a learning-disability label. The group that demonstrated the least proficiency in an oral reading and retelling task were students whose primary language at home was Spanish but who had not received ESL services. They had been required to perform as native English speakers since kindergarten. These students had also developed elaborate coping strategies for literacy and schooling in general. In a companion study (Miramontes, 1990), the reading strategies of students considered "mixed dominant" by their teachers were found to be significantly different from those of students making the transition from Spanish to English reading, and a significant number were found to have good oral reading and comprehension strategies, again seemingly unrecognized by their teachers.

The effects of "submersion" into English—instruction through English without any form of mediation—can severely impact students. It impacts their teachers as well. As one teacher in Commins's (1986) study reflected:

> I think maybe from the time they are in kindergarten until they are in
> second or third grade [the pattern develops] where the teacher feels, well,

these kids really don't understand me anyway. And so in the beginning of the year you are really trying to make a connection, a communication, but after the kids seem to be slipping, or seem to be behind, then you tend to try to make that communication less. So as the year goes on you're trying less and less to make that communication so that they can get that understandable instruction. (p. 143)

Children may interpret their teacher's loss of confidence as rejection or disapproval, which, in fact, it often is.

Intensifying the problem for language-minority students is the perception that speaking a language other than English constitutes an educational handicap. A familiar echo could be heard in the teacher interviews conducted in our research project: "Spanish holds students back." Bilingualism was not seen as a goal to be fostered or as an asset for a diverse society. Unfortunately, this perception is often shared by teachers in bilingual classrooms. In the words of one teacher: "It didn't make sense to push them back to Spanish after having advanced. They were performing more or less adequately in English, so I decided not to penalize them." When teachers view the primary language in this manner, it is not at all surprising to find that students view it in the same way. And, indeed, a student in one of our projects objected to receiving math instruction in Spanish with the comment, "Why do we have to go backwards instead of forwards?"

Home-School Connections in the Prevailing Perspective

The Vygotskian perspective that has been described in numerous chapters in this volume (see, e.g., Chapters 2 and 3) identifies the contexts of children's homes as the primary means for fostering cognitive and linguistic abilities. Although this mechanism operates in all cultures and languages, educators have typically discounted the scaffolding that has occurred in the homes of language-different children. Indeed, many teachers regard the language environments of limited-English-speaking students as a limiting factor to academic success. We have found evidence for a deficit view of homes throughout our research. At best, teachers feel that not much learning occurs in children's homes. At worst, they believe that very little occurs in students' homes that is of value in school. One teacher's comments volunteered in the context of questions about students' academic achievement (Commins, 1986) illustrate these perceptions. In describing a student's performance, the teacher stated, "I think the main problem is the learning problem at home. He never does homework, he never gets anything beyond the classroom." Later in the interview, the teacher blamed the home for yet another student's lack of achievement:

I have a hard time getting homework back from her so that the educational environment at home is lacking there also. And I think that's
probably one of the big things with a lot of the kids who appear slow
to me is that when they go home it's totally forgotten about so therefore when they come back to me the next day, it's kind of starting over
again. (p. 7)

This teacher judged parental support by students' completion of homework
assignments and those families not meeting this criterion failed their children. Finally, the nature of tasks on which teachers focus instruction can
impact parental perceptions and parent–child interaction. When homework
represents narrow definitions of literacy, such as spelling or decoding exercises, it becomes very difficult for non-English-speaking parents to contribute
to their children's literacy development.

The role of language-minority parents is undermined in other ways.
School personnel may suggest that parents speak to their children in English,
regardless of parents' facility in English. Or teachers may discourage parents
from interacting with their children about schoolwork by suggesting that the
methods of instruction in U.S. schools differ substantially from those in
which parents were educated. Such recommendations can limit the quality of
parent–child interaction severely. Compensatory perspectives and narrow definitions, thus, negatively impact not only school learning but, perhaps even
more fundamentally, the relationship between children and their families. By
discouraging parents from participating in a most significant period of their
child's development, they are robbed of the opportunity for meaningful interaction in the child's learning. The link that allows parents to guide and nurture their children's development begins to deteriorate, inevitably weakening
the family structure.

Children can perceive their parents' reluctance as rejection and may see
it as a choice between the language and culture of family and those of the
school. Gomez (1973) has articulated the growing sense of alienation as a
result of this rift between school and home: "Gradually I became aware of
feeling that what my family had to offer—language, customs, food, ways of
looking at the world . . . was not very good in comparison with others and
the other world in which I lived" (p. 10).

This debilitating circumstance can cause a gulf to form between children
and their families, between the self and the significant others in their lives.
At the same time, English begins to be seen as the language of school, an
identification that reinforces the disassociation of learning from home. This
separation can begin very early. In a home visit, Monica, the 5-year-old sister
of a student in our research, refused to play a game of translating animal
names (Commins, 1989). She was adamant that English was for school alone

and that only Spanish be used at home. Another parent reported that Jose, a fifth grader, had virtually stopped using Spanish in the home by second grade, although his father spoke no English.

In recalling how his parents had adopted the school's suggestion that they speak only English to their children, Richard Rodriguez (1981) relates his pain upon hearing his parents switch from Spanish to English in his presence:

> The gringo sounds they uttered startled me. Pushed me away. In that moment . . . I felt my throat twisted by unsounded grief. I simply turned and left the room. But I had no place to escape to where I could grieve in Spanish. My brother and sisters were speaking English in another part of the house. (p. 16)

Although strongly against the use of students' primary languages in schools, Rodriguez makes an eloquent argument for the high cost of not including (or trying to eliminate) the primary language from children's lives.

Such stresses impact learning. The attention that limited-English-speaking children might direct toward acquiring new information and knowledge is spent instead on deciphering the new language and social code, trying to be like others (Trueba, 1987; Miramontes, 1987), covering up their inadequacies, and avoiding any difficult tasks where these inadequacies might be revealed (Rueda & Mehan, 1986).

For students who live in dual-language environments, then, literacy development requires an understanding not only of how knowledge, self, and potential for cognitive growth reside in both language contexts but also of the ways in which the challenges of literacy development are compounded by psychological and emotional pressures students endure as they must shift cultural and linguistic frames. The emotions that a once monolingual Spanish-speaking fifth grader feels as he stumbles through the oral reading of a passage from a second-grade text, for example, may reflect much more than simple embarrassment. They may stem from the frustration of years of knowing the answer but not having the right words to express it (Commins & Miramontes, 1989), the shame and continued bewilderment of having been thrust into an alien environment in kindergarten (Trueba, 1988), and the lack of adequate preparation or mediation to deal with an all-English schooling experience (Miramontes, 1990; Shannon, in press).

AN ALTERNATIVE PERSPECTIVE:
THE SEARCH FOR ABILITY CUES

A view of literacy for a diverse society that encompasses multiple literacies (Chapter 8) produces a very different perception of familial contributions and of the vital continuing relationship of learning from home to school. In Chapter 3, Eisenhart and Cutts-Dougherty have described in detail the social constructionist perspective within which parents are seen as sources of information, history, points of view, and knowledge. With this shift in perspective, it is not homes that change but their value and role in school learning. A perspective that validates all of students' sources of knowledge and modes of interaction allows teachers to view everything the child knows as a departure for learning. We, therefore, suggest that teachers must become ability centered; that is, they must engage actively in a search for ability cues.

Ability-Centered Profiles

Through an examination of case studies of students from our research (Commins, 1989; Commins & Miramontes, 1989; Miramontes, 1990), the diversity among Latino children becomes apparent, as do their strengths in learning strategies and proficiencies. Although all students showed some gaps in their linguistic abilities, all demonstrated areas of strength that could be used as the building blocks for additional strategies and proficiencies. Four examples from an ability-centered perspective illustrate the nature of their strengths.

Reina: From inconcise to coherent. Reina (all student names are pseudonyms) was a fifth-grade student whose oral language fluency varied substantially depending on the language and context. Although she loved to converse, her messages were not always clear in English, and seemingly she flitted from thought to thought. In fact, her teacher described Reina as a person who used a lot of words to say nothing. For example, her response to the question, "What did you do this weekend?" in an informal context was hard to follow: "Well at first, Saturday morning I woke up at 7:30 and the telephone rang and um . . . it was my auntie, and she wa–, and my auntie said, Samuel, you know, my godfather an um I had to call my Dad."

By contrast, Reina's spontaneous discourse in Spanish was coherent, as is evident in her response to the same question about weekend activities, "Mmm si, um bueno, limpíe mi cuarto y luego fuí a ver la tele y cené y luego lavé los trastes y hice mi tarea y luego fuí a dormir." [Mmm yes, um well. I cleaned my room and then I watched TV and I ate supper and then I washed the dishes, I did my homework and then I went to bed.] When asked to tell a story in Spanish, Reina's narrative included a broad range of vocabulary and elaboration on the setting.

Whereas Reina's retelling of a story with a wordless book prompt

Figure 6.1 Miscue Analysis of Irene's Oral Reading

"Well," said Ramon, "we sure don't want a stranger with a mean-looking dog fooling around our house. If he comes over here again let's see if we can scare him

away."

"I can make weird noises with that creaky toolbox upstairs—and by clapping my hands," said Bill.

"That's right," said Ramon. "And I can stand at the door wearing a sheet with eyeholes and waving my arms, so he'll think there are ghosts in the house! That will get rid of him in no time!" said Ramon.

∧ = inserted;   ℓ = omitted;   ①/② = first and second responses

showed the some disjointedness as her spontaneous use of English, she demonstrated an ability to give a focused retelling with details when asked to retell an English story she had read. Reina included information on the critical elements of the story such as characters, setting, and plot and much of the dialogue between characters. Thus, with a structure, Reina demonstrated the same clarity and attention to detail in English that was evident in her use of Spanish across a variety of situations, informal and formal. Instruction could be targeted to providing varied and consistent opportunities for her spontaneously to use English orally, that is, telling stories and organizing and defending points of view without specific prompts.

Irene: Poor oral reader, good meaning-maker. Students are often asked to read orally during literacy periods and content-area ones as well. As was suggested by Hiebert and Fisher in Chapter 10, teachers often make judgments about language-minority students' reading ability on the basis of these oral renditions. Irene illustrates the situation where a language-minority student's lack of fluency in oral reading masks underlying competence at making meaning from text. A miscue analysis of her oral reading (see Figure 6.1) showed that she skipped many words, mispronounced others, and generally sounded as though she couldn't possibly have comprehended the text that she was reading.

Yet, Irene's answers to questions about the story and her retelling of it indicated good comprehension of the text and use of information from reading to form opinions. Because of her excellent comprehension abilities, it would be particularly important that reading not be the only vehicle through which Irene had access to information in other curriculum areas. Providing multiple ways of gaining access to information (e.g., through audiotapes, shared reading) would ensure her continued cognitive growth. In Irene's case the ability cue of good comprehension was easily overlooked in the face of her fractured oral reading performance.

Marta: A reluctant classroom reader, an excited home reader.
Marta was a student whose true interest in learning only became apparent by looking outside of school. In school, Marta did not seem at all concerned about her work. She was easily distracted by her classmates and played with papers in her desk when the teacher presented material. According to her teacher, Marta lacked interest and was slow to retain information.

Visits with Marta outside of school and at home produced an opposite picture. On two trips to a researcher's home, Marta asked to be taken to the public library where she looked specifically for books by Judy Blume and Beverly Cleary. During a visit to her home, Marta proudly displayed a box that she had decorated by following the written instructions from a library book. On yet another occasion, she brought out a pile of *Ranger Rick* magazines she borrowed from the library and animatedly described an article about snakes. Her wish for a subscription had been vetoed by her mother because of the expense (Commins, 1989).

Marta suffered from the lack of communication between different facets of school programs that Allington describes in Chapter 17. Marta's remedial reading teacher described Marta as an eager learner, as evidenced by a prize for her story writing. Furthermore, Marta regularly visited the school library and checked out magazines, stories, and how-to books. However, the views of Marta in the remedial reading class and library did not reach the classroom teacher.

Ignacio and Marta: Inauthentic school tasks.   The nature of school tasks themselves often contributes to negative perceptions of students. Ignacio's favorite subject was math and he claimed to hate reading and spelling, which he did because he had no other choice. Every week, he dutifully followed the classroom routine for spelling: Take pretest, copy words five times each, write definitions, do exercises, and take posttest. But, in explaining spelling exercises to a research team member, Ignacio was clear that the exercises were an end in themselves. When asked what the spelling words were needed for, Ignacio simply pointed to the exercises in the workbook.

Marta responded to the same inauthentic task by memorizing many definitions but failing to associate most of them with the correct word. Without authentic reasons for using the words, she had no links for their meaning. For example, Marta confused *precede* with *produce* and defined the former as "to make something grow." Her definitions were short and concise (though wrong) in contrast to those of other students who gave roundabout, lengthy (and often incorrect) explanations of word meanings. She had the form but no one had guided her in the functions of using these words. Like Laura, the student whom Shannon (in press) studied, these language-minority students had to find ways to succeed on their own.

School Programs From an Ability-Centered Perspective

A shift in perspective to one in which teachers are actively engaged in focusing on what students *can* rather than *can't* do produces fundamental changes in instruction. In such a view, children's existing strategies and knowledge are recognized and accepted, becoming the basis for extending learning. Information about student strategies and knowledge can be gained through daily classroom activities, as Garcia and Pearson describe in Chapter 18.

Process-oriented approaches to writing offer many possibilities for finding and building on existing strengths. For example, the writers' workshop approach (Calkins, 1986) encourages conferences between teacher and individual students. This context is ideal for a number of different functions including the scaffolding that is so vital for all learning but that is fundamental for the thinking, writing, and talking of students working in their nonnative language. It also facilitates the monitoring and information gathering that is required for teachers to establish strengths and areas of emphasis. An additional benefit is that the writers' workshop offers opportunities for teachers to learn about their students as individuals and provides a legitimate forum for students' world views in the classroom.

A literature-based reading approach is another avenue to literacy that can link children's school experiences with their backgrounds and ethnic heritages. As Bishop (1987) argues, literature allows teachers and students to tap into the rich literary traditions of ethnic and cultural groups.

Many individual teachers have moved to activities based on the writing process and literature, but it is extremely difficult to implement broad-based changes alone. Although individual teachers are important in creating a climate that values diversity, efforts are limited without school-wide programs that build on these principles. By working together, teachers can make a difference. Our current research illustrates the manner in which such joint efforts can occur. This project is in a school that serves a substantial population of culturally and linguistically diverse learners. Three second-grade teachers have joined forces with the school's reading resource teacher and special education teacher to implement a writer's workshop approach benefiting both children and teachers. By extending the same activities across several contexts (i.e., regular classroom, resource rooms), teachers were able to compare students' accomplishments. By pooling resources, they also had increased opportunities to observe their students in these different contexts. A significant feature of the collaborative project involved weekly meetings in which teachers discussed children's accomplishments and mutual problems. The teachers, who began these early morning meetings sleepy and pressed for time, left 20 minutes later excitedly sharing comments about students' writing and strategies and topics for the week's instruction.

Enhancing Home–School Connections

Through paying attention to ability cues, teachers have the potential to acknowledge and integrate parents and the community. Children who write in their native language and English can share their work with parents. Teachers who do not speak the children's home language can nevertheless actively encourage parents to interact with their children in the native language. For example, parents can read children's literature and share it with one another and with their children (Moll, 1988). In Chapter 14, Edwards also describes a program in which parents are integrated into the school context through children's literature activities.

Teachers who are actively searching for ability cues value children's experiences in their primary language as a cognitive asset. Parents are supported in interacting with their children on a variety of topics. And, as Saville-Troike (1984) found, limited-English-proficient students who had achieved best in content areas as measured by English tests were those who had had opportunities to discuss the concepts in their native language. Other projects describe ways in which students gather oral histories from the community and write reports based on information gathered from community members (Moll & Diaz, 1987). Such activities connect homes and schools, validating children's out-of-school learning.

SUMMARY

For many years, educators have been urged to shift away from a deficit perspective (Cummins, 1986). However, widespread changes in attitudes and programs have been slow in coming. Many children find themselves engaged in the reductionist activities described by Rueda in Chapter 7. The consequences of a watered-down curriculum of repetitive skills, rote memorization, and an emphasis on correctness are costly, both in terms of students' school learning and of their relationships and learning in home settings.

From a deficit perspective, language-minority students are seen to be lacking and are blamed for their failure. Our recent work, grounded in a social constructionist model, has developed profiles of Latino bilingual students as proficient language users whose displayed competence varies as a function of language and context. With broader assessment measures and an ability-centered perspective, language-minority students show proficiency and interest in learning.

To look at strengths is a philosophical choice. The skillful teaching of children who are diverse in their languages and backgrounds comes from the ability to hold high expectations while providing the means whereby students can reach those expectations: modulating instruction to keep students stretching to grow. Children do not really "look" different when perspectives are shifted; it is educators' interpretations of students' skills and performances that change.

REFERENCES

Bishop, R. S. (1987). Extending multicultural understanding through children's books. In B. Cullinan (Ed.), *Children's literature in the reading program*. Newark, DE: International Reading Association.

Calkins, L. (1986). *The art of teaching writing*. Portsmouth, NH: Heinemann.

Commins, N. L. (1986). *A descriptive study of the linguistic abilities of four Hispanic bilingual students*. Unpublished doctoral dissertation, University of Colorado, Boulder.

Commins, N. L. (1989). Language and affect: Bilingual students at home and at school. *Language Arts, 66*, 29–43.

Commins, N. L., & Miramontes, O. B. (1989). A descriptive study of the linguistic abilities of a selected group of low achieving Hispanic bilingual students. *American Educational Research Journal, 26*, 443–472.

Cummins, J. (1986). Empowering minority students: A framework for intervention. *Harvard Educational Review, 56*, 18–36.

Delgado-Gaitan, C. (1986). Teacher attitudes on diversity affecting student socio-academic responses: An ethnographic view. *Journal of Adolescent Research, 1*, 104–114.

Dunn, L. M. (1987). Bilingual Hispanic children on the U.S. mainland: A review of research on their cognitive, linguistic, and scholastic development. *AGS Monograph*. Circle Pines, NM: American Guidance Service.

Gomez, D. F. (1973). *Somos Chicanos: Strangers in our own land*. Boston: Beacon.

Grosjean, F. (1982). *Life with two languages: An introduction to bilingualism*. Cambridge, MA: Harvard University Press.

Hymes, D. (1974). Ways of speaking. In R. Bauman & J. Sherzer (Eds.), *Explorations in the ethnography of speaking* (pp. 433–451). New York: Cambridge University Press.

Labov, W. (1969). The logic of nonstandard English. In R. D. Abrahams & R. C. Troike (Eds.), *Language and cultural diversity in American education* (pp. 225–261). Englewood Cliffs, NJ: Prentice Hall.

Miramontes, O. B. (1987). Oral reading miscues of Hispanic good and learning disabled students: Implications for second language reading. In S. B. Goldman & H. T. Trueba (Eds.), *Becoming literate in English as a second language* (pp. 127–154). Norwood, NJ: Ablex.

Miramontes, O. B. (1990). A comparative study of the English oral reading skills in differently schooled groups of Hispanic students. *Journal of Reading Behavior, 22*, 373–394.

Miramontes, O. B. (1991). Organizing for effective paraprofessional services in special education: A multi-lingual/multi-ethnic instructional service (MMIS) team model. *Remedial and Special Education. 12*, 29–36.

Moll, L. (1988). Some key issues in teaching Latino students. *Language Arts, 65*, 465–472.

Moll, L., & Diaz, E. (1987). Change as the goal of educational research. *Anthropology and Education Quarterly, 18*, 300–311.

Moynihan, D. (1967). *The Negro family*. Cambridge, MA: M.I.T. Press.

Nadeau, A., & Miramontes, O. (1988). The reclassification of limited English proficient students: Assessing the inter-relationship of selected variables. *NABE Journal, 12*, 219–242.

Oakes, J. (1985). *Keeping Track*. New Haven, CT: Yale University Press.

Olson, L. (1986). Many bilingual pupils unaided, study finds. *Education Week, V*, 1.

Rodriguez, R. (1981). Memories of a bilingual childhood. *American Educator, 50*, 12–21.

Rueda, R., & Mehan, H. (1986). Metacognition and passing: Strategic interactions in the lives of students with learning disabilities. *Anthropology and Education Quarterly, 17*, 146–165.

Ruiz, N. T. (1989). An optimal learning environment for Rosemary. *Exceptional Children, 56*, 130–144.

Sanchez, G. (1932). *The age-grade status of the rural child in New Mexico, 1931–1932*. Santa Fe, NM: State Department of Education.

Saville-Troike, M. (1984). What really matters in second language learning for academic achievement. *TESOL Quarterly, 18*, 199–219.

Shannon, S. M. (in press). Transition from bilingual programs to all-English programs: Issues about and beyond language. *Linguistics and Education*.

Trueba, H. T. (1987). Organizing classroom instruction in specific sociocultural contexts: Teaching Mexican youth to write in English. In S. Goldman & H. Trueba (Eds.), *Becoming literate in English as a second language: Advances in research and theory* (pp. 235–252). Norwood, NJ: Ablex.

Trueba, H. T. (1988). English literacy acquisition: From cultural trauma to learning disabilities in minority students. *Linguistics & Education, 1,* 125–151.

Vygotsky, L. S. (1978). *Mind in society: The development of higher psychological processes*. Cambridge, MA: Harvard University Press.

Part II
PRACTICES

Here in Part II, and throughout the book, there are many descriptions of classrooms where practices are heavily influenced by constructivist views of learning. In most cases, the classroom practices themselves are fully described, as well as the underlying ideas on which they are based. These descriptions, portraying the efforts of many teachers, show that these views of learning are both theoretically and practically sound, not the wild dreams of academic Don Quixotes. Many authors, in describing practices that stem from a constructivist perspective, also describe contrasting practices and their underlying rationales.

Chapter 7 foreshadows the themes of the remaining chapters. In this overview, Rueda contrasts features that support literacy acquisition in classrooms serving students with diverse backgrounds with those that obliterate or sabotage it. The remaining chapters cluster in three groups, each attending to one, or more, of the features outlined by Rueda.

The first cluster of chapters explicates ways in which classroom interaction can be created to support or hinder literacy acquisition. Chapter 8 by McCollum and Chapter 9 by Palincsar and David, drawing heavily on the work of Vygotsky, describe two different, though compatible, dimensions of social interaction. McCollum examines the role of cultural interaction patterns in the social interaction surrounding classroom literacy events. Palincsar and David explore how specific literacy processes, such as questioning and summarizing, are developed in classroom dialogue. Both aspects of social interaction are critical to a comprehensive literacy program. These chapters have been placed side by side to emphasize the complex nature of social interaction in classrooms and its influence on literacy acquisition.

In the second cluster, Chapter 10 by Hiebert and Fisher examines "talk" structures during literacy instruction and the qualities and quantities of literacy tasks in which classroom talk is embedded. Implications of distributions of task and talk structures are presented for students with diverse social, cultural, and linguistic experiences. Chapters 11 and 12 in this cluster extend analysis of classroom task structures

91

during literacy instruction. Describing the use of dialogue journals and literature logs by linguistically and culturally different students, Reyes shows some inappropriate effects when diversity in students' backgrounds is not taken into account. Meloth discusses the effects of cooperative learning tasks in classroom instruction.

In the third cluster of chapters, analysis of literacy acquisition is extended beyond the boundaries represented by classroom and school walls. Constructivist themes are applied to the learning of those who create learning contexts for children—teachers and parents. In Chapter 13 Gaffney and Anderson analyze teachers' development resulting from participation in the Reading Recovery program, and in Chapter 14 Edwards reports on working with parents to create learning contexts around books at home.

Part II documents the workability of constructivist themes in classroom literacy experiences for students with diverse backgrounds. In these programs, diversity among students is viewed as a major source of support for, and an arena in which to pursue, literacy acquisition rather than as a barrier to be reduced or overcome.

7 | Characteristics of Literacy Programs for Language-Minority Students

ROBERT RUEDA
University of Southern California

A major issue currently facing public schools is how to prepare all students to function in a social system that requires increasingly sophisticated uses of literacy. This problem is especially challenging in the face of the increasing linguistic and ethnic diversity of public schools. This challenge has not been adequately addressed, as is evident in the nonrandom ways in which academic achievement indicators differ among certain ethnic and linguistic minority groups. On almost any indicator of academic success, such as test scores, retention, referral for special education, and dropout rates, substantial discrepancies are found between Hispanic and non-Hispanic students (Arias, 1986). The National Assessment of Educational Progress (1986) reported that, overall, language-minority students, especially Hispanics, were considerably below the national average at grades 4, 8, and 11. At the same time, cultural and linguistic diversity is becoming the norm rather than the exception. In California, it is predicted that an absolute majority of public school students will be Hispanic in the early part of the next century (McCarthy & Valdez, 1986).

In spite of increased levels of underachievement in the face of growing diversity, there are indications that much of this failure is preventable. Advances in theories of literacy and research on its acquisition, instruction, and use with diverse groups suggest optimism in reversing this trend (Garcia & August, 1988). This chapter highlights these current understandings about the best ways to promote literacy with language-minority students.

In a sense, this task will be approached in a backwards fashion, by organizing around factors that are most problematic in literacy acquisition. For organizational purposes, these factors are divided into those at the individual student and classroom instructional level and those related to the institutional level. Where appropriate, exemplary or promising approaches that address the issues will be discussed.

INDIVIDUAL STUDENT AND INSTRUCTIONAL FACTORS

Although the problem of underachievement is systematically related to ethnic and linguistic minority status, both between-group and within-group variance serve to dismiss simplistic explanations. For example, what can account for the fact that some low socioeconomic status (SES) Hispanic students become proficient readers and writers while so many experience problems? Although early explanations for these systematic differences focused exclusively on perceived deficits within the child (e.g., language, culture), these have been justly criticized. More recent conceptualizations suggest that the interaction between child- and school-based factors is a more fruitful indicator in understanding eventual academic outcomes. Three of these factors are considered here: inactive teaching, previous and current experience, and mismatches between school and out-of-school experiences.

The Role of Inactive Teaching

Although approaches that de-emphasize the active role of the learner are not the exclusive domain of language-minority students, minority and low-achieving poor students tend to "get less" in the classroom (see Chapter 10). Their instruction focuses on low-level mechanics or pronunciation at the letter or word level, with minimal or no attention to comprehension of meaningful texts (Moll & Diaz, in press). Moreover, because there is a long-standing assumption that learning to read in Spanish is synonymous with sound-symbol correspondence, this emphasis is even more pronounced in Spanish reading lessons (Barrera, 1983). In spite of a recognized need for balance between word recognition and comprehension (Anderson, Hiebert, Scott, & Wilkinson, 1985), many programs for language-minority students provide little time for constructing meaning from text or for writing to communicate meaningful information. What children receive instead can be best characterized as "reductionistic" (Poplin, 1988) or "transmission oriented" (Cummins, 1989).

Low-level basal reading materials with controlled vocabularies tend to provide little motivation for many students, especially those who arrive at school without a highly developed schema for decontextualized literacy activities. Similarly, teacher-directed writing assignments that focus on the "correct" production of mechanics engender little enthusiasm in students. Although lack of motivation has been a common explanatory mechanism for school failure, only recently has attention been given to the nature of the activities themselves (see Chapters 10 and 12). Simply put, lack of interest and motivation is likely a sensible response for many students in view of school tasks.

In contrast, recent conceptualizations of learning suggest that learners must be actively involved in the learning process, actively constructing meaning and purposefully integrating new and old information (Segal, Chipman, & Glaser, 1985; Vygotsky, 1978). Cognitive psychologists have illustrated the importance of the learner's active efforts in processing, storing, and recalling information in complex tasks like reading or writing. Nowhere has the importance of the learner's active role in constructing meaning been more clear than in the area of literacy (Chapter 13).

Out of this theory have come approaches that emphasize the student's role in constructing meaning in authentic and personally relevant activities, sometimes labeled interactive/experiential (Cummins, 1989), holistic/constructivist (Poplin, 1988), or interactionist/constructivist (Tharp & Gallimore, 1988). In practice, this philosophy is implemented as whole-language (Flores et al., 1986; Goodman, 1986) or neo-Vygotskian approaches that emphasize assisted performance (Chapter 9; Tharp & Gallimore, 1988). Programs with such features appear to be particularly successful in promoting literacy with language-minority students. For example, interactive process writing (Chapter 11), computer-mediated writing (Rosa & Moll, 1985), comprehension-based strategy training (Hernandez, 1987), and whole language (Bird, 1989) have all proved successful with language-minority students. In each of these cases, discarding of traditional inactive approaches has led to the documentation of significant literacy improvement.

The social organization of activities is important, not just their content. Work on collaborative learning, for example, shows positive effects for academic gains and motivation. Kagan's (1986) review of literature led to the conclusion: "Minority students may lack motivation to learn, but only when they are placed in traditional, competitive/individualistic classroom structures. As demonstrated so clearly by the . . . [research], in a relatively short time what appears to be a long term minority student deficiency in basic language skills can be overcome by transforming the social organization of the classroom" (pp. 246–247).

The nature of activities and the manner in which they are socially organized demand closer attention before student motivation is attributed as the source of problems in literacy acquisition. Evidence is mounting that much of the low achievement of language-minority students may be pedagogically induced or exacerbated and therefore amenable to change.

Insufficient Previous and Current Experience

A common notion about student failure pertains to developmental readiness. The biological version of this view, common in special education, suggests that learning problems result from developmental delays in neurological processing. The social version of this view points to more cognitive or socially based factors. Although few would argue against individual differences in learning, a focus on limitations has not been successful in guiding instruction (Coles, 1987).

One positive contribution of a developmental perspective can be found in emergent literacy, where literacy is seen as a developmental (although not rigidly fixed) phenomenon with roots long before students enter school (Ferreiro & Teberosky, 1982). Within this view, students experiment with writing and environmental print at a very early age, and these experiences can be built upon in the design of school literacy programs.

The current nature of public schooling means that not all students come to school equally equipped to negotiate school tasks on the basis of earlier experiences. For example, ethnographic work shows that all students do not experience the same literacy-related activities at home (Anderson & Stokes, 1984; Heath, 1983). The home literacy events of working-class and language-minority students may differ systematically from those of middle-class students. These studies show that literacy is not absent and does play a part in the home lives of these children. However, the decontextualized use of language around written text, discussions of differing interpretations of stories, and other "school-like" literacy activities that have been linked with school success may not appear as frequently as in middle-class homes.

In spite of these findings, there is room for optimism. A review by Rueda, Ruiz, and Figueroa (1989) suggests that the traditional explanation of lowered parental aspirations does not account for achievement differences. Goldenberg (1987) and Delgado-Gaitan (1990) report that low-income Hispanic parents have high aspirations for their children, and many view school as a vehicle for the improvement of life circumstances. On the other hand, many of these families have a "radical bottom up" view of reading (*juntar letras*) (Goldenberg, 1987), similar to the "bottom up" practices of many school programs for low achievers. As a consequence, some parents may be unaware of how to promote discussion around written text and may even promote relatively low-level skills. Parents of language-minority students may be more than willing to facilitate their children's literacy growth but may be limited by lack of knowledge of how to proceed. Nevertheless, even with minimal interventions, the sorts of home-based literacy experiences that appear to facilitate school-based literacy seem to be highly amenable to change under the right conditions (Chapter 14).

In one project (Goldenberg & Gallimore, 1990), kindergarten teachers sent home short *libritos* every 2 or 3 weeks for parents and children to read jointly, because there were relatively few children's books at home. In the control classrooms, more conventional homework such as copying went home. Videotaping in homes indicated a substantial range in the interactions prompted by the *libritos,* with many episodes having a high level of interaction about reading. Goldenberg and Gallimore concluded that parents in these homes merely lacked information, not interest, to promote literacy.

Ada (1988) took a different approach with low-income, mostly rural Spanish-speaking parents by organizing them regularly to dialogue about high-quality children's literature and to share literature written by themselves and their children. The model emphasizes a collaborative relationship between school and home in a culturally relevant fashion. Not surprisingly, Ada documented a high degree of satisfaction among participants and an increase in home experiences thought to be advantageous for school success.

Mismatch of Out-of-School and Classroom Experience

Increasingly, cognitive psychologists and other theorists have moved from a reliance on decontextualized tasks (characteristic of many school programs) as a means of understanding how learning and transfer occur to a study of problem solving and learning in out-of-school, everyday contexts. For example, Resnick (1987) characterizes out-of-school learning as involving shared cognition, external supports in the form of various "tools," contextualized reasoning, and situation-specific competencies and school learning as lacking many of these features. Others have argued that knowledge is "situated," that is, a product of the activity, context, and culture in which it is developed and used (Brown, Collins, & Duguid, 1989).

A context-specific view of competence has been especially important in conceptualizing the achievement of language-minority students, because ability and performance have been shown to vary considerably as a function of context (Diaz, Moll, & Mehan, 1986; Rueda, 1986). Aside from the uniqueness of school as a teaching–learning setting, an additional discontinuity for language-minority students may be found in behaviors and understandings that are unique to their culture and inconsistent with the school context.

Many have studied the unique culturally based interactional styles or discourse patterns of various groups and attempted to relate them to academic outcomes as a function of real or hypothesized mismatches (Tharp, 1989). Perhaps the best documented example of a systematic attempt to accommodate cultural learning patterns is the Kamehameha Early Education Program (KEEP) with native Hawaiian students (Tharp & Gallimore, 1988). In the early phases of KEEP, cultural interactional patterns endemic of children's home settings such as "talk story" were emphasized. Gains in student literacy were documented. However, the foci on higher-order reading comprehension and on an "assisted performance" approach to help integrate background knowledge have proved to be the critical elements of the program.

Although the explanatory power of the cultural mismatch hypothesis is limited in explaining differential student outcomes (Tharp, 1989), some evidence documents the potentially devastating effects of culturally based mismatches. This is brought out clearly in a recent ethnographic study that investigated learning difficulties of a diverse group of language-minority students. Trueba (1988) studied Hispanic, Laotian, Hmong, Vietnamese, and Sudanese students across home and school settings and concluded that, among these recently immigrated students, cultural conflict was a major explanatory factor for their lack of school achievement. Classroom literacy activities (in English) presupposed cultural knowledge and values that students did not have, resulting in "cultural trauma" that disabled learning. Trueba described the students as passive during classroom activities and as likely to produce homework or other text in a fragmented fashion. Yet, even with this group of students, Trueba was able to document situational variability in performance under certain conditions. The same students, when encouraged to select the content of the task in small group settings, "produced imaginative text (albeit full of errors) describing experiences (real or fictitious) in their home countries" (p. 141).

This discussion has shown that a number of factors must be considered in arranging instructional contexts for language-minority students. In essence, to the extent that these factors characterize the instructional experiences to which students are exposed, the development of proficiency in literacy will be promoted. The major support for this hypothesis is found in the contextual variability of student output, especially the elevated levels of task engagement and performance outcomes when these conditions are met.

However, there is increasing evidence that student and classroom factors cannot be considered in isolation. Individual instructional activity settings do not operate in social vacuums but within school, community, and societal contexts. "Macrolevel" variables at the policy and organizational levels, such as current institutional mechanisms for dealing with school failure, measurement of literacy outcomes, and the role of primary language support as a policy issue, can be critical in fostering literacy.

PROGRAM AND INSTITUTIONAL FACTORS

Unlike "deficit" theorists who attribute literacy problems to perceived shortcomings in the child, more recent conceptualizations view the problem in a multifaceted fashion, with equal attention not only to student attributes but to the larger school and societal contexts as well (Cortes, 1986). One area of the institutional context of schooling relates to ways that schools handle failure. That is, when student performance falls below certain accepted norms, what institutional mechanisms are in place to address the problem, and how is this important with respect to literacy?

Institutional Responses to Problems in Literary Acquisition: The Role of Special Education

Within the typical large groups of most classrooms, teachers seem to gear instruction to an estimated median ability level. The constraints operating against individual assistance are in most cases formidable. What happens when a given student experiences prolonged difficulty in reading and writing? One possibility is referral to the special education system, a likely possibility for children with cultural and linguistic differences.

Although special education was originally designed to serve students with serious impairments such as blindness, deafness, and severe cases of mental retardation, currently most students served are "slow learners" with no demonstrable organic impairments. The special education system has come to represent the primary institutional mechanism for prolonged problems in the acquisition of literacy and other academic areas.

In theory such a system could provide needed assistance to individual students in a more specialized setting so that reading and writing could be advanced in innovative ways. Unfortunately, there are serious problems with the system as currently structured at both the conceptual and organizational levels. As Rueda (1989, in press) and others (e.g., see Chapters 17 and 19) have pointed out, the system is costly and is characterized by a medicalized notion of learning problems, by lack of coordination or competition between programs (such as with Chapter 1 programs), and by problems such as reliance on imprecise definitions and inappropriate assessment tools and practices. Perhaps most important of all, much of the instruction in these settings is characterized by "reductionistic" practices and activities, where isolated skills are presented and practiced until mastery is achieved (Flores, Rueda, & Porter, 1986; Poplin, 1988). In many cases, it is as if once students are labeled, the already described principles that facilitate the acquisition of literacy no longer apply.

At least one report underscores the need to conceptualize how underachievement is treated as an institutional problem. Wang and Reynolds (1985) have described a restructured special education system that addressed many of the problems noted above. This particular program was designed to minimize the distinctions between "regular" and "special" learners by modifying conditions in the learning environment. "Special" staff were moved into regular classrooms along with the special students they served. There were no pullout aspects of the program, and categorical distinctions between students were eliminated. The "experimental" students in this project demonstrated 1-year gains for *both* regular and special education participants, whereas control students showed only half as much gain. Additional improvements in student behavior led to recommendations of decertification for about a third of the previously labeled students, whereas the district at large averaged about 3%. In spite of strong positive evaluations of the program by administrative and instructional staff, the local school board voted to discontinue the project at the end of the year. Why was this action taken? The system was structured in such a way that only students with at least a part-time special education placement were eligible for reimbursement for services. In essence, because of institutional constraints, the schools were penalized for providing innovative educational environments. The demise of this project and what it represented was not simply the result of an isolated or singular bureaucratic regulation. Rather, this state of affairs is reflective of the larger institutionalized conceptualization of learning and learning problems.

Assessment of Student Outcomes: The Role of Standardized Tests

Normally, testing practices focused on monitoring academic outcomes can legitimately be considered an individual teacher activity. However, testing (more specifically achievement testing) here is treated within the context of a larger policy issue, which it has become with an increasing demand on the part of the public, politicians, and others for "accountability" in "basic" school skills. How do current testing policies impact testing practices and therefore the acquisition of literacy?

A complete review of the characteristics and uses of standardized tests is beyond the scope of this chapter (see Chapter 18 for an extended discussion). Although the use of standardized tests has been criticized for many reasons, there are two issues most germane to the present discussion. These include the issues of content validity and relationship of the test to instruction.

One of the major problems with present standardized tests is that they are embedded in a model of literacy that is incompatible with emerging theory and knowledge on literacy acquisition (Anderson et al., 1985). That is, such tests focus on decontextualized, hierarchically ordered discrete skills in a way that is inconsistent with how children naturally learn and use literacy. The higher-order critical-thinking skills and problem-solving behaviors given so much emphasis in recent cognitive approaches to learning (Brown et al., 1989; Resnick, 1987) are relatively ignored. Moreover, the relationship between what is taught in any given classroom and what is tested may vary considerably. If there were a national curriculum that was uniformly taught in all classrooms at the same grade levels, this point would be moot. However, whatever variability now exists is likely to increase with the spread of less standardized and more holistic approaches (e.g., Bird, 1989; Chapter 10). As it stands, the issue of content validity is a problematic aspect of current large-scale assessment procedures.

A not unrelated issue is the observation by some that in an attempt to reduce the gap between what is tested and what is taught, some schools in effect use the tests as a curriculum guide. In essence, what is tested is used to drive what is taught. A more reasonable state of affairs would suggest the reverse. Even if this practice were more defensible, however, schools with low-scoring students are left to their own devices in remedying the situation. That is, global summary scores provide little or no information as to what the problem is. Thus, although there is pressure from many social and political arenas for "accountability" in the form of standardized test scores, solutions to the problem of low reading and writing scores are elusive. Moreover, when institutional pressures fuel an increased focus on "basics" due to low test scores, there is a danger of over-reliance on the inactive teaching and curriculum described earlier in the chapter. In essence, a self-perpetuating cycle is created.

The issue of assessment and evaluation is complex, especially where language-minority students are involved. Although there is fairly wide agreement on the necessity of monitoring student learning, there is less agreement on the form it should take. However, as practice begins to reflect theory more closely, more emphasis is being placed on alternative forms of monitoring, such as examining student work products in context over reextended periods of time (see Chapter 18). At present, institutionalized policies and pressures with respect to the assessment of student achievement can have a deleterious effect on promoting literacy in both direct and indirect ways.

The Role of Institutional Support for Primary Language Instruction in Promoting Literacy

Despite ambivalence about primary language instruction, theoretical and empirical support for such an approach to promoting literacy has increased (e.g., California State Department of Education, 1984; Cummins, 1989; Wong-Fillmore, Ammon, McLaughlin, & Ammon, 1985). A complete review of this literature is beyond the scope of this chapter, but the principle is described because institutionalized policy and attitudes can have a significant impact on individual classroom practices (Garcia & August, 1988). In particular, the value placed on students' native language within the school social setting has been theorized to play a major part in the eventual mastery of literacy (Quality Education for Minorities Project, 1990).

As the literature on effective schooling emphasizes, the climate of a school or district has a powerful effect on teachers and students (Anderson et al., 1985; Carter & Chatfield, 1986). As Cummins (1989) has noted, the greater the degree to which schools promote an advocacy-based agenda, especially in placing value on student native language and culture, the more positive the outcomes. Features of schools can be isolated that appear more favorable to language-minority student outcomes. The microlevel teacher–student or student–student interactions that form the basis for most school literacy activities do not operate in a vacuum. All instructional contexts are embedded in larger social and institutional settings. Moreover, it is unlikely that microlevel contexts can successfully promote literacy in the absence of a larger arena dedicated to supporting instructional activities.

AN OPTIMAL LEARNING ENVIRONMENT
FOR THE ACQUISITION OF LITERACY:
EXAMPLES FROM A CURRENT STUDY

The efforts of my colleagues and me are presently focused on providing an optimal learning environment (OLE) for literacy development of language-minority special education students in pullout programs (see Ruiz, 1989). Initial observations in these classrooms are similar to those of Trueba (1988), although not as pronounced. Prior to the intervention, high levels of off-task and oppositional behavior and other indices of student failure to engage in learning activities are common. Activities are dominated by individual seatwork, drill and practice exercises, and decoding and writing activities that emphasize mechanics and form.

Students who continually perform exercises such as these fail to internalize the notion of literacy as a useful communicative tool. An excerpt from an interview with a student in the OLE project (Luis, a sixth grader who is considered learning disabled) illustrates this phenomenon:

INTERVIEWER: When you are writing, what kinds of troubles do you have?

LUIS: I cannot write the words correctly . . . I just don't know how. I can't spell them correctly.

INTERVIEWER: What do you do about them?

LUIS: Nothing. Sometimes I ask the teacher how to write that word.

INTERVIEWER: Do you ever make changes in what you have written?

LUIS: Yes, because I know they are wrong, but then I make it worse.

INTERVIEWER: Who is the best writer that you know?

LUIS: My friend Carlos.

INTERVIEWER: What makes him/her a good writer?

LUIS: Because he always gets the words correct and his handwriting is very nice and pretty.

INTERVIEWER: How did you learn to write?

LUIS: By writing over and over, and practicing my handwriting so that others can understand what I write.

Luis has a notion of written language that is almost entirely centered on mechanics, surface structure, and errors. Moreover, his strategy for improving his writing is to seek outside assistance rather than rely on his own approximations, and his confidence in his own ability to control written language in the form of revision is minimal. Not surprisingly, his teacher-assigned story about Abraham Lincoln is unimaginative and consists of a very brief series of unconnected details: "Abraham Lincoln was a good man. He was a special man for the people. Every book that he got ahold of he read" (translated from Spanish).

His first approximation of this story contained a number of surface mistakes that were corrected by the teacher. His second version had neater writing that he labored over. The teacher assigned five points for correctness of individual surface features.

Interestingly, a research assistant on the project was able to form a trusting relationship with this student and frequently conversed with him about his out-of-school experiences. On one occasion, the student related an incident in which his cousin was involved in a shooting and had to be taken to the hospital. With a little encouragement, the student uncharacteristically immersed himself in the task, producing a two-and-a-half-page narrative, and stopping only when time ran out. Although the text was full of invented spellings and colloquialisms, the contrast in the student's output as well as his level of task engagement between the two writing contexts was notable.

It is misleading to suggest that this student does not have significant problems in the area of literacy. However, in this project the student's output in the first context is treated as the lower range of the "zone of proximal development" (Diaz et al., 1986; Trueba, in press; Vygotsky, 1978). In general, it is characterized by many of the features identified as obstacles to literacy development earlier in the chapter. The second context is thought to reflect the upper range of the zone, or what the student can produce in a facilitating environment with assistance from a more capable "other" in a personally meaningful task.

Increasingly, evidence such as that described above suggests that the literacy development of language-minority students is best promoted in contexts in which attention to the factors outlined thus far are embedded. Unfortunately, both microlevel factors such as inactive teaching as well as macrolevel factors such as ineffective support programs provide major obstacles for the continued growth of many students.

SUMMARY

This chapter has examined characteristics of programs and instructional practices that have generally been associated with negative student outcomes and provided examples of how those problems potentially can be addressed. Since the acquisition and use of literacy is a multifaceted and complex phenomenon, neither problems nor solutions are unidimensional in nature. In the face of somewhat alarming data on the lowered academic achievement of linguistic-minority students, however, there is increased optimism. The literature increasingly shows the relatively powerful effects that can be engineered through the application of relevant theoretical frameworks and in conjunction with socially responsive and supportive program structures.

REFERENCES

Ada, A. F. (1988). The Pajaro Valley experience: Working with Spanish-speaking parents to develop children's reading and writing skills in the home through the use of children's literature. In T. Skutnabb-Kangas & J. Cummins (Eds.), *Minority education: From shame to struggle* (pp. 223–238). Clevedon, England: Multilingual Matters.

Anderson, A. B., & Stokes, S. J. (1984). Social and institutional influences on the development and practice of literacy. In H. Goelman, A. Oberg, & F. Smith (Eds.), *Awakening to literacy* (pp. 24–37). Portsmouth, NH: Heinemann.

Anderson, R. C., Hiebert, E. H., Scott, J. A., & Wilkinson, I. A. G. (1985). *Becoming a nation of readers*. Champaign, IL: Center for the Study of Reading.

Arias, M. B. (1986). The context of education for Hispanic students: An overview. *American Journal of Education, 95*, 26–57.

Barrera, R. B. (1983). Bilingual reading in the primary grades: Some questions about questionable views and practices. In T. A. Escobedo (Ed.), *Early childhood bilingual education: A Hispanic perspective* (pp. 164–184). New York: Teachers College Press.

Bird, L. B. (Ed.). (1989). *Becoming a whole language school: The Fair Oaks story.* New York: Richard C. Owen.

Brown, J. S., Collins, A., & Duguid, P. (1989). Situated cognition and the culture of learning. *Educational Researcher, 18*(1), 32–42.

California State Department of Education. (1984). *Studies on immersion education.* Sacramento: Author.

Carter, T. P., & Chatfield, M. L. (1986). Effective bilingual schools: Implications for policy and practice. *American Journal of Education, 94,* 200–234.

Coles, G. (1987). *The learning mystique: A critical look at learning disabilities.* New York: Pantheon.

Cortes, C. E. (1986). The education of language minority students: A contextual interaction model. In California State Department of Education, *Beyond language: Social and cultural factors in schooling language minority students* (pp. 3–34). Los Angeles: Evaluation, Dissemination, and Assessment Center, California State University.

Cummins, J. (1989). *Empowering minority students.* Sacramento: California Association for Bilingual Education.

Delgado-Gaitan, C. (1990). *Literacy for empowerment: The role of Mexican parents in their children's education.* London: Falmer Press.

Diaz, S., Moll, L. C., & Mehan, H. (1986). Sociocultural resources in instruction: A context-specific approach. In *Beyond language: Social and cultural factors in schooling language minority students* (pp. 187–230). Los Angeles Evaluation, Dissemination, and Assessment Center, California State University.

Ferreiro, E. M., & Teberosky, A. (1982). *Literacy before schooling.* Exeter, NH: Heinemann.

Flores, G., Garcia, E., Gonzalez, S., Hidalgo, G., Kaczmarek, K., & Romero, T. (1986). *Holistic bilingual instructional strategies.* Phoenix, AZ: Exito.

Flores, B., Rueda, R., & Porter, B. (1986). Examining assumptions and instructional practices related to the acquisition of literacy with bilingual special education students. In A. Willig & H. Greenberg (Eds.), *Bilingualism and learning disabilities* (pp. 149–165). New York: American Library.

Garcia, E., & August, D. (1988). *The education of language minority students in the United States.* Springfield, IL: Charles C. Thomas.

Goldenberg, C. (1987). Low-income Hispanic parents' contributions to their first-grade children's work-recognition skills. *Anthropology and Education Quarterly, 18*(3), 149–179.

Goldenberg, C., & Gallimore, R. (1990, April). *Local knowledge, research knowledge, and educational achievement: A case study of early Spanish reading improvement.* Paper presented at the annual meeting of the American Educational Research Association, Boston, MA.

Goodman, K. (1986). *What's whole in whole language?* Portsmouth, NH: Heinemann.

Heath, S. B. (1983). *Ways with words.* New York: Cambridge University Press.

Hernandez, J. S. (1987, August). Strategy learning and use by non-English proficient students. Paper presented at the Institute on Literacy and Learning: Linguistic Minority Research Project, University of California at Santa Barbara.

Kagan, S. (1986). Cooperative learning and sociocultural factors in schooling. In California State Department of Education, *Beyond language: Social and cultural factors in schooling language minority students* (pp. 231–298). Los Angeles: Evaluation, Dissemination, and Assessment Center, California State University.

McCarthy, K. F., & Valdez, R. B. (1986). *Current and future effects of Mexican immigration in California (R-3365-CR).* Santa Monica, CA: Rand.

Moll, L., & Diaz, E. (in press). Bilingual communication and reading: The importance of Spanish in learning to read in English. *Elementary School Journal.*

National Assessment of Educational Progress. (1986). *Literacy: Profiles of America's young adults.* Princeton, NJ: Educational Testing Service.

Poplin, M. S. (1988). The reductionist fallacy in learning disabilities: Replicating the past by reducing the present. *Journal of Learning Disabilities, 21*(7), 389–400.

Quality Education for Minorities Project. (1990). *Education that works: An action plan for the education of minorities.* Cambridge, MA: M.I.T. Press.

Resnick, L. B. (1987). Learning in school and out. *Educational Researcher, 16*(9), 13–20.

Rosa, A., & Moll, L. C. (1985). Computadoras, communicación y edución: una colaboración internacional en la intervención e investigación educativa. *Infancia y Aprendizaje, 30,* 1–17.

Rueda, R. (1986). Metacognition and passing: Strategic interactions in the lives of students with learning disabilities. *Anthropology and Education Quarterly, 17*(3), 145–165.

Rueda, R. (1989). Defining mild disabilities with language minority students. *Exceptional Children, 56*(2), 121–129.

Rueda, R. (in press). An analysis of special education as a response to the academic achievement and underachievement of Chicano students. In R. Valencia (Ed.), *Chicano school failure and success: Research and policy agendas for the 1990s.* London: Falmer Press.

Rueda, R., Ruiz, N., & Figueroa, R. (1989, March). *Home language and learning practices among Mexican American children: Review of the literature.* Paper presented at the annual meeting of the American Educational Research Association, San Francisco, CA.

Ruiz, N. T. (1989). An optimal learning environment for Rosemary. *Exceptional Children, 56*(2), 130–144.

Segal, J. W., Chipman, S. F., & Glaser, R. (Eds.). (1985). *Thinking and learning skills: Vol. 2. Research and open questions.* Hillsdale, NJ: Erlbaum.

Tharp, R. (1989). Psychocultural variables and constants: Effects on teaching and learning in schools. *American Psychologist, 44*(2), 349–359.

Tharp, R., & Gallimore, R. (1988). *Rousing minds to life: Teaching, learning, and schooling in social context.* New York: Cambridge University Press.

Trueba, H. (1988). English literacy acquisition: From cultural trauma to learning disabilities in minority students. *Linguistics and Education, 1,* 125–152.

Trueba, H. (in press). *Raising silent voices: Educating the linguistic minorities for the 21st century.* New York: Harper & Row.

Vygotsky, L. S. (1978). *Mind in society: the development of higher psychological processes.* Cambridge, MA: Harvard University Press.

Wang, M. C., & Reynolds, M. C. (1985). Avoiding the "Catch 22" in special education reform. *Exceptional Children, 51,* 497–502.

Wong-Fillmore, L., Ammon, P., McLaughlin, B., & Ammon, M. S. (1985). *Final report for learning English through bilingual instruction.* Washington, DC: National Institute of Education.

8 | Cross-Cultural Perspectives on Classroom Discourse and Literacy

PAMELA McCOLLUM
University of Colorado, Boulder

Many children, especially language-minority students, read and write below acceptable levels. The National Assessment of Educational Progress (NAEP) data show that 36% of all 9-year-olds and 40% of 13-year-olds in American schools are reading below expected levels (Kennedy, Jung, & Orland, 1986). Furthermore, the reading and writing scores of African-American and Hispanic children are considerably lower than those of white children in grades 3, 7, and 11 (Beaton, 1986). An even more sobering statistic indicates that language-minority students are 1.5 times more likely to drop out of school than native English speakers (Cárdenas, Robledo, & Waggoner, 1988).

As Rueda argues in Chapter 7, a growing body of theory and research shows that this failure is preventable. This chapter attends to the restructuring of one characteristic of school contexts—the nature of classroom discourse. At the basis of this restructuring is a view of "multiple literacies," which comes from work in anthropology and cross-cultural psychology. This definition of literacy used in conjunction with a theory of instruction based on Vygotskian principles provides students who are generally excluded from instruction with voice and opportunities for increased levels of participation.

CROSS-CULTURAL PERSPECTIVES ON LITERACY

Cross-cultural psychologists Scribner and Cole (1981) speak of literacy not simply as a matter of learning how to read and write a particular script but rather in the much broader sense of being able to apply knowledge for specific purposes in particular contexts of use. As the specific purposes and contexts for literacy use change, the possibility of multiple literacies arises (Erickson, 1984). Learning-task environments vary and are composed of the tools, symbols (words or numbers), and particular forms of social relation-

108

ships in which learning tasks are situated. If any of the elements of the learning-task environment are altered, one's ability to perform at customary levels may also change. Viewed from this perspective, language and the social relations that are embedded within language use become important for the execution of learning tasks.

A theory of multiple literacies or abilities differs from traditional views in educational psychology that pose ability as a "fixed" quantity that is unchanging and context independent. Rather, ability to perform is influenced by the learning-task environment in which performance occurs and is not uniform across all contexts. Such a perspective also moves away from using psychological interpretations that use mainstream norms as the only metric for measuring minority performance. A theory of multiple literacies provides a fresh perspective for examining cross-cultural data on classroom discourse, literacy, and achievement and precludes using uniform, unchanging standards of behavior against which all are measured and increasingly large numbers fail.

Non-Western Literacies

Studies done in non-Western societies support a view of literacy in the broader sense of "ability" rather than in the Western sense of using letters for reading and writing or of being "lettered," connoting higher social-class status (Erickson, 1984). Gladwin (1970) investigated reasoning in Polynesian sailors and found that although they use the stars for navigation, their navigational system differs greatly from Western systems. Observation of experienced sailors teaching novices showed that the system was taught orally without the aid of reading or writing to explain the process. Although traditional definitions of literacy would not acknowledge that as literacy because the sailors did not read and write, Scribner and Cole's (1981) definition encompasses this as literacy because the novice sailors learned to apply knowledge in specific contexts of use, in this case correctly navigating between the Pacific atolls.

In a similar vein, Childs and Greenfield (1980) studied how master weavers in Mexico teach others to weave, and Lave (1977) investigated how tailors in Liberia apply their craft. Although both groups performed complex mathematical operations as part of their craft, they were unable to perform the same type of reasoning on tests. These and other similar cross-cultural data led Erickson (1984) to pose that "people's ability to reason seems to be domain specific rather than generalizable across task domains that differ in surface form" (p. 528).

There are those who would respond that the previous examples are invalid by virtue of the fact that the subjects in the studies were not literate and therefore were unable to reason in the same way literates do. Scribner and Cole (1981) disproved such charges in their investigations of a Liberian tribe, the Vai, who use a script informally outside of school that differs from the script taught in school. The only difference in the behavior of the two groups during testing was that the schooled Vai were superior in talking about what they had done in "schooled" ways. Their behavior was therefore a function of school experience, not literacy.

Multiple Literacies in Western Societies

Examples of the context-dependent nature of learning tasks are not limited to non-Western cultures. Studies of cognition that focus on how thinking is done in everyday situations have shown that ability to perform tasks is context dependent. Lave, Murtaugh, and de la Rocha (1984) investigated the accuracy of American adults in making calculations while shopping in a supermarket. When shopping, their subjects were able to make virtually error-free price comparisons in the supermarket, but when faced with the same calculations on paper-and-pencil tests, all made errors regardless of their level of education or number of years since completing school. The main difference in the two situations was in the nature of task environments. In the former, the definition of the problem was created by shoppers who calculated unit price comparisons for objects they wanted to buy. In the latter, the problems were imposed upon the subjects. Their roles, the tools, and the social relations surrounding the execution of each task differed greatly in each environment.

Another example of expert–novice teaching events are the mother–child interactions where children are taught something new. Rogoff and Garner (1984) studied mothers teaching children classification tasks in everyday situations. Observation of the mothers teaching children how to put away groceries in a simulated kitchen showed that their interaction was characterized by support. The mothers implicitly transferred information necessary for the solution of the problem to the children as they were actively engaged in problem solving. Such interaction during teaching/learning has been referred to as scaffolding (Wood, Bruner, & Ross, 1976) or proleptic instruction (Wertsch, 1979). The interactions of children and mothers in learning situations in the home differ greatly, however, from those of teachers and students in traditional classrooms where such scaffolding does not occur. Traditional forms of classroom discourse do not encourage reciprocal interaction between teachers and students or mutual problem solving.

Classroom Discourse

The importance of classroom instructional discourse and its relationship to student performance has not been recognized outside the disciplines of sociolinguistics and anthropology until recently. Instead, educational researchers have tended to investigate how new curricular materials or instructional methods affect student achievement, assuming that classroom discourse had no effect on student learning or performance. However, classroom discourse becomes critical to learning and for displaying abilities when performance is interpreted using a theory of multiple literacies. Two of the three requisite components of learning-task environments, words (symbols) and the social relationship that surrounds the performance of a task, are expressed in the discourse and discourse rules governing the interaction.

In traditional American classrooms, teacher-centered lessons are the norm and strict adherence to turn-taking rules during lessons eliminates the opportunity for teachers and students to reach accommodation on points of mutual interest. Traditional classrooms reflect a transmission model of learning where teachers pass knowledge on to students who, for the most part, respond to the teacher in very proscribed ways as governed by tacitly learned discourse rules. During lessons, the teacher's role is to direct, elicit, and comment upon student response, whereas students are cast in the role of performers who are to supply answers to questions and respond to teacher directives (Lindfors, 1980).

Cross-cultural comparisons of classroom discourse patterns demonstrate that participation structures employed in each system represent different sets of rights and obligations that govern teachers and students during interactions. Differences between features of classroom discourse and home language use in ethnic communities have been shown to affect minority students' learning adversely (Au & Jordan, 1981; Au & Mason, 1981; Barnhardt, 1982; Erickson & Mohatt, 1981, 1982; Heath, 1983; Michaels, 1981; Philips, 1972, 1983). Exemplary of that genre of research, Michaels (1981) found that the narratives of African-American children during "sharing time" took the form of "topic associating" and were not valued by the white teacher who expected "topic-centered" narratives. White students who produced narratives in a style consonant with the teacher's spoke longer during "sharing time" and thus gained more valuable practice in preliteracy skills.

Such differences in language use in ethnically mixed classes often result in differential access to literacy experiences. Nonmainstream students are excluded from instruction in two ways. First, they lack the requisite knowledge to participate in instructional interaction to display knowledge or clarify misunderstandings, and second, teachers often unknowingly exclude or reduce the time minority students participate in literacy activities because features of their discourse do not conform to teachers' expectations or match their speaking style.

Initially, educational classroom research on cross-cultural miscommunication was criticized as providing simplistic explanations of minority students' underachievement and was often dismissed as being interesting but lacking in applicability and theoretical rigor. However, recently the issue of the importance of instructional discourse and the quality of student–teacher interactions during lessons has been raised again. In particular, neo-Vygotskian or constructivist approaches to learning, which stress the importance of mediated learning between the child and a knowledgeable adult or peer initially on the social plane, have once again raised the issue of the importance of the quality of student–teacher interactions and talk during learning.

Tharp and Gallimore (1988) articulate a theory of instruction based on Vygotskian theory that evolved from their research and collaboration with the Kamehameha Early Education Program (KEEP) in Hawaii. (For other views on Vygotskian perspectives related to literacy, see Chapters 3, 9, 10, and 13.) The instructional method that evolved in KEEP initially centered on the incorporation of a Hawaiian conversational form, the talk story, into pre-reading activities. That modification allowed students to participate in literacy activities in culturally appropriate ways and also changed the social relations during instruction by equalizing conversational rights between the teacher and students (Au & Mason, 1981). More importantly, the talk-story structure equalized access to literacy, allowing Hawaiian students to achieve at levels commensurate with their ability.

According to Tharp and Gallimore (1988), classrooms should be structured so that the interaction between teachers and students takes the form of instructional conversations where each can learn from the other in a reciprocal fashion as children proceed from socially mediated interaction to higher levels of independent work. It is important to note that in order for this approach to be effective, teachers must provide students with not only more open discourse structures for talk during learning but also assisted performance (similar to scaffolding) through verbal prompts to guide them as they learn.

Traditional teacher–student interactions during whole-group instruction do not allow mediated learning to occur but rather establish social relations whereby the teacher is cast in the role of the transmitter of knowledge and the student is cast in the role of performer, signaling comprehension or learning by reciting correct responses in concert with the teachers' system of questioning and turn allocation.

In the following section, data from a comparative study of turn alloca-tion in a traditional American classroom and a Puerto Rican classroom (McCollum, 1989) are compared to illustrate how literacy instruction is con-structed among different social groups. Those differences emphasize the need for viewing children's abilities within a "multiple literacies" framework and attest to the need for modifying traditional classroom structures to admit a wider range of discourse styles.

DIFFERENCES IN CLASSROOM DISCOURSE: A CASE IN POINT

The examples of student–teacher interaction come from four half-hour videotapes of teacher-directed whole-group lessons in two third-grade class-rooms—one in Chicago, Illinois, and the other in Rio Piedras, Puerto Rico. They form part of a larger data set of videotaped and observed classroom interaction that was gathered over several weeks. The Chicago classroom consisted of an English-speaking teacher and students and the Puerto Rican class was composed of a Spanish-speaking teacher and students. Both teach-ers were recommended by their principals as superior teachers, and the stu-dents in each class were at grade level or above. Microethnographic methods were used to analyze the tapes following Mehan's (1979) model of lesson structure and turn allocation. That framework of analysis was chosen because it employed microethnographic methods and viewed lessons as socially con-structed by those participating in the interaction.

A comparison of teacher-directed whole-group lessons in the American and Puerto Rican classrooms showed that the rules for turn allocation and the underlying social relations between teachers and students were very different. Those differences in lesson structure can be described best in broad terms as a contrast between "lessons as recitation" and "lessons as instructional con-versations" (Tharp & Gallimore, 1988). Recitation lessons are governed by strict turn-taking rules that are managed by the teacher who orchestrates who will speak to whom and at what times. Student participation generally hinges on following teacher cues and responding to them in appropriate ways. Vio-lation of turn-taking rules can lead to students' being unable to get the floor to speak, failing to enter information into lessons, or being reprimanded for being out of sync with the turn-taking machinery in effect. Instructional con-versations, on the other hand, are not bound by strict turn-taking rules and are characterized by assisted performance where the teacher's interactions with students provide different forms of modeling and feedback, expand ut-terances, and provide purposeful questioning to guide and support students' learning.

Preferring more open structures, Mrs. Ortiz, the Puerto Rican teacher, frequently engaged her students as conversational partners. She most often framed questions with the *invitation to reply* turn-allocation device, which is the least controlling strategy and opens the floor to everyone by using wh-questions, chorus elicitations, or sentence-completion forms. Mrs. Thomas, however, cast lessons in the recitation mode most frequently, using the most controlling strategies, *individual nomination* and *invitation to bid,* to elicit student responses during lessons. When individually nominating a student, the teacher simply selects and names the student who is to speak next in the lesson. Invitations to bid are two-stage procedures whereby students must raise their hands in response to the teacher's question and then be selected from the group of respondents before being given the floor to speak. The discourse in lessons in Mrs. Thomas's class was characteristic of traditional "lessons as recitation," whereas those in Mrs. Ortiz's more resembled "instructional conversations."

A comparison of who initiated interactions during lessons showed that Mrs. Thomas initiated 91% of all interactions. In contrast, in the Puerto Rican class, the contributions of the teacher and students to talk during lessons were much more evenly balanced, with students initiating 38% of all student–teacher interactions. This more balanced level of teacher–student interaction produced lessons that were more conversational in character. Further indication of the conversational character of lessons in the Puerto Rican class was demonstrated by students' frequent comments to the teacher during lessons. In Mrs. Thomas's room, the rare student-initiated interaction was restricted to questions on procedural matters related to lesson content, or assignments.

Mrs. Thomas and Mrs. Ortiz differed greatly in their degree of openness to student initiation. Students initiated interaction with Mrs. Ortiz almost twice as often during lessons as did students in Mrs. Thomas's class. A further indicator of Mrs. Ortiz's openness to student talk is demonstrated by contrasting her reactions to student initiations during lessons with those of Mrs. Thomas. Mrs. Ortiz never sanctioned (negatively evaluated) students for initiating interactions during lessons and only ignored them 8% of the time. She most frequently responded to student initiations by acknowledging them (44%) (briefly commenting on them) or incorporating their comments into lessons (33%). Mrs. Thomas, on the other hand, most frequently responded to students' comments during lessons by ignoring them (44%). She frequently acknowledged student initiations (27%) but rarely incorporated students' comments (2%) into lessons. Furthermore, as Mehan (1979) found, for student comments to be incorporated into lessons the following conditions had to be met: (a) They had to be strategically placed before or after an initiation-response-evaluation sequence; and (b) comments had to relate to the topic of the lesson. In Mrs. Ortiz's room, students were never sanctioned for trying to enter information into lessons, whereas in Mrs. Thomas' class, students who tried to initiate interaction during lessons were sanctioned 7% of the time. The Puerto Rican students also did not have to make initiations in certain parts of the stream of discourse to successfully get the floor to speak.

The conversational character of lessons in Mrs. Ortiz's class was further highlighted by the topics that arose during lessons. Whereas students in Mrs. Thomas's room were strictly limited to talking about the topic of the lesson, talk during lessons in Mrs. Ortiz's room consisted of a mix of curricular, social, and personal topics. Students would often introduce a personal topic into the lesson and be allowed to expound upon it at great length. Many times, Mrs. Ortiz would introduce information from her personal life or childhood into the lessons as well. The following excerpts of lesson discourse from Mrs. Ortiz's room were taken from a social studies reading lesson and demonstrate the conversational character of talk during lessons in her room and the incorporation of students' comments on social and personal topics into lessons. It should also be noted that Mrs. Ortiz contributed personal information about her childhood that related to the students' experiences, resulting in the high "cultural load" of this particular passage, which is based on mutually shared knowledge.

In this lesson, Mrs. Ortiz was conducting a review of a reading selection entitled "El Cangrejito de Oro" ("The Golden Crab") that told the story of a young Taino Indian boy, Cetí, who was learning to fish. After one of the students, José, told the teacher he had been fishing for crabs with his cousin the day before, a 9-minute segment of talk resulted where the teacher and students shared their experiences about fishing for crabs.

> JOSÉ: Misi, Misi, ayer yo estaba en Piñones y habían unas cuevitas así por la playa y habian cangrejitos chiquitos. [Teacher, teacher, yesterday I was at Piñones Beach and there were little caves like this on the beach and there were little crabs there.]
>
> MRS. O: Están llevando a cabo muy bien la pesca de cangrejitos. Bien. [Now is the time for fishing for crabs. Good.]
>
> JOSÉ: Saqué un pez y un cangrejito y una buruquena (a Daniel). [I caught a fish, a crab and a ( ) (to Daniel).]
>
> MRS. O: Y es bueno porque uno le echa agua a los hoyitos de los cangrejitos y entonces espera que venga saliendo un cangrejito . . . [And it's good because one pours water into the crab's holes and then waits for the crab to come out . . .]

JOSÉ: ¿Por qué, Misi? [Why, teacher?]

MRS. O: . . . y le le pone el cuchillo así por el lado y le tapa la cuevita
         y el cangrejito no le puede volver a meter y uno lo coge. [. . .
         and you put the knife like this on the side and cover up the hole
         and the crab can't go back and get inside and you catch him.]

JOSÉ: ¿Misi, por qué, misi por qué el agua, el agua, por qué el agua
         no puede, no pueden vivir en agua? [Teacher why, teacher why
         is the water, the water, the water . . . why can't it, why can't
         they live in the water?]

MRS. O: Aha. Miren Ustedes ven una cuevita de un cangrejito, ¿veldá?
         ¿Ustedes quieren que salga? Ustedes cogen agua . . . [Ah huh.
         Look you see a little crab's cave, right? You want it to come
         out? You take take . . .]

JOSÉ: Agua [Water]

MRS. O: . . . y le echen a la cuevita y tan pronto se llena la cuevita de
         agua el, el cangrejito sale. [. . . and you throw water in the
         little cave and as soon as it fills up with water, the little crab
         comes out.]

This segment continued as Mrs. Ortiz explained in detail how she used to
catch crabs at the beach when she was a little girl. She told how she used to
pour water into the opening of the crab's hole in the sand and the crab would
run out. Then she would place a machete over the opening so it would be
unable to return inside. José was afraid that using a machete would kill the
crab, and he explained how he and his cousin caught them by getting them
to bite on to pieces of algae. He tried to get the floor several times unsuc-
cessfully, and Mrs. Ortiz finally gave him the floor by directing everyone's
attention to him.

JOSÉ: Misi, yo vine y puse. . . Como yo estaba con mi primo le dije
         que pusiera el vaso. [Teacher, I came and put . . . Since I was
         with my cousin I told him to put the glass down.]

MRS. O.: Vamos a escuchar a José. [Let's listen to José.]

JOSÉ: . . . que pusiera el vaso le eche con una tacita como amarilla y
         como estaba, era bajito yo estaba en la arena. Yo cogí agua y
         le tiraba agua y le tiraba ya el iba saliendo. Después cogía con
         una alga y se lo ponía y el la pinchaba. [. . . that he should
         put the glass down and I threw water down from a yellow glass
         and it was down low and I was on the sand. I took water and
         threw it on him again and again and he finally came out.]

MRS. O: (no se oye) [inaudible]

JOSÉ: El venía y la pinchaba y parece que me veía con los ojos. [He came out and pinched it (the alga) and he seemed like he looked at me with his eyes.]

José continued his story for another two turns and was followed by four other students who shared their experiences about fishing for crabs with the class. Their stories demonstrated that each had a rich store of knowledge and experiences to share. Mrs. Ortiz's manner of conducting lessons allowed those who may not have participated in lessons by contributing factual information about the content of the story to interact with the teacher and to receive feedback on or recognition of their ideas. José shared another story about fishing for crabs with the class, and then Mrs. Ortiz closed this segment of talk by redirecting students to the story they were reviewing, saying, "Bien, vamos a seguir." (OK, let's continue.) The students, however, continued to engage her in conversation for another six turns of talk. She finally terminated the segment by saying the following:

MRS. O: Bien vamos a terminar ya de resumir el cuentecito, ¿veldá? Bien así que tenemos que Cetí fue de pesca. Pescó con su papá. ¿Pescó con que? [OK, let's finish reviewing the little story, OK? So we know that Cetí went fishing. He fished with his father. What did he fish with?]
WANDA: Un cangrejo. [A crab.]

These examples of student–teacher interaction were not presented to demonstrate assisted performance, mediated learning, or scaffolding but rather to show how a Puerto Rican teacher and her class constructed lessons using a discourse structure very different than that commonly used in American classrooms. The contrasts that arose when Mehan's (1979) model of lesson structure was applied to talk in both classes showed that different sets of rules, both verbal and interactional, were used to construct lessons.

Posing a hypothetical situation, students from either class would be at a disadvantage trying to interact effectively in the other's environment. Perhaps the most severe mismatch would occur if a Puerto Rican student from this study were placed in one of Mrs. Thomas's whole-group lessons. The Puerto Rican student would likely be seen as socially inappropriate for speaking out of turn on topics that are not admissible to lessons. The rich store of knowledge that was shared with the teacher would become meaningless, and the student's frequent initiations into lessons would generally be ignored or even reprimanded. Furthermore, not knowing the rules for getting the floor would make entering information into lessons difficult. In short, the highly interactive and collaborative learning environment the student was accustomed to would no longer exist.

Analyzed from a multiple-literacies framework, the Puerto Rican student might have problems rising to customary levels of performance because two components of the learning-task environment are different. First, the language (symbols) used for instruction, if it were English, might be incomprehensible to a Spanish-dominant student. If comprehending spoken English presented no problem, even more subtle issues such as language use (when and how language is used) might lead a student to be socially inappropriate, unsuccessful in clarifying questions, or unable to display what has been learned. The second and perhaps the greatest difference in the contexts of the two classes lies in the social relations between teacher and students. In the Puerto Rican classroom, students interact with the teacher as conversational partners who are free to explore topics of mutual interest with the teacher. The speaking rights between the teacher and students are more equalized, with each having the ability to discuss a variety of topics related to the lesson during whole-group lessons. Students thus become active participants in lessons even though they may not possess specific academic information. Their participation is valued and they are reinforced for cultural information in addition to the school's curriculum.

Differences in learning-task environments for culturally and linguistically different students can affect their ability to learn or to display knowledge. Equally important is the consideration that, when participation structures are altered from customary patterns, children's usual ways of thinking and interacting are also altered. From this perspective, one can see how such a mismatch could affect academic performance.

CLASSROOM DISCOURSE AND LITERACY: ISSUES

At this point, two questions that generally arise in discussions of this sort receive attention: (a) Should culturally appropriate participation structures be adopted for all nonmainstream students? and (b) Does culturally congruent instruction have to be linked to achievement to be worthwhile? In response to the first question, ideally it would be best if all culturally and linguistically different students could receive initial instruction in a participation structure culturally congruent with their background. However, considering that language-minority students often tend to be members of very heterogeneous student bodies, such an approach is neither practical nor feasible.

Furthermore, research documenting cross-cultural differences in instructional discourse is not available for all the groups in schools. A feasible and recommended solution is eliminating the lesson as recitation format, replacing it with more open discourse structures that allow mediated learning to occur. Adopting instructional conversations for literacy instruction would give voice to all learners, mainstream and nonmainstream, and provide for a variety of social relations that are necessary for establishing equitable learning opportunities for the diverse populations of schools. The form of successful instruction in KEEP essentially consisted of such a change; when the talk story was adopted, reading achievement scores improved dramatically.

There are those who do not feel that culturally appropriate interactional styles should be adopted for instruction unless a link can be made between the adoption of those styles and improved student academic achievement. This position distorts how such links are established through research. Barnhardt's (1982) experimental study with Athabaskan Indians proved that students who received culturally congruent instruction achieved at higher levels than those who did not. What preceded that study was a line of research that originated with Philips's (1972) ethnographic research on the Warm Springs Indian Reservation in Oregon, which compared how Athabaskan children learned and used language at home and in school. Based on that research, Erickson & Mohatt (1981, 1982) did a microethnographic analysis comparing the teaching styles of a Native Athabaskan and an Anglo-Canadian teacher with Odawa and Objibwa students. Their results were congruent with Philips's data in that the native Canadian teachers taught in ways that were compatible with how native Canadian children were accustomed to learning. Viewed in this perspective, Barnhardt's (1982) finding of a link between classroom discourse styles and academic achievement was based on 10 years of prior qualitative research.

SUMMARY

The comparative analysis of instructional discourse in a Puerto Rican and an Anglo-American classroom highlights the need for operating from a perspective of multiple literacies coupled with a theory of instruction based on Vygotskian principles. Both perspectives emphasize the importance of social interaction and talk between participants in learning and teaching. It is seen as an initial step in unraveling the complex system of social relations that surrounds learning in multicultural contexts. It is time to stop viewing literacy as merely decoding graphemes and learning facts through text. Literacy should be seen as learning to decode and accommodate multiple levels of meaning through a complex system of social relations. This redefinition of literacy means a restructuring of instruction, including discourse patterns, instead of reusing old approaches that have never recognized or heard minority voices.

REFERENCES

Au, K. H., & Jordan, C. (1981). Teaching reading to Hawaiian children: Analysis of a culturally appropriate instructional event. *Anthropology and Education Quarterly, 11,* 91–115.

Au, K. H., & Mason, J. (1981). Social organizational factors in learning to read: The balance of rights hypothesis. *Reading Research Quarterly, 17*(1), 115–152.

Barnhardt, C. (1982). Tuning-in: Athabaskan teachers and Athabaskan students. In R. Barnhardt (Ed.), *Cross-cultural issues in Alaskan education* (Vol. 2). Fairbanks: Centers for Cross-Cultural Studies, University of Alaska.

Beaton, A. E. (1986). *National Assessment of Education Progress 1983–84: A technical report.* Princeton, NJ: National Assessment of Educational Progress, ETS.

Cárdenas, J. A., Robledo, M. R., & Waggoner, D. W. (1988). *The undereducation of American youth.* San Antonio, TX: Intercultural Development Research Association.

Childs, C. P., & Greenfield, P. M. (1980). Informal modes of learning and teaching: The case of Zinacanteco weaving. In N. Warren (Ed.), *Studies in cross-cultural psychology* (Vol. 2, pp. 269–316). London: Academic Press.

Erickson, F. (1984). School literacy, reasoning and civility: An anthropologist's perspective. *Review of Educational Research, 54*(4), 525–544.

Erickson, F., & Mohatt, G. (1981). Cultural differences in teaching styles in an Odawa school: A sociolinguistic approach. In H. T. Trueba, G. P. Gutherie, & K. H. Au (Eds.), *Culture in the bilingual classroom: Studies in classroom ethnography* (pp. 105–119). Rowley, MA: Newbury House.

Erickson, F., & Mohatt, G. (1982). Cultural organization of participant structures in two classrooms of Indian students. In G. D. Spindler (Ed.), *Doing the ethnography of schooling: Educational anthropology in action* (pp. 132–174). New York: Holt, Rinehart and Winston.

Gladwin, T. (1970). *East is a big bird.* Boston: Belknap Press.

Heath, S. B. (1983). *Ways with words.* New York: Cambridge University Press.

Kennedy, M. M., Jung, R. K., & Orland, M. E. (1986). *Poverty, achievement and the distribution of compensatory education services.* Washington, DC: U.S. Department of Educational Research and Improvement.

Lave, J. (1977). Tailor-made experiments and evaluating the intellectual consequences of apprenticeship training. *Quarterly Newsletter of the Institute for Comparative Human Development, 1*(2), 1–5.

Lave, J. L., Murtaugh, M., & de la Rocha, O. (1984). The dialectic of arithmetic in grocery shopping. In B. Rogoff & J. Lave (Eds.), *Everyday cognition: Its development in social context* (pp. 67–94). Cambridge, MA: Harvard University Press.

Lindfors, J. W. (1980). *Children's language and learning.* Englewood Cliffs, NJ: Prentice Hall.

McCollum, P. (1989). A comparative study of turn-allocation during lessons with North American and Puerto Rican students. *Anthropology and Education Quarterly, 20*(2), 133–156.

Mehan, H. (1979). *Learning lessons.* Cambridge, MA: Harvard University Press.

Michaels, S. (1981). "Sharing time": Children's narrative styles and differential access to literacy. *Language in Society, 10,* 423–442.

Philips, S. U. (1972). Participant structures and communicative competence: Warm Springs children in community and classroom. In C. B. Cazden, V. P. John, & D. Hymes (Eds.), *Functions of language in the classroom* (pp. 370–394). New York: Teachers College Press.

Philips, S. U. (1983). *The invisible culture: Communication in the classroom and community on the Warm Springs Indian Reservation.* New York & London: Longman.

Rogoff, B., & Garner, W. (1984). Adult guidance of cognitive development. In B. Rogoff & J. Lave (Eds.), *Everyday cognition: Its development in social context* (pp. 95–116). Cambridge, MA: Harvard University Press.

Scribner, S., & Cole, M. (1981). *The psychology of literacy.* Cambridge, MA: Harvard University Press.

Tharp, R., & Gallimore, R. (1988). *Rousing minds to life: Teaching learning and schooling in social context.* New York: Cambridge University Press.

Wertsch, J. (1979). From social interaction to higher psychological processes. *Human Development, 22,* 1–22.

Wood, B., Bruner, J. S., & Ross, G. (1976). The role of tutoring in problem solving. *Journal of Child Psychology and Psychiatry, 17,* 89–100.

9 | Promoting Literacy Through Classroom Dialogue

ANNEMARIE SULLIVAN PALINCSAR
YVONNE MARIE DAVID
University of Michigan

One of the striking characteristics of dialogues surrounding literacy instruction for diverse groups of learners is how often these dialogues are fraught with tensions. In this chapter we consider three of these tensions: instruction in the basic skills versus high or critical literacy, natural versus taught literacy, and reductionist versus holistic/constructivist instruction. We then describe and illustrate an instructional procedure—reciprocal teaching—designed to teach heterogeneous groups of learners how to approach text in a thoughtful manner. Finally, we describe the outcomes of this instruction.

BASIC SKILLS VERSUS CRITICAL LITERACY

Fueled by concerns that American students have failed to maintain the competitive edge in a world economy, there is the argument that educators ought to return to basic skill instruction. Reports such as *A Nation at Risk* (National Commission of Excellence in Education, 1983) urge that teachers be held accountable for students' achieving minimal levels of competence. In juxtaposition to the "back to basics" movement is the call for "high literacy" or literacy instruction in the pursuit of learning that is beyond that of adapting to the goals of the prevailing culture (Bereiter & Scardamalia, 1987; Resnick & Resnick, 1977). There is also the call for "critical literacy," the ability to use reading and writing to go beyond the demands associated with minimal competency (McGinley & Tierney, 1989). Such a movement demands the use of what Hilliard (1988) has referred to as "maximum-competency criteria" (p. 199). One problem that arises when basic skills are contrasted with higher order skills in the reading domain is the faulty impression that not all students are entitled to instruction in both sets of skills. In fact, traditionally there has been the trend to target basic skill instruction for younger and disadvantaged students while reserving the "higher order" or reasoning skills for older and more successful students. (See Chapters 7, 10, and 17 for fuller descriptions of the manner in which tasks differ across students.)

However, if one maintains that the goal of literacy instruction is to prepare learners who are independent and able to assume responsibility for life-long learning, then this "tension" between basic and higher order skills makes little sense. Children, regardless of age or level of achievement, should be taught effective reasoning and the skills to learn from text.

One hallmark of the critical reader is a repertoire of strategies for gaining knowledge from text and simultaneously monitoring levels of understanding (Brown, 1980; Paris, Wasik, & Turner, in press). Referred to as the "metacognitive skills of reading," these strategies enable students to:

1. Clarify the purposes of reading
2. Make use of relevant background knowledge
3. Allocate attention to focus on major content at the expense of trivia
4. Critically evaluate content for internal consistency and compatibility with prior knowledge and common sense
5. Monitor to ensure that comprehension is occurring
6. Draw and test inferences

In this chapter, we examine how children can be taught to engage in the metacognitive skills of reading even before they have acquired the basic skills of reading. We will make the point that as important as identifying the skills to be taught is the choice of instructional context.

NATURAL VERSUS TAUGHT LITERACY

A second tension that figures in the dialogue is the tension between natural and taught literacy. The question raised by this tension is: To what extent should literacy instruction be represented as the transfer of literacy skill and knowledge from teacher to child? The natural literacy argument would suggest that, given a literate culture, young humans make sense of written language in much the same natural, effortless, and unconscious way that they learn spoken language (Phelps, 1988). Phelps suggests that, from this perspective, the culture supports this natural process by providing "the meaningful contexts and experiences of written language events that stimulate the learner's own construction of the symbol systems and strategies we call literacy" (p. 108).

Indeed, cross-cultural research, particularly in the writing domain, shows that children exposed to written language begin reinventing and appropriating the literacy of their culture long before formal schooling. What emerges from the natural literacy tradition is a partial explanation regarding the diversity of practices and attitudes displayed by children from various ethnic and socioeconomic backgrounds. However, the teacher is left dangling in the natural literacy argument. What is the place of conscious teaching of the means to deal with written text? Is the teacher merely the facilitator for the activities of rather autonomous learners? Or, should classrooms be the place where the teacher, by virtue of relative expertise, with deliberate intention, enables the learner to acquire knowledge and procedures? Delpit (1988) has argued that the tenets of the natural literacy tradition unwittingly serve to deny African-American students entry into the "culture of power." Delpit speculates that this occurs when students are denied access to teachers as sources of knowledge because of the teachers' fears that "exhibiting personal power as expert source" somehow serves to disempower one's students (p. 288). We explore how it is possible for both teacher and students to assume active roles in instructional activity so that students can profit from the relative expertise of the teacher and from the expertise of one another.

REDUCTIONIST VERSUS HOLISTIC/CONSTRUCTIVIST INSTRUCTION

A final tension that reflects the spirit (and spirited nature) of contemporary dialogue is the tension between reductionist and holistic/constructivist theories of learning and teaching. Central to this tension are issues regarding the content and purpose of instruction, the roles of teacher and learner in instruction. Poplin (1988) suggests that reductionist perspectives support segmenting the content to be learned into parts, each of which is taught to some level of mastery. The content of lessons from this perspective is determined through task analysis with little attention paid to the experiences students have had with this content or the sense that they make of it. In the case of strategy instruction, there is segmentation of the strategy into steps and emphasis on students' following procedural steps in utilizing the strategies. Finally, little attention is paid to the social interactions among students and teachers or among students themselves in the learning process. Illustrative of a reductionist approach to strategy instruction (summarization) would be a lesson in which children are asked to underline an explicit main idea sentence in an abbreviated, simplistic piece of text. Poplin (1988) and Heshusius (1989) argue that this perspective has been particularly prevalent in the design of "remedial," "compensatory," and "special" education for children at risk for academic difficulty or failure.

The alternative holistic/social-constructivist perspective (Gavelek & Palincsar, 1988; Vygotsky, 1962, 1978; Wertsch, 1980) urges that tasks be presented in a goal-embedded context; for example, in strategy instruction, the goal would be to develop a strategic conception of reading rather than to master the steps of a strategy. This goal would be pursued through instruction conducted during meaningful reading activity. Additionally, from this perspective, social interactions have a prominent role to play in learning.

In this chapter, we describe our investigations of an instructional procedure that was designed to teach young children, principally those considered at risk for academic difficulty, how to approach reading in a thoughtful manner. The instruction is designed to provide students practice in a coherent and meaningful way. Finally, the instruction occurs in the natural social context of discussion.

RECIPROCAL TEACHING

Reciprocal teaching is a procedure featuring guided practice in the application of four concrete strategies for the purpose of understanding text. Students and their teachers take turns leading discussions about shared text, which they have read silently or listened to (depending upon their reading skill). These are not, however, opened-ended discussions. The dialogue leader (adult or child) begins the discussion by *asking questions* about the content of the text. The group discusses these questions, raises additional ones, and, in the case of disagreement or misunderstanding, rereads the text. Although questions are used to stimulate discussion, *summarizing* is used to identify the gist of what has been read and discussed and to prepare the students to move on to the next portion of text. Once again, there is discussion for the purpose of achieving consensus regarding the summary. The third strategy, *clarification,* is used opportunistically for the purpose of restoring meaning when a concept, word, or phrase has been misunderstood or is unfamiliar to someone. Finally, the discussion leader provides the opportunity for *predictions* regarding upcoming content. Group members generate their predictions based on their prior knowledge of the topic of the text as well as clues that are provided in the text itself. The following excerpt from a reciprocal teaching lesson conducted by a first-grade teacher illustrates the role of the strategies in supporting the dialogue.

MRS. MACKEY: (reading the following text) "The pipefish change their color and movements to blend with their surroundings.

For example, pipefish that live among green plants change their color to a shade of green to match the plants."

CLARE: (leading the discussion) One *question* that I had about this paragraph is: What is special about the way that the pipefish looks?

KEITH: (clarifying) Do you mean the way that it is green?

ANDY: (elaborating) It's not just that it's green; it's that it's the same color as the plants around it, all around it.

CLARE: (resuming) Yes. That's it. My *summary* is this part tells how the pipefish looks and that it looks like what is around it. My *prediction* is that this is about its enemies and how it protects itself and who the enemies are.

MONTY: (adding to Clare's summary) They also talked about how the pipefish moves . . .

KEITH: (rejoining) It sways back and forth.

ANDY: (adding) Along with the other plants.

MRS. MACKEY: (interjecting) What do we call it when something looks like and acts like something else? The way that the walkingstick was yesterday? We *clarified* this word when we talked about the walkingstick.

ANGEL: "Mimic."

MRS. MACKEY: That's right! We said/ we would say/ that the pipefish mimics the _____

STUDENTS: "Plants."

MRS. MACKEY: OK! Let's see if Clare's predictions come true.

The Role of Dialogue in Reciprocal Teaching

To examine the use of dialogues in comprehension instruction, it is useful to consider the tenets of a Vygotskian perspective on teaching and learning (Vygotsky, 1962, 1978; Wertsch, 1980). Vygotsky maintained that the inner speech that is used by humans to plan, as well as to regulate, their own activity is a consequence of earlier participation in social activity. Thus, the strategic patterns of reasoning exercised at an intrapsychological plane (within the individual) are a reflection of the strategies that the child was encouraged to follow earlier as a participant at an *interpsychological* plane (between or among individuals). Indeed, Vygotsky argued that through social dialogue it is possible for a child to participate in strategic activity without understanding it completely, Through repeated and shared social dialogues, the child comes to discover the import of the more experienced individual's utterances and his or her own responses. Having experienced this social dialogue, the child is then able to engage in private speech or speech that is spoken aloud but addressed to himself or herself for the purpose of directing cognitive activity. This private speech finally leads to inner, self-guiding speech that, as the child matures and acquires expertise, is internalized as verbal thought.

In addition to the interesting instructional opportunities that dialogues can provide in classrooms, they can also serve as a window on the verbal thought in which children are engaged as they attempt to understand text, providing unique diagnostic opportunities.

As McCollum shows in Chapter 8, research on classroom interaction illustrates how often dialogue among teachers and students is thwarted. Teacher–child interactions are dominated by adults in both amount and direction of the conversation. Most "discussion" that is held in classrooms is, in fact, recitation where there are recurring sequences of teacher questions and student responses, with most questions of the "known-answer" variety that offer little opportunity for the exchange of ideas and opinions (Gall, 1984). Impeding conversation are the asymmetry of power and knowledge between teacher and child (Bloome & Greene, 1984); sociocultural differences among children and teachers (Heath, 1981); and organizational constraints in classrooms (Cohen, 1986).

These observations suggest that one important key to the successful use of dialogues in classrooms is to determine ways in which students can assume and teachers can impart a voice to children in these dialogues. The discourse structure in reciprocal teaching, determined principally through the use of the four strategies, and the explicit instructional goal of turning these dialogues over to the children serve these very purposes.

The Role of the Strategies in Reciprocal Teaching

The four activities (question generating, summarizing, clarifying, and predicting) were selected on the basis of several features. First, they are examples of strategic activities that good readers routinely bring to bear when learning from text (Bereiter & Bird, 1985) but poor readers fail to use (Garner, 1987). Second, when employed intelligently, they both improve comprehension and provide the alert reader an opportunity to monitor for understanding. For example, if one attempts to paraphrase a section of text and fails, this may be a good indication that comprehension and retention have not been achieved and that remedial action, such as rereading, is required. Finally, as illustrated above, these particular strategies lend themselves well to supporting a discussion.

The Role of the Teacher in Reciprocal Teaching

Although the strategies serve to structure and support the dialogue, it is the teacher who supports the children's participation in the dialogue. This support varies, naturally, according to such features as the ability of the students and the difficulty of the text. In the course of reciprocal teaching instruction, the teacher assumes many roles by:

1. Modeling competent use of the strategies for the purposes of constructing meaning and monitoring comprehension
2. Engaging in on-line diagnosis of the students' emerging competence with the comprehension activity
3. Supporting students' efforts to understand the text
4. Pushing for deeper understanding
5. Consciously releasing control of the dialogue to the students as they indicate the ability to assume responsibility for their own learning

In describing a quite comparable role for the teacher of mathematics, Lampert (1986) has characterized the teacher as "building a culture of sense-making" (p. 340).

Collaborating With Teachers on Implementation of Reciprocal Teaching

Because many of the teachers with whom we have worked have not used dialogue for instructional purposes, a critical step in the implementation of reciprocal teaching has been the preparation of the teachers. Over the years, with our teachers' advice, we refined this process to include the following steps.

First, the teachers were encouraged to reflect on and discuss their current instructional goals and activities related to improving students' comprehension of text. Similarities between the processes and outcomes of their current programs and reciprocal teaching were highlighted. For example, most teachers with whom we worked already engaged in the teaching of strategies. The differences between teaching strategies as isolated skills and teaching strategies for the purpose of self-regulating one's learning activity were discussed and demonstrated.

Second, the theory informing the design of reciprocal teaching was introduced to the teachers. The following points were emphasized:

1. The acquisition of the strategies employed in reciprocal teaching is a joint responsibility shared by the teacher and students.

2. The teacher initially assumes major responsibility for instructing these strategies (i.e., the teachers "think aloud" how they generate a summary, what cues they use to make predictions, how rereading or reading ahead is useful when encountering something unclear in the text), but gradually transfers responsibility to the students for demonstrating use of the strategies.
3. All students are expected to participate in this discussion; that is, all students are to be given the opportunity to lead the discussion. The teacher will enable the students' successful participation by supporting the students in a variety of ways. For example, the teacher might prompt the student, provide the student additional information, or alter the demand on the student.
4. Throughout each day of instruction there is a conscious attempt to release control of the dialogue to the students.
5. The aim of reciprocal teaching is to construct the meaning of the text and to monitor the success with which comprehension occurs.

Following this explanation and description, the teachers were shown tapes in which reciprocal teaching was demonstrated with students of an age comparable to that of children with whom the teachers would work. Following these introductory activities, the teachers participated in several sessions where the reciprocal teaching dialogues were role-played, simulating situations that had arisen in previous research. Transcripts of reciprocal teaching sessions were shared for the purpose of discussing some of the finer points of the dialogue; for example, how teachers adjusted the support given to individual members in the instructional group. Finally, there was a demonstration lesson in which the investigator and a teacher conducted a reciprocal teaching lesson followed by a debriefing with all of the teachers involved in the study. Following these formal sessions to prepare the teachers, additional coaching was provided to each of the teachers as they implemented the dialogues in their respective settings.

Introducing Students to Reciprocal Teaching

In the initial investigations of reciprocal teaching (Palincsar & Brown, 1984), instruction started with the dialogues. When we began to investigate its use with larger instructional groups and younger children (Palincsar & Brown, 1989), we added a procedure to introduce the students to reciprocal teaching. The procedure included discussion regarding the purpose of reciprocal teaching, the features of reciprocal teaching, and a structured overview of each of the strategies that would be used in the discussion with the use of teacher-led activities. For example, summarizing was introduced by discussing how summarizing is useful (e.g., in a quick telephone conversation). The students then generated summaries of familiar stories, movies, and television programs. This provided the teachers the opportunity to evaluate how well their students could frame summaries. The students were then introduced to basic guidelines useful in constructing summaries (e.g., think about what is important). These teacher-led activities were included principally to introduce the students to the language of the reciprocal teaching dialogues and to provide the teacher with diagnostic information suggesting how much support the individual children in the group might need in the dialogue, based on their performance with these isolated activities.

Evaluating the Effectiveness of Reciprocal Teaching

The initial research on reciprocal teaching was conducted with junior high students who were adequate decoders but poor comprehenders (Palincsar & Brown, 1984). Implementing the reciprocal teaching procedure on a small-group basis (the groups averaged five students) with remedial reading teachers, for a period of 20 days, we observed that

(a) students' ability to summarize, generate questions, clarify, and predict improved markedly;
(b) quantitative improvements on comprehension measures were large, reliable, and durable;
(c) the benefits of the intervention generalized to classroom settings; and
(d) there was transfer to tasks that were similar but distinct from the instructional tasks.

Having determined that reciprocal teaching was an effective intervention for poor readers in junior high school, we began a series of comparative studies to determine the essential features of the practice. In the first of this series we compared reciprocal teaching with other interventions that included instruction regarding the same strategies but not conducted in a dialogic manner. We compared reciprocal teaching with

(a) modeling, in which the teacher modeled the four strategies as she read the text while the students observed and responded to her questions;
(b) isolated skill practice, in which the students completed worksheet

activities on each of the four strategies and received extensive feed-back from the teacher; and

(c) reciprocal teaching/practice, during which the students received the reciprocal teaching intervention for the initial four days of instruction, followed by eight days of independently applying the strategies, in writing, to segments of text.

Only the traditional reciprocal teaching procedure resulted in large and reliable gains (Brown & Palincsar, 1989).

In the second comparative study, we asked whether the four strategies were necessary to effect improvement on the comprehension measures or whether a subset of the strategies would suffice. Ten days of either reciprocal questioning or reciprocal summarizing alone did not result in the same gains as ten days of the full reciprocal teaching procedure (Brown & Palincsar, 1989; Palincsar & Brown, 1989).

Satisfied that this was not a procedure that could be streamlined readily and still maintain the same effectiveness, we implemented the reciprocal teaching procedure in a series of classroom studies in which all six middle-school remedial reading teachers from an urban district, working in groups that ranged in number from seven to fifteen, compared reciprocal teaching with an individualized program of reading skill instruction. Although the results were not as dramatic as our earlier work, over 70% of students participating in the experimental groups met our criterion as compared with 19% of the control students (Palincsar & Brown, 1989).

Case Study

In this chapter, we focus on the research conducted with first-grade students. This research was motivated by our interest in determining what comprehension instruction might look like when conducted with students who were, as yet, nonreaders (in the sense that they were not yet decoding words). We chose to work with students who are often identified as at risk for academic difficulty (i.e., children from disadvantaged families, children referred for special education or remedial services). We were particularly interested in these children in light of the evidence that, although considerable educational efforts are spent on teaching them decoding skills, such instruction is often at the expense of comprehension instruction. In reporting the results of this research, we will first describe the activity that occurred between the children and teachers and then characterize the concomitant changes that were observed on the part of the children in these instructional groups.

The students were selected by asking each of 3 first-grade teachers to nominate at least 12 of their 27 to 30 students who might be at risk for academic difficulty, based on previous school histories, referrals for remedial education, and current classroom performance. The teachers were also asked to identify up to four students who were not experiencing any school-related difficulty who might serve as catalysts to the discussions. All nominated children were then assessed using an array of procedures. The students were first administered the Stanford Early Assessment of School Achievement Test (SESAT). This test measures listening comprehension by asking the students to circle the picture that best represents the statement that has been read to them. The children were below the 50th percentile on the SESAT. To collect a measure of listening comprehension in a task more representative of learning from extended text, the teachers administered a series of comprehension assessments in the following manner. The children were told that they were going to hear a story and that, as the story was read, they would be asked to answer questions about what they were learning. The stories were read, paragraph by paragraph. The mean length of each story was five paragraphs, each paragraph averaging 80 words. There were a total of 10 questions designed to assess recall as well as the ability to draw inferences from the text. These questions were interspersed so that the children generally answered two questions per paragraph. In addition, following the story, the students were asked one question that required them to identify the gist of the passage and one question that measured their ability and inclination to use information that had been presented in the story to solve a novel problem. For example, following a passage that described how camouflage is useful to deer, the children were asked to suggest why an American Indian would dress in deerskins when hunting. Three of these comprehension assessments were administered to each child before the instruction began. On the recall and inference questions the children were averaging about 50% correct. On the gist questions, they averaged 27% correct and on the application questions, 25% correct.

As an additional measure of listening comprehension activity, we asked the students to engage in the isolated use of the four strategies. First, we read the title of the passage to the children and asked them to tell three things they would expect or would like to hear about in a story with this title (predicting). Next, we asked the students to listen carefully as we read the first part of the story and to think of a question they might ask other children to make sure they understood the story (questioning). We then asked them to listen once again so that they could tell what the story was mainly about (summarizing). The students were told, with each reading, that they should ask for help if there were any words or ideas that they could not understand (clarifying). Each story was constructed to include one difficult vocabulary word for young children. There were two such assessments of strategy knowledge administered during pretesting. The students earned 26% of the total points possible for executing each of these strategies.

To increase our understanding of these children's listening comprehension activity, we asked them what they did while listening to the stories to help them understand and remember what they were hearing. Typical responses for the majority of students included: "I don't know this. I'm only 7 years old!" "I do nothing." "I stay still." These responses contrast with those of a few students selected by their teachers as potential catalysts to the discussion, who answered: "I keep thinking about it." "I keep running my mind over it." "I picture it in my head, I catch the picture."

Following this evaluation, the 10 children whose individual composite scores suggested that they were most in need of comprehension instruction were matched and randomly assigned to either the experimental or control group for each of the three teachers. In addition, two students (generally from the four each teacher had nominated as possible catalysts to the discussions) who fared well on the assessments were selected and randomly assigned to either the experimental or the control group. Each of the three instructional and control groups then consisted of five at-risk children and one child not experiencing difficulty.

The three teachers in this replication had each taught for more than 15 years in the primary grades and had successfully participated in two earlier studies of reciprocal teaching. Instruction took place in each teacher's classroom during that time of day when the teachers generally met for small-group instruction. Prior to beginning the dialogues, children in experimental groups were introduced to reciprocal teaching using the activities described earlier. The introductory activities required five consecutive days of instruction, each lasting 20 to 30 minutes.

The teachers then began the dialogues. Instruction was conducted for 20 to 30 minutes a day for 30 consecutive school days. The teachers read expository and narrative passages derived from third-grade basal reading materials and covering a range of topics such as plants that glow, chimps that use sign language, and the production of cartoons.

Examining the Dialogue

Each day the teachers audio-recorded the reciprocal teaching dialogues. Days 1, 5, 10, 15, 20, 25, and 28 through 30 were transcribed for each teacher. In addition, the teachers were invited to indicate any tape they would like transcribed for their own interest.

In previous research (Palincsar, 1986), we have asked such general questions as: How does the dialogue change over time? What differences are observed among the groups engaged in the dialogue? We have also inquired into the kinds of opportunities that are created when instruction features structured discourse (Palincsar & Brown, 1989). For this chapter, we present excerpts from one reciprocal teaching lesson illustrating how the dialogue fosters reasoning about text, facilitates an active role for teachers and learners, and represents holistic/constructivist instruction.

As illustrated in the following section of transcript, the teachers regularly reviewed the strategies with children and reported that children enjoyed using these "big words." Labeling the activities assisted the children to use these strategies in contexts other than listening time; for example, teachers reported that the children would label predictions and tell the teacher that they had thought of a good question during reading time. Children requested clarifications during whole-class discussion times and when films were shown. In addition, when the dialogue began to stray, it was not uncommon for a child, frustrated that the direction of the discourse was unclear, to demand, "What is it we're doing now? Is this our summary?"

The children were listening to a story called "Living Lights." It was the 15th day of reciprocal teaching.

> TEACHER: So, what are we learning to do as we listen to stories?
> KEISHA: Ask questions.
> TRAVIS: About the important things that we learn in the story.
> RICHARD: Clarify.
> TEACHER: Anytime there is a word that you don't understand or something doesn't make sense in the story, give me a signal, so we'll stop and clarify.
> TRAVIS: We'll predict.
> TEACHER: You know that sometimes right in the middle of the story . . . I'll stop and say, "I think I can make a prediction . . ."
> KEISHA: I think I know what is going to happen next.
> TEACHER: And the last thing that we have talked about . . .
> MISSY: We summarize what we have learned. How it was, was we ask question, summarize, and I think it was then predicting and then clarifying.
> TEACHER: Well, that's right; but we don't always need to do it in that order. We can use these strategies whenever they are needed.

In the next segment, the group pools their assorted recollections about the opening paragraph introducing fireflies, which was read the previous day. They also discuss their personal experiences with fireflies.

TEACHER: Let's summarize what we learned yesterday.

RODNEY: Fireflies.

MISSY: They are beetles.

TERRANCE: Lightning bugs.

TEACHER: Yes, a firefly is a beetle and another name for it is a lightning bug.

KEISHA: It has a chemical that can make it glow.

TEACHER: Yes. When the chemical in the lightning bug mixes with air, the lightning bug can glow. OK Here we go!

TERRANCE: This might be about how to catch a firefly.

RICHARD: I used to catch some and I'd put em in a mayonnaise jar but my mom poked a hole in em.

TEACHER: Why would your mom put holes in the lid?

RICHARD: Because, so they can breathe.

MISSY: They need air because they are called *living* lights.
[The teacher begins reading when Rodney stops the reading for a clarification, provided not only by the teacher but by the students as well.]

TEACHER: (reading) "People like to watch the winking lights of the fireflies in the summer nighttime sky. Did you know that fireflies really use their lights as signals? At twilight . . ."

RODNEY: Twilight. What's that?

TRAVIS: It means night.

TEACHER: When day turns to night.

MISSY: When it's still kinda day but it's kinda night.

TEACHER: (reading) "At twilight the male fireflies begin to fly and flash their lights. The females flash their lights as an answer. The flashing lights are a signal that help the male and female fireflies find each other."

TEACHER: Who will be our teacher and summarize? Keisha?

KEISHA: It means that they are trying to find each other.

RICHARD: By their lightnings.

TERRANCE: Talking by their lightnings.

MISSY: Communicating.

TEACHER: They were communicating. Excellent.

RICHARD: When they flash them things, kids see em and they try to get em.

TEACHER: Did you ever stop to think that when you were seeing them flashing their lights, flashing their bottoms, that they were trying to find each other? Help me again, how do those lights happen?

TRAVIS: They got stuff inside of em.

TEACHER: What was that special word for the stuff inside them?

KEISHA: Chemicals.

RODNEY: Chemicals mixing in the air.

TEACHER: Let's see what happens. Any predictions?

TERRANCE: Maybe they will talk about how the light turns on.
[The children then generate a number of predictions regarding the possible topics the author will discuss, including how fireflies fly, drink, read, and tell time.]

TEACHER: You're being silly now, aren't you? Do you think a firefly can read? Is this a pretend story?

CHILDREN: NO!

MISSY: This is a real story, like maybe it will talk about how they sleep.

TEACHER: Let's find out.

The interaction continued, with the teacher reading from the text and students and teacher intermittently employing the strategies as they discussed the content of the text.

Evaluating the Outcomes of Dialogic Instruction

We have maintained that by participating in learning dialogues, children acquire a thoughtful approach to text. We have suggested that, from a sociohistorical account of learning, what the child learns while participating in the dialogue is internalized over time. To examine this hypothesis, we will discuss data provided by the transcripts, anecdotes, and posttests for the children in the three instructional groups involved in the research reported in this chapter.

The transcripts for these three groups suggest that the discussions, over the course of the 30 days of instruction, became more spontaneous, less labored, and less teacher-directed. Furthermore, the children increasingly monitored their understanding of the text (e.g., by requesting clarifications with greater frequency or asking the teacher to reread). Finally, the transcripts indicate that the children began to make distinctions regarding the information that was provided in the text and information that either was derived from personal experience or would have to be sought elsewhere.

This last observation requires some explanation. In contrast to the seventh graders with whom we had done the earliest reciprocal teaching research, one of the difficulties experienced by these first graders was distancing themselves from the text as a source of information (Mason, McCormick, & Bhavnagri, 1986). This difficulty manifested itself in two ways. First, the children often would indicate that they could not answer a question (either in the discussion or in the assessment sessions) because of the relationship between this information and their personal experience. For example, after hearing a story about how manatees have cleared the Florida water canals, the children were asked several general questions about the story. It was not uncommon for children to indicate that they knew nothing about this because they had never seen a manatee, or to indicate that they ought to know something about this because they had just visited their grandmother in Florida. Second, when these first graders initially began to generate their questions, an unusual number of these questions (compared once again with those generated by seventh graders) could not be answered from the text but rather seemed to reflect general knowledge the children possessed related to the topic of the text. The teachers were careful to acknowledge these question types as "good and interesting questions" and then ask the children to indicate whether this was a question that could be answered using the text or one dependent on the knowledge the children already possessed. Over time, the children began to distinguish between text and background knowledge; they asked more text-based questions. However, at the same time, they began using their background knowledge to make predictions about the text.

Anecdotal evidence of internalization on the part of the students is indicated in the teachers' reports, mentioned earlier in this chapter, that the children began to use the strategies employed in the dialogue, unprompted, in contexts other than the listening comprehension lessons. In addition to this collective evidence, individual students' responses to the intervention are reflected in the results of the comprehension assessments administered throughout the intervention. These were the assessments in which the children listened to an expository passage and answered 10 questions that were interspersed throughout the story and one gist-and-application question following the story. These assessment materials were independent from the materials that were used during the instruction. The results of these assessments indicate that during baseline, on the three assessments that were administered prior to instruction, the mean for the three experimental groups was 51% and for the three control groups, 49%. Following the first half of intervention, the experimental mean was 62% and the control was 49%. The experimental mean for the last phase was 72% and the second-phase mean for the control students was 55%. Multivariate analyses of variance, using a design on dependent measures and decomposing the gains made from baseline to the first half of intervention and from the first to the second half of intervention indicated that there was a significant difference between the gains of the experimental and control students following the first half of the intervention, $F(1, 33) = 4.75$, $p < 0.02$. Although there were no significant differences detected on the gist questions as a function of the intervention (both the experimental and control groups showed gains on this measure, simply as a function of practice answering these questions), there were significant differences indicated on the analogy questions (i.e., those questions that required the students to use information in the text to solve a novel problem). The gains made by the experimental students between the first and second half of intervention were significantly greater than those of the control students on these measures, $F(1, 33) = 5.02, p < 0.02$.

Finally, we have suggested that, although mastering the strategies is not the principal goal of instruction, the ability to engage in independent use of the strategies is certainly a desirable by-product of instruction. Whereas both groups were earning about 26% of the total points possible on the strategy pretest measure, the experimental group earned 48% of the points possible on the posttest measure compared with 33% by the control group. This represents a significant difference between experimental and control groups, $F(1, 33) = 4.16, p < 0.03$.

In summary, students participating in the reciprocal teaching dialogues outperformed matched, control children on measures of independent listening comprehension, strategy use, and ability to use the information in text to solve novel problems.

SUMMARY

Reciprocal teaching is a collaborative learning procedure, in which children receive guided practice in the use of metacognitive skills of reading designed to improve their ability to understand text. The theoretical underpinnings of reciprocal teaching attribute learning to the process of internalizing cognitive activities that were originally experienced in a social context. The children use the strategies to generate their own questions about the text, to relate their own knowledge to the new knowledge posed in the text, to summarize what they have learned, and to identify what they found confusing in the text and how they might proceed to render the text more meaningful. The teacher's role in supporting the students' participation in the learning dialogues is, without question, a demanding one. The dialogue provides rich opportunities for the teacher to model the processes of successful comprehension and to conduct diagnoses of the impediments to comprehension. The teacher proceeds, with deliberate intention, to enable the children to acquire knowledge that will be useful to them. Because of the diversity of experiences and knowledge the children bring to these texts, each participant can make a useful contribution to the emerging understanding of the content at hand. In such a context, classrooms of diverse learners become communities of literate thinkers.

ACKNOWLEDGEMENT. The research reported in this chapter was supported by PHS Grant 95951 from the National Institute of Child Health and Human Development and OSE Grant G008400648 from the Department of Education. Special thanks are due Kathryn Ransom, Reading Coordinator, School District #186, Springfield, Illinois; her enthusiastic support of reciprocal teaching has contributed enormously to the success of this research program. In addition, we wish to acknowledge the many fine teachers who have participated in our research, including Mrs. Derber, Ms. Hagerman, Ms. Johnson, and Mrs. Mackey—the teachers conducting the research reported in this chapter. Finally, we are grateful to Ann Brown for our ongoing collaboration.

REFERENCES

Bereiter, C., & Bird, M. (1985). Use of thinking aloud in identification and teaching of reading comprehension strategies. *Cognition and Instruction, 2*(2), 131–156.

Bereiter, C., & Scardamalia, M. (1987). An attainable version of high literacy: Approaches to teaching higher-order skills in reading and writing. *Curriculum Inquiry, 17*(1), 9–30.

Bloome, D., & Green, J. (1984). Directions in the social sociolinguistic study of reading. In P. D. Pearson, M. Hamil, R. Barr, & P. Mosenthal (Eds.), *Handbook of reading research* (pp. 395–421). New York: Longman.

Brown, A. L. (1980). Metacognitive development and reading. In R. J. Spiro, B. C. Bruce, & W. F. Brewer (Eds.), *Theoretical issues in reading comprehension* (pp. 453–481). Hillsdale, NJ: Erlbaum.

Brown, A. L., & Palincsar, A. S. (1989). Guided, cooperative learning and individual knowledge acquisition. In L. Resnick (Ed.), *Knowing, learning, and instruction: Essays in honor of Robert Glaser* (pp. 393–451). Hillsdale, NJ: Erlbaum.

Cohen, E. (1986). *Designing groupwork: Strategies for heterogeneous classrooms.* New York: Teachers College Press.

Delpit, L. D. (1988). The silenced dialogue: Power and pedagogy in educating other people's children. *Harvard Educational Review, 58,* 280–298.

Gall, M. D. (1984). Synthesis of research on questioning in recitation. *Educational Leadership, 42*(3).

Garner, R. (1987). *Metacognition and reading comprehension.* Norwood, NJ: Ablex.

Gavelek, J. R., & Palincsar, A. S. (1988). Contextualism as an alternative world view of learning disabilities. *Journal of Learning Disabilities, 21*(5), 278–281.

Heath, S. B. (1981). Questioning at home and at school: A comparative study. In
G. Spindler (Ed.), *Doing ethnography: Educational anthropology in action.*
New York: Holt, Rinehart and Winston.

Heshusius, L. (1989). Holistic principles: Not enhancing the old but seeing a-new:
A rejoinder. *Journal of Learning Disabilities, 22*(10), 595–602.

Hilliard, A. (1988). Public support for successful instructional practices for at-risk
students. In *School success for students at-risk* (pp. 195–208). A report com-
missioned by the Council of Chief State School Officers. Orlando, FL: Har-
court Brace Jovanovich.

Lampert, M. (1986). Knowing, doing, and teaching multiplication. *Cognition and
Instruction, 3*(4), 305–342.

Mason, J. M., McCormick, C., & Bhavnagri, N. (1986). How are you going to help
me learn? Lesson negotiations between a teacher and preschool children. In
D. B. Yaden, Jr. & S. Templeton (Eds.), *Metalinguistic awareness and beginning literacy: Conceptualizing what it means to read and write.* Portsmouth,
NH: Heinemann.

McGinley, W., & Tierney, R. J. (1989). Traversing the topical landscape. *Written
Communication, 6*(3), 243–269.

National Commission on Excellence in Education (1983). *Nation at risk: The imperative for educational reform.* Washington, DC: U.S. Department of Education.

Palincsar, A. S. (1986). The role of dialogue in providing scaffolded instruction.
Educational Psychologist, 21(1, 2), 73–98.

Palincsar, A. S., & Brown, A. L. (1984). Reciprocal teaching of comprehension-
fostering and comprehension-monitoring activities. *Cognition and Instruction,
1*(2), 117–175.

Palincsar, A. S., & Brown, A. L. (1989). Classroom dialogues to promote self-
regulated comprehension. In J. Brophy (Ed.), *Teaching for understanding and
self-regulated learning: Vol. I* (pp. 35–72). Greenwich, CT: JAI.

Paris, S. G., Wasik, B. A., & Turner, J. C. (in press). The development of strategic
readers. In P. D. Pearson (Ed.), *Handbook of reading research* (2nd ed.). New
York: Longman.

Phelps, L. W. (1988). *Composition as a human science.* London: Oxford Press.

Poplin, M. S. (1988). The reductionist fallacy in learning disabilities: Replicating
the past by reducing the present. *Journal of Learning Disabilities, 21*(7), 389–
400.

Resnick, D. P., & Resnick, L. B. (1977). The nature of literacy: An historical exploration. *Harvard Educational Review 47*(3), 370–385.

Vygotsky, L. S. (1962). *Thought and language.* Cambridge, MA: M.I.T. Press.

Vygotsky, L. S. (1978). *Mind in society: The development of higher psychological
processes.* Cambridge, MA: Harvard University Press.

Wertsch, J. V. (1980). The significance of dialogue in Vygotsky's account of social,
egocentric, and inner speech. In A. J. Edwards (Ed.), *Contemporary Educational Psychology, 5*(2), 150–162.

10 | Task and Talk Structures That Foster Literacy

ELFRIEDA H. HIEBERT
University of Colorado, Boulder

CHARLES W. FISHER
University of Northern Colorado

Reports of schools' failures to improve levels of literacy among America's youth are numerous. The most recent National Assessment of Educational Progress shows that many seventh and eleventh graders are unable to write an adequate summary of a short narrative passage (Applebee, Langer, & Mullis, 1988). When it comes to more complex tasks, like making inferences from text, performance by many students is also disturbingly poor (Applebee, Langer, & Mullis, 1989). Moreover, failure of our schools to promote high levels of literacy, though by no means restricted to specific groups, occurs more frequently among students from some racial and cultural minorities, economically disadvantaged students, and students for whom English is a second language. Because low levels of literacy, among other factors, reduce the range of educational and career opportunities for students, this issue continues to be a barrier to both social and economic progress.

An increasing number of studies of classroom learning indicate that acquisition of literacy can be improved by restructuring certain aspects of learning environments (see, e.g., Chapter 7). This chapter focuses on changes in two aspects of classroom life—task and talk structures. Together, task and talk structures regulate the quality and quantity of classroom learning opportunities. If not thoughtfully designed, these structures can create favorable learning environments for some students while restricting the participation of others. Appropriate changes in these structures can create more productive and equitable classrooms where literacy is the rule rather than the exception.

TASK AND TALK STRUCTURES: A CONCEPTUAL BACKGROUND

Although task and talk structures are conceptually distinct, they operate simultaneously in classrooms. Most teachers regularly set learning goals and design sequences of activities to achieve these goals. That is, an agenda with children "doing" something such as listening to a story or completing a worksheet is typically on the table at all times. As a result, teacher decisions about tasks are more conscious than those about talk. Whereas talk is always performed within the context of some task, talk structures are unlikely to be at the center of teacher planning. It would be a rare teacher, for example, who designs a class day around talk structures such as student-led large-group or dyadic discussions. Talk structures, however, are critical to accomplishing the goals of schooling. Task and talk structures, when taken together, provide insights into why and how classroom literacy experiences are productive.

Structures of Tasks

The task perspective, that is, viewing schooling as an extended sequence of tasks, draws heavily on the work of the ecological psychologists (Barker, 1963) and more recently on work by Doyle (1983) (see, e.g., Mergendoller, 1988). A task, according to Doyle, involves a goal, resources for accomplishing the goal, and a set of cognitive operations that are adequate to reach the goal. Academic tasks in schools are defined by the products students are requested to produce and the routes that can be used to attain these products. Task goals may be very concrete, as in completing a summary of a passage, or somewhat more ephemeral, as in listening to the teacher read a story. Tasks influence learners by directing their attention to particular aspects of content and by specifying ways of processing information. From this perspective, tasks form the basic treatment unit in classrooms; students learn what tasks lead them to do.

Blumenfeld, Mergendoller, and Swarthout (1987) have extended Doyle's notions about tasks by stressing task form as well as task content. Academic content is embedded in tasks whose forms vary in terms of types of activities, products, and social organization. These forms can be as critical to learning as the cognitive operations and goals of tasks. The form of the task (e.g., collaboration with peers or collaboration explicitly outlawed) restricts the range of what students are to do, and when, where, how, and with whom they are to do it. Empirical work by Blumenfeld and her colleagues has focused on explicating the manner in which motivational dimensions of tasks influence student engagement and achievement (e.g., Blumenfeld & Meece, 1988).

Fisher and Hiebert (1990a; 1990b) examined both the content and form of task structures in elementary classrooms over full days of schoolwork. In comparing task structures in two approaches to literacy instruction, they explored several aspects of task form. By describing the function of each component of schoolwork tasks, explicit opportunities for students to structure and restructure knowledge were identified. In addition, dimensions of task content, including cognitive complexity and the "function-infrastructure" dimension (Valencia, McGinley, & Pearson, 1990) were considered. This latter term refers to the specificity of content, that is, the extent to which the task relates to the overall functions of a discipline. For example, literacy tasks could address story composition on the one hand or specific exercises related to writing mechanics on the other. Levels of function-infrastructure constitute one way of describing the authenticity of school tasks (Brown, Collins, & Duguid, 1989). Task structures, especially when viewed over weeks and years of students' school careers, act as powerful treatments on acquisition of content knowledge and development of dispositions toward learning, school, and work.

Structures of Talk

All classroom events are embedded in oral language. At one level, oral language is the means for conveying the parameters of literacy tasks (e.g., "You've got 15 minutes to finish writing your summaries."). At a more profound level, as meaning is negotiated through classroom discourse, oral language provides the medium for structuring and restructuring meaning. Because the latter function may be overlooked during teacher planning, it is considered more extensively.

An early and powerful argument for the effects of social interaction on children's literacy development comes from the work of Vygotsky (1962) and its extensions (Edwards & Mercer, 1987; Wertsch, 1985). Vygotsky saw social interaction as the primary mechanism for acquiring the symbol systems and practices of a culture. In his view, the distinctive properties of human knowledge and thought are derived from various aspects of social activity. While thought is not considered to be equivalent to language, children's internal thought processes are profoundly shaped through social interaction.

Children's thought processes are initially shaped through interactions with parents. When children attend school, their thinking, especially thinking about the academic content of school, is further influenced by interactions with teachers. Ideally, conversations between teachers and students include support or "scaffolding" that allows children to engage new ideas and construct appropriate meanings from their experiences. With this support, children perform near the upper boundaries of their capabilities. Without this support, learning, at best, will occur more slowly. At worst, children may develop misconceptions about both the content of instruction and methods of meaning-making. Through regulation of the amount of structural support or scaffolding in conversations, students function in their "zone of proximal development," resulting in productive learning.

When reading is viewed as active participation in the construction of a text's meaning, and when writing is viewed as a means for individuals to convey meanings, opportunities for interaction become essential ingredients in classroom reading and writing experiences. In classrooms, modification of support structures in conversations becomes problematic because the level of support that is appropriate for one student may not be appropriate for others. When teacher–student and student–student talk contexts are considered, in addition to substantial differences in students' linguistic and cultural experiences, the situation is extremely complex.

When participation in social interaction is viewed as crucial to children's learning, as it is from a Vygotskian perspective, studies of classroom participant structures provide insight into children's opportunities to learn. Rules for interaction among participants in classrooms have been identified in a number of studies (e.g., Au & Mason, 1981; Michaels, 1981). Verbal interaction in classrooms is often dominated by repeated recitation-like triads, each consisting of a "teacher initiation" followed by a "student response" and concluded by a "teacher evaluation." For some children more than others, participation structures in classrooms mirror interactions at home (Heath, 1983). For children who have not had frequent experiences with the dominant participant structures, life at school may seem alien and portray children as inarticulate. From a Vygotskian perspective, differences in participation structures represent more and less effective opportunities for students to structure and restructure meaning.

THE NATURE OF TASK AND TALK STRUCTURES
IN CLASSROOMS

As diversity among students within a classroom increases, thoughtful design of task and talk structures becomes essential for providing productive and equitable instructional opportunities. The relationship between task and talk structures is remarkably complex. At times, talk structures appear to be subordinate to tasks, but at other times, these appear to drive classroom tasks. An understanding of task and talk structures is very useful in changing, as well as explaining, classroom learning experiences.

Within a given classroom, both task and talk structures appear to follow reasonably stable daily and weekly patterns. When talk and task structures are examined across classrooms, two fundamentally different scenarios can be identified. The first, or traditional, scenario typifies the experiences of most children who have attended American schools in the last several decades. This scenario emanates from a reductionist or skills-oriented perspective in which learning is viewed as the transmission of static objective knowledge from one person to another in incremental steps. The second, or transformative, scenario has its philosophical basis in constructivism, where learning is viewed as the construction of knowledge through dynamic interaction among learners about ideas and experiences.

In describing literacy instruction in the two scenarios, we emphasize task and talk structures rather than the standardized achievement scores that are typically taken as evidence of learning in American schools. The inadequacy of standardized tests as the exclusive indicators of students' literacy accomplishments is well-documented (see Chapter 18). Although a few tests require students to write responses to passages or grapple with multiple interpretations of text (Valencia & Pearson, 1987), there are neither sufficient examples of paper-and-pencil tests that move beyond a single multiple-choice answer nor adequate reports on alternative assessments such as portfolios. When literacy acquisition, as measured by conventional tests, is compared between classrooms implementing the traditional and transformative approaches, there is some evidence that outcomes are similar (Hagerty, Hiebert, & Owens, 1989). However, in this chapter, task and talk structures per se are taken to be important short-term outcomes of schooling.

Tasks and Talk: A Traditional Scenario

A typical scene in a sixth-grade classroom studied by Fisher and Hiebert (1990a) illustrates task and talk structures in traditional skills-oriented classrooms. The teacher announced the beginning of reading period and directed students to work on their weekly assignments. Although the assigned pages were different for students in each of three ability groups, all students were responsible for reading a passage or two in the textbook, completing related workbook pages, and responding to questions in the textbook. By week's end, students were to have the teacher's verification of correct responses on these workbook pages and questions. This requirement for teacher grading meant that most students stood in line by the teacher's desk for 10 to 15 minutes of the reading period, waiting to have their work evaluated or to ask questions about assignments.

The structures in this classroom were common to other skills-oriented classrooms in the study, regardless of achievement or grade level. Students spent long periods of time completing low-level cognitive tasks that had been highly specified by their teachers. Talk before tasks consisted primarily of directions from the teacher on how to perform them. Occasions for teachers and students to talk about knowledge and perceptions of curriculum topics before either reading or writing were rare. Opportunities for restructuring knowledge by talking with the teacher or other students after reading or writing were even less frequent. Oral interaction following reading and writing typically evaluated "right" and "wrong" answers as opposed to discussion of alternative interpretations of text.

In the traditional scenario, literacy tasks direct student's attention to small pieces of text. For students who are proficient readers and writers, most tasks are small, cognitively simple, and highly specified by someone other than the student. However, for those who are not proficient readers and writers, the entire diet consists of low-level tasks.

Regardless of the reason for limited proficiency (e.g., age, learning English as a second language), the traditional skills-oriented view mandates low-level, incremental tasks. Students are required to master individual letters before words and individual words before sentences in stories. Analysis of kindergarten and readiness materials in textbook programs confirms this task sequence for beginning readers (Hiebert & Papierz, 1990). Hiebert and Papierz conclude that children could go through their entire first year of "reading" instruction without encountering words in text. When children finally face text, after months of struggling through letter-sound matching exercises, a typical page might contain only two small words. Ironically, a fairly sophisticated literacy schema is required to recognize that "It is"— perhaps the only symbols on a preprimer page—is text.

Some children, as preschoolers, have logged hundreds of hours listening to an adult read and playing with print-related toys. For these children, the traditional task sequence may delay additional literacy acquisition. However, their engagement in these tasks can be sustained by drawing on previous home experiences and ongoing parental encouragement. For other children, home literacy experiences may have consisted of watching family members read magazines or marquees (see Anderson & Stokes, 1984) or being read advertisements and cartoons (Pellegrini, Perlmutter, Galda, & Brophy, 1990). For children with such alternative literacy experiences, their initial inability to succeed in the unfamiliar tasks of traditional school literacy programs can quickly mark them for special reading programs or, at minimum, assignment to low-ability groups.

Once in a low-ability group, children receive an endless string of letter–sound matching activities, sight word-recognition activities, and other low-level tasks that emphasize decoding and literal comprehension, whereas students who know how to read engage in higher level tasks like discussions about stories (Allington, 1983; Cazden, 1986; Hiebert, 1983). Those who are least successful receive special attention, often in the form of pullout programs, where a philosophy of "more of the same is better" reigns. For example, children in Chapter 1 and special education programs often receive additional drill on low-level tasks, while their peers in the classroom read books (Rowan & Guthrie, 1989).

Opportunities for participation in higher level reading and writing tasks may be reduced even more if children attend school in a low-income neighborhood (Anyon, 1981; Fraatz, 1987) or if children are proficient in a language other than English. Moll, Estrada, Diaz, and Lopes (1980) found that bilingual children, like children who are proficient in dialects other than standard American English, participate almost exclusively in low-level tasks during English reading periods.

Judgments about children's reading proficiency and reading-group placement are often based on dialect (Burke, Pflaum, & Krafle, 1982; Deniston & Hiebert, 1983). Subsequent reading instruction frequently becomes a context for correction of pronunciation rather than reading and talking about text (Piestrup, 1973). When there are large numbers of minority children in a school, the entire program of the school may focus on low-level reading and writing skills. In addition, reading programs in schools with high numbers of African-American students are paced more slowly than those in schools with white students (Dreeben, 1987).

Talk in traditional skills-oriented classrooms often pertains to procedures rather than to concepts. Several analyses of oral discourse in classrooms (e.g., Heap, 1985; Wells, 1986; Edwards & Mercer, 1987) suggest that students develop many misconceptions rather than shared understandings in these circumstances. In reading groups, oral discourse most often conforms to the teacher-initiation/student-response/teacher-evaluation pattern described earlier (Cazden, 1986). Research on both tasks and talk in the traditional approach to instruction reveals that teachers do most of the talking while children watch, listen, and work on tasks that are highly specified by the teacher or textbook.

Tasks and Talk: A Transformative Scenario

According to Jackson (1986), the transformative tradition of teaching attempts "a transformation of one kind or another in the person being taught—a qualitative change often of dramatic proportion, a metamorphosis, so to speak" (pp. 120–121). The term "transformative" seems appropriate for describing the development of true literacy in students, that is, where students avidly use reading and writing as vehicles for thinking and living.

The transformative tradition is distinguished from the traditional approach by a particular conceptualization of the change process. In the transformative tradition, change is viewed as an internal process that, to a considerable degree, is initiated and controlled by the learner, thereby making the learner primarily responsible for his or her own learning. In contrast, the traditional view places responsibility for initiation and control of the change process primarily with external agents.

Transformative and traditional approaches are also differentiated in terms of the role played by social learning. In the transformative scenario, social interaction among classroom participants and between the class and the community of which it is a part are viewed to be critical factors determining what and how much is learned. In this scenario, knowledge is acquired through interactions with a relatively large number of knowledge sources. In the traditional scenario, the relationship between the teacher and individual students is viewed as the primary mechanism for knowledge transmission. In this sense, the teacher is the single most important source of knowledge. Consequently, interaction among students, and the relation between the classroom and the broader community of the school, is viewed as relatively unimportant to knowledge acquisition.

These fundamentally different views have implications for how teaching, learning, and knowledge itself are construed within each of the scenarios. Almost all learning in complex environments contains elements from both traditions; however, substantially different "mixes" can be identified relatively easily. These mixes show up in the task and talk structures that characterize particular environments. Moreover, change within a learning environment can be indexed by shifts in distributions of talk and task structures.

Classrooms in the literature-based approach to literacy instruction studied by Fisher and Hiebert (1990a) manifest some characteristics of the transformative scenario. For example, a reading period in a sixth-grade classroom began with a discussion among students and teacher about the ways in which authors create settings for their stories. After listening to the teacher read from two of her favorite authors, students identified mechanisms used by these authors to create specific settings. Following the discussion, students began (or continued) independent reading of self-selected books with an eye out for ways in which their authors created settings. The last portion of the reading period consisted of discussions of students' findings about creation of setting, first in groups of twos or threes and subsequently as a whole class. Later in the morning, students implemented their ideas about setting while writing stories of their own.

Generally, occasions for reading and writing in the literature-based classrooms were interspersed with talk among teacher and peers about what was to be read or written or what had been read or written. Approximately a quarter of all literacy periods was devoted to oral language activities that provided opportunities for students to speak about the meaning of their schoolwork. Occasions for structuring and restructuring understandings through talk were abundant after, as well as prior to, reading and writing of text. Sometimes, especially in writing tasks, students led the discussion of the whole group, whereas at other times students met in small groups.

Changes described in the task and talk structures studied by Fisher and Hiebert were restricted to a relatively small number of classrooms in one district. In this case, changes were initiated by the teachers themselves and local administrators. Elements of the transformative scenario can also be seen in larger change efforts and with diverse student populations. A prime example of system-wide change is that of the Kamehameha Early Education Program (KEEP) (Au & Jordan, 1981). The KEEP example is especially important because it represents a concerted study of the task and talk structures of a culture and the translation of this information into classroom practices. The KEEP efforts are described elsewhere (see Chapters 3 and 8).

Approximations of the transformative scenario through changes in task and talk structures have also been successful with native Spanish-speaking children in American schools (Moll, 1988; Moll & Diaz, 1987). Moll and colleagues have shown that deft alterations to these classroom structures can increase the quality and quantity of both participation and learning by Spanish-speaking children. In these case studies, talk structures provided opportunities for students to be proficient in two languages and task structures provided opportunities to exchange ideas about issues that were relevant to the students, school, and community. Moll's work also illustrates that changes in task and talk structures can be made by small groups of people in a manner that makes substantial differences to many students.

One case study describes shifts in reading instruction (Moll & Diaz, 1987). Initially, reading lessons in English consisted of large amounts of decoding but limited comprehension activities, as described in the traditional scenario. Subsequently, members of a bilingual research team changed the task and talk structures dramatically. The grade-level textbook was substituted for material that was several levels below grade, and the focus of instruction shifted from word-by-word reading to discussions of story content. New passages were read to students to facilitate story comprehension. In discussions, students and teachers switched to Spanish when needed to clarify the meaning of the text. By the third lesson, students were reading passages by themselves and answering comprehension questions at a comparable level to English monolingual readers at grade level.

In a case study of writing (Moll & Diaz, 1987), a similarly composed research team worked with teachers from several junior high schools in the same community. Researchers and teachers focused on writing instruction in bi-weekly sessions. When the project started, students were not doing any extended writing; rather, their writing consisted of copying and paraphrasing activities similar to those described by Bridge and Hiebert (1985).

From a study of writing in the community, researchers knew that writing in students' homes included functional tasks such as taking telephone messages, completing various forms, and responding to homework assignments. Parents valued education highly and viewed proficiency in writing as an essential part of literacy. Parental and community interests became the basis for a switch in the content and process of writing. Consequently, writing activities centered around information on community views that was collected through homework assignments. In one instance, widespread adoption of bilingualism was identified through class discussion as a significant community issue. Students created a questionnaire on the topic that they used to interview parents, peers, siblings, neighbors, and adults in the school. When data had been gathered, students compiled the information and described their findings in articles. There were differences in levels of involvement by teachers and peers in drafting, revising, and editing articles. Articles also differed as a function of students' fluency. However, all students, regardless of English fluency, took part in demanding and meaningful intellectual activities.

An increasing number of studies report growth in children's learning as a function of changes in task and talk structures. In each case, these studies involve an adjustment toward the transformative tradition by increasing diversity of the task diet, student generation of oral and written language, use of students' prior knowledge, or authenticity of school tasks. Goldenberg (1990) reports that changing the tasks of beginning literacy instruction for Spanish-speaking students involves them in participating as readers much more effectively than Spanish literacy programs that emphasize only the code. Feitelson, Kita, and Goldstein (1986) show that integrating a task like teacher read-aloud on a regular basis can increase low-income students' involvement as readers and writers. Elley and Mangubhai (1983) report increased participation of English-as-a-second-language students in reading trade books, resulting in reading and listening comprehension at twice the previous rate. Allen and Mason (1989) present a series of projects that document the effects of increases in generative writing and shared reading tasks. Cochran-Smith and Lytle (1990), in their review of studies involving teachers-as-researchers, point to shifts in the task and talk structures of reading and writing experiences. In Chapter 2, Langer provides additional examples of classrooms where task and talk structures have been restructured to draw on students' communication strengths in the context of authentic tasks.

RESTRUCTURING TASKS AND TALK:
CHALLENGES AND ISSUES

In a broad array of studies, task and talk structures have been shown to influence the effects of literacy instruction. In presenting evidence for this statement, instruction was examined from two distinctly different viewpoints. A traditional scenario, representing the lion's share of literacy instruction in American schools, was contrasted with a transformative scenario. In its essential form, the latter approach occurs infrequently in practice, and therefore several studies were described as moving toward the transformative scenario. Neither of these scenarios is considered ideal, though each serves a heuristic purpose in representing complex instructional environments. If neither scenario is to be aimed for, then what is the appropriate architecture of task and talk structures to foster literacy acquisition?

Distributions of Tasks and Talk

Task and talk structures can be productively addressed in terms of the teaching and learning "diet" that students experience in schools. It may be tempting to view particular task and talk structures as always preferable (at this point in time, structures that give precedence to meaning over form) and other structures as less preferable (such as tasks that focus on decontextualized skills). The crux of the issue lies not in determining which single task and talk configuration is universally superior. Because specific task and talk structures tend to "pull for" or enhance some educational outcomes more than others, choice of literacy goals must drive instructional architecture. Furthermore, achievement of multiple goals demands successful experiences in multiple task and talk structures. The situation is further complicated because the fit between task and talk structures, on the one hand, and educational outcomes, on the other, is not necessarily similar for students from different gender, racial, or sociocultural groups. Although it may never be possible to prescribe precise relationships between task and talk structures and outcomes for specific groups of students, the effects of distributions of these structures should be the focus of inquiry.

The authenticity of task and talk structures for particular groups of students presents another challenge. Although it may be desirable to have authentic task and talk structures operating in the classroom as often as possible, what constitutes authenticity in one context may be rendered unauthentic by marginal changes in the context. That is to say, authenticity pertains not to the task itself but to an interaction between task and context. This interaction effect was dramatically illustrated in the attempt to extrapolate the KEEP model to Navajo children (Vogt, Jordan, & Tharp, 1987). The talk structures that had worked with native Hawaiian children did not work with Navajo children. Both talk structures and forms of tasks needed to be changed, especially for contexts involving group cooperation. Reyes in Chapter 11 and Delpit (1986) raise analogous questions about use of certain whole-language and process-writing task and talk structures, such as use of dialogue journals in response to literature books and use of peer writing conferences, for students who do not bring particular strategies and experiences to the classroom.

By conceptualizing literacy instruction in terms of distributions of task and talk structures, the long-standing debate over skills-oriented versus meaningful-use-oriented strategies can be placed in a larger context. With this shift in perspective, the debate may become less oppositional as strands from both instructional approaches are woven together. In the classrooms studied by Fisher and Hiebert (1990a), activities that focused on skills generally were embedded within larger tasks. For example, students in both the skills-oriented and literature-based classrooms spent part of each day on spelling tasks (practicing spellings of words) that, on the surface, appeared to be similar. However, in the literature-based classrooms, most of the words were identified and selected by students after they had had difficulty with them in their reading or story writing. Practicing spelling of these words represents a learning task quite different from practicing words from a list that may have little or no relation to other current classroom learning activities. This embedding of skills within larger tasks grounded the acquisition and application of skills in a somewhat broader and more meaningful context. In the literature-based approach, students acquired skills in the context of one or more of the outcomes that constitute the reason for acquiring the skills in the first place. In the skills-oriented approach, acquisition of skills was the end point of instruction. The absence of scaffolding to support connections between skills and applications subsequently results in generally poor performance when skills are indirectly called for in problem-solving situations.

The distribution of task and talk structures is critical for all learners but may be particularly so for novices. It may be that appropriate distributions of task and talk structures are a function of unit of language or level of teacher guidance. Recent reviews of what works in beginning reading instruction by Adams (1990) and Stahl and Miller (1989) continue to recommend explicit guidance for beginning readers. This is not to suggest that instruction for young children should be didactic and unauthentic but rather that distributions of task and talk structures of effective beginning literacy experiences need to be examined in a variety of contexts and with a variety of student populations.

SUMMARY

Low levels of performance on literacy measures, rapid changes in the demography of the school population, and increasing differences in out-of-school literacy experiences among students have contributed to a pedagogical crisis. As the student population becomes more diverse, on several levels, traditional practices of literacy instruction are proving inappropriate for larger and larger numbers of children. The situation demands a significant shift in many practices of literacy instruction. This chapter has reviewed recent research that offers substantial guidance for restructuring literacy programs. Current literacy practices, as well as restructured practices for a more diverse student population, are framed in terms of schoolwork task and talk structures. The required shift in literacy instruction is outlined by contrasting task and talk structures in a traditional and a transformative scenario. Rather than attempting to identify a single best approach to literacy instruction, we argue for attending to the distributions of task and talk structures and for tuning these distributions to local pedagogical contexts.

REFERENCES

Adams, M. (1990). *Beginning to read: Thinking and learning about print.* Cambridge, MA: M.I.T. Press.

Allen, J., & Mason, J. M. (1989). *Risk makers, risk takers, risk breakers: Reducing the risks for young literacy learners.* Portsmouth, NH: Heinemann.

Allington, R. L. (1983). The reading instruction provided readers of different reading abilities. *Elementary School Journal, 83,* 549–559.

Anderson, A. B., & Stokes, S.&J. (1984). Social and institutional influences on the development and practice of literacy. In H. Goelman, A. Oberg, & F. Smith (Eds.), *Awakening to literacy* (pp. 24–37). Portsmouth, NH: Heinemann.

Anyon, J. (1981). Elementary schooling and distinctions of social class. *Interchange, 12,* 118–132.

Applebee, A. N., Langer, J. A., & Mullis, I. V. S. (1988) *Who reads best? Factors related to reading achievement in grades 3, 7, & 11.* Princeton, NJ: National Assessment of Educational Progress, ETS.

Applebee, A. N., Langer, J. A., & Mullis, I. V. S. (1989). *Crossroads in American education.* Princeton, NJ: National Assessment of Educational Progress, ETS.

Au, K. H., & Jordan, C. (1981). Teaching reading to Hawaiian children: Finding a culturally appropriate solution. In H. T. Treuba, G. P. Guthrie, & K. H. Au (Eds.), *Culture and the bilingual classroom: Studies in classroom ethnography* (pp. 139–152). Rowley, MA: Newbury House.

Au, K. H., & Mason, J. M. (1981). Social organizational factors in learning to read: The balance of rights hypothesis. *Reading Research Quarterly, 17,* 115–152.

Barker, R. G. (Ed.). (1963). *The stream of behavior: Exploration of its structure and content*. New York: Meredith.

Blumenfeld, P. C., & Meece, J. L. (1988). Task factors, teacher behavior, and students' involvement and use on learning strategies in science. *Elementary School Journal, 88,* 236–250.

Blumenfeld, P. C., Mergendoller, J., & Swarthout, D. (1987). Cumulative experience of task form: Its impact of students as thinkers and workers. *Journal of Curriculum Studies, 19,* 135–148.

Bridge, C. A., & Hiebert, E. H. (1985). A comparison of classroom writing practices, teachers' perceptions of their writing instruction, and textbook recommendations of writing practices. *Elementary School Journal, 86,* 155–172.

Brown, J. S., Collins, A., & Duguid, P. (1989). Situated cognition and the culture of learning. *Educational Researcher, 18,* 32–42.

Burke, S. M., Pflaum, S. W., & Krafle, J. D. (1982). The influence of black English on diagnosis of reading in learning-disabled and normal readers. *Journal of Learning Disabilities, 15,* 19–22.

Cazden, C. B. (1986). Classroom discourse. In M. Wittrock (Ed.), *Handbook of research on teaching* (3rd ed., pp. 432–463). New York: Macmillan.

Cochran-Smith, M., & Lytle, S. L. (1990). Research on teaching and teacher research: The issues that divide. *Educational Researcher, 19,* 2–11.

Delpit, L. D. (1986). Skills and other dilemmas of a progressive black educator. *Harvard Educational Review, 56,* 379–385.

Deniston, B. R., & Hiebert, E. H. (1983, October). *Teachers evaluations of children's reading and dialect differences*. Paper presented at the annual meeting of the College Reading Association, Atlanta, GA.

Doyle, W. (1983). Academic work. *Review of Educational Research, 53,* 159–199.

Dreeben, R. (1987). Closing the divide: What teachers and administrators can do to help black students reach their potential. *American Educator, 11,* 28–35.

Edwards, D., & Mercer, N. (1987). *Common knowledge: The development of understanding in the classroom*. New York: Methuen.

Elley, W. B., & Mangubhai, F. (1983). The impact of reading on second language learning. *Reading Research Quarterly, 19,* 53–67.

Feitelson, D., Kita, B., & Goldstein, Z. (1986). Effects of listening to series stories on first graders' comprehension and use of language. *Research in the Teaching of English, 20,* 339–356.

Fisher, C. W., & Hiebert, E. H. (1990a). Characteristics of tasks in two approaches to literacy instruction. *Elementary School Journal, 91,* 3–18.

Fisher, C. W., & Hiebert, E. H. (1990b, April). *Shifts in reading and writing tasks: Do they extend to social studies, science, and mathematics?* Paper presented at the annual meeting of the American Educational Research Association, Boston, MA.

Fraatz, J. M. B. (1987). *The politics of reading: Power, opportunity, and prospects for change in America's public schools*. New York: Teachers College Press.

Goldenberg, C. (1990). Beginning literacy instruction for Spanish-speaking children: Searching for a balanced approach. *Language Arts, 67,* 590–598.

Hagerty, P., Hiebert, E. H., & Owens, M. K. (1989). Students' comprehension, writing, and perceptions in two approaches to literacy instruction. In S. McCormick & J. Zutell (Eds.), *Cognitive and social perspectives for literacy research and instruction* (pp. 453–460). Chicago: National Reading Conference.

Heap, J. L. (1985). Discourse in the production of classroom knowledge: Reading lessons. *Curriculum Inquiry, 15,* 245–279.

Heath, S. B. (1983). *Ways with words.* New York: Cambridge University Press.

Hiebert, E. H. (1983). An examination of ability grouping for reading instruction. *Reading Research Quarterly, 18,* 231–255.

Hiebert, E. H., & Papierz, J. M. (1990). The emergent literacy construct and kindergarten and readiness books of basal reading series. *Early Childhood Research Quarterly, 5,* 317–334.

Jackson, P. (1986). *The practice of teaching.* New York: Teachers College Press.

Mergendoller, J. R. (Ed.). (1988). School work and academic tasks [Special issue]. *Elementary School Journal, 88.*

Michaels, S. (1981). "Sharing time": Children's narrative styles and differential access to literacy. *Language in Society, 10,* 423–442.

Moll, L. C. (1988, November). *Social and instructional issues in educating "disadvantaged" students.* Paper prepared for SRI's Committee on Curriculum and Instruction for the Study of Academic Instruction for Disadvantaged Students, Palo Alto, CA.

Moll, L. C., & Diaz, S. (1987). Change as the goal of educational research. *Anthropology & Education Quarterly, 18,* 300–311.

Moll, L. C., Estrada, E., Diaz, E., & Lopes, L. M. (1980). The organization of bilingual lessons: Implications for schooling. *The Quarterly Newsletter of the Laboratory of Comparative Human Cognition, 2,* 53–58.

Pellegrini, A. D., Perlmutter, J. C., Galda, L., & Brophy, G. H. (1990). Joint bookreading between black Head Start children and their mothers. *Child Development, 61,* 443–453.

Piestrup, A. (1973). *Black dialect interference and accommodation of reading instruction in first grade* (Monograph No. 4). Berkeley, CA: Language-Behavior Research Laboratory.

Rowan, B., & Guthrie, L. F. (1989). The quality of Chapter 1 instruction: Results from a study of 24 schools. In R. E. Slavin, N. L. Karweit, & N. A. Madden (Eds.), *Effective programs for students at risk.* Boston: Allyn & Bacon.

Stahl, S., & Miller, P. (1989). Whole language and language experience approaches for beginning reading: A quantitative research synthesis. *Review of Educational Research, 59,* 87–116.

Valencia, S., & Pearson, P. D. (1987). Reading assessment: Time for a change. *The Reading Teacher, 40,* 726–732.

Valencia, S., McGinley, W., & Pearson, P. D. (1990). Assessing literacy in the middle school. In G. G. Duffy (Ed.), *Reading in the middle school* (2nd ed., pp. 124–153). Newark, DE: International Reading Association.

Vogt, L., Jordan, C., & Tharp, R. (1987). Explaining school failure, producing school success: Two cases. *Anthropology & Education Quarterly, 18,* 276–286.

Vygotsky, L. S. (1962). *Thought and language.* Cambridge, MA: M.I.T. Press.

Wells, G. (1986). *The meaning makers: Children learning language and using language to learn.* Portsmouth, NH: Heinemann.

Wertsch, J. V. (Ed.). (1985). *Culture, communication, and cognition: Vygotskian perspectives.* New York: Cambridge University Press.

11 | A Process Approach to Literacy Instruction for Spanish-Speaking Students: In Search of a Best Fit

MARÍA DE LA LUZ REYES
University of Colorado, Boulder

The current constructivist view of learning and knowledge has contributed to a shift in literacy practices. There are numerous characterizations of a constructivist philosophy in literacy instruction, but among the most prominent are the writing-process model of Graves (1983, 1985) and the whole-language view of literacy (Goodman, 1986, 1989; Harste, 1989; Smith, 1986). Many teachers implement activities that emanate from writing-process and whole-language views through literature-based instruction. Reading and writing are integrated as students write responses to literature that they have read and as they use topics, genres, and techniques from literature in compositions. In the eyes of many teachers, the writing process and whole language combine to form a holistic process approach to literacy.

A process approach to literacy has been advocated and implemented on a large scale in language-arts frameworks of states like California and Pennsylvania. In particular, a process approach to literacy has been suggested as a solution in school districts where large numbers of their students are not performing at adequate levels of reading and writing proficiency. The students who have failed most are those with linguistic and cultural backgrounds that differ from the mainstream (Applebee, Langer, & Mullis, 1988; Applebee, Langer, & Mullis, 1986).

This chapter examines issues related to the use of process approaches in literacy with bilingual Hispanic students. In particular, it considers the use of dialogue journals for writing and literature logs for written responses to trade books. Following a review of literature on the use of dialogue journals and literature logs, the results from a study of Hispanic students using these genres will be presented. Findings of the study suggest problems in extrapolating, in exact form, practices designed for mainstream classrooms to ones with second-language learners. The chapter concludes with a discussion of considerations in restructuring process approaches to literacy with second-language learners.

PROCESS APPROACHES TO LITERACY:
EXAMPLES AND EXTENSIONS

In a growing number of American classrooms, teachers are integrating reading and writing activities through a process approach (see, e.g., Chapter 10). Classroom-based research indicates that a process approach to literacy assists students in controlling the writing task and communicating their ideas more effectively (Atwell, 1987; Calkins, 1986; Giacobbe, 1984; Graves, 1983). This literature also suggests that immersion in writing activities that emphasize process rather than product increases students' control over writing conventions like grammar and spelling and helps them develop a sense of audience, voice, and fluency (Atwell, 1987; Calkins, 1986; Graves, 1985; Hansen, 1987). Two popular methods that exemplify process approaches are dialogue journals and literature logs.

Examples of Process Approaches

Dialogue journals.   The use of interactive or dialogue journals to initiate and sustain ongoing written communication between student and teacher has been reported as effective, particularly in middle school settings (Atwell, 1987; Staton, Shuy, Payton, & Reed, 1988). Dialogue journals are said to be useful because they allow students and teachers to construct a mutually interesting text (Staton, 1980). Students initiate topics of interest and determine the length of entries. As they write, students can shift topics, ask questions, and seek help. Teachers respond to students' comments but not evaluatively.

Although most research on dialogue journals has been conducted with native English speakers, research with second-language writers is beginning to appear (Groves, 1980; Flores & García, 1984; Hayes & Bahruth, 1985; McGettigan, 1987; Staton et al., 1988). This literature shows that second-language learners are also gaining fluency in writing through dialogue journals. That is, students write longer passages. The journal format seems to offer second-language learners a nonthreatening, nongraded medium for communicating without the heavy emphasis on writing mechanics that can discourage novice writers. The informal conversationlike nature of this medium allows students to be "experts" in their own topics and to set the pace and tone of the communication while they are developing fluency. Although these are all positive outcomes, the literature on dialogue journals with second-language learners does not provide strong evidence that this writing improves writing form, a benefit that many claim with mainstream students.

Literature logs.   Literature logs are direct manifestations of the reading-writing connection in that the writing of literature logs derives from the books that students have read. Often, students' writing is based on books that they have selected themselves, whereas in other instances, students respond to books from a recommended reading list or ones that teachers have presented in book talks or read-alouds. This task permits "written talk" about what students read and assists students in thinking through content, raising questions about its veracity, and comparing the text with their own experiences. The source of writing is not solely dependent on personal experiences, as is the case with dialogue journals, but relies on comprehension of reading content. Writing in literature logs, then, requires completion of several tasks: reading a book, comprehending its content, and selecting key ideas from the book to use in the written response.

Unlike dialogue journals, literature logs do not necessarily require a written response from teachers, although some teachers choose to comment on what students have read and written and to share their own interests in books (Atwell, 1987). Another uniqueness of literature logs relative to dialogue journals is that they are frequently viewed as measures of performance in literacy and may be evaluated as fulfilling an academic requirement and may even be assigned a grade.

Process Approaches with Diverse Learners

Claims of positive benefits resulting from the implementation of process approaches to literacy through dialogue journals and literature logs have been reported with mainstream students at virtually every level (Atwell, 1987; Calkins, 1986; Emig, 1983; Graves, 1985; Staton et al., 1988). Although whole-language advocates argue strongly that there is abundant research supporting its efficacy (Goodman, 1989), questions abound on the research evidence for the superiority of process approaches (see, e.g., McKenna, Robinson, & Miller, 1990). For instance, the literature is silent on the efficacy of these instructional innovations with nonmainstream students in general and with second-language learners in particular.

Delpit (1986, 1988) suggests that a process approach to literacy may be a drawback for African-American children because they do not possess the appropriate discourse styles valued and used in the classroom. Differences in discourse styles may lead to misunderstandings of both teacher and student roles and expectations in learning. Minority groups who hold teachers in high regard, for example, may rely on and expect some direct guidance from teachers—a feature not so evident in process classrooms where teachers function more as facilitators than as intervenors (Pearson, 1989). Macias's (1989) work with Hispanic students and Siddle's (1986) work with African-American students indicate that these minority pupils expected that, if they needed to learn something, teachers would point it out. Instruction based on process approaches that emphasize student choice in writing topics, book selection, and communicating ideas without concern with form may lead to misunderstanding about tasks. Students may regard teachers' failure to correct errors as approval of their work and, as a consequence, fail to show improvement.

Recent work in writing-process classrooms (Reyes, 1990a) extends Delpit's examination of process approaches with students of diverse cultural backgrounds to students who are proficient in Spanish but have limited or no English skills when entering school. The emerging evidence from this work calls for an examination of the ways in which such approaches are implemented with nonmainstream students, particularly second-language learners who must deal with different language-processing demands.

A CASE STUDY OF A PROCESS APPROACH
TO LITERACY WITH SECOND-LANGUAGE LEARNERS

Over the course of an academic year, the dialogue journals and literature logs of 10 Hispanic, bilingual sixth-grade students were examined. The students all came from a bilingual classroom in a metropolitan school district where the official policy was "whole language" in bilingual education. Mrs. Sands, the teacher, reported that she was organizing literacy experiences around the whole-language philosophy, including process-writing activities. In brief, the study explored how the construction of meaning differed in first and second language and how implementation of the process approach affected outcomes for second-language learners. Weekly observations of classroom language arts periods focused on the social context of writing, including the medium of instruction, student-teacher interactions, organization of literacy events, assignment of tasks, and use of materials. Detailed information on data gathering and analysis can be found in Reyes (1990a). Three aspects of students' writing in the two genres (literature logs and dialogue journals) are considered here.

Themes

Some recurring topics and themes emerged in the dialogue journals (in order of importance): family, culturally specific objects, events or places, personal interaction with the teacher, and school-related incidents. More complex ideas and greater writing fluency occurred when students initiated topics around their families or culturally specific events. Familiarity with the topic allowed students to write with a confident voice as "experts." In contrast, writing entries that related to school were often shorter (rarely more than two or three sentences) and, for the most part, purely functional, as in "Where can I buy another notebook?" or "I lost my library book."

Another salient feature of these bilingual students' journal writing was their close bond with the teacher and their dependence on her guidance. The teacher's promptings, encouragement, interest, or disinterest affected the length and elaboration of a topic. Students expressed an emotional bond with the teacher and depended heavily on her responses, to the point that they felt personally slighted when she missed writing in their journals. Some typical comments included, "You're the best teacher." "How come some times you don't write back?" "You forgot to write!" Sometimes, students approached interactions with the teacher seriously and respectfully, even taking the teacher's attempts at humor literally. The following exchange took place when the teacher wrote to a student explaining that she had not written in his journal because of her heavy work load. (All examples of students' writings are unedited. Pseudonyms are used throughout.)

Dear Mrs. S.
    Why don't yuo tell me about your probles.

The teacher wrote the following tongue-in-cheek response:

Dear Miguel,
    Where should I start? I'm just kidding. I do have a problem with my work. To you students it probably seems we teachers don't do much, but the truth is that we work all day and all night and never get through. I think that's my biggest problem right now. Do you think I shouldn't work as hard?
                                                                    Mrs. S.

Accepting the challenge, Miguel provided the following advice:

Mrs. S. you should tried harder with your work, like that you could finish your work. And you should tried to solve your problems. I all wes work harder with my work. And I allwes tried to solve my problems [extra space left here] you should tried what I do.

Contrary to popular perception that many Hispanic students suffer from poor self-concepts, the journal entries reflected both positive and negative self-concepts and attitudes toward school. In come cases, students expressed concern about academic tasks, for example, "Mrs. I really don't like reading I try but I never get the hang of the book or I don't read far enough . . ." In other cases, students wrote positively about school:

> Yes I do like this school, its great. Well I miss my old school. I liked it to, like I like this school . . . I had shost [just] one best friend, his name was Jose. We were the best students in the classroom. We were the best on math, science, reading, art, story, and going speling test.

In the literature logs, there were few discernible themes. The typical literature-log entry was a one- or two-line summary of the story, for example, "I'm reading (*book title*). It is about (*character*) who does (*XYZ*)." Students did not elaborate on the contents of their books. Some other responses centered around the teacher's questions about their books, "Yes, I'm finished and that's sad because she got sick and died." In general, the literature logs contained little substance or evidence of reflective thinking on their readings, suggesting little control over the task.

Language Use

The students used Spanish and English freely in their dialogue journals, and the teacher generally matched the students' language. By using the students' primary language, the teacher validated Spanish for school tasks and allowed them to develop fluency at a good comfort level. However, when the teacher imposed English before the student him- or herself initiated it, construction of meaning was affected negatively. The task of writing in their weaker language constrained students' control of the task, and their focus shifted to form rather than development of ideas. In one case, the teacher suggested that the student write in English and she would respond in Spanish so that both could practice their second language. The result was devastating, as indicated by the student's journal response: "I don't now very good the English. If I don't now how to write soting in English I will write in Espanish." Although the student eventually complied with the teacher's request to write, she stopped writing in her journal for a time, and, when she resumed, she wrote shorter, less complex ideas. This pattern confirms Moll and Diaz's (1987) finding that, when students are overly concerned with English production, higher order skills in literacy suffer.

Although English and Spanish were generally permitted in oral communication and dialogue journals, there was an unspoken rule that the literature-log entries were to be in English. The teacher responded only in English, even when students initiated their writing in Spanish.

Code switching, the alteration of Spanish and English in the same entry, appeared infrequently in either dialogue journals or literature logs. This finding is consistent with Edelsky's (1986) research with other bilingual writers. In oral communication, code switching was common for students, but in their written communication it occurred less frequently.

Skills

A notable finding from both dialogue journals and literature logs was that, even over time, the students did not attend to correct form in their writing. The classroom-based research of Atwell (1987) and Graves (1985), among others, implies that exposure to correct models of conventional form in journals, literature logs, and other writing genres helps students learn and apply correct form. This was not the case with these bilingual students. The teacher conducted daily writing conferences with individuals, peer conferences, and mini-lessons to focus on specific writing problems of students, but the students did not make any lasting improvement in using these conventions in their writing.

There was a high incidence of inventive spelling in the writing of these second-language learners. The errors were by no means arbitrary; the inventive spelling in Spanish and in English and the use of Spanish phonemes for English words and vice versa demonstrated that students were using their phonemic and orthographic knowledge of Spanish and English to construct meaning. This high frequency of inventive spelling may be symptomatic of students' juggling of two linguistic systems and the transition from Spanish to English writing. It may also be that, although oral Spanish was permitted in the classroom and many students chose to write in Spanish, they did so without the benefit of formal writing instruction in Spanish.

PROBLEMS IN IMPLEMENTING A PROCESS APPROACH WITH SECOND-LANGUAGE LEARNERS

The process approach for these bilingual students certainly had positive effects. Children were writing extensively and were exposed to good literature. The teacher was doing many exemplary things: sharing her love for books, modeling reflective writing, and matching language use in dialogue journals. However, despite extensive opportunities to write, students did not achieve the high levels of writing that Atwell (1987) and others describe of mainstream students in process classrooms. Students were not filling pages with their responses about books. Their writing in dialogue journals, while more abundant than that in literature logs, did not grow more sophisticated in the conventions of language.

Even though there were positive results and potential for even more impressive results, there were clearly problems. Determining what these problems are and how they can be alleviated is critical if optimal gains are to be obtained from constructivist approaches with an increasingly diverse student population.

An immediate explanation by advocates of process approaches may be that this teacher's efforts were not "real" whole language or writing process. The manner in which teachers transform philosophy into practice is an issue with process approaches, as it is with any instructional philosophy. However, an examination of this teacher's implementation indicates that a search for explanations must move to more deep-seated factors that are not idiosyncratic to this teacher.

The Nature of the Teacher's Implementation

The school district in which Mrs. Sands taught had adopted a process approach for bilingual instruction. Educators central to the conceptualization and dissemination of the whole-language and writing-process philosophies had provided training for the teachers in the school district over a period of time. Mrs. Sands had been part of this training and continued to attend classes and workshops. She designed her classroom literacy program around recommendations from workshops on process approaches.

In implementing these activities, Mrs. Sands encouraged students to write dialogue journals in their first or second languages. Though not Hispanic, the teacher was fluent in Spanish and English, informed about Hispanic culture, and sensitive to the backgrounds and needs of her students. By asking informed questions such as "Sabes hacer pan dulce?" (Do you know how to make [Mexican] sweet bread?), she validated students' language and culture and responded sensitively to linguistic and cultural needs when students felt unsure or embarrassed. More importantly for these bilingual students, Mrs. Sands responded affectionately and respectfully to their feelings as in statements "I'm sorry I didn't write back" or "I missed you, too." At all times, the teacher projected genuine interest in individuals as evident in her comments to students in the dialogue journals, like "I do wish you good luck on your green belt in karate" or "You seemed very tired today. Are you getting enough sleep?" She inquired about family members as in asking a student about her sister ("How does María like Lincoln High?"). She often interacted with students in a way that reminded them that she, too, was a learner, as in "You will have to explain what *kata* is. I'm not very informed." She nudged, motivated, and encouraged students to write and read more. In all respects, she was an above-average teacher.

So why were students' contributions to the literature logs weak and why did students fail to grow in conventions of language in their writing in the dialogue journals? Several underlying assumptions about literacy and language contributed to the less than optimal growth of students, the most basic of which was a view of the primacy of English as the language of academic tasks. In addition, an emphasis on several basic assumptions of whole language may act against the needs of second-language learners.

The Role of English for Academic Tasks in Bilingual Classrooms

Although the theory of bilingual learning supports opportunities for second-language learners to acquire concepts in their native languages while learning English, the use of primary language is minimal in practice (Halcón, 1983). Even in bilingual programs where native-language instruction is permitted, there is a deeply rooted fear that students will not learn English well enough or fast enough, a sentiment heard in the comments of the teachers studied by Miramontes and Commins in Chapter 6. The operating assumption is that if the task is academic, then it should be conducted in English. In traditional and bilingual programs, English is treated as though it were synonymous with literacy (Reyes, 1990b). Although this assumption is not part of underlying whole-language or writing-process philosophies, it has a great deal to do with the policies and practices of schools for minority students (see Chapters 6 and 15) and impacts the nature of minority students' experiences and performances.

This assumption was very evident in the school district in which the case-study classroom was located. District policy called for all language arts classes in the bilingual program to be treated as "English to speakers of other languages," thus establishing English as the official medium of instruction. This mandate undermined the true spirit of bilingual education and process approaches. Not only were students unable to develop proficiency in academic tasks through using their native languages, they had to struggle in academic tasks in a language in which they were not entirely fluent. For example, students' lack of proficiency in the literature logs illustrates the consequences of this assumption. The literature logs clearly fell under the purview of "formal literacy" instruction and were therefore conducted solely in English. Questions of cultural relevance, authenticity of tasks, language proficiency, and teacher guidance were ignored.

Assumptions of Teachers, Tasks, and Skill Instruction in Process Approaches

In theory, whole language allows the use of native language in literacy activities, as is evident in Goodman's (1986) statement, "Whole language programs get it all together: the language, the culture, the community, the learner, and the teacher" (p. 8). An emphasis on several fundamental assumptions within process approaches related to teachers' roles, children's knowledge of school tasks, and proportion of time spent in explicit instruction can act to the disadvantage of second-language learners. Educators with a whole-language perspective tend to emphasize these assumptions and to exclude ideas that relate to adaptations for second-language learners. The nature of these assumptions underlying process approaches and how they can act against linguistically different students are illustrated in this case study.

A fundamental assumption of process approaches is that teachers function primarily as creators of contexts and as facilitators of learning, not as the source and transmitter of knowledge. This role may create dissonance with a cultural group's expectations of teachers. The Hispanic second-language learners in the case study sought the teacher's help in selecting books, but Mrs. Sands chose not to impose her "expertise"; instead, she exhorted students to keep trying to find books to their liking. A mere invitation to keep looking for an appropriate book without explicit assistance led to some students' failure to complete the task. The teacher was left with the impression that students lacked motivation to learn. The assumption that all students flourish in classrooms where there is ample freedom to choose activities and where the teacher's role is that of facilitator raises some doubts relative to these second-language learners.

There was also evidence that students were often confused with the goals of different tasks. Most students perceived the literature logs and dialogue journals to be informal means of communicating with the teacher. They got in trouble for trying to socialize with the teacher by expressing affection, interjecting personal topics, and failing to view the literature log as a businesslike diary, which was the teacher's view of the task.

A third feature of process approaches that relates to the nature, focus, and relative emphasis of skill instruction also acts against second-language learners. Following the directions of leading process-approach educators, Mrs. Sands presented information about language conventions in minilessons and conferences. Neither context made the what, how, and when of language usage sufficiently clear to most students. The amount of time for these lessons was brief relative to that spent in process activities. Students failed to see a connection between the lessons and their writing in dialogue journals and literature logs and so continued to make the same mistakes. The teacher's attempts at indirect mediation are contrary to the explicit guidance that children from nonmainstream backgrounds may expect (Delpit, 1988).

Many whole-language educators see these assumptions to be the crux of process approaches (Goodman, 1986), and little attention is given to examining the fit of these assumptions with different groups of students. This failure for reflection was evident in the staff development that was provided by prominent whole-language and writing-process educators to the bilingual teachers in this district. These sessions paid little, if any, heed to adjustments that might need to be made for children as a function of language fluency and cultural background. The failure of these leaders to point out the need for linguistic and cultural modification when using these practices with second-language learners encouraged the notion that process instruction works equally well with all students regardless of backgrounds. Through sustained training that deemphasized the accommodations for linguistically different students, even outstanding teachers like Mrs. Sands began to distrust their own best judgments. The result was that teachers did not provide the needed mediation and scaffolding of tasks for students. The program director in the district had gone so far as to issue the directive that "no more than 10 minutes should be devoted to teaching skills in whole-language classrooms." Teachers like Mrs. Sands were left with the impression that "things take time" and that the processes would work eventually—if only they allowed the process to take its natural course.

ISSUES IN RESTRUCTURING PROCESS APPROACHES FOR SECOND-LANGUAGE LEARNERS

This preceding discussion of problems with process approaches for second-language learners should not be taken as advocating a return to a skills-oriented perspective or a departure from a constructivist view of learning. Many positive things were occurring in the case-study classroom that need to be continued. If an understanding of students' cultural and linguistic backgrounds can be gained, some shifts in the tasks and instruction of a process approach may mean more productive literacy-learning contexts for students. In redesigning process classrooms for second-language learners, a number of factors need to be considered, including a balancing of tasks, creation of culturally relevant tasks, and scaffolding of tasks.

For some students, mere exposure to correct form may be sufficient for proficient application. For many culturally different students who do not belong to the "culture of power" (Delpit, 1988), more explicit instruction and culturally relevant tasks may be necessary to apply particular strategies and skills consistently, in addition to abundant opportunities for writing and reading.

This need for guidance in conventions of language is especially critical, given the evidence on how language-minority students are measured on large-scale writing assessments (Reyes, 1990c). The use of student writing samples on such assessments does not advantage language-minority students, as García and Pearson suggest in Chapter 18. Indeed, nonmainstream students in process classrooms who have been encouraged to express themselves without regard for mechanics may be even more at a disadvantage (Delpit, 1988; Reyes, 1990c). A recent study by Reyes (1990c) shows that nonnative English speakers' writing may be judged even more harshly on the basis of mechanics because their limited English proficiency makes the errors more obvious as they struggle to control the writing task in their weaker language.

In the case study, it was evident that students did not find cultural relevance in the literature-log activities. The assumption of process approaches that the use of trade books constitutes "authentic" tasks fails to consider that authenticity is highly subjective and relative to individual interest, as well as social, cultural, and linguistic appropriateness. The lack of available books in Spanish, the lack of opportunity to write in their native language, the teacher's hesitance in assisting students in finding books, and the lack of culturally relevant books contributed to tasks that were far from authentic. Furthermore, other dimensions that would make tasks authentic for students with diverse backgrounds were not cultivated. Rarely was a topic extrapolated from the journals or literature logs for public consumption or sharing with the whole class. There were few opportunities for students to write for different audiences, learn other genres, or revise compositions for sharing with others. Moll and colleagues (Moll, 1989; Moll & Diaz, 1987) illustrate the manner in which authentic writing tasks can be created, where students interact extensively with one another on topics of cultural interest that extend into the community (see Chapters 2 and 10 for further discussions of such tasks).

Process approaches to literacy for second-language learners should also consider the importance of scaffolding of tasks, not just the scaffolding of interactions that Palincsar and David describe in Chapter 9. Scaffolding of tasks calls for guidance from teachers as students participate in new tasks. Only an array of instructional contexts that include small-group teacher-led conferences, peer groups, and whole-class instruction will ensure that a diversity of learners will be accommodated in classrooms.

SUMMARY

Through the use of literature, process approaches in reading and writing have converged. Although such approaches offer the potential for many positive benefits for all students, to date they have not yielded satisfactory results for culturally or linguistically different learners. Many implementations of process approaches, and the training of teachers to use these approaches, have assumed that the same activities can be implemented with all students regardless of social, cultural, or linguistic uniquenesses. The case study in this project suggests that this assumption cannot be made. When this assumption is coupled with the idea that English is the language of academic tasks, students with diverse backgrounds are at a disadvantage in process approaches and fail to get the full benefit. With adjustments in process approaches that attend to the balancing, authenticity, and scaffolding of tasks, students of diverse backgrounds may be able to attain the literacy levels necessary for full participation in a technological society.

The continued depressed performance of minorities on literacy assessments (Applebee, Langer, & Mullis, 1988; Applebee, Langer, & Mullis, 1986) offers a compelling argument for these adjustments in process approaches for students with diverse backgrounds. If any instructional approach is to yield optimal benefits, *it must be tailored to the academic needs of learners*. To do less is to exacerbate existing problems for subgroups within a "nation (already) at risk."

REFERENCES

Applebee, A. N., Langer, J. A., & Mullis, I. V. S. (1986). *The writing report card: Writing achievement in American schools.* Princeton, NJ: National Assessment of Educational Progress, ETS.

Applebee, A. N., Langer, J. A., & Mullis, I. V. S. (1988). *Who reads best? Factors related to reading achievement in grades 3, 7, and 11.* Princeton, NJ: National Assessment of Educational Progress, ETS.

Atwell, N. (1987). *In the middle: Writing, reading, and learning with adolescents.* Portsmouth, NH: Boynton/Cook.

Calkins, L. M. (1986). *The art of teaching writing.* Portsmouth, NH: Heinemann.

Delpit, L. D. (1986). Skills and other dilemmas of a progressive black educator. *Harvard Educational Review, 56,* 379–385.

Delpit, L. D. (1988). The silenced dialogue: Power and pedagogy in educating other people's children. *Harvard Educational Review, 58,* 280–298.

Edelsky, C. (1986). *Writing in a bilingual program: Había una vez.* Norwood, NJ: Ablex.

Emig, J. (1983). *The web of meaning: Essays on writing, teaching, learning, and thinking*. Upper Montclair, NJ: Boynton/Cook.

Flores, B. M., & García, E. A. (1984). A collaborative learning and teaching experience using journal writing. *National Association for Bilingual Education Journal, 7*, 67–83.

Giacobbe, M. E. (1984, October). Helping children become more responsible for their writing. *Live Wire*.

Goodman, K. (1986). *What's whole in whole language?* Portsmouth, NH: Heinemann.

Goodman, K. (1989). Whole-language research: Foundations and development. *Elementary School Journal, 90*, 207–221.

Graves, D. H. (1983). *Writing: Teachers & children at work*. Portsmouth, NH: Heinemann.

Graves, D. H. (1985). The reader's audience. In J. Hansen, T. Newkirk, & D. Graves (Eds.), *Breaking ground: Teachers relate reading and writing in the elementary school* (pp. 193–199). Portsmouth, NH: Heinemann.

Groves, P. L. (1980). *The writing of Micronesian ESL students* (Technical Report 143). (ERIC Document Reproduction Service No. ED 247 573)

Hansen, J. (1987). *When writers read*. Portsmouth, NH: Heinemann.

Halcón, J. J. (1983). A structural profile of basic title VII (Spanish-English) bilingual bicultural education programs. *The Journal of the National Association for Bilingual Education, 7*, 55–73.

Hayes, C. W., & Bahruth, R. (1985). Querer es poder. In J. Hansen, T. Newkirk, & D. Graves (Eds.), *Breaking ground: Teachers relate reading and writing in the elementary school* (pp. 97–108). Portsmouth, NH: Heinemann.

Harste, J. (1989). The future of whole language. *Elementary School Journal, 90*, 243–249.

Macias, J. (1989, April). *Transnational educational anthropology: The case of immigrant Mexican students*. Paper presented at the annual meeting of the American Educational Research Association, San Francisco, CA.

McGettigan, K. (1987). Dialogue journals: An initiation into writing. *Reading, Writing, & Learning Disabilities, 3*, 321–332.

McKenna, M., Robinson, R. D., & Miller, J. W. (1990). Whole language: A research agenda for the nineties. *Educational Researcher. 19* (8), 3–6.

Moll, L. C. (1989). Teaching second language students: A Vygotskian perspective. In D. M. Johnson & D. H. Roen (Eds.), *Richness in writing* (pp. 55–69). White Plains, NY: Longman.

Moll, L. C., & Diaz, S. (1987). Change as the goal of educational research. *Anthropology & Education Quarterly, 18*, 300–311.

Pearson, P. D. (1989). Reading the whole-language movement. *Elementary School Journal, 90*, 231–241.

Reyes, M. de la Luz (1990a). *A process approach to literacy with second language learners*. Boulder: University of Colorado.

Reyes, M. de la Luz (1990b). *Challenging venerable assumptions: A multicultural language arts alternative*. Boulder: University of Colorado.

Reyes, M. de la Luz (1990c, April). *Bilingual students' pre and post writing samples*. Paper presented at the annual meeting of the American Educational Research Association, Boston, MA.

Siddle, E. V. (1986). *A critical assessment of the natural process approach to teaching writing*. Unpublished qualifying paper, Harvard University.

Smith, F. (1986). *Insult to intelligence*. New York: Arbor House.

Staton, J. (1980). Writing and counseling: Using a dialogue journal. *Language Arts, 57*, 514–518.

Staton, J., Shuy, R., Payton, J. K., & Reed, L. (1988). *Dialogue journal communication*. Norwood, NJ: Ablex.

12 | Enhancing Literacy Through Cooperative Learning

MICHAEL S. MELOTH
University of Colorado, Boulder

Ruddell and Sperling (1988) recently voiced a concern of many educators when they observed that research findings rarely appear to have any direct impact on practice. Periodically, however, a method comes along that seems particularly appealing to educators and its adoption becomes widespread. A case in point is cooperative learning. The attention cooperative learning has received from the educational community has prompted Slavin (1987) to state that "the age of cooperation is approaching" (p. 7). Perhaps it is true. In contrast to teacher-centered instruction, cooperative learning encourages students to become actively involved with their learning by working together, sharing their ideas, and providing assistance to their peers. Cooperative learning also seems an equitable method because its goal is to provide *all* learners with access to important information about comprehension. In doing so, the detrimental effects of homogeneous ability grouping and gender and cultural stereotyping are reduced or eliminated. This method also appears theoretically sound in that it fits nicely within the social constructivist view of teaching and learning found throughout this volume (e.g., Chapters 9, 10, and 13).

More cynical educators, however, might caution that Slavin's optimism is a bit premature. In the past, other highly regarded instructional methods also viewed students as more than passive recipients of teacher talk, sought to make access to information more equitable, and were based on then current theories of teaching and learning. One obvious example is mastery learning, which posited that virtually all students, regardless of ability or background, could master essential information when opportunity to learn and quality of instruction were maximized (Bloom, 1985). Today, only pockets of mastery learning programs survive, although some of its basic elements, like criterion-referenced testing, remain in many schools.

Hindsight offers numerous reasons why highly regarded methods like mastery learning failed (Stallings & Stipek, 1986). One explanation is that it relied on comparative studies conducted under highly controlled conditions to establish its viability and therefore failed to address the realities of day-to-day instruction. As a result, teachers had little information to guide its implementation. At the present time, cooperative-learning research is proceeding down the same path; virtually every study is an experimental one, yet few data are available to inform educators about how this approach fits within the many competing goals, tensions, and constraints of daily classroom life. Without such information, successful implementation is likely to be difficult and the high expectations for this method may go unrealized.

The purpose of this chapter is to examine three instructional variables that can have a marked impact on how cooperative learning is used in classrooms and, ultimately, what students learn through collaboration: teachers' belief systems about cooperative learning, cooperative tasks used to promote comprehension, and ways in which instructional talk orients students' discussions in collaborative groups. Although these three variables are not exhaustive, they serve as a partial template for examining cooperative learning and other instructional practices.

The definition of cooperative learning that guides this chapter deserves attention. The practice goes by many names, such as collaborative learning, peer-group interactions, small-group discussions, and so on. Additionally, it can take many forms, although the best known to teachers are those advocated by Slavin (1989a), Johnson and Johnson (1987), and Palincsar and David (Chapter 9). This chapter is not concerned with any particular cooperative-learning approach. Therefore, the term *cooperative learning* is used in a generic sense to refer to all forms of peer-group instruction.

THE ROLE OF BELIEFS SYSTEMS IN COOPERATIVE LEARNING

Belief systems go by a variety of terms, including implicit or folk theories and concepts of instruction (Clark & Peterson, 1986). Whatever the term, they refer to teachers' knowledge about the purpose of schooling, appropriate roles for themselves and students, and the nature of knowledge acquisition. These beliefs, in turn, influence the ways teachers plan, organize, and deliver instruction. The foundations of belief systems are formed through years of observation as students (Buchmann, 1989). Through these observations, beliefs about teaching and learning become firmly ingrained and highly resistant to change (Zeichner & Liston, 1987).

Belief systems affect teachers' ability and willingness to adopt newer instructional methods (Richardson, in press) as well as determine the organization and delivery of daily instruction. For example, Rich (1990) found that teachers who received staff development training in cooperative learning often failed to implement it. This was attributed to a lack of congruence between teachers' ideologies (i.e., beliefs) about schooling and their perceptions of cooperative learning. Most teachers, according to Rich, believed the primary purpose of schooling is to ensure that students acquire academic skills; children's social and personal development are less important or even inappropriate goals of education. Cooperative learning was viewed as primarily a means to improve social skills and self-esteem. Rich concludes that the incongruence between teachers' beliefs about the purpose of schooling (academic) and the goals of collaboration (social) is deeply ingrained. As a result, teachers not only resist making changes but may actually engage in passive (and not so passive) acts that "sabotage" the implementation of cooperative learning.

Palincsar, Stevens, & Gavelek's (1989) concerns about teacher beliefs are similar to Rich's (1990). In trying to understand why an established cooperative-learning program (in this case, reciprocal teaching) did not result in any appreciable achievement gains, Palincsar et al. interviewed 25 teachers about the value of collaborative activities. Teachers mentioned that collaboration was beneficial because it helped students become more actively involved in their learning and provided opportunities to build confidence, obtain peer approval, and improve social skills. Rarely mentioned were the cognitive benefits of collaboration. When probed, these teachers surprisingly mentioned that collaborative groups were most useful for drill and practice. In effect, teachers held a "knowledge transmission" view of teaching and learning, that is, learning is best accomplished when actively transmitted from expert teachers to novice learners. First-grade teachers especially expressed skepticism about whether young children possessed academic knowledge that could be shared with other students. This mismatch between teachers' beliefs and the theory behind reciprocal teaching was identified by Palincsar et al. as a major factor likely to lead to unsuccessful implementation.

Two recent studies by Meloth and Deering (1990a, 1990b) suggest that, even when teachers report having changed in their instructional beliefs and practice substantially for several years, the academic orientation of cooperative learning may be weak. Over two studies, 12 third- through sixth-grade teachers were asked about the purposes and goals of their reading instruction. All teachers had taken at least one course each in whole-language and cooperative learning through district-sponsored staff development programs or from local universities. In addition, each reported using these methods on a consistent basis (i.e., three times per week) for a minimum of 2 years. Informal observations indicated that teachers did, indeed, use collaborative-learning methods that fit within a whole-language or literature-based framework. Further, instruction did provide students with the opportunity for collaborative discussions about literacy. Teachers reported that cooperative activities were the preferred form of instruction because they provided students with access to important information about literacy processes and a richer understanding and appreciation of literacy. When asked to describe how specific cooperative-reading activities would improve learning, teachers responded in a fashion similar to Palincsar et al.'s teachers by emphasizing social skills but rarely mentioning cognitive benefits.

Meloth and Deering (1990a, 1990b) also found support for a dilemma posed by Slavin (1989b). According to Slavin, cooperative learning appeals mainly to humanistic teachers who are uncomfortable with high levels of structure and extrinsic incentives, two of the factors that have explained achievement in cooperative learning. Only 2 of the 12 teachers studied by Meloth and Deering used grades or other forms of extrinsic rewards during cooperative learning, and these uses did not conform to the highly structured systems associated with achievement gains in cooperative-learning experiments. The remaining teachers, although aware of the emphasis on incentive systems in cooperative-learning models, used positive praise and encouragement and perceived grades to affect motivation and self-esteem detrimentally.

An implicit assumption underlying the work of Rich (1990), Palincsar et al. (1989), and Meloth and Deering (1990a, 1990b) is that teachers' failure to modify their beliefs to those of theorists may result in the ineffective use of cooperative learning. This assumption requires careful consideration. On the one hand, it seems appropriate for teachers to modify beliefs, if in so doing the likelihood is increased that students will engage in higher order thinking because of cooperative learning. On the other hand, it seems presumptuous and short-sighted to require changes if they may actually deter learning and motivation. The debate about motivation and extrinsic incentives is by no means resolved theoretically or empirically. For example, some forms of cooperation like reciprocal teaching (see Chapter 9) do not use incentive systems and yet report positive achievement gains. Thus, staff-development and teacher-education programs need to move cautiously in what they advocate.

COOPERATIVE-LITERACY TASKS

The tasks of cooperative-literacy activities, just as with other instructional modes, direct students' thinking and action (Doyle, 1983). Classroom tasks go through transformations as teachers and students define them, with participants' definitions not necessarily the same (Marx & Walsh, 1988). In other words, what a student gets from a task may be quite different from what a teacher intended.

Most classroom tasks have been characterized as requiring the reproduction of knowledge, that is, the rote memorization and recall of facts or skills. These tasks do little to promote the acquisition of cognitive and metacognitive processes necessary for independent learning skills nor do they help students make connections between the task and reading. The consequences of continuous exposure to and evaluation of reproduction tasks are that students are often left with the impression that learning may be less pressing than accomplishing work on time with a minimum of errors (Anderson, 1990).

However, not all good tasks are "higher order" ones; it is the context within which these tasks are accomplished that is important. When the context allows students to make connections between the task at hand and literacy use in general, the task is considered authentic (Chapter 10). For example, simply identifying "who, what, when, where, and why" involves routine "right there" text reinspection strategies (Raphael & Pearson, 1985). However, when students work together to discuss how strategies can provide readers with a schema for understanding stories in general, the task becomes more authentic.

A strength of the work of Palincsar (see Chapter 9) relates to the role of authenticity; only interesting and informative tasks that involve essential comprehension strategies are part of reciprocal teaching. These tasks ensure that focused discussions of text go beyond literal content to a richer understanding of the text and strategies that support meaning-making. Strategies that are critical to make meaning of a text form the starting point for group discussions. The discussion is then oriented toward acquiring the critical meanings of a text.

Other cooperative-learning programs take a quite different approach. For example, the fundamental issue for Slavin (1989a) and Johnson and Johnson (1987) centers on inducing collaboration by teaching students cooperative skills, manipulating reward structures, and/or constructing activities that require collaboration (Bossert, 1988). The nature of the task is of secondary importance in these programs; Johnson and Johnson (1987) suggest that learning will occur regardless of whether the task is an authentic one, if cooperative skills are engaged.

The differences in orientation between Palincsar and Slavin and Johnson and Johnson have a profound influence on how teachers and students define cooperative tasks. Selecting a task from a "what are they going to learn" perspective as opposed to a "how are they going to learn it" approach communicates to teachers and students that understanding is valued above doing. Although Slavin (1986) has begun to identify cooperative group structures that are appropriate for different cognitive objectives, it is still unclear how these structures ensure that the task begins, and remains, an authentic one.

One caveat to the above discussion is warranted. Just because a method like reciprocal teaching encourages authentic tasks does not mean that teachers will always be able to create the conditions for authenticity. Palincsar et al. (1989) note that this is not always the case. Nor is it being suggested that those electing to use, for example, Slavin's Student Teams Achievement Divisions (STAD) approach will do so without concern for authenticity. However, research on teacher thinking (Clark & Peterson, 1986) has long shown that teachers typically plan and implement lessons around activities and content, rarely cognitive objectives. The organization and activities in many cooperative-learning programs may pull for them to be even more activity-oriented, rather than process-oriented, encouraging teachers to select on the basis of "cooperation" rather than authentic literacy use.

Even when tasks allow for authentic literacy use, students may transform the character of the tasks based on their past experiences with cooperative learning and concerns with accountability. For example, when Meloth and Deering (1990a) asked students to define the task of their cooperative literacy group, they consistently described the procedural dimensions of tasks, such as what was required to "get it done." Few students reported that the task would help them improve their ability to collaborate effectively. These responses were in sharp contrast to teachers' reports that the primary goal of the task was the improvement of students' cooperative skills. Additionally, although most students expressed little concern about whether they would receive good grades on the task, some expressed concern for peer reactions. In one classroom, where the cooperative activity was to create a play from a fable, students were concerned about failing in front of their peers, even though their teacher was not formally evaluating the play's quality. Teachers, however, indicated no awareness of students' concerns about public failure but believed that by eliminating grades or other formal accountability forms, students would pursue tasks for their intrinsic value.

A study by Ross and Raphael (1990) supports the role of task structure in student discussions and performance. They studied two teachers who were using a version of Slavin's (1986) STAD format in science. Whereas one teacher faithfully adhered to the guidelines for using STAD, the other interpreted these guidelines loosely. For example, in the structured STAD classroom, the teacher assigned each student in a group a specific role such as recorder or manager and required groups to follow a specified sequence of activities. In the other classroom, no roles were identified or assigned, and students determined the procedure that they would use to accomplish their task. Students in the classroom where STAD guidelines were faithfully followed learned less than peers in the classroom that permitted greater leeway in determining organization of discussions. Ross and Raphael hypothesized that the different task structures in the two classrooms affected the form and content of discussions and that these different communication patterns, in turn, affected student achievement.

Two additional issues surround cooperative tasks: level of ambiguity and risk associated with accomplishing a task. Ambiguity reflects the extent to which the product (i.e., the knowledge of reading to be acquired from the task) and the strategies that can be used to produce the product are familiar or easily identifiable. Risk is closely associated with accountability and refers to the consequences of failure on a particular task. Tasks that figure into end-of-semester grades, for example, are high in risk, whereas those that go un-evaluated are usually low. As ambiguity and risk increase, students often simplify the task so that it can be "successfully" accomplished (Doyle, 1987). In doing so, they often transform it into little more than routine "tried-and-true" procedures that require little cognitive effort and result in little cognitive improvement (Marx & Walsh, 1988). Implicit in this simplification is the notion that completing work on time will be accepted as evidence of learning, as often it is (Doyle, 1987).

This simplification was evident in the comments of students interviewed by Meloth and Deering (1990a). Although the collaborative activities appeared to provide the opportunity for discussions of comprehension, students reported that the goal of the task was to produce a document and described procedural routines to accomplish the goal. This simplification did not appear to help them understand how the task would benefit them as readers. In addition, their teachers did not formally evaluate students' strategies gained from the tasks, perhaps reinforcing students' perceptions that task accomplishment is sufficient evidence for learning.

The paradox here is that cooperative tasks are, by their very nature, high in ambiguity and risk. For example, the product of discussions of texts and strategies for attaining the goal of this activity may not be easily identifiable. If goals and strategies are obvious, collaboration may not be necessary because students can easily accomplish the task independently. On the other hand, overly complex tasks make it difficult for the group to recognize what they must do to accomplish the task. When this occurs, the likelihood of task simplification increases. Even with tasks of sufficient complexity to encourage collaboration and discourage simplification, some group members may be uncomfortable with *any* ambiguity, and some students may try to reorient the groups' discussion to a comfortable level. Thus, effective cooperative tasks are constantly in danger of being transformed into low-level procedural ones that may not help students improve their comprehension.

INSTRUCTIONAL TALK AND COOPERATIVE LEARNING

Even though the discourse patterns of classrooms are critical (see Chapter 8) and a strong association between teacher talk and learning has been found (Brophy & Good, 1986), cooperative-learning research has been relatively silent about the relationship between the information that teachers communicate to students and how this information affects group discussions.

What should teachers say to prepare students to work effectively in groups? For the most part, there are only general guidelines. For example, Slavin (1989b) has noted that cooperative learning is not a substitute for direct instruction. Merely placing students into groups does not ensure that they will learn. Palincsar and David in Chapter 9 echo this concern; students must receive some form of instruction prior to collaboration. If they do not, students may be unprepared to activate the knowledge and skills that are required by the task. Despite the importance of instruction in cooperative learning, Slavin (1989b) continues to find that some teachers believe that instruction plays an unnecessary or, at best, a minor role. Although Slavin expresses dismay about this interpretation of cooperative learning, one reason may be that articles and books directed at practitioners seem to place an emphasis on group organizations, team building, social skills, and incentive systems but provide only passing reference to the nature of concomitant instruction. This emphasis is somewhat understandable, because promotion of social strategies is not commonly part of a teacher's instructional repertoire. Unfortunately, this emphasis seems to have been interpreted, rightly or wrongly, as a suggestion that the organization of cooperation takes precedence over the information that teachers communicate about content and literacy strategies.

Some teachers also seem to believe that direct instruction may actually undermine the goals of cooperative learning. Evidence for this interpretation is anecdotal and stems from staff development efforts in school districts. In these discussions, some teachers express the idea that providing information prior to group work may "give away too much," thereby reducing the amount of information to be gained through collaboration. This "discovery" as opposed to "telling" dichotomy is not new (Greene, 1986) and reflects a belief that the less information provided (within reason) increases the quality of "real learning" or, in this case, "real learning through cooperation." Concerns about the balance between providing too much and too little information during instruction are not exclusive to cooperative learning nor are they expressed solely by practitioners (see, e.g., Tierney & Cunningham, 1984). Conversely, there is strong evidence that the explicit communication of what is to be learned, how it is to be learned, why it is important to learn, and how to orchestrate knowledge and skills for learning increases the acquisition of essential cognitive and metacognitive abilities (Duffy & Roehler, 1990), which in turn increases reading comprehension (Meloth, in press).

Teachers also create the conditions for productive cooperative discussions through the feedback they give to students while monitoring groups. Again, much of the literature on cooperative learning has been silent regarding this issue. Certainly, it is important to monitor groups to ensure that they stay on task. However, just because students are working together does not mean that they are on task and does not decrease the need for the close monitoring of collaborative discussions. As Bloome and Argumedo (1983) point out, students can become very sophisticated in "mock participation" or "procedural display," appearing to be engaged when actually they are not. In addition, engagement is more than simply thinking about, or talking about, the task; students may participate in lively discussions, but these discussions may be oriented toward goals that are not intended by the teacher. Thus, teachers need continually to orient student talk toward the cognitive goals of the task. Doing so, however, can be extremely difficult. Teachers must simultaneously monitor the activities of several groups at a time, help resolve problems or disputes, keep conversations going, recognize that the dynamics of groups differ, and adjust feedback accordingly, while making sure that each group makes sufficient progress.

Researchers are only beginning to link the form and quality of instruction and monitoring with the content of student discussions. In Meloth and Deering's (1990a) observations of discourse in cooperative reading-writing groups, 69% of all teacher feedback statements to groups were procedural in nature (i.e., focusing on task completion rather than task understanding), whereas cognitively oriented feedback comprised 20% of teacher statements. Only one teacher engaged in any substantial cognitive talk (39%). Student discussions mirrored teacher feedback: 53% of discussions were procedural in nature, whereas 20% were cognitive talk. These student discussions were closely tied to teacher feedback: Where teachers provided cognitively oriented feedback, students engaged in more cognitive-oriented discussions.

The follow-up study (Meloth & Deering, 1990b) examined teacher and student talk in six additional classrooms to verify discourse patterns prior to group discussions with tasks that were similar across classrooms. Patterns were similar to those of the initial study. Teachers varied in the cognitive nature of the information communicated prior to group work. Half the teachers engaged in typical recitation exchanges with little reference to the cognitive goals of the task. These teachers then asked students to begin working but provided little information about how group work could be oriented so that the cognitive goals of the task could be accomplished. The remaining teachers engaged in greater cognitive talk prior to group work, but only one included information about how to discuss the cognitive and metacognitive aspects of the tasks when working in groups.

Teacher feedback and student talk during the cooperative-learning phase followed a similar pattern in that procedural information comprised the bulk of teacher talk in all but two classrooms. Students followed the lead of their teachers; higher levels of cognitive discussions were found only in the two classrooms where teachers provided cognitively oriented feedback. This cognitive talk continued even after the teacher moved to another group. Although Meloth and Deering correctly caution that other, uncontrolled variables may have contributed to the content of group discussions, this study offers further credence to the idea that teachers play a critical role in improving the quality of group discussions in cooperative learning through their comments before and during cooperative activities.

SUMMARY

Cooperative learning is one solution that has been proposed to promote the discussion and interchange that contribute to a literacy for a diverse society. It has also been proposed as a means for engaging students with diverse backgrounds in common contexts. A variety of factors impact whether, indeed, cooperative settings achieve these goals.

Teachers' belief systems dictate whether cooperative learning is ever adopted and how it is translated into practice. The manner in which tasks are constructed and the nature of interaction among students and between teacher and students also impact its efficacy as a context for meaning-making. Simply placing students in groups and asking them to work together is unsatisfactory, because students may have little idea exactly what they should talk about or what they should learn. Similarly, teachers need to monitor the content of these discussions continually to ensure that they are oriented toward the cognitive goals of the task. Failure to do so does not eliminate the possibility of lively discussions. However, meaning-making in cooperative settings that fosters higher level literacy and allows students with diverse backgrounds to contribute to one another depends on teachers who are active through creating appropriate tasks, modeling discussion, and monitoring group interaction.

REFERENCES

Anderson, L. (1990). Implementing instructional programs to promote meaningful, self-regulated learning. In J. Brophy (Ed.), *Advances in research on teaching* (Vol. 1, pp. 311–343). New York: JAI Press.

Bloom, B. (1985). Learning for mastery. In C. Fisher & D. Berliner (Eds.), *Perspectives on instructional time* (pp. 73–93). New York: Longman.

Bloome, D., & Argumedo, B. (1983, April). *Procedural display and classroom instruction at the middle school level: Another look at academic engaged time.* Paper presented at the annual meeting of the American Educational Research Association, Montreal.

Bossert, S. (1988). Cooperative activities in the classroom. In E. Rothkopf (Ed.), *Review of Research in Education* (Vol. 15, pp. 225–250). Washington, DC: American Educational Research Association

Brophy, J., & Good, T. (1986). Teacher behavior and student achievement. In M. Wittrock (Ed.), *Handbook of research on teaching* (3rd ed., pp. 328–375). New York: Macmillan.

Buchmann, M. (1989). *Breaking from experience in teacher education: When is it necessary, how is it possible?* Paper presented at the annual meeting of the American Educational Research Association, San Francisco, CA.

Clark, C. M., & Peterson, P. L. (1986). Teachers' thought processes. In M. C. Wittrock (Ed.), *Handbook of research on teaching* (3rd ed., pp. 255–296). New York: Macmillan.

Doyle, W. (1983). Academic work. *Review of Educational Research, 53,* 159–199.

Doyle, W. (1987). Work in mathematics classes: The context of students' thinking during instruction. *Educational Psychologist, 23,* 167–180.

Duffy, G., & Roehler, L. (1990). Why strategy instruction is so difficult and what we need to do about it. In C. McCormick, G. Miller, & M. Pressley (Eds.), *Cognitive strategy research: From basic research to educational applications* (pp. 133–154). New York: Springer-Verlag.

Greene, M. (1986). Philosophy and teaching. In M. C. Wittrock (Ed.), *Handbook of research on teaching* (3rd ed., pp. 479–501). New York: Macmillan.

Johnson, D., & Johnson, R. (1987). *Learning together and alone* (2nd ed.). Englewood Cliffs, NJ: Prentice Hall.

Marx, R., & Walsh, J. (1988). Learning from academic tasks. *Elementary School Journal, 88,* 207–219.

Meloth, M. (in press). Changes in poor readers' knowledge of cognition and its association with regulation of cognition and reading comprehension. *Journal of Educational Psychology.*

Meloth, M., & Deering, P. (1990a, April). *Cooperative reading tasks, student awareness, and group discussions.* Paper presented at the annual meeting of the American Educational Research Association, Boston, MA.

Meloth, M., & Deering, P. (1990b, November). *Teachers' interpretation and implementation of a cooperative reading task.* Paper presented at the annual meeting of the National Reading Conference, Miami, FL.

Palincsar, A., Stevens, D., & Gavelek, J. (1989). Collaborating with teachers in the interest of student collaboration. *International Journal of Educational Research, 13,* 41–54.

Rich, Y. (1990). Ideological impediments to instructional innovation: The case of cooperative learning. *Teaching and Teacher Education, 6,* 81–91.

Richardson, V. (in press). Significant and worthwhile change in teaching practice. *Educational Researcher.*

Raphael, T., & Pearson, P. D. (1985). Increasing students' awareness of sources of information for answering questions. *American Educational Research Journal, 22,* 217–235.

Ross, J., & Raphael, D. (1990). Communication and problem solving achievement in cooperative learning groups. *Journal of Curriculum Studies, 22,* 149–164.

Ruddell, R., & Sperling, M. (1988). Factors influencing the use of literacy research by the classroom teacher: Research review and new directions. In J. E. Readence & R. S. Baldwin (Eds.), *Dialogues in literacy research* (pp. 319–329). Chicago: National Reading Conference.

Slavin, R. (1986). *Using student team learning* (3rd ed.). Baltimore: Johns Hopkins University, Center for Research on Elementary and Middle Schools.

Slavin, R. (1987). Cooperative learning and the cooperative school. *Educational Leadership, 45,* 7–13.

Slavin, R. (1989a). Cooperative learning and school achievement. In R. Slavin (Ed.), *School and classroom organization* (pp. 129–156). Hillsdale, NJ: Erlbaum.

Slavin, R. (1989b). Here to stay—or gone tomorrow? *Educational Leadership, 47,* 1.

Stallings, J., & Stipek, D. (1986). Research on early childhood and elementary school teaching programs. In M. Wittrock (Ed.), *Handbook of research on teaching* (3rd ed., pp. 727–753). New York: Macmillan.

Tierney, R. J., & Cunningham, J. (1984). Research on teaching reading comprehension. In P. D. Pearson, *Handbook of Reading Research* (pp. 609–655). New York: Macmillan.

Zeichner, K., & Liston, D. (1987). Teaching student teachers to reflect. *Harvard Educational Review, 57,* 23–48.

13 | Two-Tiered Scaffolding: Congruent Processes of Teaching and Learning

JANET S. GAFFNEY
RICHARD C. ANDERSON
University of Illinois, Urbana-Champaign

Time and elements have conspired to form the richly layered landscape of the Badlands in South Dakota. The red, rust, and cream bands of oxide and ash contrast with one another and with the horizon in which they are embedded. Yet, the uneven-edged layers fit like interlocking pieces of a puzzle. The awesome beauty of the Badlands emanates from the contrast of parts with the symmetry of the whole. Likewise, as we peel away individual tiers of the teaching-learning process for examination, visualize the criss-crossed, complex landscape from which each slice is drawn.

The metaphor of "scaffolding" has been used to describe the support that enables a learner to complete a task or achieve a goal that would have been unattainable without assistance (Wood, Bruner, & Ross, 1976). The concept of scaffolding is implicit in Vygotsky's (1978) notion of the "zone of proximal development." The width of this zone "is the distance between the actual developmental level as determined by independent problem solving and the level of potential development as determined through problem solving under adult guidance or in collaboration with more capable peers" (p. 86). Inherent in this definition of the zone of proximal development is the feature of social interaction between a learner and an individual with expertise. Although this interaction may be verbal, nonverbal, or a combination, Palincsar (1986) and Stone (1989) have emphasized the critical role of dialogue in scaffolded instruction.

What we are calling the "first tier" of scaffolding is a teacher, or someone else who qualifies as a more capable other, providing support for a student. Regulating the amount and nature of scaffolding requires a high degree of craftsmanship from the teacher. From the Vygotskian perspective, a high-craft teacher provides the minimal support necessary to assist a learner to operate at the upper limits of competence. Adjustable scaffolds are temporarily used to help extend the range of work and accomplish tasks not otherwise possible (Greenfield, 1984).

Several instructional methods have been developed with varying degrees of emphasis on scaffolding, zone of proximal development, social interaction, and dialogue. These concepts have been described as features of reciprocal teaching (A. L. Brown, 1985; Palincsar, 1986; Palincsar & A. L. Brown, 1984), guided participation (Rogoff, 1984), Experience-Text-Relationship method (Au & Kawakami, 1984), language acquisition and weaving skills (Greenfield, 1984), explicit explanation (Duffy et al., 1987), proleptic instruction (Stone, 1989; Wertsch, 1979), and assisted performance (Tharp & Gallimore, 1988).

We wish to extend the scaffolding metaphor by building a second tier on the model. The second level depicts the support necessary to assist an adult in supporting a child in a manner consistent with the method located on the first tier. In other words, this second level encompasses teacher education. The construction of a connected, upper tier rather than a separate scaffold is crucial to understanding the proposed model. The two-tiered scaffold illustrates the integral, interactive relationship between the processes used to prepare experts (whether parents, educators, or peers) and the methods they use to teach novices.

Thus, our purpose is to extend the Vygotskian conceptual framework. Wertsch (1984) acknowledged Vygotsky's lack of discussion of development of the adult's role in providing the novice with assistance. Wertsch (1984) cautioned that poor definition of these functions could render the construct of the zone of proximal development too broad to be useful.

It is said that there's nothing so practical as good theory. It may also be said that there's nothing so theoretically interesting as good practice. We will highlight the critical features of our proposed extension of Vygotskian theory using examples from Reading Recovery, a program with demonstrated success with young children who are at risk for reading failure. Although Reading Recovery was not developed on the basis of Vygotsky's theory, features of the program may be interpreted in Vygotskian terms (Clay & Cazden, 1990). The stories from Reading Recovery reveal some perhaps generalizable truths about the interactive processes of learning and instruction.

AN INSTANTIATION OF VYGOTSKIAN THEORY

Reading Recovery is a supplemental reading and writing program for first-grade children who are at risk of reading failure. Reading Recovery was developed in New Zealand by Clay and her associates (1979, 1982, 1985) and has been successfully implemented in Ohio since 1984 (Pinnell, DeFord, & Lyons, 1988). The immediate goal of Reading Recovery is to assist the children who are most at risk of failure to read at or above the average levels of their first-grade peers in the least amount of time possible. Evaluations have indicated that children typically meet this goal after 12 to 16 weeks of intensive, one-to-one instruction for 30 minutes daily with a Reading Recovery teacher (Pinnell et al., 1988). This phenomenal rate of success of Reading Recovery children is described as accelerated progress.

The goal is for children to continue to improve their reading and writing performance after they have completed Reading Recovery. In Clay's (1985) words, teachers must "encourage a self-improving system" (p. 57). In Slavin and Madden's (1989) synthesis of effective reading programs for at-risk students by grade levels, Reading Recovery was the only first-grade program for which evidence was found of positive effects that are sustained for 2 years following discontinuation of the intervention.

Reading Recovery is not packaged in a kit of materials. Nor could one implement it by following a predetermined, instructional sequence. In other words, Reading Recovery is not a "teacher-proof" program; in fact, it is a "teacher-dependent" program. The success of the instruction appears to hinge upon the teacher's ability to make and execute the most "powerful decisions" throughout each lesson.

In a typical Reading Recovery lesson, the child rereads several familiar books; independently reads a book read for the first time the previous day; if necessary, studies letters or words; creates and writes a story; reassembles the story after the teacher has cut it up; and reads a new book.

A child usually has the opportunity to read five or more texts during a half-hour Reading Recovery lesson. This is vastly more than a first grader typically reads, especially one in the low group. The texts may be described as authentic, in the sense that such features as vocabulary and sentence structure are not closely controlled as in basal reading programs. When authentic materials are used, the probability increases that children will acquire strategies that are broadly adaptive, rather than strategies that are skewed to accommodate an artificially constrained range of features.

Reading Recovery engages children in reading *whole* books and stories. One of the instructional premises is that the teacher should focus the child's attention on the largest chunk of information that will contribute to learning. Thus, the teacher is disposed to draw the child's attention to the overall story line of a book rather than to a sentence, to a sentence rather than a word, and to a word rather than a letter. Learning to read cannot be reduced to accretion of discrete items of knowledge—such as letters, letter clusters, or words. An overemphasis on discrete items is inefficient at best and self-defeating at worst.

Scaffolding

At the heart of Reading Recovery instruction is the scaffolding the teacher provides to keep the child within his or her zone of proximal development. An important scaffold is selecting a book of just the right level of difficulty. Too difficult a book and a child may flounder. Too easy a book and the child will not have enough productive "reading work."

The difficulty of a book is affected by such factors as whether it has a predictable pattern, the extent to which the pictures illustrate the concepts, and the familiarity of the words. However, a book is not easy or difficult in and of itself. For a child having trouble learning to read, the difficulty of a book can be intelligibly discussed only in relationship to this particular child. Because Reading Recovery is implemented as a one-to-one program, the teacher does not have to compromise in making decisions about books.

Moreover, whether a particular child will find a particular book easy or difficult depends upon the context in which the book is read and the conditions surrounding its use. Specifically, the difficulty of a book is influenced by the teacher's orientation, or introduction, to the book. An orientation may include looking through the book with the child, commenting on what is significant in the pictures, and discussing the plot. The teacher may use new and important words in his or her oral orientation and may ask the child to locate one or two of these words in the text. For example, if *terrible* is important for grasping the plot, the teacher may ask, "What letter would you expect to see at the beginning of *terrible?*" And then, "Can you find *terrible* on this page?"

Or, depending upon the child, his or her level of reading development, and the book, the teacher's orientation to a book may include none of these elements. Reading Recovery operates on the principle that each child's developmental trajectory as a reader may be at least somewhat different from every other child's. Just as expedition leaders decide what route to take up a mountain based on features of that mountain, strengths of the climbers, and the weather, so, too, do Reading Recovery teachers create an individual program for each child. It is part of the lore of Reading Recovery that, among the thousands of children who have received the program, no two have ever read exactly the same books in exactly the same order.

Reading Recovery reinforces the idea that the zone of proximal development is instructionally sensitive, that it must be recalibrated constantly to take account of new learnings of the child. Thus, a teacher is always supporting a child at the "cutting edge of the child's competencies" (Clay & Cazden, 1990). This means that a child's program cannot be fixed in advance but must be adjusted from lesson to lesson and even from minute to minute within lessons.

Within the zone of proximal development, Reading Recovery teachers operate using an "implicit theory of steps" (Stone, 1989, p. 37). The teacher tries to anticipate and support the child's next steps. In mountain climbing, a piton is wedged into the mountain to help the climber stretch to a higher plane. The child-climber is able to stretch to reach the next piton because of the support provided by the scaffold. The teacher's role is to secure the next piton for the learner. Consistent with the Vygotskian perspective, in Reading Recovery, "instruction leads development rather than waiting for it" (Clay & Cazden, 1990).

In an alternative image, the scaffolding Reading Recovery teachers provide can be thought of as serving as a safety net. Because of the scaffolding, the child is enabled to take new risks at a higher level and, therefore, independence in reading is promoted. Scaffolding must be adjusted over time so that there is a shift in responsibility from the teacher to the child. The child must come to accept the responsibility for all aspects of reading. Whereas the teacher initially adjusted the scaffold relative to the learner's skill as it interacted with task difficulty, the responsibility for flexible adjustment becomes the learner's responsibility.

For example, a Reading Recovery teacher may, if needed, direct a child just beginning to read to point to the words as the child reads them. This helps the child keep his or her place and promotes one-to-one correspondence between spoken words and printed words. Later in the child's program the teacher will ask the child to read a familiar book "with your eyes" and comment approvingly if the child is able to read it with greater fluency without pointing. Then, for a period of time the teacher will occasionally ask questions prompting the child to evaluate whether or not it is necessary to keep pointing to the word. Finally, a stage will be reached where the child is in complete control of pointing. At this stage, the child will read without pointing most of the time but may point when the text is difficult or when in danger of losing his or her place.

One speaks of scaffolding as something that is provided or constructed by the teacher. From another perspective, the scaffold is built by the child in the form of emerging skills and knowledge. Sometimes the child has built the scaffold but doesn't use it for support. The teacher's role is to enlist the child's nascent abilities to support whatever is currently difficult (Clay, 1987; Greenfield, 1984).

Emphasis on Strategies

To become self-improving readers, children must consistently and independently solve problems on the fly while reading text. The premise of Reading Recovery is that for this to happen, children must learn to be strategic in their use of semantic, syntactic, orthographic, and phonological cues. They must learn to monitor their reading performance and correct errors on their own.

The emphasis in Reading Recovery on strategies is entirely consistent with Soviet developmental psychology. Drawing on this perspective, Stone (1989) suggests that an overriding goal is for children to adopt more strategic conceptions of tasks. Thus, in the case of reading, whereas the ostensible task is to construct meaning for a specific text, the goal is for the child to learn how to construct meaning for any text.

In some reading programs, strategy instruction has become decontextualized. Means have become confused with ends; the task has become learning a recipe that describes a strategy rather than acquiring functional control over a strategy. However, a child who is able to recall a five-step procedure for summarizing a story, for instance, may or may not be able to use the procedure. Presenting strategies in a "front-loaded" (Duffy et al., 1987), decontextualized manner radically changes the task and may circumscribe maintenance and generalization (Stone, 1989).

Reading Recovery teachers support the child's development and use of strategies as a means for facilitating independent learning. Teaching for strategies, self-monitoring, and cross-checking is always done in the context of reading and writing authentic texts, as is illustrated in the following vignette. Nancy, a first grader, was reading *My Grandpa* (Mitchell, 1986) for the first time following an orientation to the text by the teacher. Among other points, the teacher mentioned during her orientation that people in some countries call cookies "biscuits," while referring to a picture in the text. Nancy read:

NANCY: <u>He</u> <u>likes</u> <u>eating</u> <u>berries</u> | SC |R
TEXT: <u>He</u> <u>likes</u> <u>eating</u> biscuits.

Note that she read "berries" for "biscuits." The codes SC and R mean, respectively, that she self-corrected and reread the sentence from the beginning. When Nancy completed the sentence, which continued on the facing page, the following conversation ensued.

TEACHER: You read "berries" for "biscuits." Then, you fixed it. How did you know it was "biscuits"?

NANCY: Because it began with a "b."
TEACHER: Yes, "biscuits" begins with a "b" but so does "berries."
NANCY: They both have "s"s too.
TEACHER: So, how did you know?
NANCY: The picture! They don't look like berries.

In this segment of dialogue, the teacher is trying to help the child gain conscious realization and self-regulation of strategies for word analysis. When the emphasis is on strategies rather than discrete items of knowledge, progress may occur in leaps rather than small, cumulative steps. Leaps are promoted when the teacher is able to capitalize on examples that are "powerful," or informative and convincing, for a particular child (Clay, 1979). Within the social-interactive framework, the teacher may easily respond to leaps by the child.

EDUCATION OF READING RECOVERY TEACHERS

The second tier of scaffolding in our proposed extension of Vygotsky is the education of teachers. In the context of Reading Recovery, the first tier drives the second tier. By this we mean that teacher-child interactions form the essential content of teacher training. Without the concurrent teaching of children, there would be no fabric to weave into the in-service sessions.

Teacher education has often been criticized for the discontinuity between university course work and field experience (Joyce & Clift, 1984). The teacher education component of Reading Recovery is intended to narrow the gap between theory and practice. Trainees, who are experienced primary grade teachers, immediately begin teaching Reading Recovery to a minimum of four children on a daily basis. During an academic year, trainees work with a range of children. When children are "discontinued" from Reading Recovery, because they are now reading at the average level of their peers, other children enter the program. Over the year, the teachers usually teach two cycles of children. A teacher in training teaches over 600 Reading Recovery lessons in her first year.

In addition, the teachers have the opportunity to observe two lessons at each Reading Recovery in-service session. Each week, two of the teachers conduct 30-minute lessons with children whom they are currently teaching. The other trainees observe the lessons through a one-way mirror. The Teacher Leader, as the teacher trainer is called in Reading Recovery, engages the remaining trainees in vigorous discussion of each lesson while it is occurring. Over an academic year, teachers in training observe and discuss 40 to 50 lessons. The discussions of "behind-the-glass" lessons are intense, challenging, and synergistic.

The teacher-observers participating in behind-the-glass sessions discuss the child's behavior, teacher-child interactions, and the teacher's implementation of procedures. They are challenged to form hypotheses about the child's performance, to present evidence from the lesson unfolding in front of them that supports or disconfirms their hypotheses, to provide rationales for the teacher's decisions, and to suggest alternative instructional procedures.

Here's an example of a behind-the-glass session. As it was early in the training year, only the second in-service session, the Teacher Leader was intent on eliciting accurate descriptions of the child's performance from the teachers. Notice that the teachers are asked to support their statements with evidence from this lesson or other reasoning.

TEACHER LEADER: We are observing familiar reading, the first component of a lesson. What are some of the purposes of familiar reading?

TEACHER 4: To let the child practice what he knows.

TEACHER 1: So that the child can read fluently books he's had before.

TEACHER LEADER: Is this child reading fluently?

TEACHER 1: Yes, I think so.

TEACHER 6: I do too (two other teachers nod in agreement).

TEACHER LEADER: Think of the children you're working with in Reading Recovery. How does his reading fluency compare to theirs?

TEACHER 3: Mine read like him.

TEACHER 2: Mine, too (all other teachers nod in agreement).

TEACHER LEADER: You're all experienced teachers of Grade 1 children. Think of the average and above average readers in first grade. Does this child read this book as fluently as they would?

TEACHERS ALL: NO! (emphatically with head-shaking)

TEACHER LEADER: Is this child reading fluently?

ALL: No! (in unison)

TEACHER LEADER: It is important for you to keep in mind your purpose. Your goal is to have this child read as well as average readers in his class . . . that's your standard. Now, is fluency the only thing that's important . . . that he goes fast?

TEACHER 8: He should read with expression . . . meaning.

TEACHER 5: In phrases.

TEACHER LEADER: Why is it important that the child read with both phrasing and fluency?

The Teacher Leader is relentless in her pursuit of an accurate characterization of the child's reading. Interestingly, during the second lesson, taught by a different teacher, that immediately followed the lesson excerpted above, the observers quickly reached a consensus about the fluency with which the child read familiar books. The Teacher Leader then was able to move to a different level of questioning: She challenged the teachers to talk about why phrased and fluent reading are important and asked them to suggest procedures from *The Early Detection of Reading Difficulties* (Clay, 1985) that they could use to teach for fluency.

Compare the foregoing discussion with the one following a session in the spring, when the teachers were about 75% of the way through their training. They are observing the phase of the lesson in which the child writes a story she has composed with the support of the teacher.

TEACHER LEADER: The teacher just praised the child for getting the "ch" down in "chair." Why did she praise her?

TEACHER 9: Because that's a hard one to learn.

TEACHER 5: It's important.

TEACHER LEADER: And she isn't doing it in pieces . . .

TEACHER 7: Chunks.

TEACHER LEADER: Is getting chunks down important at this level? The teacher said she wanted to work for transfer. Why would chunks be helpful for that?

TEACHER 1: They might start . . . they might start to see patterns.

TEACHER LEADER: Why is it more important to see patterns than to talk about individual letters?

TEACHER 4: She's got a way to get to unknown words. When she goes to another word that contains the same sound cluster she's able to write more of the word.

TEACHER 1: Another suggestion I have is that I don't think she needs to look back at the practice page. She did just look back up at "chair" but I would fold the book under and have her write, or cover it or something.

TEACHER LEADER: Why would you choose to do that?

TEACHER 1: Because if she can write that many words she ought to be able to do it from memory without an example.

TEACHER 6: Seeing and retaining visual patterns.

TEACHER LEADER: And how does that help her? Why would it be beneficial for her to be doing it from memory rather than just copying it?

TEACHER 7: It indicates a certain knowledge of what she's working on and also the idea of being able to not only hear, but how to utilize the chunks—the clusters—of letters. I think the book talks about the more fluent readers are those that are able to use those chunks, at specific times and transfer them to other areas in that particular practice time.

In both lessons, the Teacher Leader was supporting as well as stretching the group. Comparing the transcripts that were recorded at different points in the training year, one notices shifts in the role of the Teacher Leader and the teachers. In the latter transcript, the Teacher Leader just states what's occurred, e.g., "The teacher just praised the child." The Teacher Leader chooses to focus her questions at a higher level of thinking requiring the teachers to reflect about the value of working with larger chunks of material. Notice the teachers have runs of sequential responses. The Teacher Leader comes in to challenge the teachers to think about the purpose of the task. Also, the teachers' comments are now longer and demonstrate that they have an increased understanding of processes and strategies, the relationship between reading and writing, and the procedures used in Reading Recovery (Clay, 1985). All of this discussion ensued because the child could chunk two letters in a writing task!

The number and diversity of lessons teachers observe over a year broaden instructional horizons. The diversity of lessons observed and discussed, as well as lessons taught, expands both breadth and depth of the teacher's experiential knowledge. This in-service process forestalls oversimplification (Spiro, 1988). That icy spots continue to be encountered by the teachers increases their cognitive agility (Burton, Brown, & Fischer, 1984).

AWARENESS OF DISCREPANCIES AND
THE SELF-IMPROVING SYSTEM

The difficulty of tasks can be calibrated in terms of the nature and frequency of discrepancies, or mismatches, between the learner's performance and some currently appropriate standard of performance. The concept of discrepancies is integral to stretching the zone of proximal development. The high-craft teacher searches for ways to engage the learner in performing tasks that are at the outer limits of the learner's potential, where the learner is working at the edge of his or her competency.

The learner's becoming aware of mismatches is a precursor to new learning. For example, a prerequisite for self-correction is awareness that an error has been made. Initially, with easy texts, self-monitoring may dawn as a result of a mismatch in the number of words read to the number of words on a page of text.

A six-year-old child just entering Reading Recovery read the book *I Can Read* (Malcolm, 1983).

CHILD: *I can read it to my sister.*
TEXT: I can read – to my sister.

The child appeared to be unaware that he had added a word to the text. The role of the teacher was to encourage his awareness of a mismatch.

Reading Recovery includes several suggestions for promoting awareness of mismatches arising from violations of one-to-one correspondence (Clay, 1985). The teacher may ask the child, simply, "Were you right?" This general prompt may be sufficient to encourage the child to reread and notice the insertion. A more specific prompt would be to ask, "Were there enough words?" or "Did you run out?" What is important is that the child learns to monitor his or her own reading, even if unsure at this point of how to correct an error.

Once the child shows evidence of awareness of errors—revealed by tentativeness, balking, or uncertainty—the teacher may ask, "What did you notice?" or "Why did you stop?" These questions further encourage the child to monitor his or her reading.

A child who is aware of mismatches of a certain kind is on the road to conquering them. When the child consistently exhibits awareness of mismatches without prompting from the teacher, then the child's zone of proximal development has expanded. And then the teacher must select the next process over which this child needs to gain control in order to be a successful reader. The teacher enthusiastically accepts attempts to resolve mismatches ("I liked the way you tried to work that out."). At the same times, he or she probes successful performance ("How did you know?"), because the real task is learning the process, or how to self-correct, not simply responding correctly to any particular item.

As soon as possible, the child must begin to correct mismatches independently. Only when the child initiates the action may it be called self-correction. In other words, the weight of the responsibility for noticing and handling discrepancies gradually shifts from the teacher to the child on increasingly difficult and complex texts. The child is afforded opportunities to solve problems with minimal assistance. Again the outer limit of the zone of proximal development is being stretched. The child is becoming a self-improving reader.

Resolving discrepancies between performance and currently appropriate standards is also integral to Reading Recovery teacher training. The lessons observed behind the glass, discussions with peers, and the procedures suggested in the *Early Detection of Reading Difficulties* (Clay, 1985) all provide standards with which teachers can compare their own understanding and performance. These comparisons allow for multiple mismatches, thereby creating tension, whose resolution results in new learning.

In observing a lesson behind the one-way mirror, discrepancies may arise between what the teachers observe during this lesson and what they are doing in their own tutoring. For example, in the first 2 weeks that they are in Reading Recovery, the children explore and gain control over what they already know. The teachers are instructed to use meaningful texts in reading and writing and to ensure that the tasks are easy for the children. The teachers are cautioned not to teach! As the new group of teachers observed an experienced Reading Recovery teacher work with a child during her initial period, cries arose, "But she's teaching!" "I thought that was teaching!" "Is that teaching?" The mismatch generated a rich discussion about the role of the teacher during this initial period and about the participants' understanding of what "teaching" is.

The mismatch created tension that led the group to generate hypotheses about the teaching going on in the lesson they were watching and about their own teaching. Whether the teachers' ideas were sound or not is not so important as that the teachers were engaged in the process of tension resolution that could lead to new learning.

The Teacher Leader sometimes confronts teacher trainees with questions or statements that contradict their present understandings or current activities. A Teacher Leader might say, "One time in Tasmania I saw a teacher who said that she had the same lesson focus for each one of her children. You wouldn't say that, would you?" Or, "Although she's having the child draw a picture to help remember the story, most of your children aren't using pictures any more. Are they?"

Thus, Reading Recovery teacher training creates many and varied mismatches. The articulation and subsequent discussion are central to teacher trainees' becoming self-improving teachers.

SUMMARY

Vygotsky (1981) contended that higher mental functions are developed first on an interpsychological plane through social interactions and second on an intrapsychological plane. An individual's potential level is not limited by that individual's endowed ability but is raised exponentially by the quality of the social interaction in which the individual participates. The social interaction not only precedes an individual's development of higher mental functions, but the organizational features of the social context are also internalized and reflected in the individual's performance (Wertsch & Rogoff, 1984).

In our two-tiered conceptualization, the conditions within which the teacher's learning is embedded not only affect the teacher but, in addition, impact upon the child. To an observer who is naive to Reading Recovery, the social interaction in a lesson may appear to be teacher driven. In reality, the expert teacher is responding to the evidence and information provided by the child; the teaching "can be likened to a conversation in which you listen to the speaker carefully before you reply" (Clay, 1985, p. 6). Thus, despite appearances, the instruction is really child driven. Not only is the child the catalyst for interactions occurring on the first tier (teacher-child), the child is the driving force for the interactions occurring on the second tier (Teacher Leader–teacher).

The focus at both tiers is on the use of strategies. One cannot directly prepare a child or a teacher for each of the infinite array of difficulties that they may confront. However, one can help another to use strategies that are effective in problem solving. At both tiers, responsibility for independent action gradually shifts from expert to novice, that is, from teacher to child and, likewise, from Teacher Leader to teacher. The goal is for both the teacher and child to function independently at increasingly higher levels on more and more difficult tasks.

REFERENCES

Au, K. H., & Kawakami, A. J. (1984). Influence of the social organization of instruction on children's text comprehension ability: A Vygotskian perspective. In T. E. Raphael & R. E. Reynolds (Eds.), *The contexts of school-based literacy* (pp. 63–77). New York: Random House.

Brown, A. L. (1985). *Teaching students to think as they read: Implications for curriculum reform* (Tech. Rep. No. 58). Champaign, IL: Center for the Study of Reading.

Burton, R. R., Brown, J. S., & Fischer, G. (1984). Skiing as a model of instruction. In B. Rogoff & J. Lave (Eds.), *Everyday cognition: Its development in social context* (pp. 139–150). Cambridge, MA: Harvard University Press.

Clay, M. M. (1979). *The early detection of reading difficulties* (2nd ed.). Auckland, New Zealand: Heinemann.

Clay, M. M. (1982). *Observing young readers: Selected papers.* Exeter, NH: Heinemann.

Clay, M. M. (1985). *The early detection of reading difficulties* (3rd ed.). Auckland, New Zealand: Heinemann.

Clay, M. M. (1987). Learning to be learning disabled. *New Zealand Journal of Educational Studies, 22,* 155–173.

Clay, M. M., & Cazden, C. B. (1990). A Vygotskian interpretation of reading recovery. In L. C. Moll (Ed.), *Vygotsky and education: Instructional implications and applications of socio-historical psychology* (pp. 206–222). New York: Cambridge University Press.

Duffy, G. G., Roehler, L. R., Siven, E., Rackliffe, G., Book, C., Meloth, M. S., Vavrus, L. G., Wesselman, R., Putnam, J., & Bassirir, D. (1987). Effects of explaining the reasoning associated with using reading strategies. *Reading Research Quarterly, 22,* 347–368.

Greenfield, P. M. (1984). A theory of the teacher in the learning activities of everyday life. In B. Rogoff & J. Lave (Eds.), *Everyday cognition: Its development in social context* (pp. 117–138). Cambridge, MA: Harvard University Press.

Joyce, B., & Clift, R. (1984). The phoenix agenda: Essential reform in teacher education. *Educational Researcher, 13*(4), 5–18.

Malcolm, M. (1983). *I can read.* Wellington, New Zealand: Department of Education.

Mitchell, G. (1986). *My grandpa.* New South Wales, Australia: Martin Educational.

Palincsar, A. S. (1986). The role of dialogue in providing scaffolded instruction. *Educational Psychologist, 21,* 73–98.

Palincsar, A. S., & Brown, A. L. (1984). Reciprocal teaching of comprehension-fostering and comprehension-monitoring activities. *Cognition and Instruction, 1,* 117–175.

Pinnell, G. S., DeFord, D. E., & Lyons, C. A. (1988). *Reading recovery: Early intervention for at-risk first graders.* Arlington, VA: Educational Research Service.

Rogoff, B. (1984). Adult assistance of children's learning. In T. E. Raphael & R. E. Reynolds (Eds.), *The contexts of school-based literacy* (pp. 27–40). New York: Random House.

Slavin, R. E., & Madden, N. A. (1989). What works for students at risk: A research synthesis. *Educational Leadership, 46*(5), 4–13.

Spiro, R. J. (1988). *Cognitive flexibility theory: Advanced knowledge acquisition in ill-structured domains* (Tech. Rep. No. 441). Champaign, IL: Center for the Study of Reading.

Stone, C. A. (1989). Improving the effectiveness of strategy training for learning disabled students: The role of communicational dynamics. *Remedial and Special Education, 10,* 35–42.

Tharp, R. G., & Gallimore, R. (1988). *Rousing minds to life: Teaching, learning, and schooling in social context.* New York: Cambridge University Press.

Vygotsky, L. S. (1978). *Mind in society: The development of higher psychological processes.* Cambridge, MA: Harvard University Press.

Vygotsky, L. S. (1981). The genesis of high mental functions. In J. V. Wertsch (Ed.), *The concept of activity in Soviet psychology* (pp. 144–188). Armonk, NY: Sharpe.

Wertsch, J. V. (1979). From social interaction to higher psychological processes: A clarification and application of Vygotsky's theory. *Human Development, 22,* 1–22.

Wertsch, J. V. (1984). The zone of proximal development: Some conceptual issues. In B. Rogoff & J. Wertsch (Eds.), *Children's learning in the zone of proximal development* (pp. 7–18). San Francisco: Jossey-Bass.

Wertsch, J. V., & Rogoff, B. (1984). Editors' notes. In B. Rogoff & J. V. Wertsch (Eds.), *Children's learning in the zone of proximal development* (pp. 1–6). San Francisco: Jossey-Bass.

Wood, D., Bruner, J. S., & Ross, G. (1976). The role of tutoring in problem solving. *Journal of Child Psychology & Psychiatry, 17,* 89–100.

14 | Fostering Early Literacy Through Parent Coaching

PATRICIA A. EDWARDS
Michigan State University

Over the last few years, researchers have focused attention on parent-child book-reading interactions in nonmainstream families (Farron, 1982; Heath & Thomas, 1984; McCormick & Mason, 1986; Ninio, 1980). One of the shortcomings of this body of research is that it describes only the nonmainstream parents' *inability* to participate successfully during book reading. It does not go to the next step of describing strategies for improving parental participation in book reading.

As demonstrated by Edwards (1989), successful models can be built for book reading from existing research. Although most of these models are derived from mainstream populations, much can be learned from these parent-child interactions to enhance the literacy development of nonmainstream families. For example, we already know that mainstream mothers focus their child's attention by pointing to and naming items on the printed page. They then ask questions about the names of items, their features, and location in the book; the child watches, listens, waits, and responds (Flood, 1977; Snow & Ferguson, 1977).

Research also shows that children whose parents read to them before they entered school tend to do better in reading than children whose parents did not (Durkin, 1966, 1984; Lartz & Mason, 1988). Teale (1981) noted that "one issue the various 'camps' in the field of [reading] are in virtually unanimous agreement: reading to preschool children is a good thing; it is an activity through which children may develop interest and skill in literacy" (p. 902). On a contrary note, Anderson and Stokes (1984) argue that book reading is not the only way of becoming literate and that nonmainstream children participate in literacy experiences that are unrelated to books. Despite this argument, they quickly agree that experiences with books are strongly considered in evaluating children's readiness for school and that nonmainstream children's lack of experience with books could be a contributing source to poor school performance. Gallimore and Goldenberg (1987) take the view one step further when they state, "If reading books and talking with children helps them succeed in school this information should be available to every parent, no matter their social, economic, or cultural circumstances" (p. 22).

Recognizing that nonmainstream children often have limited experiences with books, a number of researchers have asked aides, volunteers, and older children to read to young children or integrate storybook reading into classroom settings (Dickerson, 1989; Mason, Peterman, & Kerr, 1988; Teale, Martinez, & Glass, 1988). Although classroom storybook reading provides nonmainstream children with an excellent opportunity to have experiences with books, Teale (1987) questioned whether classroom storybook reading experience substitutes for the more intimate one-to-one interactions of homes. And Meek (1982) describes the unique role of parents as compared with teachers: "It is to encourage the child to believe that reading is within his grasp, and to provide the means for his enjoyment and success" (p. 26). According to Mason (1986), parents with marginal literacy skills can serve this critical role of reading storybooks with their children.

The thesis underlying this chapter is that parent-directed book-reading interactions will allow children to acquire literacy skills that will help them become better readers at school, a position supported by numerous scholars (e.g., Gallimore & Goldenberg, 1989; Mason, 1986; Sledge, 1987; Teale, 1981, 1987). This chapter reports on a program (Parents as Partners in Reading) developed to give nonmainstream parents the strategies to read to their children successfully. Several theoretical principles undergirded the development of the book-reading program, including the zone of proximal development, scaffolding, reciprocal teaching, guided participation, social interaction, and dialogue concepts, all of which have been discussed by others (Au & Kawakami, 1984; Rogoff, 1984; Vygotsky, 1978; Wertsch, 1979), including several researchers in this volume (see Chapters 9 and 13). This chapter presents the book-reading program, with focus on its strategies and theoretical principles.

AN OVERVIEW OF THE PROGRAM

The participants in the book-reading program were 25 lower socioeconomic-status (SES) mothers (18 African-American, 7 white) and their children. Mothers had been recommended by kindergarten and first-grade teachers on the basis of their children's performances in kindergarten and grade 1. The children's teachers were also an integral part of the project in that they created the training materials and interacted extensively with parents.

The intervention fell into three phases: Coaching, Peer Modeling, and

Parent-Child Interaction. Each phase was of approximately the same length (6 or 7 weeks). Sessions were held weekly beginning in October 1987 and ending in May 1988, and each session lasted for 2 hours. There were 23 book-reading sessions, although not all mothers attended every session.

Development of Materials

The university and school-based teams collaborated on the development of the parent-training materials, which were four videotapes on two sets of book-reading strategies. One set was derived from the mother-child obser-vational checklist of Resnick, Roth, Aaron, Scott, Wolking, Laren, and Packer (1987). This checklist pertains to four dimensions of parent-child interaction: body management (e.g., sitting opposite child), management of book (e.g., encouraging child to hold book and to turn pages), varying one's voice, language interactions (e.g., labeling and describing pictures), and af-fect (e.g., pausing for child's responses, making approving gestures). The second set, although overlapping with the first set in some cases, gives par-ents a general progression of steps to follow with a story: attention getting, questioning, labeling, and providing feedback (Ninio & Bruner, 1978). Teachers became familiar with both sets of strategies and selected particular dimensions to highlight in the particular videotapes.

Coaching

Coaching sessions consisted of the university leader modeling book-reading behaviors and introducing the videotapes. In a manner similar to that described by Gaffney and Anderson in Chapter 13, the leader-parent sessions used the model of "scaffolded dialogue." This model was also used to guide the teacher-child interaction on the videotape and was intended to be emu-lated by parents in their interactions with children. That is, when there was a breakdown in parents' understanding or use of a strategy, the leader would prompt and support them to use strategies that would have been otherwise unattainable.

The parents met with the university leader as a group. The group setting was not as threatening as a one-to-one meeting would have been. Throughout the coaching phase, parents were seen as conversational informants and part-ners in the interactions. In the initial sessions, the university leader accepted any parent's decision not to respond to questions or make comments, but as time passed each parent was encouraged to respond and make comments. As this occurred, the dialogue between the mothers and the university leader increased in complexity. Many parents frequently stayed on after sessions to review tapes and interact with the leader. Parents could come back to the school during the week and view tapes at their leisure. Parents were encouraged to become part of their children's classrooms, and several accepted the invitation. Throughout this phase (as with all other phases of the project), the leader and teachers encouraged a sense of community among the parents and between the school and the parents.

For each strategy, a videotape was presented in which a teacher explained the strategy and then demonstrated it in a videotaped lesson with one of the target children. For example, the objective of one tape was for children to engage in story reading through labeling and describing pictures. Using Ziefert's (1985) *Baby Ben Gets Dressed,* the tape began with the teacher providing a rationale for why this book was particularly appropriate for accomplishing the objective of labeling and describing pictures. Then, with one of the target children, the teacher modeled book reading with labeling and description. Throughout these interactions, teachers participated in the scaffolded dialogue that was the focus for parents' interactions as well. After parents viewed the videotape, the university leader involved them in a guided discussion on the application of the strategy. This discussion was aimed at promoting parents' ability to talk about content and strategies of book reading and to make text-to-life and life-to-text connections.

An example from an interaction from the third book-reading session illustrates the nature of the dialogue between the university leader (referred to as Pat) and the parents. The university leader selected one parent (Marinetta) to be the focus of the discussion but was intent on eliciting responses from other parents, as well. Notice that the parents were asked to describe concepts, define words, provide support for their answers, and evaluate what they had learned in this session.

> PAT: What we're going to do this morning is have a group discussion about some of the books I brought this morning. Marinetta, I want you to choose a book. (She selects *The Counting Carnival* by Ziner and Galdone, 1962.)
>
> PAT: You could have the child call out the number clustered in the balloons on the book's cover. (The parents were encouraged to count 1 through 10 as a group). Then you could ask your child how many fingers are on each hand; how many toes are on each foot. Then open the book.
>
> MARINETTA: I would have child say *The Counting Carnival.* (Using her fingers, she underscores the title. Opening the book, she holds a double spread of a neighborhood scene for all the parents to see). I would call this man the grandfather, and this is the little boy.

PAT: Okay. What else?

JEANETTE: There are ladies and a cat.

MARY: Pigeons gathered in the street.

PAT: You might want to relate this to the theme. All these people seem to be doing what?

PARENTS: Talking.

PAT: Perhaps this is a typical neighborhood scene—talking in the street. Anytime you see something in a picture you can't explain, say: Let's read to find out. Keep in mind that your children are young and lack the same level of knowledge that you may have about certain concepts. (Marinetta has just finished reading page 10. On this page is the word *carnival*). Now, we need to talk about what the word *carnival* means. What is a carnival?

JEANETTE: A place where you have fun.

PAT: What happens?

CHARLENE: Games and activities.

PAT: In our state (Louisiana), we have a lot of carnivals. You can relate the word to Mardi Gras. Most of your children have heard of Mardi Gras because we live so close to New Orleans.

The conversation proceeded in a similar dialogic fashion until Marinetta came to the end of the book. At that point, the university leader asked parents to reflect on what they had enjoyed and learned about the book.

JEANETTE: It was a counting book and I'm trying to help my daughter with counting right now. Our discussion today gave me some ideas for discussing this book and other books like it with Erica.

CHARLENE: I learned from our discussion of this book that I have to move beyond just providing a label or name of an item in the text. I need to ask my child more questions to check his understanding of the concept I'm trying to get him to understand. This book helped me to really understand this.

MARY: I realized from our discussion of this book the importance of involving my child in the book.

PAT: You are all really catching on to what I'm trying to get you to understand about the interactive nature of parent-child book-reading interactions.

By the end of the 6-week coaching phase, the parents had begun to view book-reading as a routinized and formatted language event between themselves and their children. They also had begun to adjust their language to their child's level of understanding. Furthermore, the parents were developing an interest and sophistication in book reading. For example, they were able to label and describe pictures more easily, link text to life and life to text, ask and answer questions about words and pictures, vary their voices, and make motions while interacting with the texts during the sessions. More importantly, parents in their individual ways seemed to be acquiring an internal understanding of what it meant to share books with their children.

Peer Modeling

The second phase of instruction, peer modeling, focused on promoting parents' control of the book-reading sessions and strategies. The rationale for this stage was based upon the work of Vygotsky (1978), who described the zone of proximal development as defining "those functions that have not yet matured but are in the process of maturation" (p. 86). As Palincsar and David in Chapter 9 note, Vygotsky's work suggests that the acquisition of skills progresses from a stage in which the teacher and learner jointly collaborate to perform a cognitive task (interpsychological plane) to a state in which the learner has internalized and can regulate the process him- or herself (intrapsychological plane).

Although the parents had matured in their book-reading interactions with their children, the peer-modeling stage was instituted to promote parents' further internalization and regulation of the book-reading strategies. In this stage, parents began to direct the book-reading sessions themselves, focusing on modeling particular book-reading strategies for the group and practicing the targeted strategies with one another. More specifically, one or two parents each week would model how they would read a book to their child for the entire group, and the other parents would provide feedback and coach one another in the use of the strategies. The university leader's role in this stage was supportive and served to

(a) guide parents' participation in book-reading interactions with each other,

(b) find connections between what the parents already knew and what they needed to know,

(c) model effective book-reading behaviors for the parents when such assistance was needed,

(d) encourage them to review teacher tapes, and

(e) provide praise and support for their attempts.

The process of internalization for the parents was gradual, but they began to assume more and more control of the book-reading sessions themselves. The following are examples of two parents' initial attempts at modeling for their peers what they would do in book-reading interactions with their children at home.

Displaying the book *Over and Under* by Matthias (1984), Charlene explains to the group that she thinks this is a good book for young children because the pictures are "explanatory." She begins by reading the title and the author's name. She reads each page and talks about the pictures, emphasizing that she would ask her child to tell what is in each picture so that she knows he understands. As Charlene reads, she rephrases the written language "for Kyle's understanding," she says.

Charlene illustrates how a parent can expand, extend, clarify, and even disregard the written language forms chosen by the author in favor of a more appropriate text for her child (Altwerger, Diehl-Faxon, & Dockstader-Anderson, 1985). Furthermore, she is continually adjusting her [and the author's] demands to the developing abilities of her son as she focuses on meaning rather than form (Snow & Ninio, 1986).

After Charlene finishes modeling for her peers how she would share this book with her son, she asks the mothers for suggestions for improvement. One mother asks Charlene if she allowed Kyle to hold the book. She replies "yes." Another mother comments that it was good that Charlene rephrased things in the book because she thought her son would not understand. The other parents show their approval nonverbally.

Patricia, another mother, is shy and withdrawn, and talks softly. She reads the title of her book, *Bigger and Smaller,* by Manley (1981). As she reads, she turns the pages and holds the book so the other parents may see. Her tone is so soft that it is difficult to understand what she is saying. Turning the page, she cautiously reads, "One candle on baby's cake." She then stops for a long pause. The parents and the university leader watch to see what she intends to do. Finally, in order to help Patricia move forward, the university leader suggests the need to relate the story to the child's life, "You might want to say: Remember when you were one?" The parents, including Patricia, see the humor in this statement as they realize its improbability. Laughing with them, the leader suggests that Patricia might want to ask: "Do you remember when you went to a birthday party, and the person was one?" The university leader glances at Patricia and says, "He had one candle because. . . ." And Patricia enthusiastically responds, "Because he is one year old!"

Patricia, like Charlene, asks her peers for suggestions. They praise her for her initial attempts and encourage her to be more relaxed when sharing books with her son. One mother comments that, with practice, Patricia will learn to relax. Another mother replies, "You read the title of the book and you held the book so that all of us could see it, which indicates that you have learned the importance of letting your child see the book when you are reading to him at home."

In the unfolding weeks, the parents continued to learn and mature. They jointly shared in the book-reading sessions and verbally and nonverbally corrected and guided each other. They provided each other with the same instructional scaffolding the university leader had provided for them earlier. Their story talk increased in complexity and their shyness about participating in the peer group decreased. They learned to approach the book-reading sessions with confidence.

Parent-Child Interaction

During the final phase, the university leader ceded total control to the parents and functioned primarily as a supportive and sympathetic audience: offering suggestions to the mothers as to what books to use in reading interactions with their children; evaluating the parent-child book-reading interactions; and providing feedback or modeling. In this final phase, parents actually brought their own children to the sessions and used the strategies directly with them. The examples below provide some evidence of the parents' developing knowledge of book-reading.

Jeanette shares with her four-year-old daughter, Erica, the book *Sometimes Things Change,* by Patricia Eastman (1983).

JEANETTE: And the title of our book is . . . *"Sometimes Things Change"* by Patricia Eastman. (Erica nods yes.)

JEANETTE: Let's look at the picture. What do you see in the picture?

ERICA: A little girl.

JEANETTE: What is she doing? Look at the picture. What is she doing? She's . . . is she pointing at what? She's doing what? What is this on this? A worm. Have you ever seen a worm like that before? (Erica nods no.) OK. Let's find out about this worm. OK. (Erica and Jeanette turn to the first page of the book.)

JEANETTE: OK. Sometimes things change. Once upon a time a butterfly . . . You ever seen a butterfly before? (Erica nods yes.) You know what a butterfly was before he was a butterfly? (Jean-

> ette looks at Erica and points to the book. Erica nods yes
> then no.)
>
> JEANETTE: Yeah? Yeah. Let's look quick at the pictures. OK. This is
> what a butterfly was . . .
>
> ERICA: A worm.
>
> JEANETTE: A worm! . . . or a caterpillar. OK? Let's see. (Erica nods
> yes.)
>
> JEANETTE: See? He was a caterpillar. (Jeanette points to page.)

The dialogue between Jeanette and Erica continues, following the "completion" routine observed by Doake (1986). The completion structure, together with mumble, cooperative, and echo reading, comprised the forms of participation that Doake observed in parent-child interaction as children become increasingly familiar with certain stories. The completion form is characterized by the reader's pausing at various points in a story, inviting the child to complete the sentence. After Jeanette does this, she requests a further explanation from Erica about the sentence. She accepts Erica's response and praises her efforts. Jeanette frequently repeats and extends her child's vocalization. She also defines words, clarifies text, and relates the text to Erica's background of experience. For example, she asks Erica at one point in the story, "What do you think you were before you were a baby?" Erica answers, "A little girl." Throughout the interaction, Jeanette directs Erica's attention to the text and to the details and story events within the text. Over the 7 weeks, Erica begins to ask her mother more questions and to read along as Jeanette reads to her.

Patricia, a second mother, chose to read Ziefert's (1985) *Baby Ben Gets Dressed,* a book featured in a first-grade teacher's sample given earlier in this chapter. Patricia sits in an overstuffed chair, holding Walter in her lap and positioning the book so that both can see.

> WALTER: I'm ready to read (bouncing into his mother's lap)!
>
> PATRICIA: Baby Ben Gets (pointing to title) . . .
>
> WALTER: Baby Ben Gets Dressed (taking control of the book)!
>
> PATRICIA: It's time for Baby Ben to get dressed. What's he wearing?
>
> WALTER: A shirt!
>
> PATRICIA: Where's the word shirt (trying to assist Walter)? (Negating
> any help, Walter hurriedly finds the words himself.)
>
> PATRICIA: He's wearing socks and sneakers too (pointing to the words).
> "You look funny, Teddy," said Baby Ben. Do you know
> what's funny?
>
> WALTER: Yeah, they're the wrong colors.

PATRICIA: What colors are they?

WALTER: Purple and yellow.

PATRICIA: Now, look at the pictures. Shirt, socks, sneakers, and over-
alls. (She points to each word.) Now, read the pictures to me.

WALTER: (And he does.) Shirt, socks, sneakers . . .

Patricia and Walter continue the reading of the story following the first-
grade teacher's pattern of labeling and describing pictures. Upon completion
of *Baby Ben Gets Dressed,* Walter again takes the book away from his
mother. Rapidly flipping the pages, Walter exclaims, "I 'swimming' [skim-
ming] through this book"; and using his index finger, just as his mother and
the first-grade teacher had done, he designates each item of apparel and calls
out the words.

From the above dialogue, it is evident that Walter is internalizing the
strategies and language for talking about the pictures and story that he had
heard his own parent use in the initial reading of the book. Walter's situation-
specific use of language follows the pattern that Snow and Goldfield (1983)
describe of children becoming more facile with language and concomitant
cognitive processing.

The most important result of the book-reading program was the manner
in which parents guided their children's participation in the book-reading
interactions. Their actions indicated an ever-increasing awareness of what
their children knew and, even more importantly, what they needed to know.
As the parents finely tuned and structured their book-reading interactions,
their children became more active as readers and participants. The parents'
facility meant that children extended their active participation beyond what
children would have been able to accomplish independently.

EFFECTS OF THE BOOK-READING PROGRAM

Observational data showed that the children increased in their knowledge and ability to participate in book-reading interactions with their parents.
More importantly, they became active conversational partners, and they
learned to ask and answer questions. Even though the university leader did
not observe children in their classroom reading interactions, the children's
teachers as a group reported that they had observed a difference in the children's ability to participate in classroom reading interactions. The teachers
also reported that the children's knowledge of written language, directional-
ity, and story grammar had improved since they had become a part of the
book-reading program. Further, the teachers noted achievement in grade-

appropriate subjects, like the alphabet, colors, locations, sequences, comparisons, and so forth. The university leader's observations of the children as well as the teachers' observations revealed that the book-reading program did indeed have a positive effect on the children's literacy development.

SUCCESSFUL ELEMENTS IN
THE BOOK-READING PROGRAM

A major component contributing to the success of this program that should not be overlooked was the community. Initially, the university leader asked for community support in recruiting parents for participation in the book-reading program from the Ministerial Alliance, business leaders, and ordinary townspeople (e.g., grandmothers, bus drivers, and people sitting on street corners). Overwhelming support was received from all groups, including the school superintendent. Two community leaders, in particular, surfaced as strong advocates of the program. One was a local bar owner, Ray Jacobs, who attended all of the book-reading sessions. He brought mothers to school to participate in the program and took them back home. He worked successfully with the Social Services Department to secure baby-sitters for those parents who otherwise would not come and thus not benefit from the program. Mr. Jacobs's support was echoed by Father Hogan, the priest of a predominantly African-American Catholic Church. He urged parents to participate in the book-reading program, noting in a sermon that literacy was a "tool of faith" and that children needed to be able to read the confirmation requirements.

This outpouring of support from the community was duplicated in the local school where school administrators, teachers, and the librarian staunchly supported the program. Teachers, as well as the school administrators and the librarian, enrolled in a family literacy course taught by the university leader to broaden their knowledge of literacy development in different family structures. Teachers also assisted in the development of training materials designed to show parents effective book-reading behaviors, and they also agreed to observe the participating children's classroom performance in reading. The principal and assistant principal helped to publicize the program in the community, driving parents to the program each week and creating a friendly and warm environment at the school for the parents. The librarian designed a computer program that listed the names of each child whose parent was participating in the book-reading program. For the first time in the school's history, parents were able to check out up to five books under their child's name. The librarian also kept a computerized list of types of books the parents were checking out. This information was shared with the university leader and the child's teacher. More importantly, the teachers, school administrators, and the librarian began to accept the parents as a useful and reliable resource.

Initially, the participating parents had feared coming to school because of their own past experiences. However, they soon began to enjoy coming and could actually laugh about the experiences they were encountering. The general consensus among parents was that "for the first time . . . they were being invited to school not because there was a problem with their child, but to learn how to share books with their child and to support their child's growth toward literacy" (Edwards, in review). In the past the parents noted that they were invited to school only when their children were failing or had already failed. The parents also stated that the teachers talked to them in generalities about reading to their children, and that they did not understand what the teachers meant when they were told to "read to their children" or "be a good literate model." These parents were echoing the sentiments of Lareau (1986) and Ogbu (1974) who argue that nonmainstream parents who lack knowledge do not necessarily lack interest in the schools their children attend nor in knowing how to help their children. What schools and districts lack, as McLaughlin and Shields (1987) put it, are appropriate strategies or structures for involving nonmainstream parents.

The Parents as Partners in Reading Program provided such a structure for parents to participate in book-reading interactions with their children. The obvious success of the program is evident in the comments of one parent:

> I had a lot doubts about myself and it was hard for me to make up my mind about coming. With some encouragement from another mother who was attending the program, I decided to come. She told me that "the program would help me help my kids in school." I said to her, "OK, I'll come one time," but I ended coming all year. By coming to this program, I found out that there was a lot that I didn't know and a lot of things that I wasn't doing, but I didn't know what to do. I really didn't know bookreading was so important. I wish I had known that sooner, because I would have been able to help my other children in school.

SUMMARY

Nearly 20 years ago, Swift (1970) found that "as time passed, [the nonmainstream mothers he assisted to participate in book-reading interactions] began to illustrate not only their enhanced story telling ability but their increased perception of their role in the life, education, and [literacy support] of their children, as well as of the children's dependence upon them for coping with situations they encounter" (p. 366). Similarly, this chapter serves to demonstrate that nonmainstream parents can profit from learning to engage in book-reading interactions with their young children.

Although "read to your child" is the most frequently requested parent-involvement activity in the schools (Vukelich, 1984), this directive cannot be effective until we shift from "telling" to "showing" nonmainstream parents how to read to their children (Edwards, 1989). For many nonmainstream parents, reading is not a literacy event in their home and books are not a literacy artifact. If nonmainstream parents are shown how to share books with their young children and are provided with successful models of book-reading, we will help these parents help their children grow toward literacy. Nonmainstream parents have the right to know that sharing books with their children is the most powerful and significant predicator of school achievement. Not only do they have the right to know, they have the right to receive assistance in how to participate in book-reading interactions with their young children.

REFERENCES

Altwerger, A., Diehl-Faxon, J., & Dockstader-Anderson, K. (1985). Read-aloud events as meaning construction. *Language Arts, 62,* 476–484.

Anderson, A. B., & Stokes, S. J. (1984). Social and institutional influences on the development and practice of literacy. In H. Goelman, A. Oberg, & F. Smith (Eds.), *Awakening to literacy* (pp. 24–37). Exeter, NH: Heinemann.

Au, K. H., & Kawakami, A. J. (1984). Influence of the social organization of instruction on children's text comprehension ability: A Vygotskian perspective. In T. E. Raphael (Ed.), *The contexts of school-based literacy* (pp. 63–77). New York: Random House.

Dickerson, D. K. (1989). Effects of a shared reading program in one Head Start language and literacy environment. In J. Allen & J. Mason (Eds.), *Risk makers, risk takers, risk breakers: Reducing the risks for young literacy learners* (pp. 125–153). Portsmouth, NH: Heinemann.

Doake, D. B. (1986). Learning to read: It starts in the home. In D. R. Rovey & J. E. Kerber (Eds.), *Roles in literacy learning* (pp. 2–9). Newark, DE: International Reading Association.

Durkin, D. (1966). *Children who read early.* New York: Teachers College Press.

Durkin, D. (1984). Poor black children who are successful readers: An investigation. *Urban Education, 19,* 53–76.

Eastman, P. (1983). *Sometimes things change.* Chicago: Children's Press.

Edwards, P. A. (1989). Supporting lower SES mothers' attempts to provide scaffold-ing for bookreading. In J. Allen & J. Mason (Eds.), *Risk makers, risk takers, risk breakers: Reducing the risks for young literacy learners* (pp. 222–250). Portsmouth, NH: Heinemann.

Edwards, P. A. (in review). Parents and children reading together: The library as family room. *Language Arts*.

Farron, D. C. (1982). Mother-child interaction, language development, and the school performance of poverty children. In L. Feagans & D. C. Farron (Eds.), *The language of children reared in poverty* (pp. 19–52). New York: Academic Press.

Flood, J. (1977). Parental styles in reading episodes with young children. *The reading teacher, 30,* 864–867.

Gallimore, R., & Goldenberg, C. N. (1989, March). *School effects on emergent literacy experiences in families of Spanish-speaking children.* Paper prepared at the annual meeting of the American Educational Research Association, San Francisco.

Heath, S. B., with Thomas, C. (1984). The achievement of preschool literacy for mother and child. In H. Goelman, A. Oberg, & F. Smith (Eds.), *Awakening to literacy* (pp. 51–72). London: Heinemann.

Lareau, A. (1986, April). *Social class differences in family-school relationships: The importance of cultural capital.* Unpublished manuscript, Department of Sociology, Stanford University.

Lartz, M. N., & Mason, J. M. (1988). Jamie: One child's journey from oral to written language. *Early Childhood Research Quarterly, 3,* 193–208.

Manley, D. (1981). *Bigger and smaller.* Windermire, FL: Ray Rouke.

Mason, J. M. (1986, March). *Reading stories to preliterate children: A proposed connection to reading.* Paper presented at the Conference on Early Reading, Center for Cognitive Science, University of Texas at Austin.

Mason, J. M., Peterman, C. L., & Kerr, B. M. (1988, April). *Fostering comprehension by reading books to kindergarten children* (Tech. Rep. No. 426). Urbana, IL: Center for the Study of Reading.

Matthias, C. (1984). *Over Under.* Chicago: Children's Press.

McCormick, C., & Mason, J. M. (1986). Intervention procedures for increasing preschool children's interest in and knowledge about reading. In W. Teale & E. Sulzby (Eds.), *Emergent literacy: Writing and reading* (pp. 90–115). Norwood, NJ: Ablex.

McLaughlin, M. W., & Shields, P. M. (1987). Involving low-income parents in the schools: A role for policy? *Phi Delta Kappan, 69,* 156–160.

Meek, M. (1982). *Learning to read.* London: The Bodley Head.

Ninio, A. (1980). Picturebook reading in mother-infant dyads belonging to two subgroups in Israel. *Child Development, 51,* 587–590.

Ninio, A., & Bruner, J. (1978). The achievement and antecedents of labelling. *Journal of Child Language, 5,* 1–6.

Ogbu, J. (1974). *The next generation.* New York: Academic Press.

Resnick, M. B., Roth, J., Aaron, P. M., Scott, J., Wolking, W. D., Laren, J. J., & Packer, A. B. (1987). Mothers reading to infants: A new observational tool. *The Reading Teacher, 40,* 888–895.

Rogoff, B. (1984). Adult assistance of children's learning. In T. E. Raphael (Ed.), *The contexts of school-based literacy* (pp. 27–40). New York: Random House.

Sledge, A. C. (1987, April). *Mother infant literacy knowledge.* Paper presented at the annual meeting of the American Educational Research Association, Washington, DC.

Snow, C., & Ferguson, C. (Eds.). (1977). *Talking to children.* New York: Cambridge University Press.

Snow, C. E., & Goldfield, B. (1983). Turn the page please: Situation specific language learning. *Journal of Child Language, 10,* 551–570.

Snow, C. E., & Ninio, A. (1986). The contract of literacy: What children learn from learning to read books. In W. H. Teale & E. Sulzby (Eds.), *Emergent literacy: Writing and reading.* Norwood, NJ: Ablex.

Swift, M. S. (1970). Training poverty mothers in communication skills. *The Reading Teacher, 23,* 360–367.

Teale, W. H., Martinez, M. G., & Glass, W. H. (1988). Describing classroom storybook reading. In D. Bloome (Ed.), *Classrooms and literacy* (pp. 58–188). Norwood, NJ: Ablex.

Teale, W. H. (1981). Parents reading to their children: What we know and need to know. *Language Arts, 58,* 902–911.

Teale, W. H. (1987). Emergent literacy: Reading and writing development in early childhood. In J. E. Readence & R. S. Baldwin (Eds.), *Research in Literacy: Merging Perspectives* (36th Yearbook of the National Reading Conference) (pp. 45–74). Rochester, NY: National Reading Conference.

Vukelich, C. (1984). Parents' role in the reading process: A review of practical suggestions and ways to communicate with parents. *The Reading Teacher, 37,* 472–477.

Vygotsky, L. S. (1978). *Mind in society.* Cambridge, MA: Harvard University Press.

Wertsch, J. V. (1979). From social interaction to higher psychological processes: A clarification and application of Vygotsky's theory. *Human Development, 22,* 1–22.

Ziefert, H. (1985). *Baby Ben gets dressed.* New York: Random House.

Ziner, F., & Galdone, P. (1962). *The Counting Carnival.* New York: Coward-McCann.

Part III
POLICIES

Literacy in schools is influenced by a complex, and sometimes contradictory, array of policies. Most policies are interpreted and reinterpreted several times before students, teachers, and curricula interact in instructional activities. For this and other reasons, the size and direction of the effect of a given policy, whether initiated from the district, state, or federal level, is not always obvious from its rationale. In creating learning conditions that foster literacy for diverse groups of students, it is especially important that the intended effects of policies be compared with the everyday experiences of students in schools. The chapters in Part III trace the effects of selected policies for several particularly important aspects of literacy instruction.

In Chapter 15, Brown presents a broad-ranging study of variations in policy implementation in several large school districts. In Chapter 16, in an analysis of high school literature curricula, Applebee demonstrates that relatively rapid growth of diversity in the student population has far exceeded the rate of change in curriculum content. Allington in Chapter 17 examines influences of various meanings given to literacy and learning by classroom teachers, special reading teachers, and administrators of Chapter 1 and other special reading programs. Although federal guidelines set some parameters for these programs, views of literacy and learning at local levels are shown to penalize some children.

In Chapter 18 García and Pearson review assessment practices associated with literacy programs. They argue that emphasis on standardized multiple-choice testing procedures has worked against literacy acquisition for large numbers of students, especially students for whom English is a second language and children of the poor. In place of these measures, García and Pearson suggest embedding assessment in classroom practices that provide students with a range of, and more diverse, contexts for authentic performance.

In Chapter 19, Shepard traces the effects of certain tracking, retention, and special education policies that, in fact, act against the very groups the policies are intended to benefit. These policies are often based on reductionist views of learning. Shepard suggests that policies driven by a constructivist view of learning and literacy acquisition are more likely to support higher levels of literacy for all students.

Advocacy of a constructivist perspective and its consequent changes in literacy policies and practices have been evident throughout this volume. This consensus is part of a larger phenomenon through which a "new" vision of literacy for a diverse society is being created. To achieve the goals of the higher literacies for all in a diverse society depends on extension of this vision and its enactment in classrooms, school board offices, and legislatures around the country.

15 | Policy and the Rationalization of Schooling

REXFORD BROWN
Education Commission of the States

In 1987, with a generous grant from the John D. and Catherine T. MacArthur Foundation, some colleagues and I began an intensive study of the effects of policy on efforts to develop a much higher level of literacy for a much broader range of students. We were studying a literacy of thoughtfulness, a literacy that included critical and creative thinking and problem solving, skills in analysis, synthesis, interpretation, evaluation, dispositions to apply these skills, and knowledge about how and when to do so. Much in demand as a literacy for the 21st century, thoughtfulness involves students in constructing systems of meaning and negotiating them with others collaboratively. Where we found this literacy in schools, we wanted to know how policy helped bring it about or sustain it; where we did not find it, we wanted to know what role policy played in discouraging it or preventing its proliferation throughout the system.

Webster's Third New International Dictionary (Gove, 1976) says that policy is "a definite course or method of action selected from among alternatives and in the light of given conditions to guide and usually determine present and future conditions" (p. 1754). Our first-level commonsense definition was simply an extension of that: Policy is a social agreement that has been expressed through formal public pronouncements, laws, and the rules and regulations that interpret and apply them. Official policy has to be formal, which means that certain elected and appointed officials have considered it in some public forum and ultimately written it down. To say that it is an agreement does not mean that everyone agrees with it; the opposition party may not agree with the administration's foreign policy, for instance. But once it is written down, it becomes the guiding rationale for how the administration is going to conduct itself and explain its actions.

At this first level of understanding, then, there are executive, legislative, and judicial policymakers, all of whom derive certain policy-making prerogatives from the United States Constitution or state constitutions or city char-

217

ters and all of whom can delegate certain other policy-making prerogatives to other legally constituted bodies. Education policymakers are then governors, legislators, chief state school officers, state school board members, local school board members, and others to whom they delegate policy authority. Judges have increasingly become education policymakers through desegregation rulings and detailed school district guidelines respecting equitable financing of education, civil rights, and equality of opportunity.

Besides these duly constituted policymakers, other people powerfully affect policy through their official roles as interpreters and appliers of policy. These are the rule makers and program makers: state department of education officials, for instance, or centrally housed administrators in a school district, who write regulations that are supposed to follow logically from the policies and develop programs that are supposed to carry out the intentions of policymakers. These rules and regulations and programs often touch people's lives more directly than the policies that spawned them. It is often the case that the regulations and programs developed by rule makers and program makers do not uncontroversially embody the spirit or follow the letter of the policy. Many's the slip 'twixt cup and lip.

Policymakers, rule makers, and program makers create important symbolic and practical elements of the work environments within which teachers and administrators understand and carry out their jobs. Policy does not fully constitute that environment by any means. Professional norms, beliefs, and community influences are very powerful, as are the situational imperatives to which people in the system must react every day (Wilson, 1990). But policies do contribute to the organizational cultures, if you will, that establish norms of behavior, create motivational climates, and reinforce, explicitly or implicitly, certain value systems. Administrators can sweeten or sour the environments, depending upon their management and leadership philosophies and styles.

It was at this general level of understanding that we began our studies of how people in different parts of the education system react to different policies and how those policies affect what happens in classrooms. We were particularly interested in knowing how policies in curriculum, instruction, and evaluation affected efforts to offer students far more opportunities for critical and creative thinking, problem solving, and active learning. How powerful are curricular mandates once the classroom door closes? How do mandated teacher evaluations of various kinds constrain or liberate educators' capacities to cultivate a literacy of thoughtfulness? To what degree do mandated tests drive curriculum and instruction away from or closer to the conditions necessary for broad cultivation of a literacy of thoughtfulness?

In attempting to answer these questions, we deepened our understanding of how policy works. In our case studies of school districts, we found that unambiguous, direct links between specific state or district policies and specific teacher behaviors are rare (Brown, in press). Connections between policies and symbolic environments and general understandings about roles and responsibilities are much easier to descry. We also found that policy can exacerbate or soothe natural tensions between institutional needs and practitioner needs; that policy operates as a kind of discourse—a metadiscourse, if you will—that encourages some kinds of school and classroom discourse while it discourages other kinds; and that the language of policy rationalizes the education system—that is to say, it defines what is reasonable, it creates structures of consciousness that guide the ways people tend to define problems, ask questions, talk with one another, and actually think about what they are doing.

THE STUDY

We decided at the outset that we should not attempt to study a literacy of thoughtfulness through a model of policy research and analysis as scientific undertakings in the positivist tradition. We agreed that we were engaged in cultural interpretation, not hard science; that a separation of facts and values would be both impossible and undesirable; and that case-study narratives were more appropriate for the study than modes of discourse that purport to be scientifically objective. Our approach was consequently similar to what Jennings (1987) calls "policy analysis as counsel" (p. 139). We would describe what we saw, try to make reasonable recommendations on the basis of our experience, and let policymakers and other audiences take whatever actions they saw fit.

We also assumed a hermeneutic perspective about the world we were studying: that people's actions and experience are essentially linguistic; that they are engaged in various kinds of language games and our job as researchers is to understand and describe those games. This presumption, too, was dictated by our belief that the literacy we were studying rests on what Rorty (1982) calls a pragmatist vision of "the human community as engaged in problem-solving" (p. 10). We would try to determine what problems our interviewees were trying to solve and what formal and informal kinds of community they were constituting in their efforts to solve problems.

Because a literacy of thoughtfulness draws heavily on what Bruner (1986) calls "a language of culture creating," as opposed to "a language of knowledge consuming" (p. 133), we sensitized ourselves to these and other discourse differences and analyzed school discourse captured in our interviews and observations with these distinctions in mind. In our interviews with students, teachers, administrators, and policymakers, we tried to determine what key terms such as *critical thinking* or *basic skills* meant to them. We tried to get a sense of how they talked about literacy as well as what they talked about. We enquired into perceived barriers to a more robust literacy. We tried to determine how and how well people in schools and districts communicated with each other and their external clients. We tried to grasp and characterize the kinds of conversations going on in and around schools. We listened for beliefs about knowledge, learning, and human potential. Wherever we went, we collected documents describing policy and practice and analyzed the language in which they were expressed.

In our observations of classrooms, we tried to grasp the discourse context (recitation, coaching, lecture, etc.) and describe the learning environment physically and symbolically. We characterized relationships and interactions. We looked for questioning strategies, various kinds of facilitation and probing. We analyzed discussions and nonverbal indicators of engagement and interest. We looked for various signs of courtesy, sensitivity, listening, humor, reflection, and, of course, thinking. We collected classroom materials.

Altogether, we spent about 650 hours at seven sites (three rural, four urban) and countless hours making sense out of what we saw there and integrating material and experiences external to the study. The sites were chosen because each claimed to be making a deliberate effort, through state and district policy, to offer a more robust literacy to a full range of students, not just an elite. Each interpreted literacy differently; for some, it turned out to be a basic skill; for some, it was a higher order kind of skill; for some, it was not simply a skill—it was a version of the literacy of thoughtfulness I have described. Three sites were located in some of the very poorest rural counties in some of the poorest states in the United States; their student populations were entirely either African-American or Native American. Four sites were urban districts with diverse student bodies and the full spectrum of urban woes and challenges.

The schools and classrooms we visited in each district were those described by key people as the best places to find what we were looking for. We concentrated on grades 3, 6, 8, and 11.

SOME FINDINGS

What do educators believe keeps them from giving students more opportunities to think, solve problems, and learn to use their minds more effectively? Our interviews and observations turned up a variety of perceived policy-related constraints.

Too Little Time

The reason most often cited for why schools lack instruction conducive to thoughtfulness was "time." Many said there simply was not enough time for it in a class period or a school day. Many said that what time available, is too fragmented for sustained intellectual activities. A number said that the schedule dominates decision making in their schools.

Time is perceived as a policy constraint because it is a collectively bargained commodity, because the whole enterprise of schooling is set up according to required credit hours, because pupil progress is gauged in terms of required attendance time, and because definitions of the school day and school year are determined by policy, among other reasons. Some teachers believe that for each student, learning is primarily a matter of time exposed to subjects and time available to practice and process what one has learned (see Chapter 17). The prevailing model of schooling, however—partly a creature of policy and certainly held in place by policy—does not structure or allocate time in ways that make it possible for individuals to get the time they need or that thoughtfulness requires.

So pervasive are conscious and unconscious assumptions about time in educational discourse, so thoroughly do profound and silly ideas about time penetrate educational philosophy, policy, and daily practice that one is at a loss to know where to begin a critique that could lead to new ways of using time in schools. Perhaps the most obvious thing to do is to start anywhere, so long as one starts with a question about time. Why 12 years? Why 9 months? Why 6 hours per day? Why 40 minutes per period? Why 2 weeks on the Civil War? Why a timed test? Why are we spending our time doing x and not y? What do we really know about the relationship between time and learning? Answers to these questions lead to further questions and ultimately expose the ways in which outdated cultural and educational notions are embedded in and furthered by policy. What is lacking, in most schools and districts, is a forum for just such a continuing inquiry.

Too Much to Cover

"Coverage" was the second most common reason given for why there is not more thoughtfulness in the schools. Teachers feel they must cover a sprawling and constantly expanding list of topics. They perceive the curriculum as so packed that nothing more can be shoehorned in, yet, in their view, policymakers seem to want to mandate more and more courses and services.

Although some curricular demands clearly stem from policy mandates, many result from the ways professionals have come to define their knowledge bases and lay out their instructional plans. A few teachers told us this. Clearly, so long as educators and policymakers alike view knowledge as an accretion of facts and terms to be transmitted, not constructed, it becomes mathematically impossible to teach it all. Policy documents and educator comments reveal that the relationship of curriculum and time constraints to underlying assumptions about knowledge are neither perceived nor discussed by many school people. A continuing practitioner inquiry into the nature of the knowledge we are purveying is as essential to creating a climate for thoughtfulness as is a continuing inquiry into time. But curriculum inquiry inside school districts must be joined with community discussions about what is important on the outside. What we teach is a highly political matter.

School districts that we found making progress toward a literacy of thoughtfulness had found ways to join the political and substantive, external and internal debates about what students should know and be able to do (Brown, in press). Policy documents embodied, legitimated, and promoted new kinds of community and school conversations.

Students Cannot Think

A third reason why there is so little thinking or problem solving going on is that many teachers believe that most students cannot think in sophisticated ways. Some elementary teachers told us their students were too young to think abstractly; some high school teachers told us their students were too unprepared in "the basics" to be ready to think as educated people think. Some educators believe that critical-thinking or problem-solving skills are determined by students' innate, inherited intelligence. This seems to guarantee that only a small percentage of students will be intelligent enough to be interested or engaged in a literacy of thoughtfulness.

Policies with respect to tracking and ability grouping reinforce an old-fashioned view of intelligence as a very limited resource and thinking as a function of intelligence (see, e.g., Oakes, 1985). Also problematic, we found, were compensatory education policies. Much of the research upon which compensatory education policies and practices rest either suggests or has been interpreted to suggest that many children lack capacities or motivation to do intellectual work. The basic-skills-oriented, remedial curriculum to which they are consequently exposed consumes enormous amounts of time and energy, perversely setting the stage for this negative prophecy to come true. Students raised on a steady diet of dumbed down, reductive, basic curriculum turn out as we could have predicted: uninterested in reading and writing, resistant to, or woefully unprepared for, the intellectual work of the higher grades.

Low Expectations

Expectations for minority and disadvantaged students are low. Interviewees sometimes said that schoolwork runs against the grain of minority culture or family upbringing or that asking too much of a disadvantaged student will further erode his or her self-esteem. Some also said that minorities—especially adolescent boys—resist academics as a matter of racial pride or as an act of social protest, and often taunt classmates who are academically inclined.

Other reasons given were: Minorities have unique "learning styles" and do not like to conceptualize the way Anglos do; language minorities cannot be expected to think in English (see Chapter 6); institutionalized racism undermines the motivation of minority children; minority parents prefer drill, rote memorization, and disciplined instruction for their children, distrusting progressive approaches that undermine parental authority; minority and poor parents do not provide the kind of support Anglo and affluent parents provide, so their children cannot be expected to compete. Some also said that competition, even for grades, is foreign to the cultures of some minority children. No one of these assertions was made by more than a few people and all were contradicted by other assertions and evidence to the contrary. Clearly there is much confusion about this issue. Policies with respect to fairness, compensatory education, grouping, tracking, counseling, and service provision do little to clarify or deepen understanding of how best to proceed here.

Too Little Pedagogical Knowledge

A fifth constraint upon thinking and problem solving is that most teachers do not know how to do what is necessary. They did not see it in their own educations. Models of thoughtful learning environments are rare. Teachers seldom get the chance to observe each other, and teacher in-service training seldom exemplifies the precepts of active, hands-on learning or discovery. Indeed, in-service education per se is woefully thin, fragmented, and conducted primarily in lecture modes. Policies influencing teacher professional development—preservice, certification, and in-service—are clearly salient.

Too Hard to Evaluate

Another constraint upon activities conducive to more active learning, critical thinking, or creativity is the widespread belief that these activities either cannot be evaluated at all or cannot be evaluated in ways compatible with current accountability systems. The first belief was surprisingly strong, given all the evidence available to the contrary (see, e.g., Brown, 1989a; Chapter 18). The second belief is easier to understand; testing and accountability policies have long been perceived by many educators to be formidable barriers to progress (see also Brown, 1989b; Chapter 19).

Weak Policy Framework

In general, we found that "thoughtfulness policy" (policy about critical and creative thinking, problem solving, inquiry, etc.), whether at the state or local level, is weak. Goals or objectives dealing with these matters are either absent, poorly stated, or buried among other goals. The weaknesses take a variety of forms.

Thoughtfulness policy is usually framed in terms of skills and subskills. Such "thinking skills" or even "higher-order thinking skills" can be incorporated into current teaching methodology (lecture, recitation, teacher dominance, and student passivity) without requiring significant changes in teaching or schooling. State and local policies are largely silent about active learning, a necessary ingredient in any critical- and creative-thinking effort.

Policy says *what* to teach but not *how* to teach, thus bolstering the assumption that lecture and recitation are adequate for teaching thinking and that "seat time"—number of hours of exposure to a subject—is the best measure of learning. Policies in curriculum, testing, accountability, certification, teacher evaluation, and in-service implicitly or explicitly reinforce this "transmission" model of teaching.

Policy is often contradictory or confused, leading to contradictory or confused school programs. Recent reform packages reflect the bartering and compromise necessary to pass any complex legislation. Incompatible philosophies coexist in education policy, sending mixed signals and leaving ample room for districts to interpret and implement policy in a multitude of ways.

POLICY AND RATIONALIZATION

We observed educators doing various things; we asked them why they did them that way and we listened for answers related to policy. Many teachers said they did what they did because "it will be on the [state or district] test." Many said they taught what they taught because "that's the curriculum I'm supposed to teach." Many lectured and conducted recitations because "that's all there is time to do." But in any school we visited, there were other teachers who paid no attention to mandated tests or curriculum, and who had their students working thoughtfully regardless of time constraints. In many districts we visited, some schools were very rule bound and others seemed comparatively free from constraints. So we have to conclude that particular policies are not inevitable constraints on all teachers, administrators, or schools. In our opinion, new, insecure, and heavily monitored teachers and administrators were most likely to say they were constrained by particular policies, rules, or regulations.

A number of teachers and administrators blamed policy for behaviors that seemed to us more related to their professional training and experience. Policy can be a convenient whipping boy or a plausible excuse for not trying anything new. More influential than specific policies or professional habits, however, was a general school-wide or district-wide attitude about the binding force of rules and regulations and the degree to which teachers could be trusted to interpret and apply them according to their professional judgment about students and learning situations. That attitude is heavily influenced by the language of policy—how it sounds and what values it embeds—and the ways in which leaders choose to interpret and apply it.

The language of policy turns out to be mostly what sociologists call "instrumental rationality" (Habermas, 1984, p. 11). It is a language and rationality of getting things done. It is a language about objects and processes and institutions. It embeds a presupposition that we live in an objective world that can be mastered through goal-directed actions. It is the language of hard science and law and economics and administration.

But practitioners, who depend upon policy-guided institutions for housing and sustaining their practice, "speak," if you will, a different language, think, if you will, a different rationality. The language of learning is intersubjective, not objective. It has to do with people reaching understanding, which is fundamentally different from "getting things done." The practice of teaching takes place in a context of realities and constraints very different from those faced by managers, policymakers, rule makers, or program makers. It requires a full range of discourses and rationalities—moral, practical, expressive, even aesthetic—if it is to be successful. But these ways of thinking and conversing and negotiating meanings and collaborating in the search for, and creation of, knowledges and understandings require legitimation and "space" where they can be practiced. To the extent that an instrumental rationality of administration, economics, logistics, and control crowds out and replaces a language of learning, a literacy of thoughtfulness (for adults as well as students) has no institutional legitimacy, no way to sustain and reproduce itself. This is the likely case even when a number of people in the institution say they want a literacy of thoughtfulness. So long as they are thinking and talking about it instrumentally and not actually practicing it, they are unlikely to achieve it.

A tension between institution and practice is inevitable (see MacIntyre, 1981, for an interesting discussion of this from a philosophical point of view). But in some schools and districts it is an unhealthy tension. Conversation is vague and heavily laced with jargon. Intentions are unclear. People cannot seem to get to the bottom of anything. Talk seems systematically distorted and evasive. Policy language can become the lingua franca in such a climate in the absence of leaders sensitive to the need to preserve and expand institutional space for a language of learning.

SUMMARY

Education policy influences what people do not so much because it tells them what to do but because it establishes norms of rationality and communication, ways of thinking about things, and a vocabulary with which to describe and negotiate institutional experience. It structures and, sometimes, overdetermines the discourse it engenders. Leadership requires at least an intuitive grasp of this situation. Leaders who want a well-run institution that is hospitable to robust learning opportunities for adults and students alike have created space for reflection, critique, and dialogue through which people can become aware of the structures of thought implicit in their language (Brown, in press). They have created opportunities for people to explore unthreateningly the presuppositions in their own and others' language through formal and informal conversations oriented toward reaching understanding, not compliance. They understand that the educational structures that need "restructuring" are not just inside schools or districts; they are inside people's heads.

REFERENCES

Brown, R. G. (1989a). Testing and thoughtfulness. *Educational Leadership, 46,* 31–33.
Brown, R. G. (1989b). Who is accountable for thoughtfulness?" *Phi Delta Kappan, 69,* 49–52.

Brown, R. G. (in press). *Schools of thought.* San Francisco: Jossey-Bass.

Bruner, J. (1986). *Actual minds, possible worlds.* Cambridge, MA: Harvard University Press.

Gove, P. B. (Ed.). (1976) *Webster's third new international dictionary.* Springfield, MA: G. & G. Merriam.

Habermas, J. (1984). *The theory of communicative action* (Vol. I) (Thomas McCarthy, Trans.). Boston, MA: Beacon Press.

Jennings, B. (1987). Interpretation and the practice of policy analysis. In F. Fisher & J. Forester (Eds.), *Confronting values in policy analysis* (pp. 128–152). Beverly Hills, CA: Sage.

MacIntyre, A. (1981). *After virtue.* Notre Dame, IN: University of Notre Dame Press.

Oakes, J. (1985). *Keeping track: How schools structure inequality.* New Haven, CT: Yale University Press.

Rorty, R. M. (1982). Hermeneutics, general studies, and teaching. *Synergos: Selected papers from the Synergos seminars* (Vol. 2). Washington, DC: George Mason University.

Wilson, J. Q. (1990). *Bureaucracy.* New York: Basic Books.

16 | Literature: Whose Heritage?

ARTHUR N. APPLEBEE
State University of New York, Albany

As we consider the topic of literacy for diversity, it is fitting to turn our attention to the role of literature instruction in our nation's schools. Historically, literature in the schools has played a central role in discussions of cultural assimilation and cultural differentiation; more recently, such issues have been heightened by the complaints of authors such as E. D. Hirsch (1987) and Allan Bloom (1987), whose writings represent in part a conservative reaction against perceived changes in our schools. With literature continuing at the core of English instruction in the secondary school, and beginning to reclaim its central role in reading instruction in the elementary school, issues of literacy, literature, and diversity are inevitably closely intertwined.

THE POWER OF LITERATURE

Running through past and present discussions of the role of literature has been the acknowledgment of the power of literature both to shape the values of the individual and to redirect the course of society as a whole. This power has led to a long history of attempts to control the influence of literature on the schools through careful selection of "appropriate" selections and ruthless censorship of nonconforming texts. Thus Plato banned poets from his Republic, because their writings appealed to emotion rather than to reason. And similarly Horace Mann of Massachusetts, who did so much for public education, argued that novels should not be included in the school curriculum, because emotion had no place in our schools or in the life of the intellect (Applebee, 1974).

The belief in the power of literature is deeply ingrained in American education at all levels. The *New England Primer* (circa 1686), the first widely used schoolbook, was designed to foster a very specific set of religious beliefs (Ford, 1962). The next "giants" in American schoolbooks continued that tradition of shaping students' values through the selections they were asked to read, though their goals were secular rather than religious: Webster's *Grammatical Institute of the English Language* (1783–1795) (which included his famous Blue-Backed Speller) sought to develop a common language and common Americanism, whereas *McGuffey's Readers* (1836) promulgated the development of proper attitudes, correct behavior, and the virtues of an American way of life (Johnson, 1963).

Thus the choice of America's early educators was clear: The role of literature was to reduce diversity and promote a common set of values and a common culture.

In making this choice, they listened to the voices of the Romantic poets and critics, who saw in literature a stay against the anarchy of the industrial revolution. The fullest statement of this point of view was presented in Matthew Arnold's (1867) *Culture and Anarchy* (in Culler, 1961; see also Williams, 1958), a text that was widely influential in America. As Arnold described it in 1880, "The future of poetry is immense, because in poetry, where it is worthy of its high destinies, our race, as time goes on, will find an ever surer and surer stay. . . . The stronger part of our religion to-day is its unconscious poetry" (Culler, 1961, p. 306). Arlo Bates (1897), an early professor and teacher of literature, was specific about which poetry filled this role. In his words, "One would hesitate to ask to dinner a man who confessed complete ignorance of *The Canterbury Tales*" (p. 125).

THE EMERGENCE OF A LITERARY CANON

English literature found a firm place in our high schools in the late 19th century, and it did so against a backdrop of attitudes such as these. Given such attitudes, a predictable canon emerged, one that reflected a particular British and American literary heritage, though the specific sources of selections in the high school were diffuse. As we think about the issue of literacy and diversity, it is useful to remind ourselves just how haphazard these influences were. They included:

1. Grammar instruction, which brought us Milton and the Augustan poets, whose Latinate styles had made them useful texts for analysis in early English grammar texts modeled on Latin predecessors
2. The preeminence of Shakespeare in popular culture long before Shakespeare became the particular provenance of the literary and cultural elite (Levine, 1988)
3. A concern to support contemporary literature (thus Addison, Steele, and

the English Romantics appeared initially as samples of contemporary literature in school readers, and then made their way into the high school)

4. A concern to include some literature that would be easily accessible to the adolescent reader, providing a place for texts such as Sir Walter Scott's *Ivanhoe*

5. The Latin and Greek training of most early English teachers, which led them to structure the English curriculum to reflect that of the "classical" languages that English replaced; the influences of this heritage are evident in the term "classics" itself, as well as in the placement of Shakespeare's *Julius Caesar* in the same year with Caesar's *Chronicles,* the Latin or Greek epic with Longfellow or *Paradise Lost,* and British and American orators with Cicero and Demosthenes

6. The influence of the familiar (thus Charles Cleveland (1851) explained the basis of selection in a preface to one of the early literature texts: "I have constantly endeavored to bear in mind a truth, which even those engaged in education may sometimes forget, that what is well known to us, must be new to every successive generation; and, therefore, that all books of selections designed for them should contain a portion of such pieces as all of any pretensions to taste have united to admire. Milton's 'Invocation to Light,' Pope's 'Messiah,' Goldsmith's 'Village Pastor,' and Gray's 'Elegy' are illustrations of my meaning").

The effects of these various influences are clear in a study of the literature curriculum as it was played out in American schools at the turn of the century (Tanner, 1907). The 10 most popular selections, in descending order of frequency, included *Julius Caesar, Macbeth, Silas Marner,* Milton's *Minor Poems, Merchant of Venice,* Burke's *Speech on Conciliation With the Colonies,* Lowell's *The Vision of Sir Launfal, Rime of the Ancient Mariner, Ivanhoe,* Macaulay's *Essay on Addison.*

Granting literature such power, and turning so firmly to a particular heritage, diversity had little place in the early teaching of literature. The unfamiliar, the unconventional, the new fared poorly. Thus we can listen to a professor of English, writing in 1923 in the pages of the official journal of the National Council of Teachers of English:

> If we know anything worth knowing about past literature, we can say something sensible about that much over-praised novel, *Main Street,* or about the blatant productions of the Vulgarian School of versifying, headed by Vachel Lindsay, Carl Sandburg, and a few nondescript immigrants, and sponsored by strong-minded ladies like Harriet Monroe and Amy Lowell. . . . The most noticeable feature of their curious volumes is that they need the services of a delousing station. (Baker, 1923)

With the wisdom of hindsight, we can laugh at the narrowness and shortsightedness of Professor Baker's comments, but such strong sentiments flow naturally from our deeply rooted beliefs in the power of literature to shape the individual as well as society. We may laugh less comfortably when we remind ourselves of contemporary manifestations of the same basic beliefs, in the attempts to censor the movie version of *The Last Temptation of Christ,* or in the violent Iranian reaction to Rushdie's *Satanic Verses.*

But the new and unfamiliar are often also vigorous and enlivening. The books and authors attacked so vociferously by Professor Baker claimed their own place in our culture and our society, and the schools built new rationales to justify them.

The belief in the power of literature to shape our values and beliefs continues, however. More recently, this same belief in the power of literature to empower readers has led to a different line of argument, one that emphasizes the need for greater diversity in the characters, settings, and authors included in texts used at elementary and secondary school levels to reflect the diverse cultural traditions that have found their place within our nation. Gaining impetus from the civil rights and women's movements in the 1960s, such voices have found their place within the academy itself as a new generation of scholars has sought to legitimate a wider range of critical studies.

Schools and publishers have been responsive to such calls for more broadly representative instructional materials, but just as in the past, such changes in the content of the curriculum are seen by advocates on all sides as involving fundamental questions about the nature of the individual and of society. As the perception has grown that the curriculum is being broadened, so has the virulence of the reaction against those changes. In a widely cited critique, E. D. Hirsch (1987) proclaimed the disappearance of cultural literacy from American schools. William Bennett (1988), as U.S. Secretary of Education, called similarly for a reassertion of the values of Western culture, arguing the timeliness and importance of the classics.

Both Hirsch and Bennett stand firmly within a tradition that goes back directly to Matthew Arnold, espousing one heritage (largely white, male, Anglo-Saxon) as the proper heritage of all of our citizens.

BUT WHAT OF THE SCHOOLS?

Where do our schools stand after two decades or more of attempts to provide more fully for the diverse groups of students they serve? Here we can turn to some of the recent studies carried out at the Center for the Learning and Teaching of Literature as part of a series of analyses designed to provide a comprehensive portrait of secondary school literature instruction.

In one study, we used teams of teachers and university-based researchers to visit schools with reputations for excellence, in a diverse set of communities across the United States (Applebee, 1989a). The teachers in these schools were well-prepared, experienced, and dedicated to their profession. The departments within which they taught were coherent and supportive, and had given thought and attention to the English curriculum for which they were responsible. Overall, these departments were appropriate places to study how the conventional wisdom about effective teaching of English works itself out in practice.

Among the many findings, perhaps the one most relevant in the context of our present concern with diversity was that these departments work best for their college-bound, primarily white, middle-class students. Students in non-college-bound tracks are the orphans of the system. Rewards and recognition, for individual teachers as well as for the department as a whole, usually come from their advanced-placement and college-bound students. These are the ones who raise average SAT scores, who win awards, and who generate favorable publicity in the local papers. Success with non-college-bound students, when it occurred, was attributed to the individual "outstanding" teacher, who was "dedicated," "caring," "devoted," or "sympathetic." In a telling difference from descriptions of success with the college-bound, such success was rarely attributed to the quality of the program, to careful planning, or to the systematic efforts of the department as a whole.

Indeed, the college-bound students even *look* like their teachers, sharing similar backgrounds, interests, and goals; students in the non-college-bound tracks, on the other hand, tend to diverge. Thus in our study when we asked students for their comments on authors that they had found "personally significant," the titles mentioned by the college-bound students echoed their teachers: Shakespeare and Steinbeck headed the list. Responses from the nonacademic tracks diverged: Stephen King and Judy Blume topped their list.

The result of these various factors is that the students who need the most help get the least attention in curriculum planning and curriculum revision.

A second point was also clear in our study of schools with reputations for excellent English programs: In spite of 20 years of efforts to broaden the curriculum, the selections for study were dominated by traditional British and American literature. The observers who visited the schools, as well as the teachers themselves, reported only token attention to world literature, contemporary literature, and to literature by women or minorities.

In another study sponsored by the Literature Center, we looked directly at the book-length works required of any students (Applebee, 1989b). Replicating a study conducted by the Educational Testing Service in 1963 (Anderson, 1964), we surveyed representative national samples of public, private, Catholic, and urban secondary schools, asking the department chairs to list titles of book-length works required of all students in any class at each of the high school grades. This survey, conducted in the spring of 1988, yielded results that look remarkably like those from secondary schools at the turn of the century. The most frequently required book-length works in public schools (grades 9–12) included *Romeo and Juliet, Macbeth, Huckleberry Finn, Julius Caesar, To Kill a Mockingbird, The Scarlet Letter, Of Mice and Men, Hamlet, The Great Gatsby, Lord of the Flies.*

All but one of these are the work of white, male, Anglo-Saxon authors—a situation that has changed not at all since Tanner's survey in 1907. (It is curious that the two women in these lists—Harper Lee in 1988 and George Eliot in 1907—both have gender-ambiguous or misleading names.) Although it was discouraging to see so little diversity in the top 10 titles, it was even more discouraging to find a similar homogeneity in the top 30 and top 50.

These are overall figures, however, and we were also interested in how they would vary in response to some of the diversity that was built into the schools in our sample. To explore this, we looked separately at public, private, and Catholic schools, at assignments by track within school, and at schools varying in ethnic composition.

Approached in this way, there were some differences in the titles required: Private schools, for example, were more likely to require the *Odyssey;* Catholic schools were less likely to include adolescent novels in the required curriculum; and lower-track students were less likely to be required to read at all—though when they were asked to read, the titles were again white, primarily male, and Anglo-Saxon. Shakespeare and Steinbeck continued to lead, joined, however by Zindel (*The Pigman*) and one woman, S. E. Hinton (*The Outsiders*).

The findings that were most surprising came from schools with high proportions of minority students. Again, Shakespeare, Steinbeck, and Dickens led the ranks of most frequently required authors. When we look specifically for minority authors, only two showed up at all: Lorraine Hansberry and Richard Wright. In the overall public school sample, they ranked 42nd and 53rd, respectively. In the sample of schools from major urban centers, their popularity increased, to 25th and 37th; in schools with 50% or more minority students, they ranked higher still, at 14th and 17th. No other minority author appeared in the top 50 in any of these lists.

The selections examined in this study were limited to book-length works—a restriction that in practice limited it to epics, novels, and plays. It is clear from our other studies that there is considerably more diversity in selections of short stories, poems, and nonfiction, and that commercial literature anthologies in particular have been making conscious efforts to broaden the basis of their selections. The curriculum as a whole, then, looks noticeably better than do the book-length works. On the other hand, it is the book-length works that are at the heart of the curriculum; these are the texts that receive the most time and attention and around which other selections are often organized and introduced. As long as these texts remain unchanged, there will be no "canonicity" for minority authors or for women; their place will continue to be at the margins of the culture that is legitimated by its place in the school.

There is another bit of evidence that is relevant to the argument here, evidence about what students know. Student achievement, as reflected in a recent National Assessment of literature and U.S. history, shows a similar pattern (Applebee, Langer, & Mullis, 1987). The assessment itself was a multiple-choice examination of knowledge of literature. On this examination, what students got right resembles the texts they are required to read. The best known aspects of literature included biblical stories, Shakespeare, Dickens, Greek mythology, and children's classics ("Cinderella," *Alice in Wonderland*)—literature that reflects the same Western heritage as the book-length required texts.

But such overall results are misleading in their suggestion that students are somehow "homogeneous" in what they know. The most interesting, if commonsense, finding from the National Assessment is that students' knowledge of literature is clearly linked to the diversity of their backgrounds. In particular, students are more likely to be knowledgeable about the literature and culture of their own racial and ethnic groups. African-American students, for example, did less well overall than did their white peers. But they did better than whites on questions dealing with literature by or about African-Americans. To take a typical example, 53% of African-American black students answered a question about Langston Hughes correctly, compared with only 35% of white students and 27% of Hispanics.

Such patterns of differential achievement raise interesting and troubling issues: What would patterns of racial and ethnic achievement look like if the content of our tests were dominated by African-American, Hispanic, Asian, or Native American literatures? And could we claim that such tests would be any less representative of knowledge of literature than are the tests we use now?

The issue, of course, is not one of simply ensuring that students read works from their own heritage. It is an issue of finding the proper balance among the many traditions, separate and intertwined, that make up the complex and changing fabric of American society. In our instruction, as well as our testing, we need to find better ways to ensure that our programs are culturally relevant as well as culturally fair—that no group is privileged while others are marginalized by the selections we choose to teach and the tests we choose to use. At the same time, we must also be wary of a curriculum that becomes too "particularized" (Ravitch, 1990), polarizing the separate traditions that contribute to our diversity, rather than increasing our understanding of and respect for other alternative traditions.

SUMMARY: WHAT IS OUR ANSWER TO DIVERSITY?

Whether intentional or not, schools have chosen to ignore diversity and assimilate everyone to the "classical" culture that found its way into the schools before the turn of the century. The roots of such an approach run deep—in Matthew Arnold's rationalization of the power of literature as a stay against anarchy, William McGuffey's attempts to develop proper values and a common Americanism in his *Readers,* and William Bennett's recent appeals to "our one great heritage."

But the dangers are also real. Louise Rosenblatt, writing in 1938, said of literature:

> Literature treats the whole range of choices and aspirations and values out of which the individual must weave [a] personal philosophy. The literary works that students are urged to read offer not only "literary" values, . . . but also some approach to life, some image of people working out a common fate, or some assertion that certain kinds of experiences, certain modes of feeling, are valuable. (p. 20)

But what happens to the students who find that their lives and values have been marginalized, if they have any place at all, in the curriculum we require them to study? What kind of multicultural society are we building that privileges one segment of society to the virtual exclusion of others? Where do our young African-American, Hispanic, or Asian students, or our young women of any ethnic background, find their role models and personal philosophy in the canon we presently offer?

The answer seems clear that they don't. And until they can, I must believe that we are failing in a fundamental way to open the gates of literacy to the majority of the students we teach.

This is the problem, and the challenge: to overcome our own reliance on the familiar, to step outside the narrowness of our own traditions, to open ourselves to the richness of the many cultures that offer great art and great literature—to find the approaches and the curriculum that will ensure that all of our students will find both a common culture and the unique voice that assures them that they, too, come from a tradition that gives them roots and have a future that offers them hope.

REFERENCES

Anderson, S. (1964). *Between the Grimms and 'The Group': Literature in American high schools*. Princeton, NJ: Educational Testing Service.

Applebee, A. N. (1974). *Tradition and reform in the teaching of English: A history.* Urbana, IL: National Council of Teachers of English.

Applebee, A. N. (1989a). *The teaching of literature in programs with reputations for excellence in English* (Report No. 1.1). Albany, NY: Center for the Learning and Teaching of Literature.

Applebee, A. N. (1989b). *A study of book-length works taught in high school English courses* (Report No. 1.2). Albany, NY: Center for the Learning and Teaching of English.

Applebee, A. N., Langer, J. A., & Mullis, I. V. S. (1987). *Literature and U.S. history: The instructional experience and factual knowledge of high school juniors*. Princeton, NJ: National Assessment of Educational Progress, ETS.

Baker, H. T. (1923). The criticism and teaching of contemporary literature. *English Journal, 12*, 459–463.

Bates, A. (1897). *Talks on the study of literature*. Boston: Houghton-Mifflin.

Bennett, W. (1988). *American education: Making it work*. Washington, DC: U.S. Government Printing Office.

Bloom, A. (1987). *The closing of the American mind*. New York: Simon & Schuster.

Cleveland, C. (1851). *A compendium of English literature, chronologically arranged, from Sir John Mandeville to William Cowper*. Philadelphia: E. C. and J. Biddle. (First edition, 1849)

Culler, A. D. (Ed.). (1961). *The poetry and criticism of Matthew Arnold*. Boston: Houghton-Mifflin.

Ford, P. L. (1962). *The New England primer.* New York: Teachers College Press.

Hirsch, E. D. (1987). *Cultural literacy: What every American needs to know*. Boston: Houghton-Mifflin.

Johnson, C. (1963). *Old time schools and school books*. New York: Dover.

Levine, L. (1988). *Highbrow, lowbrow.* Cambridge, MA: Harvard University Press.

Ravitch, D. (1990). Diversity and democracy: Multicultural education in America. *American Educator, 14*, 16–20, 46–48.

Rosenblatt, L. (1938). *Literature as exploration*. New York: D. Appleton Century.

Tanner, G. W. (1907). Report of the committee appointed by the English Conference to inquire into the teaching of English in the high schools of the middle west. *School Review, 15*, 37–45.

Williams, R. (1958). *Culture and society 1780–1950*. London: Chatto and Windus.

17 | Children Who Find Learning to Read Difficult: School Responses to Diversity

RICHARD L. ALLINGTON
State University of New York at Albany

In every school some children find learning to read difficult, and such difficulties are, unfortunately, too often predictable. It is the children of poverty who are most likely to have literacy-learning difficulties. These are the children who are most likely to experience retention in grade, transition-room placement, remedial or special education program participation, and permanent assignment to a "bottom track." Such experiences increase the likelihood that one will never become truly literate, will leave school before graduation, will become a teen parent, and will be unemployed as a young adult (Edelmann, 1988). The most prevalent explanations for the failure of schools to educate poor children revolve around criticisms of the home environment. Unfortunately, children rarely have the option of selecting, or changing, their parents.

Although children of poverty are most at risk of being failed by our schools, there yet exists a remarkable diversity in the children who find learning to read difficult. First, children of poverty are diverse, with one-third from racial/ethnic minorities. Poor children reside in virtually every community, although our large cities have the greatest concentrations. However, even though school failure is most predictable for children of poverty, other children experience failure in our schools as well. These are children from working-class and middle-class families, and they too are diverse, although boys from these families seem more at risk than their sisters. We have created a number of hypotheses to explain the school failure of middle-class children—hypotheses that are less likely to indict the home environment than the hypotheses offered for poor children. Some are said to be unready for school, some immature or small for their age, some are said to be learning disabled, some are tagged as hyperactive. These diverse children are failed by schools, but the children have something else in common. The primary reason for their school failure is that they do not acquire reading and writing

237

abilities on the same schedule as their peers—these children find learning to read difficult.

SCHOOL RESPONSES TO AT-RISK CHILDREN

Over the past decade we have reported on the school experiences of children who find learning to read difficult. The majority of these children have been from economically disadvantaged families, but not all. We have examined the literacy instruction offered these children and concluded that few schools organize instructional resources such that low-achieving children are provided access to larger amounts of high-quality literacy instruction. Our findings suggest why the most common responses of schools (e.g., retention, remediation, and special education services) rarely substantially alter the academic status of children who do not acquire literacy early and easily (e.g., Birman, 1988; Juel, 1988; Slavin, 1989). The instructional programs organized for children who find learning to read difficult too often provide no out-of-the-ordinary instruction or provide only the minimum amount of the least expensive instruction required under federal and state program regulations (Allington & McGill-Franzen, 1989b). Although schools with fewer children of poverty typically have fewer children experiencing difficulty acquiring reading abilities, we have found that schools too often respond to these children in very similar and largely unsuccessful ways.

Nonetheless, some schools do manage successfully to teach large numbers of poor children to read. Our work has attempted to discover the nature of those few school programs that work and the many that do not. Successful programs and effective instruction have many characteristics, but we have focused primarily upon program organization and academic work presented students. Generally, we have been concerned with various aspects of opportunity to learn and, specifically, with examining whether schools respond to literacy learning difficulties with programs that enhance access to more and better instruction.

More and better instruction may be defined in a number of ways. We examined time allocations for literacy instruction and the engagement of learners during that time. School programs that do not increase reading instructional time allocations for children who find learning to read difficult are inadequate responses. These children need and benefit from larger amounts of instructional time, especially in the regular classroom (Kiesling, 1978). Second, in an attempt to capture aspects of the quality of instructional experiences, we have examined the academic work that children do across the school day and across instructional settings. The amount of actual reading and writing children do, the difficulty, and the coherence of the literacy tasks they are assigned are important aspects of instructional quality. Third, instructional interactions are important aspects of instructional quality, particularly adult–child verbal interactions. We simply attempt to describe how teachers (and paraprofessionals) go about teaching literacy to children who find learning to read difficult. These interactions are important to the learning fostered by the academic work that children are given to do (see Chapter 8).

The remainder of this chapter presents a general summary of our findings and those of others who have studied similar educational efforts. This summary focuses on issues of instructional time, academic work, and curricular coherence and concludes with an explanation of why schools respond as they do to children who find learning to read difficult.

Instructional Time

The quantity of time available for literacy learning is demonstrably important (Denham & Liberman, 1980), but children who find learning to read difficult rarely participate in programs that reliably increase instructional time available for teaching or learning to read (e.g., Allington & McGill-Franzen, 1989b; Ysseldyke, Thurlow, Mecklenburg, & Graden, 1984). In fact, Birman (1988) reports that schools with high concentrations of poor children routinely schedule significantly less classroom literacy instruction than schools with few poor children. When children of poverty are provided with substantially less reading instruction, we do not need to blame the home environment for their lack of success.

A common school response to literacy-learning difficulties is the development of remedial and special education instructional support programs. It is often thought that such programs expand the opportunity to learn by increasing the time allocated to literacy instruction. Although it seems feasible that the common small group pullout instructional design used in most remedial, compensatory, and special education programs could increase allocated time, it rarely does (Allington & McGill-Franzen, 1989b; Ysseldyke et al., 1984).

Because most schools offer remedial and special education support instruction during the school day, participating children have no expanded allocation of instructional time generally. Because the most commonly scheduled time period for such support instruction is during the time period when the same subject is being taught in the classroom (e.g., remedial or resource-room reading instruction is scheduled during all or part of the classroom reading period), participating children have no larger period of time allocated for reading instruction than other children. Because the most common design for remedial and special education resource-room instruction involves sending participating children to a different teacher in a different room, participants lose available instructional time in transitions from one setting to the other. Even when these transition periods fall in a 10- to 15-minute-a-day range, about an hour of potential instructional time is lost each week (these 15-minute transitions add up to 50 hours a year, or 10 weeks of daily 1-hour lessons each year, and the loss of a year of daily 1-hour lessons every 4 years). Even more distressing is the fact that in many cases far larger amounts of time are lost to transitions (Allington & McGill-Franzen, 1989a).

Even if the amount of time allocated to reading instruction is not expanded, remedial and special education support instruction might improve upon the classroom instruction if participating children are actually more likely to be engaged in academic work in the specialist's class. It seems feasible that the small-group pullout design could result in higher student engagement, but the evidence suggests that this is not normally the case. Instead, the proportion of time spend in nonacademic activities is greater (or not substantially different) in remedial or resource rooms compared with time-use regular classroom instruction (Allington, Stuetzel, Shake, & Lamarche, 1986; Allington & McGill-Franzen, 1989b; Haynes & Jenkins, 1986). Children spend much time in transition to and from support instruction classes and much time in these classes waiting for teacher attention.

Studies of school responses to literacy-learning difficulties suggest that

1. schools with many poor children schedule less classroom instructional time for literacy lessons than schools with few poor children,
2. remedial or special education programs are organized in ways that rarely increase time allocated for literacy lessons, and
3. the support instruction offered by specialist teachers infrequently results in more active student involvement in literacy lessons.

Instead of responding to children who find learning to read difficult with programs that provide access to more and better instruction, too often schools respond with interventions that meet the minimum regulatory requirements and that result in less literacy instruction with lower levels of student involvement in the academic work assigned. Such interventions seem more likely to maintain the child's status as an underachiever than to produce a substantial acceleration in literacy development.

We have assumed, after Carroll (1963), that by comparing the amount of time spent with the amount of learning achieved, one can begin to estimate the varying rates of literacy learning by different children. Time allocated and even time engaged in instruction are but very crude indicators of "opportunity" to learn and assume that most children receive a generally similar literacy curriculum exposure. Nonetheless, this view posits that some children will simply need access to more instruction than others if they are to achieve "average" rates of acquisition. Only unequal instructional inputs will produce comparable achievement outcomes across different groups of children. Unfortunately, at-risk children are more likely to be scheduled for fewer minutes of literacy instruction than their peers. Instructional interventions that reduce the time allocated for instruction must be considered odd strategies for enhancing achievement of children whose literacy acquisition has not kept pace with that of their peers.

It takes time to learn and time to teach. When instructional time is reduced, instructional quality must increase, even to maintain the current level of achievement deficit. The quality of instruction can be examined from several perspectives, but we have concentrated our analyses on but two. First, we have detailed the nature of the academic work, the experienced curriculum of at-risk, low-achieving children. Second, we have examined the coherence of the academic work assigned students across settings, programs, and teachers. In addition, these analyses lead us to reconsider the notion of individualization of instruction.

Academic Work

The academic work done by "good" and "poor" reader groups in the same classrooms is not very similar, except in time allocated for completion (Allington, 1977; 1980; 1983). We identified two primary differences almost immediately: distribution of oral and silent reading opportunities and differences in text reading opportunities. Poor readers were most likely to be assigned round-robin oral reading, whereas good readers were more likely to be asked to read silently for comprehension. These studies described how teachers interrupted poor readers more often, asked them fewer comprehension questions, assigned more skill-in-isolation work, and so on. These data suggested that poor readers learned what was taught—and that what they were taught was strikingly different from what better readers were taught (see also Hiebert, 1983). For instance, differences in the oral and silent reading practices we observed created two types of readers—one group learned to self-monitor comprehension while reading and the other learned to pronounce words aloud while relying on external monitors—their teacher or peers. Some children were taught to be teacher-dependent readers, and others were taught to be something quite different.

We have attempted to capture the conceptualization that the academic work that children do is a good indicator of what they are likely to learn and that the thinking children do during their academic work is central to their learning (Marx & Walsh, 1988; Chapter 12). The analyses of the instructional experiences of low-achievement children indicate that low-level task completion dominates their literacy work (e.g., McGill-Franzen & Allington, 1990; Rowan & Guthrie, 1989; Chapter 7). It seems that comprehension is not often the focus of the literacy lessons of low-achievement children. Likewise, neither the reading nor writing of extended texts is commonly included in their academic work (see Chapter 10).

Curricular Coherence

Although the importance of silent, comprehension-focused, extended text reading was emphasized in our earlier classroom-based work, the issue of the match between the curriculum of the classroom and the curriculum of instructional support programs emerged as we began to follow children across the school day (Allington, et al., 1986). The most common situation encountered—at-risk learners working in different, and often philosophically incompatible, literacy curricula in the two settings—is difficult to support with any existing theory or model of learning (Johnston, Allington, & Afflerbach, 1985). Children who participate in remedial and special education are more likely to experience cognitive confusion as a result of this "planned fragmentation" of the literacy curriculum (Allington & McGill-Franzen, 1989a).

The issue is one of curricular coherence across the literacy lessons in the regular education program as well as the coherence across the academic work assigned in the regular and support programs (Allington & Johnston, 1989). Basically, curriculum coherence can be viewed as planned arrays of literacy lessons that offer interrelated academic tasks across instructional episodes and settings.

Curricular coherence is not simply an issue that arises when children receive literacy instruction in the classroom and in a support program. All too often classroom literacy instruction alone provides a planned fragmentation. The curricular materials for reading, phonics, spelling, language arts, handwriting, and so on, often present no coherent array of literacy-learning tasks. In most schools at-risk learners spend substantially more time working on several unrelated skill tasks than they spend actually reading and composing. Little has been written about the incoherence in the array of literacy tasks presented in the several literacy curricula found in most classrooms. The fragmentation of literacy lessons observed in the regular education program is obvious (Allington et al., 1986; McGill-Franzen & Allington, 1990). We find many word-level tasks, for instance, in reading, spelling, phonics, and language arts materials, but only coincidentally have we found any coherent array of these activities across a school day. The fragmentation is simply compounded with the additional curricular materials and academic tasks presented at-risk children in remedial and special education instruction during the day.

For instance, the grade 2 reading/language arts curriculum in one district included a meaning-oriented basal, a phonics skills text from another publisher, a spelling workbook from a third publisher, a handwriting workbook from a fourth, and a language arts basal series from a fifth. In addition, this district promoted a "process-approach" to writing with twice-weekly composing sessions suggested. Classroom reading/language arts activities were scheduled daily with separate time periods for each of the curriculum materials and a twice-weekly session for process writing. Although we found considerable overlap in specific word-level skills practice exercises in the curriculum materials (e.g., affixes, blends, pronouns, possessives, contractions, synonyms, etc.), this overlap occurred across the year and rarely resulted in daily, or weekly, lessons that offered any coherent array of word-level instruction. In other words, the point and sequence of instruction varied across these curricular materials, and, often, the labels for the skills, the technical language used to talk about them, and the paper-pencil formats provided for practice differed considerably. The reading/language arts periods in this school offered children an enormously fragmented array of academic work, as one might expect from materials from five different publishers.

Each of the several periods in the larger reading/language arts block was brief as well as isolated from the remaining academic work during other periods. Learners went from skill to skill, task to task, worksheet to worksheet, to 15 minutes of writing 2 days a week. The decoding lesson in the basal was unrelated to the phonics skills text assignment and to the spelling lesson, which was unrelated to the handwriting worksheet, which was unrelated to the composing, which was unrelated to the basal reading selection. The language arts skill was compound words, but this lesson was not related to spelling, reading, phonics, or writing tasks.

Now add into this melange even more curricular fragmentation for children participating in remedial or resource-room instruction. In the former, there was no district-mandated curriculum, so individual specialist teachers selected their own materials, which were always different from those used in classrooms. For special education resource rooms, the district mandated a code-emphasis reading program that employed a different orthography and a different focus on text reading. Thus, low-achievement children went from a well-fragmented classroom reading/language arts program in the classroom to more intensive levels of fragmentation when they participated in instructional support programs.

It is unlikely that this curricular fragmentation was purposely designed to make literacy learning difficult. However, it seems that is the ultimate effect. We know that when classroom and specialist teachers emphasize the same literacy skills, mastery of those skills improves (e.g., Winfield, 1987), and we have evidence that achievement improves when classroom and remedial programs emphasize congruent skills and strategies (Gelzheiser, Meyer, & Pruzek, in press; Walmsley & Walp, 1990). However, such coordination occurs only when planned (as opposed to left to chance) and cannot be expected when incoherent curricula are mandated across different programs (Allington & McGill-Franzen, 1989a).

It is a little-examined hypothesis that the achievement of at-risk children is negatively affected when planned sets of instructional activities hinder the development of an awareness of the interrelationships of various literacy-learning tasks. Nonetheless, we would argue that children who find learning to read difficult are those children with the least tolerance for the curricular fragmentation that currently defines their literacy instruction. These are the children who seem to benefit most from curriculum plans that feature a coherent array of literacy-learning activities that extend, refine, and support each other. These are the children who benefit not only from greater quantities of instruction but who also need instruction that is consistently focused and clarifies the essential tasks of literacy learning.

Current concerns about curricular fragmentation and the lack of coordination between regular education and instructional support programs (Allington & Johnston, 1989) have led to proposals for the rethinking of current federal- and state-funded efforts to enhance the academic achievement of at-risk learners. The regular education initiative (Wang, Reynolds, & Walberg, 1988) proposes to merge regular, remedial, and special education into a single instructional support system. The "unified" instructional support programs (Jenkins, Pious, & Peterson, 1988) combine regular, remedial, special, and migrant education support efforts into a single comprehensive effort. The California School-Based Program Coordination Act, the New York "congruence" model for remedial and classroom instructional programs, and the recent revisions in the federal regulations for Chapter 1 projects are each evidence of policymakers' interest in moderating, if not eliminating, the fragmentation and segregation inherent in categorical programs today.

Schools today vary substantially in the philosophical and instructional coherence of their literacy curriculum. Some schools have mandated different and incompatible curricula for regular, remedial, special, and bilingual education literacy efforts. Others offer coherent curricular plans across programs (e.g., Walmsley & Walp, 1990). Some schools segregate their teaching staffs, whereas others produce collaborative efforts. If Hyde and Moore (1988) are correct, and our experience suggests they are (Allington & McGill-Franzen, 1989a), such differences reflect variations in the plans developed by central office administrators rather than differences in schools per se. Unfortunately, plans developed for schools with concentrations of at-risk children seem usually more fragmented than coherent.

Individualization

A final aspect of the academic work assigned children who find learning to read difficult involves the long-standing notion of "individualization" of instruction. Individualization has a long history in discussions of interventions with at-risk learners, regardless of which label is assigned. However, as noted earlier, there is little evidence that we individualize instruction by varying the amount of instruction children are offered. In addition, few reliable effects for individualized instruction have been reported in school-based research (e.g., Leinhardt, Zigmond, & Cooley, 1981). Using a detailed instructional analysis (McGill-Franzen & Allington, 1990), we examined what "individualization" meant for remedial and special education students and concluded that it usually meant the at-risk learner was working alone on low-level skills tasks. Individualization was not typically individually appropriate instructional interactions or tasks. There was little evidence of differentiation of academic work in remedial and special education rooms by difficulty, instructional need, or classroom curricula. These children who participated in instructional support programs spent much time working alone (individually), typically on low-level skills-sheets tasks. This remedial and resource-room instruction was "routinized" (much like classroom instruction), wherein the learners had to adapt to another teacher's routine. The "individualized" instruction offered was often identical for all children in the remedial or resource-room group.

Fraatz (1987) discusses the "paradox of collective instruction"—that schools attempt to teach each child similarly to ensure equity but would need to teach each differently to assure individualization. If we are to individualize, we must differentiate between issues such as differences in the time allocated to different students, curriculum materials, pacing, performance standards, and so on (Johnston & Allington, 1991). But at what point might such "individualization" become potentially discriminatory (McGill-Franzen, 1988; Chapter 19)? Little of what is done in the name of individualization in schools seems to address an individual child's instructional needs. When decisions about individual needs lead to smaller amounts of instruction, to reduced curricular coverage, to the neglect of comprehension development, and to perpetuation of low-achievement status for some children, one must question whether those children are well served. Current attempts at individualization seem more likely to inhibit literacy acquisition than to advance it.

WHAT SHAPES SCHOOL RESPONSES?

Children who find learning to read difficult routinely participate in instructional programs that seem designed in ways that make participation unlikely to resolve their difficulties. Many programs, very simply, are not designed to accelerate learning such that achievement lags can be overcome in the short term. We have been attempting to understand how such programs come to exist and why they are typically maintained even though ineffective. In our view, the most influential factor in developing effective school literacy programs is, very simply, district commitment to the effective education of all children—the poor, the handicapped, the minority, those different from the mainstream. School districts typically offer mandated programs, but few seem to routinely provide local funds necessary to support or extend the minimum regulatory requirements. Instead, districts too often optimize fiscal returns through excessive labeling, cross-subsidy, and triple- or quadruple-dipping into various external education funds (Allington & McGill-Franzen, 1989a; Hyde & Moore, 1988; Kimbrough & Hill, 1981; McGill-Franzen, 1987). Most often, however, children who earn money from multiple sources are served by only one support program and are often excluded from some or all of their regular education literacy instruction. In these schools children received whatever minimum services were available, not the instructional intervention they needed to overcome their learning difficulties.

McGill-Franzen (1987) reported that schools in states that offered high rates of fiscal reimbursements for mildly handicapped children identified substantially more children as handicapped than schools in states with low reimbursement rates. The number of handicapped children was influenced substantially by the money available to support special programs. She also noted the apparent shift of 1.5 million children from Chapter 1 remediation to learning-disabled special education between 1975 and 1985. This shift occurred as Chapter 1 funding declined and special education funding expanded. As more funding became available for special education services, more children were identified as being handicapped, even though few, if any, psychometric differences existed between the children participating in remedial programs and those in special education resource-room instruction for the mildly handicapped (e.g., Algozzine & Ysseldyke, 1983). Currently, some districts have 20% or more of their student population identified as handicapped, whereas other districts, which draw students from similar communities, have fewer than 5% who are so identified. Whether a child is considered learning disabled, remedial, or simply immature and whether that child will be well served by rich classroom and, perhaps, supportive remedial or resource-room instruction will depend more on which district the child lives in than on the child's needs. However, regardless of which funding source the district may have tapped, it is likely that the district is better served by the program funds than is the child.

For instance, like Kimbrough & Hill (1981), we observed cross-subsidization, the use of money from one fund to pay for other programs. In our schools the subsidy usually went from externally funded programs to locally funded programs. For example, most often paraprofessionals paid out of federal Chapter 1 funds worked in classrooms to monitor the behavior of low-achieving youngsters. This allowed the classroom teacher to work uninterrupted with the better readers. This use of the paraprofessional did not seem to benefit the low-achieving students nearly as much as it benefited the teacher and higher achieving students. Few schools elected to use paraprofessionals to work with the better readers in order to provide time for the classroom teacher to work with Chapter 1 children, though this was done in one district studied. In addition, most Chapter 1 and special education programs provided no additional reading instruction for participating children but simply replaced part, or all, of the regular classroom reading period. Very simply, we found very many instances where external funds from state and federal sources provided no additional services and instead simply replaced any local effort.

We have also found it useful to examine commitment by noting attributions for success or failure of students offered by teachers and administrators. We found Winfield's (1986) study of urban teachers instructive here. Winfield reported that such attributions varied on two dimensions: possibility and accountability. The classroom teachers in that study reported that either (a) children could be expected to learn to read or not, and (b) teachers felt reading instruction was primarily their responsibility, or that it was someone else's. It should not be surprising that teachers who believe in children's potential as learners and who accept responsibility for children's learning are more likely to offer children more and better instruction than teachers who do not share these beliefs. Likewise, it should not be surprising to find few intensive instructional efforts in the classrooms of teachers who believe that some children cannot learn and, additionally, that the responsibility for teaching belongs to someone else. In several schools we studied, for instance, over half of the classroom teachers reported that the "primary responsibility for reading instruction" of Chapter 1 students belonged to the Chapter 1 pullout teachers. Likewise, over three quarters of the classroom teachers felt that the primary responsibility for the reading instruction of mainstreamed learning-disabled children fell to the special education teacher. What seems unappreciated here is that the specialist teachers had these children for only 60 to 150 minutes per week, whereas the children spent 25 to 30 hours in their regular classrooms! In order to adequately address the instructional needs of children who find learning to read difficult, classroom teachers must necessarily accept primary responsibility for all children including those served in instructional support programs.

District Plans

One must temper notions that teachers are key players in such scenarios. Our work has shown that in most school districts similar attitudes flow from district administrators, building principals, and teachers. These attitudes are typically reflected in district plans for responding to children who find learning to read difficult. For instance, administrators in one district admitted that some schools served significantly larger populations of students who were less academically advantaged than other children but continued to support the idea that all schools be allocated the same fiscal resources. If we admit that some children need more and better teaching, we must create district-level plans that allocate larger shares of fiscal resources to such schools. In addition, when district-level administrators create fragmented instructional programs, we should not be surprised to find teachers reenacting that fragmentation in their activities.

Similarly, when a building principal disavows both responsibility for and knowledge of the remedial and special education instruction ("That's Mary's program, I don't even observe in those rooms"), one should not be surprised to find a segregated support program and a regular education staff less than wholly committed to resolving the learning failures of at-risk children. When district and building administrators attribute learning difficulties to deficient parents, homes, or children, we find a similar response from the teachers. When district administrators responsible for the various instructional programs (regular education, Chapter 1, special education, bilingual) have little shared knowledge of the various programs, principals and teachers typically reflect this situation in their admitted ignorance of the instructional activities of each other. ("I couldn't tell you what they might do down there.")

We have concluded, however, that most teachers simply follow the district plan (Allington & McGill-Franzen, 1989a). That is, when the district classroom reading/language arts curriculum plan offered five separate and incompatible commercial reading/language arts materials, most teachers offered an incoherent array of instructional tasks drawn from these materials. When the district plan mandated a different and incompatible curricular approach to reading in remedial or special education, teachers followed that mandate. When districts sought to optimize the amount of external funding, teachers referred many children to special programs. On the other hand, when district plans called for coherent and collaborative approaches to remedial and special education, teachers collaboratively planned coherent instructional sessions. When district plans included literature in their reading curriculum and made appropriate resources available, teachers used them. When trade books were largely unavailable, but workbooks and photocopy machines were in plentiful supply, teachers filled up the day with low-level skills sheets.

District-level plans are important. When districts make resources accessible to support certain activities, one should not be surprised to see those activities. The point here is one that Barr and Dreeben (1984) have addressed far more elegantly—that decisions made at other levels do have enormous potential for constraining the actions of teachers. Most teachers we have observed spend their days doing exactly what they believe those in charge want them to do.

SUMMARY

Many children do not find learning to read easy. Unfortunately, we have spent far more time and energy attempting to discover defects, deficits, and differences in such children than we have spent on careful examinations of the classroom and instructional support programs we have created (and of the effects of these programs, intended or unintended). Although many children find learning to read difficult, it is the children of poverty who experience the most predictable difficulties. We have created categories for classifying these children and categorical programs to which they get assigned. We have not often studied the nature of these programs, nor have we responded vigorously to the few reports that suggest that children are not well served. We have substantial evidence that the most common school responses to literacy-learning difficulties (retention, remediation, and special education) do not reliably alter children's status as poor readers. We have substantial evidence that once literacy-learning difficulties appear, little of what we most commonly do actually accelerates children's literacy development to the point where they are on par with their peers. On the other hand, we do have good evidence that programs can be designed to virtually assure that all children acquire literacy with their peers (Madden, Slavin, Karweit, Livermon, & Dolan, 1989; Pinnell, 1989; Walmsley & Walp, 1990). In these efforts school responses were fundamentally redesigned with an emphasis on early intervention to accelerate literacy acquisition by providing children access to necessarily large amounts of substantially improved instruction. These successful school responses suggest that tinkering with our current programs may be insufficient to the task of developing real readers. Tinkering may improve the most common school responses, but it may be the case that a whole-scale restructuring of our beliefs, our regulations, and our programs is what is truly necessary.

Our work has suggested the centrality of district-level plans rather than school- or classroom-level efforts, especially in the literacy-learning experiences of children who participate in remedial and special education programs (Allington & McGill-Franzen, 1989a). Although principals and teachers are obviously important players, these participants seem to follow district-level plans more often than they create unique school or individual plans (though one does see such principals and teachers). This position is similar to that expressed by Barr and Dreeben (1984) and Hyde and Moore (1988) and points to the need to understand the influence of district-level constraints and opportunities on school and classroom behavior. At the most basic level, we must develop district plans that reliably enhance access to more and better instruction for children who find learning to read difficult. Such plans are not easily achieved. However, we will better serve children who find learning to read difficult if we redirect our energies from looking for deficits in these children and their families and, instead, put that effort into redesigning our programs.

REFERENCES

Algozzine, B., & Ysseldyke, J. E. (1983). Learning disabilities as a subset of school failure: The oversophistication of a concept. *Exceptional Children, 50,* 242–246.

Allington, R. L. (1977). If they don't read much, how they ever gonna get good? *Journal of Reading, 21,* 57–61.

Allington, R. L. (1980). Teacher interruption during primary grade oral reading. *Journal of Educational Psychology, 72,* 371–377.

Allington, R. L. (1983). The reading instruction provided readers of different reading abilities. *Elementary School Journal, 83,* 549–559.

Allington, R. L., & Johnston, P. (1989). Coordination, collaboration, and consistency: The redesign of compensatory and special education interventions. In R. Slavin, N. Karweit, & N. Madden (Eds.), *Effective programs for students at risk* (pp. 320–354). Boston: Allyn & Bacon.

Allington, R. L., & McGill-Franzen, A. (1989a). Different programs, indifferent instruction. In D. Lipsky & A. Gartner (Eds.), *Beyond separate education* (pp. 75–98). New York: Brookes.

Allington, R. L., & McGill-Franzen, A. (1989b). School response to reading failure: Chapter 1 and special education students in grades 2, 4, and 8. *Elementary School Journal, 89,* 529–542.

Allington, R. L., Stuetzel, H., Shake, M. C., & Lamarche, S. (1986). What is remedial reading? A descriptive study. *Reading Research and Instruction, 26,* 15–30.

Barr, R., & Dreeben, R. (1984). *How schools work.* Chicago: University of Chicago Press.

Birman, B. F. (1988). Chapter 1: How to improve a successful program. *American Educator, 12,* 22–29.

Carroll, J. (1963). A model for school learning. *Teachers College Record, 64,* 723–733.

Denham, C., & Lieberman, A. (1980). *Time to learn.* Washington, DC: U.S. Government Printing Office.

Edelmann, M. W. (1988). Forward. *Childrens' Defense Budget.* Washington, DC: Childrens' Defense Fund.

Fraatz, J. M. B. (1987). *The politics of reading: Power, opportunity, and prospect for change in America's public schools.* New York: Teachers College Press.

Gelzheiser, L., Meyers, J., & Pruzek, R. (in press). Effects of pull-in and pull-out models of reading instruction provided to resource and remedial students. *Journal of Educational and Psychological Consultation.*

Haynes, M. C., & Jenkins, J. R. (1986). Reading instruction in special education resource rooms. *American Educational Research Journal, 23,* 161–190.

Hiebert, E. (1983). An examination of ability grouping for reading instruction. *Reading Research Quarterly, 18,* 231–255.

Hyde, A. A., & Moore, D. R. (1988). Reading services and the classification of students in two school districts. *Journal of Reading Behavior, 20,* 301–338.

Jenkins, J. R., Pious, C., & Peterson, D. (1988). Categorical programs for remedial and handicapped students: Issues of validity. *Exceptional Children, 55,* 147–155.

Johnston, P. H., & Allington, R. L. (1991). Remediation. In R. Barr, M. L. Kamil, P. B. Mosenthal, & P. D. Pearson (Eds.), *Handbook of Reading Research (Vol. 2, pp. 984–1012).* New York: Longman.

Johnston, P. H., Allington, R. L., & Afflerbach, P. (1985). The congruence of classroom and remedial reading instruction. *Elementary School Journal, 85,* 465–478.

Juel, C. (1988). Learning to read and write: A longitudinal study of 54 children from first through fourth grade. *Journal of Educational Psychology, 80,* 437–447.

Kiesling, H. (1978). Productivity of instructional time by mode of instruction for students at varying levels of reading skill. *Reading Research Quarterly, 13,* 554–582.

Kimbrough, P., & Hill, P. T. (1981). *The aggregate effects of federal education programs.* Santa Monica, CA: Rand.

Leinhardt, G., Zigmond, N., & Cooley, W. (1981). Reading instruction and its effects. *American Educational Research Journal, 18,* 343–361.

Madden, N. A., Slavin, R. E., Karweit, N., Livermon, B., & Dolan, L. (1989). *Success for all: Effects on student achievement, retentions, and special education referrals* (Report No. 30). Baltimore, MD: Johns Hopkins University, Center for Research on Elementary and Middle Schools.

Marx, R. W., & Walsh, J. (1988). Learning from academic tasks. *Elementary School Journal, 88,* 207–219.

McGill-Franzen, A. (1987). Failure to learn to read: Formulating a policy problem. *Reading Research Quarterly, 22,* 475–490.

McGill-Franzen, A. (1988). Review: The politics of reading. *Journal of Reading Behavior, 20,* 379–384.

McGill-Franzen, A., & Allington, R. L. (1990). Comprehension and coherence: Neglected elements of literacy instruction in remedial and resource room services. *Journal of Reading, Writing and Learning Disabilities, 6,* 149–180.

Pinnell, G. S. (1989). Reading Recovery: Helping at-risk children learn to read. *Elementary School Journal, 90,* 161–184.

Rowan, B., & Guthrie, L. F. (1989). The quality of Chapter 1 instruction: A study of 24 schools. In R. Slavin, N. Karweit, & N. Madden (Eds.), *Effective programs for students at risk* (pp. 320–354). Boston: Allyn & Bacon.

Slavin, R. E. (1989). Students at risk of school failure: The problem and its dimensions. In R. Slavin, N. Karweit, & N. Madden (Eds.), *Effective programs for students at risk* (pp. 3–22). Boston: Allyn & Bacon.

Walmsley, S. A., & Walp, T. P. (1990). Integrating literature and composing into the language arts curriculum. *Elementary School Journal, 90*(3), 251–274.

Wang, M., Reynolds, M., & Walberg, H. (1988). Integrating the children of the second system. *Phi Delta Kappan, 70,* 248–251.

Winfield, L. (1986). Teachers' beliefs toward academically at-risk students in inner urban schools, *Urban Review, 18,* 253–268.

Winfield, L. (1987). Teachers' estimates of test content covered in class on first grade students' reading achievement. *Elementary School Journal, 87,* 437–454.

Ysseldyke, J. E., Thurlow, M. L., Mecklenburg, C., & Graden, J. (1984). Opportunity to learn for regular and special education students during reading instruction. *Remedial and Special Education, 5,* 29–37.

18 | The Role of Assessment in a Diverse Society

GEORGIA EARNEST GARCÍA
P. DAVID PEARSON
University of Illinois, Urbana-Champaign

Constructivist views of comprehension have dominated our thinking about reading since the early 1980s. The rhetorical trilogy of reader, text, and context is played out almost daily in journals, state curriculum guides, basal reader philosophy statements, and methods textbooks.

Along with the constructivist view of reading has come a call for assessment measures that focus on how readers construct meaning (see Pearson & Valencia, 1987; Wixson, Peters, Weber, & Roeber, 1987). Among reading educators, process has replaced product as the primary focus for assessment, bringing into question the wide range of performance measures that have dominated the reading field for the last 40 years. Interestingly, in their pursuit of alternative measures, several reading researchers are beginning to take on an "emic," or insiders', perspective regarding assessment (Johnston, 1989) that until recently was the purview of qualitative sociologists, educational anthropologists, and sociolinguists (Cicourel, 1974; Ogbu, 1982; Troike, 1984). This shift in orientation toward understanding how individuals within a culture construct and interpret meanings has led to the realization that all performance measures, even those with the most impeccable reputations for objectivity, are inherently interpretive; at the very least, they reflect the values, norms, and mores of the test writers who developed them and the educators who requested or authorized them. It also has caused some educators to reject the "sorting" and "gatekeeping" functions of many of the commercially produced assessment measures (see Chapter 19).

Increasingly, the rhetoric of the field calls for assessments that tell us how students approach, monitor, and process text. Critics of the conventional wisdom call for classroom-based assessment that is useful to the teachers and students involved (Goodman, Goodman, & Hood, 1989; Johnston, 1989; Resnick, 1989; Valencia et al., 1990).

Although these developments may be positive for the field of reading, new forms of assessment will not, in and of themselves, improve the education of students from diverse linguistic, cultural, and economic backgrounds. Such an improvement requires a new multicultural awareness among educators in general and reading educators in particular. They must confront the legacy of three-quarters of a century of racism and discrimination inherent in literacy assessment. They must understand how tests (and, for that matter, many forms of classroom-based assessment) have been used, albeit not always intentionally, to blame students' diversity (themselves, their families, or their communities) for their lack of growth in school-based literacy. They must understand that schools, programs, and teachers contribute to the failure of many students to become literate. Without this awareness, it is possible that new assessment measures, even those based on a constructivist view of reading, even those that "empower" teacher decision making, will hinder rather than aid students' literacy development.

Our basic thesis here is that the keys to meeting the assessment needs of a diverse student population are *a flexible approach to assessment* and a *dramatically improved teacher knowledge base*. We need to grant teachers greater latitude in deciding what is appropriate for a given student in a given group for a given text and a given task; in other words, teachers need the freedom to "situate" or "contextualize" assessment. But the minute we suggest greater freedom of choice, we are confronted with issues of accountability (really responsibility), and the only guarantee against malpractice that we can offer our constituents is greater teacher knowledge.

The first step in developing this knowledge base is to persuade educators to consider the extent to which assessment methods distort or reflect the literacy development of students from diverse linguistic, cultural, and/or economic backgrounds. To that end, we begin with a quick review of the purposes of various forms of reading assessment. Then, we describe some of the different assessment tasks that have been used to evaluate children's literacy development. We point out how the assessment tasks themselves or educators' interpretations of the tasks have differentially affected and/or reflected the literacy performance of students from diverse backgrounds. Then, based on this review, we take the second important step in developing this knowledge base: We present a set of principles or guidelines that we think will be helpful in creating or evaluating the usefulness of different assessment approaches for different populations.

THE ROLE OF ASSESSMENT IN DECISION MAKING

Educators evaluate students' literacy performances for a variety of purposes. As Shepard points out in Chapter 19, commercially developed tests have been used to determine if programs are effective or if schools and teachers have been doing their jobs. They also have been used to direct children's placement and to document individual children's progress (Aronson & Farr, 1989; Slavin & Madden, 1989). Standardized test scores have played a major role in determining who attends college, who is placed in college-bound tracks in our secondary schools, and who is eligible for special programs (Durán, 1983; Mercer, 1977)—even, as recent history has documented, special kindergarten programs (Faculty Senate, 1988).

Commercially developed tests, including those found in basal reader programs, also have guided instruction (Dorr-Bremme & Herman, 1986). Many teachers rely on the pre- and posttests in the basal programs to determine when children are ready to progress to higher levels or to new skills (Barr & Dreeben, 1983).

One reason that commercially developed measures have had such a powerful influence on American education is that traditionally they have been viewed as "objective" and "nonbiased" (Johnston, 1989; Stallman & Pearson, 1990). Informal measures used by teachers to make daily instructional decisions in the classroom have not been viewed with the same type of deference and respect as commercial tests. The reluctance of the educational community to privilege informal measures is due in part to those measures' heavy reliance on teacher judgment. For some, teacher judgment is a thin disguise for subjectivity, potentially biasing assessment.

A third type of assessment, teacher-made tests, has not been thoroughly investigated. The limited information available suggests that these tests do not differ much from commercially developed tests in format and content emphases (Calfee & Hiebert, 1991). Given the plethora of commercial models available, this similarity should not be surprising.

Interestingly, as reading researchers have juxtaposed what they know about the reading process with what they see being measured on commercially developed tests, they have begun to emphasize the importance of holistic evaluations of how students approach, interpret, and engage in authentic literacy tasks (among others, see Goodman et al., 1989; Johnston, 1989; Valencia et al., 1990). Unquestionably, the whole-language movement, with its emphasis on classroom control of curricular decision making and empowerment for teachers and students, has propelled this movement toward more situated assessments. Because the school environment for authentic literacy tasks is the classroom, considerable attention has been directed toward ongoing assessment tasks that are part of the literate classroom environment. Some of these tasks include conferencing, dialogue or response journals, oral readings and retellings, portfolios, reader logs, and student think-alouds. One characteristic shared in the use of these situated indices is that students participate in their own evaluations by helping to select representative samples of their work.

DIFFERENT TYPES OF ASSESSMENT

To facilitate our review of assessment measures, we have chosen to focus on two types of assessment—formal and informal. By formal measures, we refer to those literacy tests that have been based on or at least strongly influenced by the standardized testing paradigm. Most of these tests are commercial and include curriculum-based tests, such as those found in basal reader programs, although both standardized test publishers and basal publishers will tell you that their tests serve different decision-making functions. Informal or situated literacy measures refer to the different types of evidence that a teacher uses or could collect in daily interactions with students. Although teacher-made tests are another category of assessment commonly used in the classroom, we have not chosen to discuss them in our review because so little is known about them.

Formal Literacy Tests

Early reading tests.   In a content analysis of reading readiness and early reading measures, Stallman and Pearson (1990) report that almost all of the tests reviewed measured children's performances on isolated skills in a decontextualized setting far removed from the book and print awareness features that have been emphasized in recent work within the emergent literacy tradition. The reading-readiness tests placed considerable emphasis on skills that many test publishers consider to be prerequisite to reading (hence, the term *readiness*): letters, sound-symbol correspondences, oral vocabulary, key sight words, perception of shapes. Children were asked to recognize words, letters, sounds, or what they thought they heard being read. They were not asked to actively produce or identify language, nor were they asked to actively construct meaning. This was true for both standardized reading-readiness tests and for basal-readiness tests. The remarkable similarity between these two types of readiness tests suggests that developers of these tests work with an eye on what the other is up to. Early reading tests at the first-grade level were very similar to the readiness tests, except that the former focused more on reading comprehension and asked children to recognize information that they had read instead of heard being read.

Clearly, a subskills approach to reading is implicit in both the reading-readiness and early reading tests. Edelsky and Harman (1988) point out that many of the skills tested (e.g., ability to re-sort syllables) are not needed for reading. The emphasis on recognition tasks also means that no information is provided as to how students operationalize these tasks when they read.

Problems occur when children are asked to identify unfamiliar pictures or vocabulary or when their prereading potential is based on their pronunciation of standard English (Edelsky & Harman, 1988). Because of differences in language and/or literacy experiences, children from diverse backgrounds frequently are placed in transitional kindergarten and first-grade programs where they are exposed to the same type of activities that are measured on the readiness tests in an attempt to get them "ready" to read (Karweit, 1989). The unfortunate consequence has been that these children are not exposed to the types of literacy activities that are thought to help promote emergent literacy (Edwards & García, in press; Mason, 1980; Teale & Sulzby, 1986). In addition, they have been given the message that a principal goal of early reading is to be able to recognize letters, sounds, and sound-symbol correspondencies (Stallman & Pearson, 1990).

Standardized reading achievement tests.   Reading educators from a variety of perspectives have questioned the wisdom of overrelying on standardized reading test scores for placement and instructional purposes (Edelsky & Harman, 1988; Johnston, 1984b; Valencia et al., 1990; Royer & Cunningham, 1981). Current versions of these tests typically present students with relatively short passages reflecting a variety of genres (fiction, expository text, poetry, advertisements, and letters to the editors) followed by a series of multiple-choice questions to which there is only one correct answer. Children are asked to complete the tests within a prescribed time period, and their performances typically are judged against those of other children who have taken similar versions of the tests. Test developers have tried to offset the differential influence of background knowledge by including a wide range of topics, eliminating questions that could be answered without reading the passages, and/or statistically controlling the influence of prior knowledge through latent trait theory based on population-level differences (Johnston, 1984a). Nonverbal tests scores frequently are included with standardized test reports in an effort to differentiate between children's reading and reasoning abilities (Johnston, 1981).

A major problem with these tests is that they obscure rather than confront the influence of students' prior knowledge, reading strategies, or reasoning strategies (Johnston, 1984a; Royer & Cunningham, 1981). As a result, it is difficult to know why any individual child does poorly on these tests. Other critics have pointed out that the brief and contrived test passages only simulate reading (Edelsky & Harman, 1988) and do not show what children can do with authentic literacy tasks. Furthermore, qualitative analyses of how students determine their test answers revealed that the answer selections do not always reflect the quality of students' ongoing construction of meaning and problem-solving strategies (Cicourel, 1974; García, 1988; Langer, 1987); a common thread in these studies is that there are lots of "right" reasons why students select "wrong" answers.

The historically weak performance of linguistic and culturally diverse students on such tests (Mullis & Jenkins, 1990; Durán, 1983) has prompted complaints of cultural test bias. Test bias may occur when the test procedures and test content "reflect the dominant culture's standards of language function and shared knowledge and behavior" (Tyler & White, 1979, p. 3). Test-wiseness, or the "student's capacity to utilize characteristics and formats of the test and/or the test-taking situation to receive a high score" (Millman, Bishop, & Ebel, 1965, p. 707), is a factor that may confound students' reading test performance. Most critics stress the likelihood that majority students will be more test-wise than minority students. Cicourel (1974) warns that some children "may view the task or language used as strange, yet provide a response the adult interprets as fitting the framework of the test" (p. 303). Test developers have tried to eliminate bias by examining concurrent or predictive validity of individual tests and by looking at the possible bias in item selection procedures, examiner characteristics, and language factors (Linn, 1983; Oakland & Matsuzek, 1977).

A number of researchers have suggested that standardized tests such as the Scholastic Aptitude Test and the Graduate Records Examination do not have the same predictive validity for Hispanic and African-American students' college performance as they do for Anglo (non-Hispanic white) students (Durán, 1983; Goldman & Hewitt, 1975). In a study comparing the expository test performances of Hispanic and Anglo students at the upper primary levels, García (1988) found that the predictive validity of the students' scores on prior knowledge, vocabulary, and standardized reading tests was greater for Anglo children than it was for Hispanic children. One reason that some Hispanic students' expository reading test performance might have been underpredicted was that they knew less about the passage topics and test vocabulary prior to reading the test than did Anglo students. Their lower performance on these two variables is consistent with other researchers' claims that the standardized test performance of linguistically and culturally diverse students is adversely affected by their differential knowledge of test vocabulary (Durán, 1983; Hall, Nagy, & Linn, 1984) and test topics (Royer & Cunningham, 1981).

The role of English language proficiency in second-language children's test performance is also reflected in the higher scores that they generally attain on nonverbal tests of intelligence (Durán, 1983). Yet, attempts to translate achievement tests from English to another language or to use nonverbal test scores to interpret second-language children's achievement have not always been successful. A dilemma with translated tests is that concepts do not always translate directly from one language to another (Cabello, 1984). Likewise, juxtaposing children's standardized achievement test scores with their nonverbal test scores does not necessarily explain performance discrepancies. In one case, a computerized printout sent to the parents of a Thai child enrolled in an all-English medium school stated that, based on the child's relatively high nonverbal performance and low standardized achievement performance, the child was not working up to his potential and, therefore, needed to be encouraged to work harder. This juxtaposition of scores did not take into account that the child was learning English as a second language, and that this situation, rather than the child's lack of effort, probably accounted for the test score discrepancy.

Domain-referenced/basal reading tests. Whereas criterion- and domain-referenced tests may differ from norm-referenced tests in their purpose and use, they do not differ much in their format and content (Calfee & Hiebert, 1991; Stallman & Pearson, 1990). Criterion- and domain-referenced tests do not aim to interpret children's academic performances in terms of their relative position in a representative sample or norm group. The content of such tests is based on the test developer's specification of the objectives (criteria) that the children are expected to attain, or on the knowledge that the test developer generally assumes is pertinent to a particular domain (Johnston, 1984b). The student's performance is judged against a preestablished standard, with 80% typically used as the cutoff criterion. These tests frequently are used by districts and teachers to set the pace of instruction or to group and place children.

One of the problems with content or domain-referenced tests turns on how they are interpreted, or on the meaning that parents or educators attribute to them. Although the tests reflect the curriculum taught in basal programs, they do not always reflect how well children can comprehend text; indeed, an analysis of basal tests across grades 1 through 6 revealed that only about 30% to 50% of the items focused on comprehension activities (Foertsch & Pearson, 1988). Because these tests are so similar to standardized reading tests in their format and content emphases, they are subject to many of the same criticisms. In addition, inherent in these tests is the assumption that the children taking them are familiar with the test content and format. According to one bilingual teacher, this has been a problem for second-language children who are "transitioned out" of bilingual classrooms into all-English classrooms. For a variety of reasons, it is not unusual for bilingual children to receive reading instruction in the bilingual classroom based on some variation of a language-experience approach. Yet, when these children enter the monolingual classroom, many of their teachers use basal reading tests to determine where they should be placed in the basal reading series. These series tend to assume that children have acquired a certain range of vocabulary and background knowledge. Although children from the bilingual classroom may have developed the necessary comprehension strategies needed to read, they will not necessarily have the required vocabulary or background knowledge to do well on the basal tests.

New statewide reading tests.   In an attempt to reflect current reading research, new statewide tests have been developed (Pearson & Valencia, 1987; Wixson et al., 1987). These tests assess children's prior knowledge of the topics, ask questions based on inferencing and text structure taxonomies, and evaluate children's awareness of reading strategies. Authors of the tests also have responded to criticisms that traditional reading achievement tests simulate reading but do not test it, owing to the brevity and lack of authenticity of the test passages, by providing longer, noncontrived passages. On some of the tests multiple answers are elicited to allow for multiple interpretations or partial interpretations of the text. Children's attitudes and interests in reading also are assessed.

Although these tests conform more to current reading comprehension theory, they still are product measures based on "mainstream" reading performance and are subject to the same complaints of bias that plague standardized tests. So far, no one has studied the extent to which they help to explain the relationship between linguistically and culturally diverse children's reading test performance and literacy development. In fact, a potential problem with these statewide assessments is their "level playing field" mentality. Because they are usually given at specific grade levels (e.g., grades 4, 8, and 12), there tends to be a single grade-level test for all students. With the push for longer passages, there is not usually a range of difficulty or topics in the passages used at a particular grade level. Obviously, then, the passages used at any given grade level will be incredibly difficult for students reading below grade level or for students who happen to be unfamiliar with the passage topics. Some students may give up, complete the task with overt hostility in mind, or otherwise subvert the testing process; hence, inferences drawn about individuals are likely to be based upon measurement errors associated with extremely low or random performance. As long as inferences from these assessments are limited to school or district programs, they are less prone to these criticisms and are less likely to have a negative impact on individual children. On the positive side, when scores are limited to classroom or school averages, they are more likely to focus educators' attention on aspects of the classroom or school program that might be contributing to low individual performance.

Informal Reading Measures

Since 1987, when critiques of commercial tests intensified (and as the emergent literacy, literature-based reading, and whole-language movements gathered momentum), the field has witnessed a significant increase in articles describing informal measures—practices that teachers can engage in daily to evaluate how their students are developing as literate individuals. We address these measures in this section. We have included somewhat more "formal" techniques, such as oral miscue analysis and the informal reading inventory, because these measures involve teacher judgment and lend themselves to teacher modification and personalization.

Anecdotal records.   An assessment method frequently touted in the whole-language literature is that of keeping anecdotal records of individual children's ongoing development (Goodman et al., 1989). For instance, a kindergarten teacher might record on a checklist when individual children read and write their first and/or last names or read certain signs or logos. This type of assessment encourages teachers to focus on what children *can* do at different points in time instead of focusing on what they cannot do.

Although anecdotal records may avoid the cultural bias implicit in many of the commercial measures that ask young children to respond to predetermined vocabulary items (Hall et al., 1984), this type of assessment clearly is dependent on the teacher's ability to recognize how individual children are responding to the classroom environment or defining the literacy tasks at hand. How well this type of assessment will work for culturally and linguistically diverse children may well depend on teachers' abilities to create a risk-free environment for these children.

In a Public Broadcasting television special, *First Things First* (WQED Pittsburgh, 1988), viewers see a little girl from white Appalachia at home and at school. At home, she takes the film crew around her yard, showing them her family's strawberry patch and telling them about the apples that are sweet and good to eat. She is very verbal and clearly at ease talking to the film crew about where she lives. In the scene at school, she is reluctant to talk during a game, pointing instead of verbalizing. In a later scene, the teacher tells the viewers that because children like Holly are allowed to grunt at home, they do not talk in school. Clearly, the teacher has not seen Holly at home. If she were to keep an anecdotal record of Holly's literacy development, she might very well underestimate it.

Teacher-student interactions.   Observing how a child interacts with the teacher and reading materials during storybook reading is another way of assessing children's literacy development (Morrow, 1990). Morrow points out that the interactive dialogue engaged in by both the adult reader and the child reveals what the child knows about the story, how well the child understands the story, what the child is focusing on during the story reading, and how the child is integrating background knowledge with information from the story to comprehend it.

Before teachers can use adult-child storybook interactions, however, they need to make sure that all of the children who are participating are accustomed to this type of literacy event. Apparently, this type of activity is more common in some subcultures than it is in others (see Chapter 3). Heath's (1983) comparisons of the literacy events and adult-child interactions around these events in three subcultures in the rural south (working-class whites, working class African-Americans, and middle-class whites) revealed that storybook interactions similar to those in school classrooms characterized the middle-class families but not the other two working-class families.

Even observing how children respond to teacher questioning in whole- or small-group sessions may not accurately reflect what some children know about the reading task at hand (see Chapter 8). As Hymes (1972) has noted: "It is not that a child cannot answer questions but that questions and answers are defined for [the child] in terms of one set of community norms rather than another, as to what counts as questions and answers, and as to what it means to be asked or to answer" (p. xxxi).

Philips's (1983) work with Native American children on the Warm Springs Indian Reservation and Boggs's (1972) research with Hawaiian children indicated that these children were used to participant structures (adult-child verbal interactions) that differed from those characteristic of the typical classroom. Philips warns that the reluctance of the Native American children to participate in the structures preferred by the teachers meant that the teachers were unable to use their normal means of assessment, that is, sequencing of questions and answers, to determine the appropriate levels of instruction for the children.

Story retellings.   Story retellings recently have been heralded as one way for teachers not only to facilitate children's comprehension but also to assess it (Morrow, 1989). Morrow spells out several ways for teachers to use children's story retellings to assess children's reconstruction of meaning.

However, as with classroom observational data, story retellings need to

be contextualized so that *all* children in the classroom are invited to participate. Leap (1982), in a microanalysis of a Native American student's classroom behavior, found that the student barely responded when she was asked
to retell a story she had read in class. On the other hand, when she was asked
to make up a story about a picture drawn by a classmate, she produced an
extensive narrative.

If retellings are used to assess the English reading performance of bilingual students, then teachers need to understand that some children may present richer protocols if they are allowed to present their retellings in their first
language. Miramontes and Commins in Chapter 6 illustrate how bilingual
children think and learn in two languages. García (1988) found that bilingual
children participating in all-English classrooms demonstrated greater comprehension of an English reading test than their scores indicated when she
translated unknown words in the test questions into Spanish and allowed the
students to code switch or use Spanish when they explained their answers or
talked about what they had read. These findings obviously pose a dilemma
for the monolingual English-speaking teacher who may be working with bilingual children in a monolingual setting.

Portfolios. The sampling of student work is another type of assessment measure that is commonly used by teachers to determine individual
student's progress and grades. Examples of student writing frequently are
stored in a folder, which the teacher can use to evaluate the student's written
literacy development. This method differs from the type of writing assessment that increasingly is included on commercially developed tests where
students write on a prescribed topic within a set time period. In a portfolio
approach, students frequently are allowed to choose their own topics, have
time for planning and reflection, make revisions, and, in some instances,
choose representative samples of what they consider to be their best work.

Atwell (1987) has developed a similar approach for reading. Students
record their self-selected readings in a reader's log and keep a literary response journal. This information, along with the student's goals, becomes
the focus of an individual student-teacher conference held at the end of each
grading period. Other types of activities that could provide the documents
for a portfolio are taped oral readings and a collection of responses to reading
assignments.

An advantage of portfolio assessment is that it allows children to display
what they have learned. If artifacts are collected throughout the school year,
then the progress and effort that children have made over time are revealed.
For this type of assessment to work, however, children have to be motivated
to perform, and drafts of the children's work have to be kept.

Motivation is an important issue and crucial to the participation of low-achieving readers. Johnston and Allington (1991) point out that task-involving activities motivate the child to become involved in the activity for the sake of carrying it out, not for the sake of competing or displaying knowledge as in an ego-involving activity. If the task is viewed as ego-involving, then low achievers are likely to avoid it, will not ask for help, or will set unrealistic goals for themselves. If children come from diverse linguistic and cultural backgrounds, then the teacher also has to be aware of the cultural mores and norms that may influence the children's participation. It was not until the Kamehameha Early Education Program (KEEP) in Hawaii adopted "talk story" (verbal interaction patterns based on Hawaiian culture) as an integral part of their reading comprehension instruction that the Hawaiian children in the program began to participate fully (Au, 1981).

For portfolio assessment to work, the portfolio has to be more than a folder of end-products; portfolios need to document the evolutionary nature of a piece as well as the history of progress of the individual child. Teachers need to keep drafts of children's work. Without drafts, teachers may not see the individual progress that children have made, nor will they know where their input is needed. Drafts also may reveal some of the conflicting demands that are inherent in the literacy development of linguistically diverse students (Delpit, 1988). This point is poignantly illustrated in a young African-American woman's effort to obtain a passing grade on an essay that was a major prerequisite for entrance into a required rhetoric course at the college level. On her first attempt, when she was not worried about dialect features, her writing was more fluid and complex, the relationships among ideas were clearer, and she wrote with "voice":

> *First attempt:* When I am alone, I dream about the man I want to be with. He *a* man that every woman wants, and every woman needs.

When she proofed her writing on the second and third attempts, she didn't seem to know what to change and, in the process of eliminating dialect features, turned to cliches and broke her thoughts down into simple sentences. Granted the end result was a dialect-free piece, but it was also a choppy piece of voiceless prose.

> *Second attempt:* I daydream alot about what my knight in shining armor will be like. He has to be everything rolled all in one and nothing *suppose* to be wrong with him.

> *Third attempt, and the beginning of the essay she ultimately turned in:* My make-believe man is everything. He is perfect from his head down to his toes. He's handsome, romantic and intelligent.

In such a situation, a teacher who had not kept drafts would have been unaware of the student's struggle and may even have attributed the choppiness of the last draft to a lack of sophistication rather than an attempt on the part of the student to make her writing look "conventional."

Oral miscue analysis. Several different methods have been developed to assess students' oral reading. Both oral miscue analysis (Y. M. Goodman, Watson, & Burke, 1987) and running records used in Reading Recovery (Clay, 1987) attempt to document the different types of strategies that children use when they read orally. The two procedures involve recording the child's variation from the text, noting repetitions, substitutions, insertions, omissions, and self-corrections. In oral miscue analysis, the children's miscues are evaluated in terms of the extent to which they preserve syntactic and semantic consistency at the sentence and discourse levels. Children's reading comprehension also is assessed through their retellings.

The authors of the newest manual on oral miscue analysis warn teachers to be careful in their analysis of oral miscues produced by dialect or second-language speakers of English (Y. M. Goodman, et al., 1987). They point out that dialect features and pronunciation errors need to be evaluated in terms of semantic and discourse consistency. This assumes that most teachers will be aware of these features and will know when variations such as "he be" for "he is" are consistent in meaning. Unfortunately, teachers' lack of sophistication regarding these matters continuously is demonstrated throughout the literature on the reading of linguistically diverse children (see Cazden, 1988; García & Pearson, 1990; Chapter 10). In a study comparing the reading instruction of bilingual children in Spanish and English, Moll, Estrada, Diaz, and Lopes (1980) discovered that bilingual children who were good readers in Spanish received limited comprehension instruction in English because their English teacher was misled by the children's non-native pronunciation of English and thought that they were not ready for English comprehension instruction.

The extent to which the assessment of oral reading is a valuable tool may also depend on children's past experiences with oral reading and the extent to which their oral reading matches their silent reading. García (1988) found that the performance of fifth- and sixth-grade Anglo children across a variety of silent and oral reading tasks was relatively consistent, whereas the performance of fifth- and sixth-grade Spanish-English bilingual children across the same tasks was inconsistent. During the miscue analysis, one of the more adept bilingual readers stopped at words she could not pronounce and waited for the researcher to provide her with the word. When the researcher told her to continue with the reading, the child skipped over the words that she could not pronounce correctly. In an interview with the researcher, the student explained that she could understand some words even though she could not pronounce them:

RESEARCHER: Is it easier for you to read it, or is it easier for you to pronounce it?

STUDENT: Easier for me to read it cause I can't pronounce.

RESEARCHER: You can recognize words by reading them even though you can't pronounce them?

STUDENT: Uh-huh.

This student's behavior should not be too surprising, given what we know about teachers' tendencies to overcorrect the oral reading of low readers (Chapter 17) and that of children who do not speak fluent standard English (Chapter 6).

Teachers working with second-language children also need to understand how children acquire a second language. For example, Indochinese children learning English as a second language may have difficulty with gender and tense markers because these constructs are marked differently in their native languages. Instead of considering such miscues to be errors, teachers need to check children's understanding of what is being read. Children's difficulty producing certain constructs does not necessarily mean that they are not comprehending them (Savignon, 1983; Troike, 1969). Overemphasis on such errors ignores the developmental nature of children's second-language acquisition and shifts the emphasis of the lesson from reading to English-as-a-second-language instruction.

Informal reading inventories. These assessment measures are commercially produced and include brief passages and vocabulary lists that are graded. The usual procedure is for individual children to read word lists and passages orally and to answer comprehension questions based on the passages. The teacher has individual children begin at a level that is comfortable for them and continue to read more difficult lists and passages until they reach a level where they cannot recognize 95% of the words or answer 75% of the comprehension questions. Sometimes, children's silent reading and/or listening comprehension is assessed. Retellings and probing questions also may be used to evaluate comprehension. Some type of miscue analysis generally is used with the oral reading.

We have listed these inventories under informal measures because some element of teacher judgment is allowed in their administration. For example, if children are accustomed to reading a passage silently before they read it orally, the teacher can accommodate this practice. In order to get an accurate reading of students' comprehension of "new" text, teachers also are supposed to select passages with topics relatively unfamiliar to their students.

Despite their popularity, informal reading inventories are fraught with many of the problems characteristic of the formal and informal measures that we already have discussed. Implicit in them is the assumption that the passages and vocabulary selected do indeed characterize the type of reading found at a particular grade level. Further, their sequential framework implies a linear development in children's reading ability and suggests that all children have equal access to the same materials and instruction. The emphasis on oral vocabulary reading and passage decoding assumes that children cannot understand what they cannot say (a point that we already have discussed in the section on oral miscue analysis). In addition, the setting in which the informal reading inventory is administered, where an individual student interacts on a one-to-one basis with an adult, does not always guarantee a risk-free environment (Labov, 1969).

A major drawback in the use of this type of assessment with children from diverse backgrounds is that their reading comprehension potential may be seriously underpredicted. It is likely that these children will be more adversely affected by the inventory's reliance on oral reading then will children who speak fluent standard English. They also may be less familiar than their middle-class Anglo counterparts with the topics and vocabulary included in the inventories (García, 1988; Bruce, Rubin, Starr, & Liebling, 1984). Readability formulas based on word-frequency counts tend to reflect more of the spoken vocabulary of middle-class students than they do that of low-income students (see Bruce et al., 1984).

Finally, although this type of assessment may sample aspects of children's reading, it does not reveal what students can and cannot do with authentic text in a noncontrived setting. It specifically does not tell us how students comprehend and process both familiar and unfamiliar text, nor does it tell us how they adjust their reading according to the purpose of the task or to their interest in the topic.

FUTURE ASSESSMENT DIRECTIONS

Those who point out flaws in the conventional wisdom bear the obligation to suggest and, ultimately, validate alternatives. Our review reveals our clear preference for a move toward situated assessment. We prefer assessment that is grounded in the local realities of schools, classrooms, teachers, and students. We prefer assessment systems in which teachers, students, parents, and the community have a voice in deciding what is being assessed and how it is being interpreted. The reliance on standardized and criterion-referenced tests for assessment purposes has not been informative regarding the literacy development of students in general, but it has been particularly misleading for students from non-middle-class backgrounds. As we have pointed out, these measures do a splendid job of pointing out the obvious—that these students do not do as well as their mainstream counterparts—but they do not tell us why this occurs, nor do they tell us what these students *can do* when they are confronted with authentic literary tasks.

Sadly, considerable evidence suggests that teachers' and administrators' reliance on conventional measures for instructional guidance and placement has resulted in a steady diet of isolated, low-level, decontextualized tasks for children of diversity. In a survey of test use in schools, Dorr-Bremme and Herman (1986) concluded that the education of low-income elementary students had been more influenced by the commercial norm- and criterion-referenced tests used to meet federal and state program-evaluation requirements than had the education of other students. Although they report that part of this was in response to the general public's negative reaction to these students' traditionally low test scores and to the large numbers of low-income children who participate in specialized programs receiving state and federal funding, they note that a good part of it was due to principals' and teachers' concerns about low-income students' basic skills development, and their reliance on commercial tests to assess this development. The end result is that teachers of low-income students reported spending more time and resources teaching their students the material on the tests than did teachers of other students.

These facts and conclusions lead us to several recommendations about changes in assessment practices and policies:

1. *We (meaning the educational community at large) should reduce our reliance on group testing as indices of individual, school, district, or state accountability.* Exactly how we reached our current state of excessive reliance on indirect measures of reading is not altogether clear. Surely the wedding of our incessant quest for efficiency and our desire to instill in everyone a greater sense of both personal and communal responsibility has led us to hold students, teachers, and administrators accountable to measures that take as little time as possible to administer and score. School officials understandably want to look good on these high-stakes measures (especially when scores get published in the local media or when students can fail to advance or graduate); hence they resort to one of the oldest traditions in education—

teaching to the test. What this insidious practice does is to ask a test that was probably designed to serve as a simple, indirect index of progress on a phenomenon, like reading, to serve the role of an implicit, or sometimes an explicit, blueprint for a curriculum. And the simple fact is that tests are not up to that strain.

2. *We should privilege assessment traditions that are grounded in classrooms and schools.* If assessment tools are going to be used to serve this high-stakes accountability function (and, by implication, the curriculum blueprint function), then we need very different assessments. If assessment is going to drive school improvement, then we need methods reminiscent of responsive evaluation approaches (Stake, 1976). Such approaches would likely involve site visitations by independent reviewers at different intervals throughout the school year. In the process of helping the school staff, students, and community evaluate the school, these reviewers would visit classrooms, talk to participants (students, teachers, administrators, parents, and community leaders), and examine a wide range of artifacts that, taken together, tell the story of literacy performance, instruction, and use within the school and community. The approach we are suggesting is also similar to portfolio assessment systems that have been discussed recently by literacy researchers (Valencia et al., 1990) and school reformers (Wiggins, 1989). Local involvement could be guaranteed by insisting that school participants select many, if not most, of the portfolio entries.

Although we have concerns about situated assessment, we think that it should dominate teachers' attempts to evaluate and nurture children's literacy development. Anecdotal records, oral readings, portfolios, story retellings, and teacher-student interactions all provide useful information—windows into children's literacy progress in performance and disposition. These methods allow us to see what students can and cannot do across different tasks at different points in time. With situated assessment, teachers can support students' efforts as they provide important feedback. Documenting the extent to which students perform literacy tasks or utilize different types of strategies to construct meaning with and without "scaffolding" from teachers or peers can help inform teacher decision making at the same time that it starts students on the road to independent self-evaluation. Self-evaluation is an important goal if we want students to be active literacy participants. If students are to construct meaning both in and out of the school setting, then they have to be able to monitor their own reading and writing without the assistance of a teacher.

3. *We should take steps to ensure that teachers and administrators are knowledgeable about issues of language and culture.* For situated assessment to work with students from diverse backgrounds, administrators and teachers

need to take on an "emic" perspective. They need to become concerned about how students interpret (if you prefer, how they "read") the classroom context and the literacy events before them. This requires considerable knowledge and effort on the part of administrators and teachers.

First of all, educators need to know more about the influence of language and culture on children's learning. They need to understand that it is not language and cultural differences in themselves that cause learning difficulties. Rather, it is educators' misinterpretation of language and culture, as reflected in misguided remedial practices or unwarranted conclusions about children's motivation and behavior (as illustrated in Chapters 3, 6, and 8). Clearly, teacher education, both preservice and in-service, is the primary means available to the profession for helping educators to acquire this knowledge.

Second, lines of communication have to be opened to parents and other community leaders. Parents have to feel comfortable in the school context and know that it is acceptable for them to tell a teacher that they don't understand why their child is viewed as verbally unresponsive in school when the child constantly talks at home. Teachers, in turn, have to be willing to accept parents' observations. Perhaps, most importantly, teachers have to expand the range of explanations they consider to understand why some children are not performing well in the classroom. They have to be willing to seek out answers, not just by sharing information with their middle-class colleagues but also by sharing information with participants in the child's culture (as Miramontes & Commins suggest in Chapter 6). The latter may be one of the most difficult tasks at hand because it requires teachers to acknowledge that their own behavior is conditioned by their own socialization and that there are alternative ways of learning, interacting, and behaving.

4. *We should promote new criteria for evaluating assessment tools.* Traditionally, four criteria have dominated our evaluation of tests and other assessment devices: reliability, validity, objectivity, and efficiency. Reliability, which indexes the consistency with which an assessment device measures whatever it measures, and validity, which indexes the degree to which a tool is a true measure of what it purports to measure, have served as the cornerstones of measurement in American education. Objectivity (Is the test fair, unbiased, and independent of the views or whims of the test creators or administrators?) and efficiency (Is this the least expensive and intrusive index to be found?) have been only slightly less important in our selection of assessment tools. In fact, one of the reasons that situated assessments are often discredited hinges on their perceived lack of objectivity. Because such assessments rely on the interpretation of individual teachers, they are viewed as being rife with opportunities for bias and even ethnic discrimination.

Hence, one often hears the plea for a "level playing field" in which all students, regardless of background, have an equal opportunity to succeed. In most cases, the level field turns out to be another multiple-choice standardized test.

Efficiency exercises considerable muscle in an age when schools are literally inundated by assessment requirements from state mandates, federal funding agencies, and local districts. It often comes in the guise of an appeal for more emphasis on instruction: "We have to minimize the time we take away from instruction, so give us a simple, uncomplicated, and unintrusive test." Such a demand promotes the continued dominance of multiple-choice standardized tests.

If we are to reduce our reliance on these four traditional criteria, what criteria will we use as alternatives? In fact, we really do not want to suggest that reliability and validity should be diminished in importance. Unreliable measures just cannot be trusted, especially when it comes to making entry and exit decisions for individuals. Without validity, a test could measure something other than what it purports to measure, and its use could be downright harmful for decision-making purposes. It may be only a slight semantic variation, but we like the meaning conveyed by the term *trustworthiness,* a term we have borrowed from qualitative evaluation (see Guba, 1981). In a sense, trustworthiness encompasses both reliability and validity; we could not *trust* a decision based on an unreliable or invalid assessment tool. Another reason we like the term *trustworthiness* is that it already has a history of application to more qualitative measures. And we think that all assessments, both formal and informal, should be trustworthy.

A second criterion that we would like to see applied to assessment tools is *authenticity.* Authenticity is more than face validity (Does the task look like a reading task?) or curricular validity (Is the task consistent with the manner in which it is presented in the current curriculum?). A literacy assessment task is authentic to the degree that it resembles the way literacy is used in real life. It is not enough to be consistent with the curriculum, which itself may be disconnected from real-life literacy. A slightly less rigorous version of the authenticity criterion would be this: An assessment task is authentic to the degree that it promotes the use of literacy in the ways students are expected to use it in genuine communication acts.

A derivative (perhaps a slight variation) of authenticity is what has been called *instructional validity* (Pearson & Valencia, 1987). Instructional validity is almost the logical complement of curricular validity. Recall that an assessment task is curricularly valid to the degree that it resembles the form and manner in which the phenomenon is used within the curriculum. An assessment task is instructionally valid to the degree that it promotes instruction that is known to lead to student mastery over authentic literacy performance (i.e., in genuine acts of communication). In a sense, instructional validity requires us to turn our traditional approach to instructional research on its ear. Normally, in instructional research, we assume the validity of a test and then proceed to evaluate the validity of competing instructional approaches. We are suggesting just the opposite: We should assume (on the basis of cumulative experience) the validity of the instruction and evaluate the validity of the assessment task (by measuring the degree to which it is sensitive to assumed growth in the target behavior).

5. *We should change conventional assessments.* Although we remain firm in our conviction that situated assessments should dominate our instructional decision making, we recognize the fact that "big" (i.e., wide-scale) assessment is likely to remain a part of our educational system for the foreseeable future. Thus, we need to improve this tool, however flawed in basic conception and purpose we may think it is. We applaud the efforts in Michigan (Wixson et al., 1987), Illinois (Pearson & Valencia, 1987), and many other states to reform wide-scale assessments. What is significant about these efforts is their use of "authentic" texts and more "authentic" tasks; they are more firmly grounded in a constructive model of the reading process. As tools for program evaluation, these new assessments are likely to promote exciting, alternative literacy curriculum reforms. We have also seen changes in recent editions of commercially available standardized tests. Even the SAT is being revised to include longer passages, more thoughtful questions, and more instructionally valid tasks (Fiske, 1989). In terms of the diverse populations who have been the focus of our review, the jury is still out on the question of whether these sorts of changes will result in more valid assessments.

6. *We should take a more realistic perspective on what assessment tasks, especially commercially available tests, can do.* Sometimes we act as though tests were magic or divine in origin. We would be better off if we remembered a few simple facts and rules of thumb about how to use tests.

- *All tests are samples of performance.* Because tests are samples, we need to admit that they never capture the range of texts and situations to which we expect the behavior to apply.
- *Tests are surrogates for the real thing, not the thing itself.* A test is nothing but an indirect index of progress on a phenomenon we happen to care about and for which our resources for evaluation are limited. In fact it is the limited resources that force us to rely upon tests (indirect samples) rather than direct observation of the thing itself. If we remembered this fact, we might escape the utter idiocy involved in teaching directly to tests and return to teaching to thoughtful conceptualizations of curriculum.

- *Multiple indices are both desirable and necessary.* Anyone would be a fool to rely on a single measure of anything that mattered to him or her. What we want are converging indices of progress (or the lack of progress) so that we can place greater trust in our decisions.
- *Subjectivity can never be avoided, only masked.* One of the great illusions of standardized assessments is that they are more objective, and hence more trustworthy, than assessments for which teachers have to make interpretations and judgments. Yet, someone has to decide what passages to use, what questions to ask, what choices to provide for multiple-choice items, what the "right" answers are. Those "someones" are people who are subject to the same biases as those who make judgments in classrooms. And even if we granted, for the sake of argument, that tests could be developed in a nonsubjective manner, someone would still have to decide what a score meant, and that decision inevitably requires interpretation. We would all be better off if we admitted that judgment is an inherent part of any assessment activity and, in the very next breath, suggested that the best and only guarantee against poor judgment is greater professional knowledge of literacy processes, instruction, and assessment.

SUMMARY

These are the future directions that we would like to see assessment take. In developing and evaluating new literacy assessment methods or procedures, we think that it is especially important to keep in mind what we know about the reading/writing process, the test performance of students from diverse backgrounds, and the potential pitfalls that all assessments pose for these students. To meet these problems, we must concern ourselves with the development of teachers and administrators' knowledge base. As a summary to our essay, we close with a list of criteria that we hope educators would use in evaluating and creating literacy assessments. Such assessments should

- Engage students in authentic literacy tasks
- Reflect a constructivist view of reading and writing
- Reveal student progress over time
- Emphasize what students can and cannot do (with and without help from the teacher, other adults, or their peers)
- Take advantage of rather than ignore or, even worse, penalize students' diversity
- Provide multiple indices of students' literacy use and interests

- Acknowledge students' interpretations (i.e., their "readings") of literacy tasks
- Encourage the involvement of students, parents, and community participants

Without these characteristics, "new" methods of assessment will be no more useful to a diverse society than the "old" methods.

ACKNOWLEDGMENT. The work upon which this publication was based was funded in part by the Mellon Foundation and by the Office of Educational Research and Improvement under Cooperative Agreement No. G0087-C1001-90 with the Reading Research and Education Center. The publication does not necessarily reflect the views of the agency supporting the research.

REFERENCES

Aronson, E., & Farr, R. (1988). Issues in assessment. *Journal of Reading, 32*(2), 174–177.

Atwell, N. (1987). *In the middle: Writing, reading, and learning with adolescents.* Portsmouth, NH: Heinemann.

Au, K. H. (1981). Participation structures in a reading lesson with Hawaiian children: Analysis of a culturally appropriate instructional event. *Anthropology and Education Quarterly 11*, 91–115.

Barr, R., & Dreeben, R., with Wiratchai, N. (1983). *How schools work.* Chicago: University of Chicago Press.

Boggs, S. T. (1972). The meaning of questions and narratives to Hawaiian children. In V. P. John & D. Hymes (Eds.), *Functions of language in the classroom* (pp. 299–327). New York: Teachers College Press.

Bruce, B., Rubin, A., Starr, K., & Liebling, C. (1984). Sociocultural differences in oral vocabulary and reading material. In W. S. Hall, W. E. Nagy, & R. Linn (Eds.), *Spoken words: Effects of situation and social group on oral word use and frequency* (pp. 466–480). Hillsdale, NJ: Erlbaum.

Cabello, B. (1984). Cultural interface in reading comprehension: An alternative explanation. *Bilingual Review, 2*(1), 12–20.

Calfee, R., & Hiebert, E. (1991). Classroom assessment of reading. In R. Barr, M. L. Kamil, P. Mosenthal, & P. D. Pearson (Eds.), *The handbook of reading research* (Vol. 2, pp. 281–309). New York: Longman.

Cazden, C. B. (1988). *Classroom discourse: The language of teaching and learning.* Portsmouth, NH: Heinemann.

Cicourel, A. (1974). Some basic theoretical issues in the assessment of the child's performance in testing and classroom settings. In A. Cicourel, K. H. Jennings, S. H. M. Jennings, K. C. W. Leiter, R. Mackay, H. Mehan, & D. Roth

(Eds.), *Language use and school performance* (pp. 300–351). New York: Academic Press.

Clay, M. M. (1987). *The early detection of reading difficulties* (3rd ed.). Auckland, New Zealand: Heinemann.

Delpit, L. D. (1988). The silenced dialogue: Power and pedagogy in educating other people's children. *Harvard Educational Review, 58*(3), 280–298.

Dorr-Bremme, D. W., & Herman, J. L. (1986). *Assessing student achievement: A profile of classroom practices.* Los Angeles: University of California, Center for the Study of Evaluation.

Durán, R. P. (1983). *Hispanics' education and background: Predictors of college achievement.* New York: College Entrance Examination Board.

Edelsky, C., & Harman, S. (1988). One more critique of reading tests—with two differences. *English Education, 20*(3), 157–171.

Edwards, P. A., & García, G. E. (in press). Parental involvement in mainstream schools: An issue of equity. In M. Foster & S. S. Goldberg (Eds.), *Readings on equal education* (Vol. II). New York: AMS Press.

Faculty Senate position paper on the Georgia kindergarten testing/first grade readiness policy. (1988). Unpublished manuscript, University of Georgia, Athens.

Fiske, E. B. (1989, January 3). Changes planned in entrance tests used by colleges. *New York Times,* pp. 1, 16.

Foertsch, M., & Pearson, P. D. (1987, December). *Reading assessment in basal reading series and standardized tests.* Paper presented at the annual meeting of the National Reading Conference, St. Petersburg, FL.

García, G. E. (1988). *Factors influencing the English reading test performance of Spanish-English bilingual children.* Unpublished doctoral dissertation, University of Illinois at Urbana-Champaign.

García, G. E., & Pearson, P. D. (1990). *Modifying reading instruction to maximize its effectiveness for all students* (Tech. Rep. No. 489). Urbana-Champaign, IL: Center for the Study of Reading.

Goldman, R. E., & Hewitt, B. (1975). An investigation of test bias for Mexican American college students. *Journal of Educational Measurement, 12*(3), 187–196.

Goodman, K. S., Goodman, Y. M., & Hood, W. J. (1989). *The whole language evaluation book.* Portsmouth, NH: Heinemann.

Goodman, Y. M., Watson, D. J., & Burke, C. L. (1987). *Reading miscue inventory: Alternative procedures.* New York: Richard C. Owen.

Guba, E. G. (1981). Criteria for assessing the trustworthiness of naturalistic inquiries. *Educational Communication and Technology Journal, 29,* 75–92.

Hall, W. S., Nagy, W. E., & Linn, R. (1984). *Spoken words: Effects of situation and social group on oral word usage and frequency.* Hillsdale, NJ: Erlbaum.

Heath, S. B. (1983). *Ways with words: Language, life, and work in communities and classrooms.* New York: Cambridge University Press.

Hymes, D. (1972). Introduction. In C. B. Cazden, V. P. John, & D. Hymes (Eds.), *Functions of language in the classroom* (pp. xi–lvii). New York: Teachers College Press.

Johnston, P. (1981). *Prior knowledge and reading comprehension test bias.* Unpublished doctoral dissertation, University of Illinois, Urbana-Champaign.

Johnston, P. (1984a). Prior knowledge and reading comprehension test bias. *Reading Research Quarterly, 19*(2), 219–239.

Johnston, P. (1984b). *Reading comprehension assessment: A cognitive basis.* Newark, DE: International Reading Association.

Johnston, P. (1989). Constructive evaluation and the improvement of teaching and learning. *Teachers College Record 90*(4), 509–528.

Johnston, P., & Allington, R. (1991). Remediation. In R. Barr, M. L. Kamil, P. B. Mosenthal, & P. D. Pearson (Eds.), *Handbook of Reading Research* (Vol. 2, pp. 984–1012). New York: Longman.

Karweit, N. (1989). Effective kindergarten programs and practices for students at risk. In R. Slavin, N. Karweit, & N. Madden (Eds.), *Effective programs for students at risk* (pp. 103–142). Boston: Allyn & Bacon.

Labov, W. (1969). The logic of nonstandard English. In R. D. Abrahams & R. C. Troike (Eds.), *Language and cultural diversity in American education* (pp. 225–261). Englewood Cliffs, NJ: Prentice Hall.

Langer, J. A. (1987). The construction of meaning and the assessment of comprehension: An analysis of reader performance on standardized test items. In R. O. Freedle & R. P. Durán (Eds.), *Cognitive and linguistic analyses of text performance* (pp. 225–244). Norwood, NJ: Ablex.

Leap, W. L. (1982). The study of Indian English in the U.S. Southwest: Retrospect and prospect. In F. Barken, E. A. Brandt, & J. Ornstein-Galicia (Eds.), *Bilingualism and language contact: Spanish, English and Native American languages* (pp. 101–119). New York: Teachers College Press.

Linn, R. L. (1983). Predictive bias as an artifact of selection procedures. In H. Wainer & S. Messick (Eds.), *Principles of modern psychological measurement: A Festschrift for Frederic M. Lord* (pp. 27–40). Hillsdale, NJ: Erlbaum.

Mason, J. (1980). When do children begin to read: An exploration of four year old children's letter and word reading competencies. *Reading Research Quarterly, 15,* 203–227.

Mercer, J. R. (1977). Identifying the gifted Chicano child. In J. L. Martinez (Ed.), *Chicano psychology* (pp. 155–173). New York: Academic Press.

Millman, J., Bishop, C. H., & Ebel, R. (1965). An analysis of test-wiseness. *Educational and Psychological Measurement, 25,* 707–726.

Moll, L. C., Estrada, E., Diaz, E., & Lopes, L. M. (1980). The organization of bilingual lessons: Implications for schooling. *Quarterly Newsletter of the Laboratory of Comparative Human Cognition, 2*(3), 53–58.

Morrow, L. M. (1989). Using story retelling to develop comprehension. In K. D. Muth (Ed.), *Children's comprehension of text: Research into practice* (pp. 37–58). Newark, DE: International Reading Association.

Morrow, L. M. (1990). Assessing children's understanding of story through their construction and recognition of narrative. In L. M. Morrow & J. V. Smith (Eds.), *Assessment for instruction in early literacy* (pp. 110–134). Englewood Cliffs, NJ: Prentice Hall.

Mullis, I. V. S., & Jenkins, L. B. (1990). *The reading report card, 1971–88: Trends from the nation's report card*. Princeton, NJ: National Assessment of Educational Progress, ETS.

Oakland, T., & Matsuzek, P. (1977). Using tests in nondiscriminatory assessment. In T. Oakland (Ed.), *Psychological and educational assessment of minority children* (pp. 52–69). New York: Brunner/Mazel.

Ogbu, J. (1982). Cultural discontinuities and schooling. *Anthropology and Education Quarterly, 13*(4), 291–307.

Pearson, P. D., & Valencia, S. (1987). Assessment, accountability, and professional prerogative. In J. E. Readence & R. S. Baldwin (Eds.), *Research in literacy: Merging perspectives: Thirty-sixth yearbook of the National Reading Conference* (pp. 3–16). Rochester, NY: The National Reading Conference.

Philips, S. U. (1983). *The invisible culture: Communication in classroom and community on the Warm Springs Indian Reservation*. New York: Longman.

Resnick, L. B. (1989, October). *Tests as standards of achivement in schools*. Prepared for the Educational Testing Service Conference, The Uses of Standardized Tests in American Education, New York.

Royer, J. M., & Cunningham, D. J. (1981). On the theory and measurement of reading comprehension. *Contemporary Educational Psychology, 6,* 187–216.

Savignon, S. J. (1983). *Communicative competence: Theory and classroom practice: Texts and contexts in second language learning*. Reading, MA: Addison-Wesley.

Slavin, R. E., & Madden, N. A. (1989). Effective classroom programs for students at risk. In R. E. Slavin, N. L. Karweit, & N. A. Madden (Eds.), *Effective programs for students at risk* (pp. 23–51). Boston: Allyn & Bacon.

Stake, R. E. (1976). A theoretical statement of responsive evaluation. *Studies in Educational Evaluation, 2,* 19–22.

Stallman, A. C., & Pearson, P. D. (1990). Formal measures of early literacy. In L. M. Morrow & J. K. Smith (Eds.), *Assessment for instruction in early literacy* (p. 7–44). Englewood Cliffs, NJ: Prentice Hall.

Teale, W. H., & Sulzby, E. (1986). Emergent literacy as a perspective for examining how young children become writers and readers. In W. H. Teale & E. Sulzby (Eds.), *Emergent literacy: Writing and reading* (pp. vii–xxv). Norwood, NJ: Ablex.

Troike, R. C. (1969). Receptive competence, productive competence, and performance. In J. E. Alatis (Ed.), *Monograph series on language and linguistics, 22,* 63–73.

Troike, R. C. (1984). SCALP: Social and cultural aspects of language proficiency. In C. Rivera (Ed.), *Language proficiency and academic achievement* (pp. 44–54). Avon, England: Multi-Lingual Matters.

Tyler, R. W., & White, S. H. (1979). Chairmen's report. In National Institute of Education, *Testing, teaching, and learning: Report of a conference on research on testing* (pp. 3–32). U.S. Department of Health, Education, and Welfare. Washington, DC: Government Printing Office.

Valencia, S., McGinley, W., and Pearson, P. D. (1990). Assessing reading and writing: Building a more complete picture. In G. Duffy (Ed.), *Reading in the middle school* (2nd ed., pp. 124–146). Newark, DE: International Reading Association.

WQED Pittsburgh (Producer). (1988). *First things first* [Film]. Presented by Public Television Outreach Alliance.

Wiggins, G. (1989). Teaching to the (authentic) test. *Educational Leadership, 46*(7), 41–47.

Wixson, K. K., Peters, C. W., Weber, E. M., & Roeber, E. D. (1987). New directions in statewide reading assessment. *The Reading Teacher,* pp. 747–754.

19 | Negative Policies for Dealing With Diversity: When Does Assessment and Diagnosis Turn Into Sorting and Segregation?

LORRIE A. SHEPARD
University of Colorado, Boulder

The perspective presented in this chapter derives from a series of policy research studies that we have conducted over the past decade aimed at understanding several different school placement practices: the identification of children as learning disabled, grade retention, and special kindergarten placements for unready children. How might the findings from our work and the respective research literatures inform the discussion in this volume, where the authors are interested in providing meaningful literacy instruction to a diverse population of students? Simply put, these placement practices can be seen as part of a recurring pattern in the U.S. educational system to deal with children who have trouble learning by assigning them to a special place where, despite good intentions, they receive systematically poor instruction that lessens their chances for important learning gains. As documented repeatedly in the preceding chapters, children from nonmainstream cultural and linguistic backgrounds are disproportionately the victims of these ineffective instructional practices.

The other contributors to the volume cite the detrimental aspects of current practice but focus primarily on the arguments for and substantive details of alternative approaches to literacy education. My purpose here is to elaborate more explicitly on the arguments for rejecting current practice. Why are present institutional arrangements harmful? Is there a theoretical basis for understanding the consistent lack of instructional benefits from special placements? I begin by reviewing briefly similarities in the research conclusions from the respective literatures on tracking, special education placements for the mildly handicapped, grade retention, and special kindergarten programs.

In my view each of these practices is based on a clinical or instructional model of assessment and diagnosis where the intention is to provide instructional help specifically targeted to the individual student's needs. Although the idea is to individualize instruction, negative side effects accrue as soon as students are removed from their peers and assigned to a special place to receive help. Hence the title of the chapter is meant to suggest that assessment and diagnosis turn into sorting and segregation when special help implies special placement. The special placement response is especially pernicious when it also means receiving dumbed-down instruction.

Why are students who are doing poorly in school consigned to bad instruction? In the second section of this chapter I examine the theoretical models and assumptions underlying current practice, characterizing them as old and outmoded psychological theories about human ability and learning. If we understand how the old theories were flawed, why practices derived from them don't work and are even harmful becomes transparent. It should also be clear, so long as they remain as the implicit theories guiding decisions, that new versions of the old practices will continue to be reinvented until the majority of practitioners make the same shift in perspective that has been made in the research community. Practitioners have the right to point out, of course, that the views they now hold were taught to them adamantly by a different group of researchers 10 to 40 years ago. Nonetheless we can now explain with a great deal of evidential support how it is that these old theories were mistaken.

My characterizations of "old" and "new" theories are especially intended for the uninitiated reader who might not know what to make of the constant references in this volume to Vygotsky or to the social construction of meaning. The authors in this volume all speak from the perspective of the new theories, which are based on the last 20 years of research in cognitive psychology, a resurgent interest in constructivist developmental psychology (from the work of Piaget and Vygotsky), and a broader framework for studying social, cultural, and linguistic influences on learning. The shared viewpoints among these authors are not the result of a selection bias on the part of the editor but are, in fact, representative of the larger educational research community—affecting all areas of subject-matter learning including math and science and early childhood education. In the concluding section of the chapter, I summarize the key features of the new theories of learning. Drawing from the work in the preceding chapters, I point to the kinds of changes in instructional practices that are likely to improve substantially students' ability to learn. In addition—because many of these ideas are as unfamiliar to teachers as the oddities of classroom discourse are to some groups of students—I consider the kind of support that teachers might need to make these transformations possible.

RESEARCH ON SORTING PRACTICES: TRACKING, SPECIAL EDUCATION, GRADE RETENTION, AND READINESS ROOMS

Tracking

Tracking is one of the most pervasive practices in 20th-century American schools. It was developed early in the century in response to universal public education. Once schools were expected to teach all students instead of a homogeneous, elite group, institutional arrangements were created to deal with their heterogeneous learning levels. At the time, apparent differences among students were believed to be caused by permanent differences in students' capacity to learn. Therefore, students were assigned to different classes in elementary schools and to different course sequences in high schools to receive instruction consistent with their abilities. Grouping by ability is expected to improve achievement by tailoring instruction to what students are capable of learning. It is also believed that separating slow learners from fast learners will improve their self-concepts by providing successful rather than failing experiences.

Research on tracking does not confirm the happy intention of the practice. Although results from controlled studies are mixed—with some studies showing no differences in achievement between homogeneous classrooms and heterogeneously placed controls, and some studies showing benefits for students in the fast track—there is consistent evidence showing that children in the middle and slow groups generally lose academically (Good & Marshall, 1984; Slavin, 1987). Separate classrooms also do not protect children from negative inferences about their own abilities but rather create a social stigma because of the very public nature of being in the class for "dummies." In a meta-analysis of 50 studies, Noland (1985) found that ability grouping had an average negative effect on students' self-concept.

More to the point of this volume, countless research studies show that tracking affects the quality of learning opportunities provided. Teachers would rather teach high-ability students. They hold higher expectations for them, spend more time preparing class instruction, expect more homework, and ask more challenging questions (Oakes, 1985). In the section on psychological theories I discuss why it is that teachers deliver a simplified curriculum to students in low-ability classes. In addition to content differences, however, there are also effects on learning created by the cultural norms that develop in the separate classrooms. The businesslike atmosphere in high-ability classes keeps students focused on academic content, thus not eliciting a pattern of control and reprimand from teachers. In contrast, students in lower-track classrooms must actually transgress the norms of the group to pay attention and try to learn (see Oakes, 1985; Chapter 3).

Other points should also be made about the persistent findings from research on tracking. Tests used to make placement decisions are necessarily fallible. But two students who are initially indistinguishable from each other except for measurement error will become more like the mean of their respective ability groups. Children from poor and minority backgrounds are overrepresented in lower tracks.

Special Education Placement for Mild Handicaps

Special education was developed originally to serve populations of physically handicapped, that is, deaf and blind, children, and the mentally retarded. Its boundaries have continually expanded to serve a larger and larger population of children with more mild (and more vaguely defined) learning problems. Special education is so called because it is intended to provide special instruction that acknowledges and accommodates a child's disability.

Beginning in the 1960s, a number of educational researchers and sociologists investigated the validity of claims that being placed in a separate educational system was beneficial. Their findings closely paralleled the negative evidence on tracking. Special education teachers were not necessarily better trained. Once assigned, children received a watered-down curriculum and lost ground academically compared with control children in the regular classroom. Furthermore, the negative effects of placement were greatest for the less severely (or less genuinely) handicapped students (see the meta-analysis of 50 studies by Carlberg & Kavale, 1980). A disproportionate number of special education students were (and continue to be) minority students. And more significantly, the disproportion of minority students increased as the number of mildly handicapped students increased (i.e., the more the definition of handicapped was expanded to include vaguely defined learning problems, the more minority children were captured by the definition).

Researchers have also documented the effects of labeling students as mentally handicapped. Not only are children stigmatized by negative labels, but labeling may also change how adults interact with a student. Labels are often reified so that they become the complete explanation of a child's learning problems. Because of its origins, special education placements naturally assume a medical model or deficit model of educational difficulties (Chapter 6), which means that problems are thought to be the result of the child's intrinsic disorders rather than problems that might have arisen because of the instructional context.

Research findings of negative effects are the basis for current federal requirements that children be placed in the "least restrictive environment." However, the enactment of federal legislation in 1975 has not necessarily alleviated the harmful effects of special education identification. Although a smaller percentage of children are now being placed in full-time self-contained classrooms, the total number of children being labeled as handicapped has grown markedly in the last 15 years, especially in the learning-disabilities category. We investigated the identification of children as learning disabled (LD) in a series of studies (see Shepard & Smith, 1983; Shepard, Smith, & Vojir, 1983; Smith, 1982). Our methods included interviews with directors of special education, surveys of test use and clinicians' knowledge, examination of the histories of a representative sample of 1,000 LD pupils, qualitative case studies, and observations at staffing meetings. Our conclusions from this research included the following: Most of the tests used in the diagnosis of LD are technically inadequate. Many clinicians are unaware of the difference between technically adequate and inadequate tests. Also clinicians interpret as signs of disorder patterns that occur in a large proportion of normal children (this tendency helps to explain why children are almost certain to be placed once referred to special education). Despite the tremendous costs of involving an average of six professionals in the assessment and staffing process leading to LD placement, only 7% of staffings showed any attempt to reconcile the findings from different professionals—that is, the school psychologist, LD teacher, speech pathologist, social worker, etc. More than half of the children labeled LD in the schools do not match either technical or clinical definitions of LD but are more accurately described as slow learners, children from non-English backgrounds, highly mobile children or those with frequent absences, naughty boys, and average achievers in high-achieving districts. From the available evidence it would be fair to say that most clinicians have abandoned a "scientific" definition of LD and ask instead, "Does this child need special help? If so, he must be LD." Believing that special education placement is an added benefit, educators are willing to place children with no restraint except that imposed by legal or funding limits.

The evidence does not warrant such a completely sanguine view of special education placement for "anyone who needs it." Although educators are nearly unanimous in their assertions that the LD label does not create a social stigma among a child's peers, it is nonetheless true that labeling a child changes the nature of the classroom teacher's responsibility for that child's learning in both subtle and explicit ways. For example, once a child is labeled for even part-time placement, some standardized testing programs excuse that child from participation. Consistent with findings from other pull-out programs, special education resource-room help usually supplants rather than augments regular classroom instruction. Although it is assumed that the reduced pupil–teacher ratio in resource rooms automatically produces corresponding educational gains, this is not necessarily the case. For example, Thurlow, Ysseldyke, Graden, and Algozzine (1983) found that LD students were just as distracted in resource rooms (i.e., had poor time on task) as in the regular classroom. Most significantly, as documented by Allington in Chapter 17, the instruction in resource rooms is often deadly drill on worksheets, which offers little hope of helping children become more active and effective in their learning.

Grade Retention

Grade retention is another mechanism of inequality that predates both tracking and special education. Nonpromotion was the 19th century's answer to diversity, developed when the urban poor and immigrant populations began to attend public schools. The extent of these three practices has tended to ebb and flow historically; sometimes one practice has taken on more of the sorting function when other practices were quiescent. For example, grade retention was discouraged from the time of the depression through the 1960s for philosophical reasons and to keep youths out of the work force. During the same period tracking flourished. Since the 1970s tracking practices have been greatly reduced in elementary schools; concurrently there has been a dramatic increase in special education placements and retention.

Once schools were organized into grades with the expectation that children would pass as groups through material sequentially ordered by difficulty, then repeating a grade became the remedy for students who were not keeping pace with instruction. In the present day, absent a slow track, retention is most often the intervention of choice for children who lack prerequisite skills for the next grade but whose problems are not serious enough to trigger special education placement. It is believed that the repeat year will allow students to catch up and be better prepared to go on to new material.

Contrary to popular beliefs, adhered to by both educators and the public at large, repeating a grade does not improve achievement. Holmes (1989) recently conducted a meta-analysis of 63 controlled studies. In the years following retention, retained students have lower achievement (by one quarter of a standard deviation) than control students who went directly on to the next grade. Although researchers have reported the counterintuitive and harmful effects of retention since 1909 (Ayers), the research has often been criticized on the grounds that the nonrandomized control groups might have been better off initially given that they were promoted despite their low achievement. However, Holmes isolated the 25 studies with the greatest degree of initial matching and still found the same negative effects for retention.

Because the beliefs about the efficacy of retention are so strong, educational reformers in the 1980s have also seen it as a direct remedy for school dropout problems. For example, the chancellor of New York City Schools inaugurated the Gates testing program with the following statement:

> Student promotion will be determined by the degree to which the student has mastered the basic skills required in each grade. Automatic advancement from grade to grade without evidence of achieving required performance standards in basic skills places an unfair burden on students in succeeding grades. The early mastery of basic skills will help to ensure that today's elementary school student is not tomorrow's high school dropout. The current dropout rate is intolerable and a program to attack this problem must be mounted immediately. (Macchiarola, 1981, as cited in Association for Supervision and Curriculum Development, 1984, p. 6)

Rather than reducing the risk of dropping out, however, the best evidence is that retention exacerbates the problem. Research on dropouts has always shown that a hugely disproportionate number had been retained compared with graduates. In studies where controls were introduced for prior achievement and background characteristics, retainees were 20% to 30% more likely to leave school without graduating than similar students who had never been retained (Grissom & Shepard, 1989).

The conventional wisdom on the social-emotional effects of grade retention is more congruent with research findings. Almost everyone acknowledges that there is a social stigma associated with flunking, and Holmes's (1989) synthesis confirms a negative effect on personal adjustment measures in the majority of studies. Some researchers speculate, in fact, that the humiliation of retention is one of the reasons for its lack of instructional benefit. However, such a conclusion cannot be confirmed or disconfirmed from the existing literature. It is just as plausible to conjecture that retention doesn't work because of bad instruction. Realigning a student by a 12-month relocation on a fixed achievement continuum is not any more likely to address an individual student's understandings and learning needs than occurred the first time through.

Of the three placement practices considered thus far, retention relies the least on testing. However, formal testing programs to determine grade-to-grade promotion have increased substantially during the 1980s. In addition, there is some evidence that retention increases as an indirect effect of accountability testing; for example, children may be retained in the year preceding a high-stakes test. By whatever selection method, teacher recommendation or formal test, minority children are retained at higher rates than other groups.

Kindergarten Retention and Programs for At-Risk Kindergartners

Unlike tracking, special education, and retention that have century-long histories, kindergarten retention and special programs for at-risk kindergartners are very recent phenomena. They are of particular interest here because they illustrate the extent to which the powerful belief systems underlying the old practices persist and are the basis for inventing new programs in the same mold, without any recognition on the part of practitioners that they are recreating new forms of tracking and special placement. Special kindergarten programs have burgeoned in the 1980s, but only in approximately the past 2 years have policy groups such as the National Forum on the Future of Children and Families sponsored by the National Research Council begun to use terms like *tracking*, when talking about the advisability of such programs.

In a brief space, it is very difficult to do justice to the variety of special programs that have been created to deal with children judged to be unready for kindergarten. Programs differ in form, underlying philosophy, and type of children defined to be at risk. The generic term for these special placement practices is kindergarten retention, which includes 2-year programs like developmental kindergarten before regular kindergarten, transition room before first grade, as well as straight repeating of kindergarten. Depending on local philosophy, the children may be selected for immaturity or academic deficiencies. When philosophical positions are congruent with instructional approach, there is a tendency for those who believe in biologically caused unreadiness to provide the gift of an extra year and wait for time to promote readiness; conversely, those who define unreadiness as environmentally caused skill deficiencies provide remediation following a curriculum that closely resembles readiness skills tests. We have also observed philosophically incongruent practices, however, where children were selected for 2-year placement because of developmental immaturity but given a highly regimented rule-oriented curriculum to prepare for first grade (Smith & Shepard, 1988). The names given to 2-year programs do not help to distinguish them substantively. For example, *junior-first, prefirst, transition*, and *readiness room* are all used to refer to the grade between kindergarten and first grade and are used interchangeably regardless of philosophical assumptions or instructional approach.

The purpose of 2-year kindergarten placements of whatever stripe is to foster "readiness" for first grade as defined locally. By placing similar children together and gearing instruction to their needs, the intention is to ensure a more successful, less stressful experience in first grade. Advocates for 2-year programs promise parents that their children will become leaders because of the extra year and insist that there is no stigma associated with kindergarten retention if "it is handled properly." Research evidence disputes these claims, however. A review of 16 controlled studies now available shows typically no difference academically between unready children who spent an extra year before first grade and at-risk controls who went directly on to first grade (Shepard, 1989). The findings of no benefit are consistent regardless of whether children were placed on the basis of immaturity or academic deficiency. In the few studies that included any measure of social or emotional effects there is evidence of some short-term or long-term trauma associated with the retention decision for a majority of retained children.

In our research that examined the larger context of kindergarten retention practices, we also reached the following conclusions:

1. Increasing rates of kindergarten retention (50% is not uncommon) can be attributed to dramatic shifts in the kindergarten and first-grade curriculum toward narrow emphasis on reading and numeracy skills.
2. Tests used to make readiness and retention decisions are not technically accurate enough to justify making special placement.
3. Removing unready children from regular kindergarten actually feeds the cycle of curriculum escalation as teachers adjust their expectations to the attention spans of 6-year-olds.
4. Matched schools that do not practice kindergarten retention have just as high average achievement as those that do but tend to provide more individualized instruction within normal grade placements (Shepard & Smith, 1988).

We have also noted that readiness tests are either thinly disguised IQ tests (called developmental screening measures) or academic skills tests (see Chapter 18); both types of tests tend to identify disproportionate numbers of poor and minority children as unready for school (see Ellwein & Eads, 1990; Shepard, in press).

In addition to 2-year kindergartens, there has been a tendency in recent years to group at-risk children together in regular kindergartens. This occurs, for example, when there are limited funds for extended-day programs so all of the children who need the extra resource are placed in one classroom. Apparently educators do not think of this as tracking or as a potentially harmful practice. Otherwise they might think of other arrangements, such as placing children in heterogeneous regular kindergartens in the morning followed by additional, enrichment activities in the afternoon. But these special placements do lead to a familiar outcome. As documented by Garcia and Pearson in Chapter 18, the curriculum in these special rooms is dominated by drill on isolated readiness skills with little opportunity for the kinds of literacy activities and experience with texts that would truly foster reading readiness.

Conclusions

Conclusions from the research literatures on these several sorting practices read like variations on the same theme. Each involves the use of fallible tests (or sometimes teacher judgments) to assign children to treatments that are ineffective or harmful. Tracking, special education, grade retention, and special kindergartens are all intended to individualize instruction by placing children in homogeneous groups where their needs are thought to be closer to the group average. The logic of these schemes to match instruction to student ability is so compelling that they are highly resistant to change even in the face of research evidence. Contrary to the promise of special help, however, children placed under each of these arrangements are likely to receive poorer instruction than if their problems had remained undiagnosed. Because there are socially understood connotations of incompetence associated with each of these special placements, children are likely to suffer embarrassment and have less confidence in their own abilities to learn as a result of placement. Children from linguistically and culturally different backgrounds are selected more frequently than white, middle-class children to participate in the groups with slowed instruction. In the next section I summarize the old learning theories that account for the ineffective, reductionist curriculum that children receive in accord with each of these placement practices. Belief systems based on the old theories also help to explain why tracking practices continue to be reinvented under new names.

OLD SORTING THEORIES

There are two old psychological theories that continue to have pervasive influence on what educators and the public believe about learning, especially their beliefs about how much children are *able* to learn and their beliefs about how instruction should be organized to facilitate student learning. One theory, about individuals' inherited capacity to learn, is well known as a controversial theoretical perspective. The second theory, which is the behaviorist's sequential learning model, is much less publicly recognized as a theory whose assumptions guide much of current educational practice. My rendition of these two models here is necessarily brief and oversimplified. My purpose is to sketch the most salient principles of the original theories as they are carried forward or reflected in the implicit belief systems of practitioners today. By characterizing both models as old and outmoded psychological theories, I do not claim that all scientists have rejected these theories nor even that most scientists have rejected all of the elements of each theory. However, the majority of scientists today find these theories, or explanatory viewpoints, incompatible with the weight of evidence. Thus, as outlined in the concluding section of the chapter, new models and perspectives have been developed that are more compatible with contemporary research findings.

Inherited Ability to Learn

Psychology began as the study of individual differences with particular emphasis on differences in human intellectual capacity. The earliest conceptions of intelligence equated it literally with brain size. Intelligence was thought to be an innate attribute—a fixed, unitary trait passed on from father to son like height and hair color. The theory that one's ability to learn was determined by biology meant that there were naturally imposed ceilings on what different individuals could learn. Furthermore, because the theory as commonly held did not allow for the influences of past learning on current status, it was straightforward to equate capacity or potential with observed proficiency. The early history of tracking in the United States is predicated on the assumption that children with different measured potential should be provided with instruction commensurate with their abilities and designed to prepare them for their respective stations in life (see Chapman, 1988).

A view of intelligence as largely inherited has been discredited over time, first by the debunking of IQ tests as measures of potential, by evidence of the influence of environment on observed capabilities, and then by experimental demonstrations that children can be taught to think intelligently (see Brown, Campione, Webber, & McGilly, in press). This is not to deny that there are genetic contributions to manifest cognitive abilities. However, the more that scientists have learned over the last 50 years, the more they have steadily revised downward their estimates of the relative influence of heredity.

Since the controversies of the 1960s—centering on claims about IQ differences among racial groups—most laypersons have also revised their notions about the relative influence of heredity and environment on an individual's demonstrated intellectual abilities. However, revisions in the common view, shared by teachers and the public, have not kept pace with the research insights provided by cognitive psychology, sociology, or cultural anthropology. Therefore, lay conceptions about abilities tend not to include very elaborated ideas about how interactive are the events and processes that develop learning ability. Simplistically, today's view is that a person's intelligence is determined by two quantities, heredity plus environment, rather than one. But once they are added together and cemented (say, by the time a child is 5), the idea is still that the sum of these two contributions sets fairly firm limits on how much children can learn.

I suggest that a "substitute, environmental, theory" has now taken the place of the hereditarian theory in the minds of many teachers, but that this theory nonetheless preserves many of the properties of the old theory about fixed IQ. The substitute theory is another way of looking at what several authors in this volume have referred to as the deficit model. Although almost all teachers today would consider it socially and politically unacceptable to talk about a child's "limited genetic endowment for school learning," substitution of an environmental explanation for school failure, which directly denigrates the child's home experiences, is considered acceptable (see Chapter 6). In addition, although most teachers are usually willing to acknowledge that tests, particularly ability tests, are probably biased against minority children, there is little awareness of the extent to which their personal judgments about children's abilities might be distorted and limited by their own cultural experiences and perspectives. As discussed by the authors in this volume and in Heath's (1983) study, teachers very often misinterpret a lack of response from students as evidence of deficiency, rather than seeing how students' abilities to express their understanding and relevant learning are straight-jacketed by the imposition of school conventions of discourse. Because many teachers thus miss seeing the competence of culturally different children and hold implicitly to a conception of environmentally determined inability that is relatively permanent, they tend to view the problems of children from nonmainstream or non-English-speaking backgrounds as insurmountable or unalterable. This pessimistic attitude encourages the tracking practices described in the first section of the chapter and sets the stage for watered-down teaching goals, consistent with the second "old" theory discussed next.

The Sequential, Bit-by-Bit Model of Learning

The dominant learning theory affecting education from the 1950s to the present time has been behaviorism. Its assumptions pervade both curriculum materials and standardized tests; however, most educators neither describe themselves as behaviorists nor recognize that their beliefs about learning come from behaviorist principles. Behaviorism goes back to the stimulus-response conditioning of Pavlov's first experiments. The basic tenet of this theory is that all learning can be broken down into constituent skills that must be learned sequentially from the simplest to the more complex. For example, in Skinner's (1954) words, "The whole process of becoming competent in a field must be divided into a very large number of very small steps, and reinforcement must be contingent upon the accomplishment of each step" (p. 94). In practice, enactment of behaviorist theory follows the model of mastery learning, programmed instruction, and the like, where learning objectives are carefully delineated and ordered hierarchically so that students do not go on to the next objective until they have mastered the lower level skill.

These ideas have a powerful hold on how teachers think about instruction because it seems so intuitively reasonable to help a student who is failing to learn by teaching the prerequisite knowledge that appears to be missing. However appealing the premise, the sequential, bit-by-bit learning model rests on several fallacious assumptions about learning that, in the light of current research, can be seen to lead instruction in the wrong direction. First, as other critics have noted, the model of sequential mastery rests on the assumptions of *decomposibility* and *decontextualization* (Resnick & Resnick, 1990; Stallman & Pearson, 1990). It is assumed that complex understandings can be taken apart (by the teacher or curriculum developer) and given to students to practice in isolation. As described by the Resnicks, the implication is that these separate elements, once learned, can then be reassembled into a complex skill, as if one were assembling a piece of machinery from prefabricated parts. The truth is, however, that behavioral theory never explained (nor examined) how constituent parts were to be integrated so as to progress from rote skills to conceptual understanding. This "reductionist" model leads to bad instruction because it removes learning tasks from any context that would make them more meaningful (and therefore easier to learn). And, having decontextualized skill learning, it makes learning to apply school knowledge to real-world problems into a separate and onerous step.

Perhaps the most deadly assumption of all is the belief that thinking or development of "high-order" skills should be postponed until after students have mastered the basics. Notice that the original premise of behaviorism was that children should be taught prerequisite *knowledge*, which came to mean prerequisite *skills* or information, rather than prerequisite *understandings*. Behaviorists never wanted any truck with unobservable constructs like "understanding"—a principled stance against the earlier reification of intelligence. However, this led necessarily to the specification of learning objectives that could be behaviorally defined and observed but that also were narrow and often trivial. Despite overwhelming evidence from cognitive psychology that all learning involves thinking—even comprehension of simple texts (see Resnick & Resnick, 1990), instruction predicated on the old model denies "poor" students opportunities to think until they have mastered prerequisites.

Evidence of the numbing quality of instruction delivered to low-achieving students on the basis of these assumptions is cited over and over again in the foregoing chapters. For example, in a series of studies Allington (Chapter 17) found that good readers are expected to be self-directed and are given assignments that imply that the purpose of reading is comprehension of meaning. Poor readers, on the other hand, are taught in a markedly different way, emphasizing externally controlled fluent decoding, not understanding; "teachers interrupted poor readers more often, asked poor readers fewer comprehension questions, assigned more skill-in-isolation work, and so on" (p. 000). Similarly, Borko and Eisenhart (1986; see also Chapter 3) found that children who had been assigned to reading groups on the basis of standardized test results had fundamentally different views of what reading was about. "Only high group students mentioned understanding or meaning as an aspect of reading" (p. 3). During instruction, high-group readers were given the opportunity to read and discuss extended texts and were held accountable for understanding, whereas low-group readers were publicly accountable for decoding skills and appropriate classroom behaviors. Rueda in Chapter 7 documents that language-minority students in special education programs receive instruction that treats them as passive learners, with emphasis on private drill and practice using worksheets. Hiebert and Fisher in Chapter 10 comment that poor achievers (who haven't learned as the result of bad instruction) are then assigned to special placements, Chapter 1, and special education, "where a philosophy of 'more of the same is better' reigns".

I have not attempted to analyze in this chapter how the secondary aspects of tracking and special placement—for example, being separated from peers and internalizing a sense of failure—might lead to negative outcomes. It should be clear from the preceding discussion that special placements are harmful in large part because the treatments themselves limit learning. Basing their beliefs on flawed and outdated psychological theories, teachers are pessimistic about the abilities of non-middle-class children and resort to bit-by-bit teaching strategies in low-track placements, thereby constraining opportunities for children to learn. Although intended to be helpful, the practice of assigning poor achievers to special places where they receive bad instruction is analogous to sending debtors to prison in Victorian England. The only comforting thought in the face of this dismal picture is to realize that millions of public school children are failing *because of,* not *in spite of,* the concerted effort vested in special programs. The prospects for the future would be much grimmer if the evidence suggested that the educational system had already made its best effort.

SUMMARY: NEW THEORIES AND NEW PRACTICES

When Binet first invented the idea of mental measurement, he worried that teachers would find it "an excellent opportunity for getting rid of all children who trouble us" (Binet & Simon, 1905/1973, quoted in Brown et al., in press, p. 19). As noted by Brown et al. (in press), Binet foresaw the reification of individual's scores and the development of self-fulfilling prophesies: "It is really too easy to discover signs of backwardness in an individual when one is forewarned" (Binet & Simon, 1905/1973, p. 170). The sorting and segregating educational practices of the past 90 years have been the enactment of Binet's worst fears. Although there have always been voices crying against the injustice and false science of these practices, it has only been in recent decades that a major shift has occurred in the research community away from the conceptual frameworks that had given support to injurious practices such as tracking and watered-down instruction for slow learners.

The alternatives to current practices are the substance of this volume on literacy for a diverse society. Although the authors do not come from precisely the same disciplinary and research perspectives, they share common views about learning and literacy instruction. These views, which I have characterized as the "new" theories, are the culmination of findings and cross-disciplinary insights from the last 20 years of research in cognitive psychology, sociolinguistics, anthropology, and education. This new theoretical perspective—which sees learning as an active constructive process—has been adopted by researchers and curriculum specialists in all areas of subject-matter learning, not just literacy. For example, this cognitive-constructivist perspective is reflected in the new curriculum standards of the National Council of Teachers of Mathematics (1989) and in the National Research Council (1989) report *Everybody Counts*. The same perspective pervades the standards for developmentally appropriate curriculum developed by the National Association for the Education of Young Children (Bredekamp, 1987). Thus we are witnessing a profound and pervasive effort to change the shape of educational practice based on research understandings about how children learn.

The respective chapters in the volume provide detailed elaborations of current theory and implications of theory for practice. Therefore, I will not attempt to redevelop and explicate those ideas here. However, for the benefit of the novice reader, and to contrast with the old theories, let me enumerate some of the principles of the new theories:

1. *Intelligence and reasoning are developed abilities.* Intelligence is neither a biologically nor an environmentally determined trait but is the result of complex interactions of the individual with his or her social environment. Humans learn how to think based on the models of thinking that they have the opportunity to see and try out. Metacognitive processes (that are synonymous with intelligent thought) such as planning and evaluating during problem solving, self-checking for comprehension during reading, developing a mental representation of a problem, drawing analogies to previously learned concepts are learned. Furthermore, when an individual fails to learn these thinking strategies "naturally," they can be instructed explicitly. The model of reciprocal teaching described by Palincsar and David in Chapter 9 is a successful practical application of the new perspective with special attention to this principle. Notice that reciprocal teaching makes it possible to teach the metacognitive strategies involved in effective reading even before children have mastered the basic skills of reading.

2. *Developed ability and learning-to-learn strategies are largely context specific.* Although there are some habits of mind that are applied across contexts and tend to predict how individuals will behave when confronted with novel problems, most thinking strategies are highly developed within specific contexts. This means that children who have developed the language and social interaction patterns appropriate in one context will look ignorant and deficient to teachers who are unaware of the arbitrary language and learning conventions they impose on the basis of their own cultural norms. Shirley Brice Heath's (1983) work, cited by several authors here, documents how the mismatch between community and school communication patterns leads to the perception of deficit. Her work with teachers also demonstrates how much more successful children from different cultural backgrounds can be when, with greater insight, teachers make one of two accommodations: Either teach children explicitly the school conventions that are essential or change the conventions that are unnecessary and dysfunctional. For example, African-American children in Heath's study showed much more impressive story comprehension when they were invited to retell a story rather than to respond to isolated recall questions.

3. *Learning is a constructive process.* Passively taking in endless bits of unconnected information quickly exhausts the brain. The learner cannot acquire new ideas nor see the connection between ideas unless he or she actively constructs a mental schema of relations. Reading comprehension is the process of thinking and making meaning from text. It requires interpreting, retelling the story to oneself, and rereading when the thread is lost. Thus all learning involves thinking. If thinking is officially postponed until after skills are acquired, learning will be stunted.

4. *Furthermore, meaning is socially constructed.* What children learn, how they learn, and whether they are able to apply their knowledge in particular contexts are determined by cultural patterns and social arrangements (see Chapters 3 and 8).

(Regarding points 3 and 4, the reader will note that there are multiple meanings of constructivism in the field presently. Cognitive researchers are concerned primarily with the construction of meaning that goes on inside an individual's head—the building of knowledge structures, the chunking of related information, etc. Anthropologists and sociolinguists are interested in the social construction and negotiation of meaning among individuals in a culture. Vygotsky's theory, quoted so often in this volume, provides the bridge between the two levels of contructivism, because he suggested that a child's cultural development occurs first on the social plane and then is internalized to the intrapsychological plane and becomes a part of the individual's mental functioning.)

It follows from these principles that effective instruction should engage children in meaningful, contextually situated tasks where the goal is to practice and develop strategic thinking about important subject matter. The progress of instruction should be designed to help students use what they already know to arrive at new understandings. And prior knowledge is defined not just as vocabulary and information mastery but includes all of the images, language patterns, social relations, and personal experiences that a student relies on to make sense of something new. This volume is full of examples of the kinds of instructional practices that are faithful to these cognitive-constructivist principles.

One final word of caution is called for, however. Despite the extensive, powerful evidence in this volume that alternatives to present practice are possible and essential, it is not realistic to expect that practice will change quickly or easily. Even when explicit policy changes forbid practices such as tracking or retention, there is ample evidence that new ways can be found to get rid of hard-to-teach children unless fundamental changes are made in our habits of mind (see Chapter 15). The great majority of teachers are novices to the principles of constructivism and to the models of culturally responsive literacy instruction described in this book. Old beliefs die hard. It is no more reasonable to expect teachers to adopt these complex new views whole than it is reasonable for them to expect that all children bring precisely the same experiences to school learning. Teachers will need support of the kind described by Gaffney and Anderson in Chapter 13 for their own process of learning to become experts with these ideas. More importantly, if they are to be active and constructive learners, they will need support from each other to develop fully elaborated conceptions of what these ideas mean in practice and to evaluate and improve their own efforts over time. One such model of collegial support is the staff review group suggested by teacher Anne Martin (1988) as an alternative to special education labeling. Staff review groups are comprised of regular teachers coming together to help each other brainstorm about new ways to connect with a child by recognizing and capitalizing on that child's strengths. In addition to the more promising learning prospects for children treated in this way, Martin also reported that staff participants experienced a sense of exhilaration and renewed commitment to teaching. Martin's conclusion is a fitting closing to this chapter as well:

> Perhaps if schools were to drop their screening procedures, to stop sorting out children on the basis of tests' results, and to refrain from predicting success or failure for entering students, they would be free to accept all children as learners with unique and interesting abilities. Staffs and small groups of teachers could work together to support each other's strengths, and thus support children's strengths, instead of dwelling on problems. Public education can only succeed when all children are accepted equally as contributors in a classroom community and when teachers work together, trusting themselves to teach and children to learn. (p. 501)

This volume should prove to be a rich resource to groups of teachers interested in transforming their own practices by trying out new habits of mind with literacy instruction.

REFERENCES

Association for Supervision and Curriculum Development. (1984, June). *Retention policy analysis*. Alexandria, VA: Author.

Ayers, L. P. (1909). *Laggards in our schools*. New York: Russell Sage Foundation.

Binet, A., & Simon, T. (1973). Application of the new methods to the diagnosis of the intellectual level among normal and subnormal children in institutions and in the primary schools. (Reprinted from *L'Annee Psychologique*, 1905, *11*, 245–336) *The development of intelligence in children*. New York: Arno Press.

Borko, H., & Eisenhart, M. (1986). Students' conceptions of reading and their reading experiences in school. *Elementary School Journal*, *86*, 589–611.

Bredekamp, S. (Ed.). (1987). *Developmentally appropriate practice in early childhood programs serving children from birth through age 8*. Washington, DC: National Association for the Education of Young Children.

Brown, A. L., Campione, J. C., Webber, L. S., & McGilly, K. (in press). Interactive learning environments: A new look at assessment and instruction. In B. R. Gifford & M. C. O'Connor (Eds.), *Future assessments: Changing views of aptitude, achievement, and instruction*. Boston: Kluwer Academic Publishers.

Carlberg, C., & Kavale, K. (1980). The efficacy of special versus regular class placement for exceptional children: A meta-analysis. *Journal of Special Education*, *14*, 295–309.

Chapman, P. D. (1988). *Schools as sorters; Lewis M. Terman, applied psychology, and the intelligence testing movement, 1890–1930*. New York: New York University Press.

Ellwein, M. C., & Eads, G. M. (1990, April). How well do readiness tests predict future school performance? Paper presented at the annual meeting of the American Educational Research Association, Boston.

Good, T. L., & Marshall, S. (1984). Do students learn more in heterogeneous or homogeneous groups? In P. Peterson, L. Cherry Wilkinson, & M. Hallinan (Eds.), *The Social Context of Instruction: Group Organization and Group Process* (pp. 15–38). New York: Academic Press.

Grissom, J. B., & Shepard, L. A. (1989). In L. A. Shepard & M. L. Smith (Eds.), *Flunking grades: Research and policies on retention* (pp. 34–63). London: Falmer Press.

Heath, S. B. (1983). *Ways with words*. New York: Cambridge University Press.

Holmes, C. T. (1989). Grade level retention effects: A meta-analysis of research studies. In L. A. Shepard & M. L. Smith (Eds.), *Flunking grades: Research and policies on retention*. London: Falmer Press.

Macchiarola, F. J. (1981). *Promotional policy for students in grades kindergarten through grade 9*. Brooklyn, NY: Board of Education.

Martin, A. (1988). Screening, early intervention, and remediation: Obscuring children's potential. *Harvard Educational Review*, *58*, 488–501.

National Council of Teachers of Mathematics. (1989). *Curriculum and evaluation standards for school mathematics*. Reston, VA: Author.

National Research Council. (1989). *Everybody counts: A report to the nation on the future of mathematics education*. Washington, DC: National Academy Press.

Noland, T. K. (1985). *The effects of ability grouping: A meta-analysis of research findings*. Unpublished doctoral dissertation, University of Colorado, Boulder.

Oakes, J. (1985). *Keeping track: How schools structure inequality*. New Haven, CT: Yale University Press.

Resnick, L. B., & Resnick, D. P. (1990). Tests as standards of achievement in schools. In *The uses of standardized tests in American education: Proceedings of the 1989 ETS Invitational Conference*. Princeton, NJ: Educational Testing Service.

Shepard, L. A. (in press). Readiness testing in local school districts: An analysis of backdoor policies. *Journal of Education Policy*.

Shepard, L. A. (1989). A review of research on kindergarten retention. In L. A. Shepard & M. L. Smith (Eds.), *Flunking grades: Research and policies on retention* (pp. 64–107). London: Falmer Press.

Shepard, L. A., & Smith, M. L. (1983). An evaluation of the identification of learning disabled students in Colorado. *Learning Disability Quarterly, 6*, 115–127.

Shepard, L. A., & Smith, M. L. (1988). Escalating academic demand in kindergarten: Counterproductive policies. *Elementary School Journal, 89*, 135–145.

Shepard, L. A., Smith, M. L., & Vojir, C. P. (1983). Characteristics of pupils identified as learning disabled. *American Educational Research Journal, 20*, 309–331.

Skinner, B. F. (1954). The science of learning and the art of teaching. *Harvard Educational Review, 24*, 86–97.

Slavin, R. E. (1987). Ability grouping and student achievement in elementary schools: A best-evidence synthesis. *Review of Educational Research, 57*, 293–336.

Smith, M. L. (1982). *How educators decide who is learning disabled: Challenge to psychology and public policy in the schools*. Springfield, IL: Charles C. Thomas.

Smith, M. L., & Shepard, L. A. (1988). Kindergarten readiness and retention: A qualitative study of teachers' beliefs and practices. *American Educational Research Journal, 25*, 307–333.

Stallman, A. C., & Pearson, P. D. (1990). Formal measures of early literacy. In L. M. Morrow & J. K. Smith (Eds.), *Assessment for instruction in early literacy*. Englewood Cliffs, NJ: Prentice Hall.

Thurlow, M. L., Ysseldyke, J. E., Graden, J. L., & Algozzine, B. (1983). What's "special" about the special education resource room for learning disabled students? *Learning Disability Quarterly, 6*, 283–288.

About the Contributors

Richard L. Allington is Professor of Education in the Department of Reading at the State University of New York at Albany. Prior to beginning his university career and receiving his Ph.D. from Michigan State University, Dr. Allington was an elementary school teacher and a Title I director in a poor, rural district. His research interests include reading and learning disabilities and effective instructional environments. His work includes over 100 articles, chapters, monographs, and books, and he serves on the editorial advisory boards of *Reading Research Quarterly, Journal of Educational Psychology, Elementary School Journal, Reading Teacher,* and *Remedial and Special Education*. Dr. Allington is also a co-author of three K-8 reading series published by Scott, Foresman Company and a series of 14 children's books published by Raintree Children's Books.

Richard C. Anderson is Director of the Center for the Study of Reading and Professor of Psychology, Educational Psychology, and Elementary and Early Childhood Education at the University of Illinois. An honors graduate of Harvard College, Dr. Anderson earned his doctorate from the Harvard Graduate School of Education. He has received the Distinguished Research Award from the International Reading Association and the Oscar S. Causey Award for outstanding contributions to reading research from the National Reading Conference. Dr. Anderson has been elected to the National Academy of Education, and he has been president of the American Educational Research Association, an organization that has twice awarded him the Palmer O. Johnson Award for outstanding educational research. He has published over a hundred articles on topics in psycholinguistics, human learning and memory, and reading instruction. He has authored or edited nine books. The three most recent ones are *Learning to Read in American Schools, Foundations for a Literate America,* and *Becoming a Nation of Readers*.

Arthur N. Applebee is Professor of Education, State University of New York, at Albany, and director of the federally sponsored Center for Literature Teaching and Learning. Dr. Applebee specializes in studies of language use and language learning, particularly as these occur in school settings. Applebee's most recent studies have examined current practice in the teaching of literature in programs across the country. His previous works include *Tradition and Reform in the Teaching of English* (1974); *The Child's Concept of Story: Ages Two to Seventeen* (1978); *Writing in the Secondary*

School: English and the Content Areas (1981); and *Contexts for Learning to Write: Studies of Secondary School Instruction* (1984). He is co-author of *How Writing Shapes Thinking: A Study of Teaching and Learning* (1987), and of a series of reports in the 1980s on reading and writing achievement from the National Assessment of Educational Progress. Dr. Applebee has had experience in program evaluation, high school teaching (English and Drama), and clinical assessment and treatment of children with severe reading problems. He is co-editor of *Research in the Teaching of English.*

Rexford G. Brown is the Director of Communications at the Education Commission of the States (ECS) in Denver, Colorado. He came to the Commission in 1971, after having taught high school and college English for eight years. He earned a doctorate in English literature and criticism from the University of Iowa, following undergraduate work in American literature at Middlebury College in Vermont. Dr. Brown's work at ECS has included analyzing and writing about the results of the first national study of students' literary knowledge and critical skills, conducted by the National Assessment of Educational Progress. Currently, he is also director of Policy and the Higher Literacies, a five-year study of education policies that interfere with or help promote efforts to develop a high level of literacy in a broader range of American students. He has edited numerous publications on every aspect of education, and is author of *Schools of Thought.*

Robert Calfee is a cognitive psychologist with research interests in the effect of schooling on the intellectual potential of individuals and groups. He earned his Ph.D. at UCLA, did post-graduate work at Stanford, and spent five years in psychology at the University of Wisconsin, Madison. In 1969 he returned to Stanford University to join the School of Education, where he is presently a professor in the Committee on Language, Literacy, and Culture, and the Committee on Psychological Studies. His interests have evolved over the past two decades from a focus on assessment of beginning literacy skills to a concern with the broader reach of the school as a literate environment. His theoretical efforts are directed toward the nature of human thought processes, and the influence of language and literacy in the development of problem solving and communication. His research activities include Project READ, The Inquiring School, the Text Analysis Project, and Methods for Alternative Assessment. These projects all combine theoretical and practical facets directed toward understanding and facilitating school change.

Nancy L. Commins is Assistant Professor of Education at the University of Colorado at Denver. Her research has focused on the abilities of Latino students with low academic achievement as well as on the effects of classroom context on bilingual students' literacy development and displayed language proficiency. She teaches courses in curriculum development, school/community relations, and linguistic and cultural issues in testing and assessment. Dr. Commins has also taught in a variety of elementary and adult settings in both bilingual education and English as a second language.

Katharine Cutts-Dougherty is a doctoral student in education at the University of Colorado at Boulder. She received her M.A. in developmental psychology at Cornell University where she studied under Urie Bronfenbrenner and Stephen J. Ceci. She is currently interested in social identity theory as it relates to multiculturalism in the U.S., extending upon an earlier study on the development of national identity in English and Argentine schoolboys, conducted in the wake of the Falklands/Malvinas conflict.

Yvonne M. David is a doctoral candidate at the University of Michigan in the Combined Program in Education and Psychology. She has an M.A. in special education from Michigan State University. She was a research assistant on the Reciprocal Teaching research program and is currently a research assistant on a project funded by the National Science Foundation. She is interested in the relationship between student's conceptual understanding and motivation and in the educational policies that affect minority, especially Native American, students.

Patricia A. Edwards is Associate Professor of Reading at Michigan State University and author of two nationally acclaimed family literacy programs—Parents as Partners in Reading: A Family Literacy Training Program and Talking Your Way to Literacy: A Program to Help Nonreading Parents Prepare Their Children for Reading. Before receiving her Ph.D. at the University of Wisconsin-Madison, she was a field instructor at North Carolina Central University. She later taught at Grambling State University, Louisiana Tech University, Louisiana State University, and was a Visiting Assistant Professor at the Center for the Study of Reading. Her publications include articles and book chapters specifically focused on family/intergenerational literacy. Currently she is working on a family literacy component for a basal program.

Margaret Eisenhart is Associate Professor of Educational Anthropology and Research Methodology and chair of the Program in Educational Foundations at the School of Education, University of Colorado at Boulder. She received her Ph.D. in anthropology from the University of North Carolina at Chapel Hill and was a member of the education faculty at Virginia Tech before moving to Colorado. Her research and publications have focused on what students learn about gender and race in U.S. schools and the place of ethnographic methods in educational research. She is co-author of *Education in Romance: Women, Achievement, and College Culture* with Dorothy Holland and is currently working on a book about collaborative classroom research with Hilda Borko.

Carol Carson Emmer is a doctoral candidate at the University of Colorado at Boulder and is associated with the Lab for Policy Studies. She received her M.A. in Russian literature and History from the University of Texas at Austin in 1977. She has been an educator for the past twenty years and has taught at both the university and high school levels. Her current research interests include site-based management and the school restructuring movement.

Charles W. Fisher is Associate Professor of Education at the University of Northern Colorado and director of the Center for Research on Teaching and Learning. His research on teaching and learning processes has focused on uses of instructional time in a variety of classroom task structures and social organizations. His publications include articles and book chapters on classroom processes in literacy, mathematics, and science instruction, in classrooms with high access to technology, and in classrooms with students from diverse language backgrounds. He has received the Award for Outstanding Writing from the American Association of Colleges for Teacher Education and is co-editor with David Berliner of *Perspectives on Instructional Time*.

Janet S. Gaffney is Assistant Professor of Special Education at the University of Illinois at Urbana-Champaign. As director of the Illinois Reading Recovery Project at the Center for the Study of Reading, she is responsible for the Teacher Leader Training Program. Before receiving her Ph.D. at Arizona State University, Dr. Gaffney was an elementary and secondary school teacher, a reading specialist, and a Chapter 1 and Special Education coordinator. Her publications include research on the use of strategies by children with learning disabilities. Dr. Gaffney serves on the editorial boards of *Contemporary Educational Psychology, Exceptional Children,* and *Teacher Education and Special Education Communique* (November, 1989). She is currently studying teacher change processes as a result of professional development procedures and their relationships to children's progress in reading acquisition.

Georgia Earnest García is Assistant Professor of Education at the University of Illinois at Urbana-Champaign and Senior Scientist at the Center for the Study of Reading. She received her Ph.D. in education at the University of Illinois at Urbana-Champaign. Her research focuses on literacy acquisition and instruction of students from diverse linguistic, cultural, and economic backgrounds. She previously was a classroom teacher in New York and an instructor in a community college and bilingual migrant program in Illinois.

Elfrieda H. Hiebert is Professor of Education at the University of Colorado, Boulder, where she teaches courses on literacy learning and conducts research on school literacy experiences for children who enter school with few prior text literacy experiences. She began her educational career as an elementary teacher. After receiving her Ph.D. in educational psychology from the University of Wisconsin-Madison, she served on the faculty of the University of Kentucky and as a Visiting Associate Professor at the University of Illinois' Center for the Study of Reading. She has been a recipient of a Spencer Fellowship awarded through the National Academy of Education and has published numerous journal articles and book chapters.

Ernest R. House is Professor of Education at the University of Colorado at Boulder. From 1969 to 1985 he was at the Center for Instructional Research and Curriculum Evaluation at the University of Illinois, Urbana-Champaign. Earlier he was a high school teacher, teacher trainer, and curriculum developer. He served as chair of the 1976 AERA convention and of the 1983 AERA award for distinguished contributions to educational research. His primary research interests are educational evaluation, innovation, and policy. His books include *The Politics of Educational Innovation, Survival in the Classroom* (with S. Lapan), *Evaluating with Validity,* and *Jesse Jackson and the Politics of Charisma.* He is the 1989 recipient (with W. Madura) of the Harold E. Lasswell Prize for the article contributing most to the theory and practice of the policy sciences ("Race, Gender, and Jobs"), and the 1990 recipient of the Lazersfeld Award for Evaluation Theory.

Judith A. Langer is Professor of Education at the University of New York at Albany, State University of New York. Her research focuses on how people become skilled readers and writers, how they use reading and writing to learn, and what this means for instruction. Her major works examine the structure of literate knowledge—the ways in which literate understanding develops, how particular literacy contexts affect cognition and performance, and the effects of literacy instruction on academic learning. She is presently studying the processes involved in literary understanding and the contribution of literature instruction to critical thought. Langer has published widely. Her books include *Reader Meets Author: Bridging the Gap; How Writing Shapes Thinking: Studies of Teaching and Learning;* and *New Directions in Literature Instruction,* an edited volume, presently in review. Langer is editor of *Research in the Teaching of English* and co-director of the Center for Literature Teaching and Learning.

Nancy R. Lawrence is a doctoral candidate in educational policy at the University of Colorado, Boulder, where she is combining her practical experience and knowledge of electoral politics with educational issues. Her research interests include the schools of choice movement, the high school curriculum, and cultural literacy.

Pamela McCollum is Assistant Professor of Education at the University of Colorado, Boulder. She received her Ph.D. from the University of Illinois, Urbana-Champaign, where she specialized in educational psychology and linguistics. Prior to receiving her doctorate, Dr. McCollum worked as a bilingual teacher and ESL specialist in Puerto Rico and Chicago. Her publications include research and applied articles concerning bilingual language assessment, classroom interaction, and the schooling of language-minority students in American public schools. Currently, she is studying how bilingual Latino middle school students view school and their participation in a two-way maintenance bilingual program.

Michael S. Meloth is Assistant Professor of Education at the University of Colorado, Boulder. He received his Ph.D. from Michigan State University in educational psychology. While there, he worked at the Institute for Research on Teaching on projects concerned with reading comprehension instruction. He was also a research associate at the Center for Research on Learning and Schooling at the University of Michigan. Currently, he is examining the instructional factors that affect students' communication of comprehension strategies during cooperative group interactions.

Ofelia B. Miramontes is Assistant Professor of Bilingual Education and Bilingual Special Education at the University of Colorado, Boulder. She has directed several Title VII grants for teacher preparation in bilingual and special education. Before coming to the University of Colorado, she was a bilingual and special education teacher and bilingual program coordinator. Her research focuses on first and second language development programs, particularly as they impact the achievement of Hispanic bilingual students. Her publications reflect research and applied aspects of reading and writing development in bilingual and bilingual special education students. She is currently co-authoring a book entitled *Ethics in Special Education* with Kenneth R. Howe.

Sharon Nelson-Barber is Acting Assistant Professor of Anthropology at Stanford University. She received her Ed.D. in human development from Harvard University. Her publications include research and applied articles on interethnic communication and cross-cultural education. Her recent work as Associate Director of Stanford's Teacher Assessment Project focused on examining ways in which the standards and assessment procedures now in place for teachers fail to capture culturally responsive forms of excellence. Currently, she is studying the cultural learning styles and teaching practices of Athabaskan Indian and Yup'ik and Inupiaq Eskimo peoples in Alaska.

Annemarie Sullivan Palincsar is Associate Professor of Education at the University of Michigan. Prior to completing her doctoral studies at the University of Illinois, she was a special educator and school administrator. Her research interests include the acquisition of literacy by students placed at-risk and peer collaboration in solving science problems.

P. David Pearson is Professor of Curriculum and Instruction at the University of Illinois, Urbana-Champaign, and Dean of the College of Education. He earned his Ph.D. in education at the University of Minnesota, Minneapolis. Prior to becoming Dean, Dr. Pearson served as Co-Director of the Center for the Study of Reading, where he continues to pursue a line of research related to reading instruction and reading assessment policies and practices. He has been active in professional organizations, serving the International Reading Association as a member of the Board of Directors, The National Council of Teachers of English as a member of its Research Committee, and both the National Reading Conference and The National Conference of Research in English as President. He has published several books: *Teaching Reading Comprehension, Teaching Reading Vocabulary,* and editor of the *Handbook of Reading Research.* He has also published materials for teachers and children in his role as an author for the *World of Reading* and has served two terms as co-editor of *Reading Research Quarterly.*

María de la Luz Reyes is Assistant Professor of Education at the University of Colorado at Boulder. She received her Ph.D. in educational psychology with a specialization in reading and language development as well as bilingual/multicultural education from the University of California, Santa Barbara. Dr. Reyes is a former elementary and secondary classroom teacher. Her publications include research in content area reading, literacy instruction for second-language learners, and the reading and writing connection in process approach classrooms. Currently, she is studying the language and literacy development of Spanish-speaking learners in the middle grades.

Robert Rueda is Associate Professor of Counseling and Educational Psychology at the University of Southern California. He received his Ph.D. at UCLA, and later completed a postdoctoral fellowship at the Laboratory of Comparative Human Cognition at the University of California at San Diego. He has published widely in the area of special education, especially on issues affecting language-minority students. The focus of his research has been the social basis of learning and development, including interactive approaches to teaching and learning, specifically in the area of literacy with learning-handicapped students.

Lorrie Shepard is Professor of Education at the University of Colorado at Boulder and chair of the Research and Evaluation Methodology program. Her research in applied measurement has addressed issues of standard setting 2nd test bias. Her work in educational policy research has focused on the uses of tests for special school placements (identification of learning disabilities, grade retention, kindergarten screening) and on the effects of testing on teaching and student learning. Recent publications include *Flunking Grades: Research and Policies on Retention* (with Mary Lee Smith) and

"Psychometricians' Beliefs about Learning." She has served as vice-president of AERA for Division D, member of the Council's Executive Board, editor of AERJ, and chair of the Publications Committee. She has also been active in the National Council on Measurement in Education, serving as its president and as editor of the *Journal of Educational Measurement*. She has been vice-chair of the National Academy of Sciences Committee on the General Aptitude Test Battery and is a member of the National Academy of Education's Panel on Trial State Assessment.

Index